Plymouth University Library
W: http://primo.plymouth.ac.uk **T:** 01752 588588

PARKING
ISSUES AND POLICIES

TRANSPORT AND SUSTAINABILITY

Series Editors: Stephen Ison and Jon Shaw

Recent Volumes:

Volume 1: Cycling and Sustainability
Volume 2: Transport and Climate Change
Volume 3: Sustainable Transport for Chinese Cities
Volume 4: Sustainable Aviation Futures

TRANSPORT AND SUSTAINABILITY   VOLUME 5

PARKING
ISSUES AND POLICIES

EDITED BY

STEPHEN ISON
Transport Studies Group,
Loughborough University, UK

CORINNE MULLEY
Institute of Transport and Logistics Studies,
The University of Sydney Business School,
Sydney, Australia

Emerald

United Kingdom − North America − Japan
India − Malaysia − China

Emerald Group Publishing Limited
Howard House, Wagon Lane, Bingley BD16 1WA, UK

First edition 2014

Copyright © 2014 Emerald Group Publishing Limited

British Library Cataloguing in Publication Data
A catalogue record for this book is available from the British Library

ISBN: 978-1-78350-919-5
ISSN: 2044-9941 (Series)

ISOQAR certified
Management System,
awarded to Emerald
for adherence to
Environmental
standard
ISO 14001:2004.

Certificate Number 1985
ISO 14001

INVESTOR IN PEOPLE

BIG YELLOW TAXI

They paved paradise
And put up a parking lot
With a pink hotel, a boutique
And a swinging hot spot
Don't it always seem to go
That you don't know what you've got
Till it's gone
They paved paradise
And put up a parking lot.

BIG YELLOW TAXI

Words and Music by JONI MITCHELL
Copyright © 1970 (Renewed) CRAZY CROW MUSIC
All Rights Administered by SONY/ATV MUSIC PUBLISHING
8 Music Square West, Nashville, TN 37203
All Rights Reserved
Used By Permission of ALFRED MUSIC

CONTENTS

LIST OF CONTRIBUTORS   *xi*

CHAPTER 1   INTRODUCTION
    Stephen Ison and Corinne Mulley   *1*

CHAPTER 2   PARKING POLICY
    Greg Marsden   *11*

CHAPTER 3   PARKING SUPPLY AND URBAN
IMPACTS
    Christopher McCahill and Norman Garrick   *33*

CHAPTER 4   PARKING DEMAND
    John Bates   *57*

CHAPTER 5   THE HIGH COST OF MINIMUM
PARKING REQUIREMENTS
    Donald Shoup   *87*

CHAPTER 6   PARKING CHOICE
    Sarah Brooke, Stephen Ison and Mohammed Quddus   *115*

CHAPTER 7   PARKING PRICING
    Michael Manville   *137*

CHAPTER 8   PARKING MANAGEMENT
    Tom Rye and Till Koglin   *157*

CHAPTER 9   THE EFFECTIVENESS OF
PARK-AND-RIDE AS A POLICY MEASURE
FOR MORE SUSTAINABLE MOBILITY
Graham Parkhurst and Stuart Meek   185

CHAPTER 10   CARFREE AND LOW-CAR
DEVELOPMENT
Steven Melia   213

CHAPTER 11   THREE FACES OF PARKING:
EMERGING TRENDS IN THE U.S.
Rachel R. Weinberger   235

CHAPTER 12   PARKING SUPPLY AND DEMAND
IN LONDON
David Leibling   259

CHAPTER 13   EXPLORING THE IMPACT OF
THE MELBOURNE CBD PARKING LEVY ON
WHO PAYS THE LEVY, PARKING SUPPLY AND
MODE USE
William Young, Graham Currie and Paul Hamer   291

CHAPTER 14   A PARKING SPACE LEVY: A CASE
STUDY OF SYDNEY, AUSTRALIA
Stephen Ison, Corinne Mulley, Anthony Mifsud and   317
Chinh Ho

CHAPTER 15   A CASE STUDY OF THE
INTRODUCTION OF A WORKPLACE PARKING
LEVY IN NOTTINGHAM
Simon Dale, Matthew Frost, Jason Gooding,   335
Stephen Ison and Peter Warren

CHAPTER 16   ON-STREET PARKING
Wesley E. Marshall   361

CHAPTER 17   PARKING IN GUANGZHOU:
PRINCIPLES FOR CONGESTION REDUCTION
AND IMPROVING QUALITY OF LIFE IN A
GROWING CITY
Rachel R. Weinberger and Lisa Jacobson   *381*

CHAPTER 18   CONCLUSIONS
Corinne Mulley and Stephen Ison   *409*

ABOUT THE AUTHORS   *417*

INDEX   *427*

LIST OF CONTRIBUTORS

John Bates	Independent Consultant, UK
Sarah Brooke	Transport Studies Group, School of Civil and Building Engineering, Loughborough University, Loughborough, UK
Graham Currie	Institute of Transport Studies, Department of Civil Engineering, Monash University, Melbourne, Australia
Simon Dale	Nottingham City Council, Nottingham, UK
Matthew Frost	School of Civil and Building Engineering, Loughborough University, Loughborough, UK
Norman Garrick	Department of Civil and Environmental Engineering, University of Connecticut, Storrs, CT, USA
Jason Gooding	Nottingham City Council, Nottingham, UK
Paul Hamer	Department of Transport, Planning and Local Infrastructure, Melbourne, Australia
Chinh Ho	Institute of Transport and Logistics Studies, The University of Sydney Business School, Sydney, Australia
Stephen Ison	Transport Studies Group, School of Civil and Building Engineering, Loughborough University, Loughborough, UK
Lisa Jacobson	Nelson\Nygaard Consulting Associates, Boston, MA, USA

Till Koglin	Transport and Roads, Lund University, Lund, Sweden
David Leibling	Independent Consultant, UK
Michael Manville	Department of City and Regional Planning, Cornell University, Ithaca, NY, USA
Greg Marsden	Institute for Transport Studies, University of Leeds, Leeds, UK
Wesley E. Marshall	Department of Civil Engineering, University of Colorado Denver, Denver, CO, USA
Christopher McCahill	State Smart Transportation Initiative, University of Wisconsin, Madison, WI, USA
Stuart Meek	Southern Rail, London, UK
Steven Melia	Centre for Transport and Society, University of the West of England, Bristol, UK
Anthony Mifsud	City of Sydney, Sydney, Australia
Corinne Mulley	Institute of Transport and Logistics Studies, The University of Sydney Business School, Sydney, Australia
Graham Parkhurst	Centre for Transport and Society, University of the West of England, Bristol, UK
Mohammed Quddus	Transport Studies Group, School of Civil and Building Engineering, Loughborough University, Loughborough, UK
Tom Rye	Transport and Roads, Lund University, Lund, Sweden
Donald Shoup	Department of Urban Planning, University of California, Los Angeles, CA, USA

Peter Warren	Nottingham City Council, Nottingham, UK
Rachel R. Weinberger	Nelson\Nygaard Consulting Associates, New York, NY, USA
William Young	Institute of Transport Studies, Department of Civil Engineering, Monash University, Melbourne, Australia

CHAPTER 1

INTRODUCTION

Stephen Ison and Corinne Mulley

ABSTRACT

Purpose – *This chapter provides an introduction to parking issues and policies. It seeks to place parking in the context of transport demand management (TDM) and takes as its tenet that parking is primarily a land-use issue. It outlines the types of parking which exist and why the management of parking is all important when addressing the policy goals of impacting on traffic congestion, tackling the issue of air pollution, stimulating economic activity or aiming to improve road safety.*

Methodology/approach – *This chapter discusses the role played by parking as a TDM measure and its various facets most notably pricing and regulation, the prioritisation of land for particular uses, such as Park and Ride, or indeed car free developments.*

Findings – *The chapter reveals the complex nature of parking from both the supply and demand side. The demand is driven by the kind of activity involved be it for commuter, retail or other reasons. Clearly, the type of housing stock and residential density impact on parking demand at the start point of the journey, whereas at the destination, the type of employment and the duration of parking are significant factors. Car parking is not homogeneous, since it can be found in various locations and provided by different bodies, be that the public or private sector.*

Parking: Issues and Policies
Transport and Sustainability, Volume 5, 1–9
Copyright © 2014 by Emerald Group Publishing Limited
ISSN: 2044-9941/doi:10.1108/S2044-994120140000005015

The cost of parking is an issue not simply in terms of the land take, cost of construction and maintenance but also searching for parking and the time involved.

Practical implications — *The management of parking is important as part of a package of measures commonly implemented by authorities and one which needs to be understood alongside land-use planning. It is an area involving conflict between parking supply, demand, revenue raising and economic development.*

Originality — *The book offers a clear understanding and insight into the area of parking and its issues and policies. The book uses case studies where appropriate providing originality in the area of parking and effective management approaches.*

Keywords: Parking; demand; supply; management; policy; planning

Car parking is an issue that everyone will have an opinion on whether it relates to the lack of available spaces, the price, parking fines or quality of provision. Parking is a sensitive area impacting on shoppers, retailers, commuters, employers, leisure users, local residents and local authority decision makers who have to manage this resource in an efficient and effective manner. Parking and its provision, pricing and regulation are part of the toolbox which form part of a package of measures that can be used to impact on traffic congestion, address traffic related air pollution, or indeed raise revenue to fund selected infrastructure investment. In managing parking, a number of issues are raised including the boundary effects resulting from the implementation of an area-wide parking policy, the impact a change in parking policy has on the economic vitality of an area, public acceptability or the responsiveness of motorists to a parking charge.

Transport Demand Management (TDM) is aimed at influencing travel behaviour (Ison & Rye, 2008) and, as stated by Meyer (1999, p. 576), it is 'any action or set of actions aimed at influencing people's travel behaviour in such a way that alternative mobility options are presented and/or congestion is reduced'. Table 1 provides a selection of TDM measures aimed at impacting on travel behaviour and seeking to address the issues of congestion, emissions and urban economic development. The table reveals a number of parking options including the economic approach of charging, the prioritisation of land for a particular use, such as Park and Ride

Table 1. TDM Measures.

Type	Measures
Economic	• Fuel tax
	• Parking charges
	• Public transport subsidisation
	• Road pricing
Land use	• Land use and transportation strategy such as Car free developments
	• Park and Ride facilities
Substitution of communications for travel	• Teleworking
	• E-shopping
Regulation	• Parking controls
	• Pedestrianised zones

Source: Adapted from Ison and Rye (2008).

facilities, the encouragement of developments which are car free or through regulation whether this is parking controls of various kinds or indeed providing no parking at all, as with pedestrianised zones.

If one takes Great Britain as an example, in 2012 643 billion passenger kilometres were undertaken by cars, vans and taxis representing 83% of all passenger kilometres travelled (Transport Statistics Great Britain, 2013). This compared to 58 billion passenger kilometres in 1952. The UK Department for Transport forecast that road traffic in England will increase by 39% from 2010 to 2040 but this is not simply a British phenomenon. A growth in vehicle kilometres will clearly link to the increased requirements for a parking space at the vehicles destination point. In undertaking a journey the availability and price of parking spaces is all important as to whether the individual chooses:

• a particular location to drive to;
• an alternative mode of travel;
• to indeed own a car in the first place.

It is perhaps not too surprising that car parking availability leads to more car trips and encourages car ownership (Weinberger, Seaman, & Johnson, 2009). Cars spend, on average, 80% of their time parked at the home of the owner, 4% in motion and 16% parked elsewhere, most notably in urban areas (Bates & Leibling, 2012). The land used to provide for parking in urban areas could be utilised for other purposes underpinning the argument that Shoup (2005) makes for there being no such thing as 'free parking'. This rationale is the starting point in Chapter 2, where Marsden identifies that parking is first and foremost a land-use issue with a decision required as to whether or not space should be allocated for its use.

It is certainly the case that the management of parking is a complex issue both in terms its supply and demand. On the supply side, The Institution of Highways and Transportation (2005, p. 20) states that the 'Control over the availability of parking spaces is a key policy instrument in limiting car trips and for the time being is the most widely available and readily accepted method of doing so'. In Chapter 3 McCahill and Garrick identify 'Parking supply has increased by anywhere from 70% to 160% in urban areas throughout the United States, thereby contributing to considerable land consumption and increases in local automobile use. These increases were driven in large part by minimum parking requirements and perceived market demand. Since 1980, parking growth has slowed considerably in cities that have implemented parking limits and parking management strategies'.

The demand side of parking clearly relates to where individuals want to park and this is driven by the type of activity involved whether for work, retail or leisure reasons, plus the time the journey is undertaken and how long the parking space is required for. At the start point of a journey, parking demand relates to the type of housing stock and indeed the residential density which is particularly an issue in urban areas. In contrast, at the destination parking demand is dominated by the demand by commuters given the demand and duration. In order to develop a parking strategy the issue of parking demand needs to be given careful consideration with an understanding of where, when and for how long parking occurs.

Chapter 4 by Bates deals with parking demand and notes that, as with supply, there is a data issue not least since a great deal of parking is informal and surveying it is time consuming and costly. As such, much of parking policy takes place at the local level and is basically reactive in nature rather than proactive. This means that schemes such as Controlled Parking Zones are only considered when there are serious capacity constraints. As stated by the House of Commons Transport Committee (2013, p. 5) in the United Kingdom, 'Effective parking strategies help to reconcile the competing demands of different road users. Parking restrictions are used to manage congestion and ensure that there is clear and fair access to public roads. The enforcement of parking restrictions should help to ensure that the needs of residents, shops and businesses are met. Local authorities have primary responsibility for setting parking policy and enforcement strategies on local roads'.

Table 2. Types of Car Parking Spaces.

Ownership	User	Location	Pricing
Local authority	a. Public	On-street	Charged and free
	b. Public either surface or multi-storey	Off-street	Predominantly charged but can be free
Privately owned	c. Public	Off-street	Charged
	d. Office parking	Off-street	Free
	e. Residential	Off-street	Free

Source: Adapted from Enoch and Ison (2006).

Car parking is not a homogeneous product since it can be found in various locations and is provided by different bodies, including both the public and private sector. Table 2 provides an indication of the types of parking which exist in the majority of urban areas world-wide.

Based on Ison (2014):

(a) *Public on-street* parking refers to parking on the side of the road. It is local authority controlled and as such its use can be influenced either by pricing or by regulation.

(b) *Public, surface or multi-storey off-street* car parks are those which the public can access but which are not on-street. They usually involve a charge and are subject to regulation such as a maximum stay.

(c) *Public owned non-residential car parks* are privately owned but are used by the general public and are operated above all to make a profit.

(d) *Office parking (private non-residential parking)* is usually available to use for free by employees of a particular organisation but are not available to the general public. The provision of such parking is a cost to the employer since there is the upkeep, land take (which might be better utilised for other uses) and the original cost of constructing the parking provision in the first place. While such parking provision can stimulate vehicle use it can also be important in recruiting and retaining employees. As such, parking can be seen as a perk and in some cases as an entitlement of the post as discussed in Chapter 2.

(e) *Residential parking* as expected is associated primarily with private accommodation whether these are houses or flats. These parking places are typically on private property and, in recent times, there has been a marked increase in the hiring out of these spaces to non-residents, for example when parking in order to access airports (see Budd, Ison, & Budd, 2013).

The cost of parking is not simply an issue for organisations but is also a question for city planners who are in a difficult position when managing off-street parking requirements. Planners in general are not aware of how much parking spaces cost or indeed how they impact on the cost of constructing new buildings. In Chapter 5 Donald Shoup estimates the impact the requirement for parking has on the cost of constructing developments such as shopping centres, housing stock and historic buildings. Searching or cruising for on-street parking (see Shoup, 2006) is a cost to the motorist and has an impact on the urban environment from a congestion, air pollution and noise perspective. Parking search is detailed in Chapter 6 by Brooke, Ison and Quddus and its impact for pricing in Chapter 7 by Manville.

The use of parking policy as a management measure can take a number of different forms, be it pricing, regulation or options such as the provision of Park and Ride facilities. Pricing policy for parking is often sub-optimal by being free or underpriced and, using the United States as an example, this is detailed in Chapter 7 by Manville together with a review of how various cities have attempted to reform pricing and its potential impact on equity- and fairness-based objections to market prices. Whilst parking controls and prices are never popular, not least with the general public, they are a policy option that is relatively well-known, understood and on the whole accepted in urban areas, particularly in the EU. Parking pricing and controls are the TDM measure most commonly implemented by authorities. However, relatively little of the academic transport literature details parking policy when compared to road pricing. This is being redressed; see, for example the Parking Special Issue of the journal *Transport Policy* (2006).

Chapter 8 by Rye and Koglin seeks to understand the issue of parking management in terms of how and why local parking policies are developed, the conflicting relationship between parking, revenue raising and economic development and the circumstances in which it may be appropriate to use parking policy as a demand management tool.

One of the policy options that have been used to address the issue of traffic congestion over the last 30 years or so has been Park and Ride sites located predominantly on the routes into certain towns and city centres, such as Cambridge, Oxford and York in the United Kingdom. The prime objective has been to encourage the diversion of private vehicles destined for the city centre into dedicated car parks where designated public transport is provided to complete the journey into the city centre. For this to occur it requires a frequent, reliable and fast service, with a cost perceived by motorists to be lower than that of fuel and parking in the city centre.

The Park and Ride sites have to be convenient and concerns in relation to users' personal safety and vehicle security have to be alleviated. Chapter 9 by Parkhurst and Meek argues that there is only a partial understanding by the authorities as to the effectiveness of Park and Ride in addressing its objectives, not least in relation to travel behaviour and the portion of Park and Ride users' car trips that are shortened. It would appear that the implementation of Park and Ride is generally more successful where they are provided explicitly for more parking in relation to economic growth or traffic management rather than an improvement in sustainable mobility.

While the provision of parking is important for the economic vitality and development of an urban area, there has been a rise in the number of car free and low-car developments and this is covered in Chapter 10 by Melia. They can be defined as the absence or reduced level of parking with the aim of lowering traffic generation in addition to creating benefits such as an increase in the socialisation between neighbours and the earlier independence for children. There are, however, issues with car free developments such as how to avoid overspill problems of cars parking on surrounding streets.

One of the key features of this book is a number of case studies relating to where parking policy has been enacted. As such, the latter half of the book includes chapters focussing on parking policy in the United States, more specifically parking policy in the city of London and schemes implemented in Melbourne and Sydney in Australia and Nottingham in the United Kingdom to address congestion issues and parking policy in Guangzhou, China. These chapters link and expand on the issues and policies identified and discussed in the first ten chapters of the book.

Weinberger in Chapter 11 explores the situation in the United States where cities are now looking at alternative approaches to the long standing policy intervention of requiring additional off-street parking to alleviate parking shortages. The belief that providing abundant parking is the key to a desirable, successful urban environment is now being questioned, not least since the use of minimum standards has created three or four parking spaces per vehicle in the United States. In Chapter 12 Leibling seeks to measure the supply and demand for parking in London, in part to ascertain whether there is sufficient provision for night-time residential needs and whether polices designed at controlling car ownership by restricting residential parking are effective. The chapter suggests that there would appear to be saturation in inner London for controlled on-street parking and high utilisation for off-street parking. In outer London, however, there is more spare capacity.

In Chapter 13 Young, Currie and Hamer explore the impact of the Melbourne CBD Parking Levy on who pays the levy, parking supply and mode use. The chapter argues that, since the introduction of the levy, the supply of commercial off-street parking spaces has declined while the growth in private, non-residential, parking spaces has slowed somewhat. There has been a decrease in the number of parking spaces provided for long-stay parking and an increase in the number of spaces provided for other uses. Another scheme found in Australia is that of Parking Space Levy (PSL) which was introduced in Sydney in 1992. Chapter 14 by Ison, Mulley, Mifsud and Ho provides a case study of the implementation of the PSL, a scheme that places a levy on business use of off-street car parking spaces with the revenues being hypothecated to public transport improvements. This chapter provides an overview of the introduction, implementation and outcomes of the PSL in Sydney, relating it to the Parking Levy in Melbourne (Chapter 13) and the Workplace Parking Levy in Nottingham (Chapter 15). In Chapter 15 Dale, Frost, Gooding, Ison and Warren detail the WPL, a TDM measure which raises a levy on private non-domestic off-street parking provided by employers to employees, regular business visitors and students. The idea is to increase the cost of commuting by car and a contraction in the supply of workplace parking places. Currently Nottingham is the only city in the UK to have implemented such a scheme and thus an understanding of the how that scheme was implemented, how it operates and the outcomes after a full year of operation are of importance to transport academics and other local authorities considering utilising a similar approach. These three chapters provide an opportunity for a comparison to be made between schemes in the United Kingdom and Australia.

In Chapter 16 Marshall provides an overview of on-street parking and the issues it raises not least in terms of parking demand, land use, vehicle speed, road safety, the pedestrian environment and travel behaviours. The chapter includes two case studies, the first exploring the impact in centres built before the advent of parking regulations as compared to more contemporary, conventional developments and the second investigates how street design factors have affected vehicle speeds and safety, based on a study of over 250 roads.

Weinberger and Jacobson provide an interesting account of parking in Guangzhou, China in Chapter 17, detailing the principles for congestion reduction and for an improvement in the quality of life in a growing city. The findings reveal that there is opportunity for Guangzhou to implement strategies so as to manage its parking supply relative to its roadway capacity and integrate its parking policies within the overall transportation system.

Overall this book is intended to offer the student, researcher and practitioner, with a real interest in the complex issues and policies related to parking, an increased knowledge of the role parking can play in the transport arena.

REFERENCES

Bates, J., & Leibling, D. (2012). *Spaced out perspectives on parking policy*. London: RAC Foundation.

Budd, L., Ison, S. G., & Budd, T. (2013). An empirical examination of the growing phenomenon of off-site residential car parking provision: The situation at UK airports. *Transportation Research A: Policy and Practice, 54*, 26–34.

Department for Transport. (2013). *Transport statistics Great Britain 2013*. London: The Stationery Office.

Enoch, M. P., & Ison, S. G. (2006). Levying charges on private parking: Lessons from existing practice. *World Transport Policy & Practice, 12*(1), 5–14.

House of Commons Transport Committee. (2013, October 23). *Local authority parking enforcement*. Seventh Report of Session 2013–2014 (Vol. I, HC 118), The House of Commons. London: The Stationery Office Limited.

Ison, S. G. (2014). Parking Management Policy: Its potential in improving urban traffic flows. Bruxelles, Belgium: European Automobile Manufacturers Association (ACEA).

Ison, S. G., & Rye, T. (2008). TDM measures and their implementation. In S. G. Ison & T. Rye (Eds.), *The implementation and effectiveness of transport demand management measures: An international perspective*. Aldershot, UK: Ashgate Publishing Limited.

Meyer, M. D. (1999). Demand management as an element of transportation policy: Using carrots and sticks to influence travel behaviour. *Transportation Research A, 33*, 575–599.

Shoup, D. C. (2005). *The high cost of free parking*. Chicago, IL: American Planning Association.

Shoup, D. C. (2006). Cruising for parking. *Transport Policy, 13*(6), 479–486.

The Institution of Highways and Transportation. (2005). Parking strategies and management, London.

Weinberger, R., Seaman, M., & Johnson, C. (2009). Residential off-street parking impacts on car ownership, vehicle miles traveled, and related carbon emissions New York city case study. *Transportation Research Record, 2118*, 24–30.

CHAPTER 2

PARKING POLICY

Greg Marsden

ABSTRACT

Purpose — *This chapter provides an overview of parking policy. The chapter takes as its start point that parking is first and foremost a land-use issue. It looks at the conflicts and synergies between parking policy for the purposes of traffic management and parking policy to support various key land-uses and policy objectives.*

Methodology/approach — *This chapter discusses the main practice-oriented viewpoints on what is meant by parking policy and what it aims to achieve. It then provides a state-of-art review of the evidence base on residential, retail and workplace parking as the three key parking desti-nations before drawing together these findings.*

Findings — *The reviews reveal that there has been an overemphasis on the importance of the impact of parking pricing to trip frequency, desti-nation and walk times in the literature. Much greater emphasis should be given to establishing the extent to which parking restraint supports the economy, the environment and social equity. Only then will we be able to develop a consistent policy framing within which good parking manage-ment policy can play out and make a long-term difference to travel patterns and the quality of life in our cities.*

Parking: Issues and Policies
Transport and Sustainability, Volume 5, 11–32
Copyright © 2014 by Emerald Group Publishing Limited
All rights of reproduction in any form reserved
ISSN: 2044-9941/doi:10.1108/S2044-994120140000005016

Practical implications — *If parking policy is to work well as part of an overall package of demand restraint, it needs to be applied in conjunction with land-use planning. In transport terms, this means connecting parking policy to non-car accessibility. If the overarching land-use and transport accessibility policies are right, then there is a greater possibility for other parking management policies to be effectively applied and integrated in broader transport strategies.*

Originality/value of the chapter — *This chapter suggests that without a clear understanding of the broader objectives that parking policy supports it will not be possible to design effective parking management approaches.*

Keywords: Land-use; residential; retail; integration

INTRODUCTION

This chapter provides an overview of parking policy. It aims to define what parking policy is, what it aims to achieve and to summarise the key studies in the field. The chapter takes as its start point that parking is first and foremost a land-use issue in so far as a decision has to be taken as to whether or not space should be allocated for parking. However, as one of the key users of land that glues together the land-use and transport system, parking is also a transport policy and therefore resides at the heart of an integrated land-use and transport strategy. This is where agreement ends and debate begins, since the goals of land-use and transport policy are not always clear and the role that parking plays in supporting these goals is contested. Coupled with this is the complexity of developing a coherent parking policy that covers retail, work, leisure and residential parking when these land-uses are not neatly divided and where governance arrangements can be highly fragmented.

Parking is a land-use. An estimated 12 m^2 is required to park a car in a non-disabled bay. For the 29.1 million cars currently in the United Kingdom, this equates to an area of 349 km^2 — around one quarter of Greater London and more than the whole island of Malta. It is worth noting that, in the United Kingdom, 'the average car spends about 80% of the time parked at home, is parked elsewhere for about 16% of the time, and is thus only actually in use (i.e. moving) for the remaining 3—4% of the time' (RAC, 2012, p. vi). All parking policy is a decision about how much land to give over to parking and the terms and conditions of use of that space.

Parking takes up land and in doing so it prevents an alternative use. All land has a value and, as Donald Shoup so clearly establishes, there is no such thing as free parking (Shoup, 2005). This chapter focuses on why we would wish to allocate land to parking and what is and could be done to allocate the costs of parking to users or owners of parking space.

It is tempting to treat 'parking' as a single issue, certainly in the popular press. However, parking acts are all associated with a single activity (e.g. parking at work) or a bundle of activities (e.g. parking in town to shop and eat out). These activities are different in nature and so there is a need to develop parking policies which take account of the characteristics of those activities (IHT, 2005). Whilst many single-use sites do exist (e.g. the out of town retail car park), there are often mixed use developments and conflicts can exist between the demands for parking spaces that are available (e.g. a major workplace located within a residential area). Habib, Morency, and Trepanier (2012) reflect that the transport modelling community has been slow to adapt to the complexity of parking policy and to move beyond thinking of parking policy as an influence largely on route, mode and parking duration but also to include where and when trips should occur, that is the nature of the activities and the potentially competing means by which they could be conducted.

The previous two paragraphs provide background on what parking is, but what is parking policy for? The answer to this is highly context specific. The Institution of Highways and Transportation note that the application of parking pricing and supply restrictions is 'the most widely accepted and readily accepted method' of limiting car use (IHT, 2005, p. 20). Bonsall and Young (2010) also note the role of parking in influencing transport choice, although they are more sceptical as to the extent to which local government has the levers to make this work. Parking policy is used as part of the toolkit of measures to limit congestion and air pollution in cities as well as to ensure the safe and smooth running of traffic on streets. McCahill and Garrick (2010) suggest that, applied in a consistent manner over the long term, it can be effective as a means of reducing overall demand for travel by car.

Rye, Hunton, Ison, and Kozak (2008) note, however, that parking 'is clearly an area of policy conflict since using it to manage demand may reduce revenue generation, or (be perceived to) damage the local economy. In terms of on-street and off-street parking there are a wide range of users who often have conflicting opinions, which have to be taken into account in its management' (p. 387). Parking is just one land-use; it is in competition with other land-uses and users of public space. The amount of space and its configuration relates to issues including land value, culture and

tradition, economic strength and, increasingly, the availability of supporting technologies.

This chapter aims to provide an overview of the multiple functions of
parking policy at a level of detail that highlights the main issues and outstanding questions. It relies on the published evidence base wherever possible and therefore seeks to provide insight into an often heated discussion
and suggests areas for further work, some of which are covered later in the
book. The chapter builds on a previous review (Marsden, 2006) updated
through a review of literature published on parking since 2006. By necessity, it is not possible to cover all work on parking. There has, for example,
been a rising interest in parking policy amongst emerging and developing
economies with poor regulation and inadequate supply becoming increasingly critical issues as car ownership levels rise (Al-Fouzan, 2012; Barter,
2012; Palevičius, Paliulis, Venckauskaite, & Vengrys, 2013) but this will not
be a focus here. Any reference to parking standards (e.g. space sizes)
derives from the United Kingdom and would need reinterpreting for other
contexts. The chapter focuses on car parking policy largely because there is
comparatively little written on bicycle parking policy (see Buehler, 2012 for
an exception) and not because the latter is seen as unimportant. Whilst
the chapter focuses on the place of parking in a policy context, it is not a
practitioner's guidebook (for a still excellent overview of the issues to think
through see IHT, 2005).

This chapter begins by examining residential parking policy, as this is
where vehicles spend most of their time parked. Table 1, using UK data
from the 2002 to 2008 National Travel Surveys, shows shopping and commuting to be the most important clear journey purposes which generate
parking. The chapter, therefore, then examines retail parking and workplace parking. A great deal of interest in parking comes from the focus on
workplace and commuter parking given its connection to the associated
congestion and environmental impacts of the commute. Commute parking
is shown to be largest proportion of all parking acts by purpose (28%) and
the longest average duration (excluding residential parking) of 7.5 hours.
The land-take associated with this must therefore also be significant, often
in areas with high demand from other potential uses. Each of these three
sections considers the objectives of the policy, options available and the evidence base that exists to support policy development. The chapter then
moves on to consider integrated transport policy, its role in supporting this
and the governance challenges that exist. Future challenges and opportunities are identified and discussed before the chapter concludes with what I
consider to be the main outstanding questions to be addressed.

Table 1.   Percentage of Parking Acts and Average Estimated Duration.

Purpose Category	% of Parking Acts	Average Duration (Hours)
Work	28	7.6
Employers' business	6	3.5
Education	1	5.2
Personal business	9	1.5
Shopping	17	1.5
Social/recreational	10	2.5
Holiday	<1	12.2
Visiting friends/relatives	8	3.1
Escorting passengers	20	0.8
All purposes	**100**	**3.5**

Source: RAC (2012, p. 35).

RESIDENTIAL PARKING POLICY

Residential parking policy refers to both planning policy relating to the provision of parking at the point of construction of new homes and tools which are used to manage parking in existing residential areas. Both are important since only 0.6% of the housing stock in a developed country, such as the United Kingdom, will typically be 'new build' in a given year. There are large parts of many cities which were developed in the period before mass car ownership, where parking standards were not considered at the time of construction and where managing the existing situation is critical.

The two extreme positions with regards to the role of residential parking policy are to see it as a means to accommodate current and future desired vehicles in a residential environment or as a tool to influence levels of vehicle ownership. In the absence of other supporting policies that also discourage car use, the latter approach may struggle to gain political traction and to be effective.

Options

When considering new build there are five main options available:

1. Provide parking to anticipated future needs (minimum standards[1]). In this situation, the goal of the parking policy is to avoid on-street parking

spillover with all cars located on the property. By necessity, as developers cannot know which houses will need to accommodate two or three vehicles then a situation of oversupply is created for some houses where owners would be happy with less parking. This has been demonstrated to lower the density of development and raise the average house price cost, being regressive for those seeking lower car ownership (Jia & Wachs, 1999; Litman, 2004; Shoup, 1995).

2. Limit parking to maintain densities and discourage ownership (maximum standards[2]). This policy provides a maximum level of parking which can be provided. The United Kingdom, for example had established a maximum of 1.5 spaces per property, thus seeking to increase density of development. This was somewhat difficult to deliver as it was not clear if this was over a development or a city. Critics of the approach point to the difficulties raised where the actual demand for parking exceeds the supply and where parking overspill onto the surrounding residential streets occurs. The United Kingdom has abandoned this guidance now, although local authorities will still look to match lower parking provision to areas with good public transport accessibility.

3. Decoupling car parking space from ownership is commonplace, particularly in medium and high-rise apartment developments where the amount of underground parking is far lower than the number of units. This essentially makes visible the cost of owning a parking space from within the house purchase or rental decision bundle. The ability to choose not to own a space, or to take one only as circumstances require, should act as a deterrent to vehicle ownership at the margins.

4. An extension of decoupling the parking space from ownership can be seen in the car free developments that have begun to materialise (see Chapter 10 by Melia later in this book for more in-depth review). These developments have parking available on the periphery, decoupled from home ownership. The notion is that there is a market for people who prefer to live in an area not so dominated by the car. Whilst developer uptake for these types of scheme has been slow, there are numerous examples of success.

5. The final main option is to ration and/or charge for permits to park. This can be for spaces within an off-street development, although more commonly this is used as a tool to manage the demand for on-street spaces. Typically households are allocated a baseline number of spaces and may face additional charges for fees over and above this number (see van Ommeren, Wentink, & Dekkers, 2011 for an exploration of

willingness to pay for permits). The cost of permits has, in some cities, been linked to the environmental performance of vehicles. Visitor permits are typically provided as part of the process.

Evidence

There is little evidence of the impacts of residential parking policy on car ownership levels and travel behaviour relative to the importance of the residential parking as a total of all parking acts. In a recent study in New York City, the provision of free on-street parking was estimated to increase 'private car ownership by nearly 9%; that is, the availability of free street parking explains 1 out of 11 cars owned by households with off-street parking' (Zhan, 2013). In addition to encouraging car owner-ship, the provision of convenient parking also, unsurprisingly, stimulates more trips by car (Weinberger, Seaman, & Johnson, 2009). Weinberger (2012) also explores how parking provision interacts with public transport accessibility concluding that there is 'a clear relationship between guaran-teed parking at home and a greater propensity to use the automobile for journey to work trips even between origin and destinations pairs that are reasonably well and very well served by transit' (p. 93). It is hypothesised that this will be even more pronounced for non-work trips where the des-tination set is more dispersed. Engel-Yan and Passmore (2013) conducted a study in Toronto of the impact of car sharing on requirements for dedicated parking spaces. This study is important since it considers the implications for parking standards for buildings where such schemes are in operation. Their analysis suggests that 'the presence of dedicated carshare vehicles is associated with reduced vehicle ownership and park-ing demand at the building level' (p. 82).

So, the presence of ample parking appears to have a relationship with increased vehicle ownership and use. What happens when space is con-strained? Evidence from the United Kingdom and United States suggests that where on-street parking is constrained, vehicle owners are more likely to make non-car trips and particularly to walk shorter trips (Balcombe & York, 1993; Rodriguez, Aytur, Forsyth, Oakes, & Clifton, 2008). Balcombe and York also attempted to establish the likely response to increases in parking congestion. The proportion of people that would reduce the number of vehicles held was about the same as would seek to increase ownership (although no comparator in uncongested areas was pro-vided). Importantly, the most popular responses were to consider moving to another area which suggests some limits on residential parking policy as a restraint on ownership if greater levels of supply are relatively freely available elsewhere. Balcombe and York also reported a tendency to hold on to older vehicles where residents had to frequently park some distance from home, which may stifle the uptake of cleaner technologies. As more than 30% of people normally parked more than 50 metres from home at some of the sites surveyed, this also poses challenges to electric vehicle adoption unless public charge points are available in sufficient numbers. This becomes a significant issue for the urban realm.

Discussion

Residential parking policy is one important part of the decisions of a city about its stance on vehicle ownership and use. It is a complex decision-set as cities have developed during different periods of car ownership and have areas with very different characteristics. A conscious strategy for managing the current and future supply of residential parking is essential.

Ample parking supply is correlated with increased vehicle use holding all other things equal. Limiting ownership by not providing enough spaces encourages fewer journeys by car. However, it can also create unwanted spillover effects to the surrounding area and requires managing. Work on car free developments suggest there could be an unmet demand for these types of development although the total of such stock relative to the whole housing stock is likely to remain small.

Undoubtedly, in recent years, there has been an oversupply of residential off-street parking in many places, particularly at the periphery of cities. This generates additional costs for all home owners whether or not they wish to possess a car. Planning policy has yet to catch up with developments such as car sharing clubs which offer the potential to reduce the space given over to parking.

I believe that, wherever possible, space for parking vehicles should be decoupled from the purchase cost of the residential unit. This makes the costs transparent without rationing to a degree which creates overspill. Where on-street parking is the only solution and where demand is close to supply then rationing through the use of permits which are linked to the number of vehicles which are owned seems progressive. There are also arguments in favour of those choosing to own more vehicles (than the average for the street) compensating those with fewer vehicles for the loss of amenity that their 'over parking' creates.

RETAIL PARKING POLICY

A useful start point assumption is that retailers are seeking to maximise the accessibility to their target market customers. This is where the consensus on retail parking policy ends. In particular, the tension between providing good access to car-based, bus, cycle and pedestrian customers has remained frustratingly unresolved. Indeed, following the North American model, many countries have permitted large scale out of or edge of town shopping developments which are purpose built for car-based visitors. These typically offer free parking, certainly for those that shop at the mall development. The provision of free parking for out of town developments suggests to edge of centre and city centre retailers that the parking restrictions in operation there are unfair and a clear handicap to their businesses. This section reviews the extent to which there is light as well as heat in this debate. It necessarily focuses on the evidence base published around retail choice and parking provision. A major gap or oversight in the literature is the presence of bigger picture changes such as the growth in internet shopping which is changing the competitive position of retail outlets irrespective of the presence or absence of parking in the vicinity.

Options

The options for managing retail parking are relatively straightforward although they may be applied in different ways and different combinations within a city.

1. Parking can be provided free or, more accurately, as part of the bundle of costs associated with an activity. Out of town centres, for example typically do not directly charge the users for parking but will recoup the costs of constructing and maintaining the large areas of parking through shop rental fees which indirectly filter through to the consumer. Free parking is not restricted to out of town centres but is typically applied elsewhere with a time limitation (such as 30 minutes with no return to the area within two hours). Such schemes can be used to manage the demand for spaces whilst also encouraging regular turnover of spaces. They are unlikely to be appropriate in city centres with very high levels of demand where such schemes encourage cruising activities looking for space and contributing to congestion (Shoup, 2006).

2. Paid for parking can work on or off-street where different tariffs are used to reflect the cost of the land (higher nearer busy centres) and the convenience and quality of the parking provision. Parking pricing is also often used to signal what type of users are welcome – with a distinction made between 'short-stay' and 'long-stay' parking. Here the aim is to use tariffs which discourage people parking all day for commute purposes for example, where there is a high demand from shoppers for shorter visits. High tariffs are applied for stays over a couple of hours in short-stay car parks, thus discouraging, rather than banning, longer stay parkers. One of the key aspects of short-term parking for retail is to encourage the turnover of spaces and this therefore requires active management of the use of spaces (via enforcement officers).

Park and Ride is applied in some cities with a strong emphasis on supporting visitor journeys and shopping trips. Elsewhere there is more of a focus on the commute. For insights into the choice of park and ride in cities see Dijk and Montalvo (2011) and for information on impacts see Chapter 9 later in this book.

Evidence

Hensher and King stated in 2001 that there is a 'dearth of information, locally, nationally and internationally' with respect to responses to changes in parking pricing, supply, security, access rules and in particular on their decision to select the retail centre to visit (*ibid.*, p. 177; see also Tyler, Semper, Guest, & Fieldhouse, 2012). In reviewing one of the few studies looking at the relationship between parking provision and local economic retail strength, I concluded back in 2006 that 'there appears to be no systematic relationship between the provision and convenience of parking spaces at different types of urban centres and their economic performance' (Marsden, 2006, p. 453). An update of the review work from 2006 shows that retail parking remains an under-researched topic. Kobus, Gutiérrez-i-Puigarnau, Rietveld, and Van Ommeren (2013) estimated the elasticities of demand for parking on and off-street. They suggest that on-street parking should have a premium which reflects their benefits to drivers from reduced walk times. Location specific studies have been reported from various places such as Dublin (Kelly & Clinch, 2009) and Vilnius (Klementschitz & Stark, 2008). The focus of these studies remains on the relationship between price, convenience and parking location within a centre.

As yet, comparatively little effort has been put into the study of the extent to which parking prices affect which retail centre people will visit – a matter of huge importance to the vocal retail stakeholder groups and of high political importance. Mullen and Marsden (2014) interviewed 31 stakeholders as part of a study examining whether, and if so how, cities compete with each other. The study looked at a small sample of major English cities outside London and, for each, a smaller local town or city that sits within the same functional economic area. The work revealed that major cities typically have a strong retail offer (as do some smaller historic centres) and these cities can act as price setters for parking. The main brake on price setting is the extent to which they may lose custom to out of town centres. Nonetheless, the experience of being in the city centre was critical to their distinctiveness. The smaller towns were typically struggling to maintain a healthy retail sector. Prices were generally quite low and were set with three different constraints. The authorities were aware of the difficulty of competing with out of town centres which drove prices down. The town centres were also subject to competition at the margins from neighbourhood level shopping and shopping in the major regional centre. Finally, they saw other similar towns to them in the vicinity as competitors and they were able to very accurately describe their position in a parking cost league table. Studies of retail parking policy which do not pay sufficient account of the alternatives and the impacts of prices and availability on shopping destination choice, frequency and duration are missing key variables that matter to policy makers.

Similarly, the discussion around the cost and availability of car parking spaces ignores the many shopping trips that are non-car-based. A euro spent in a shop by a cyclist has the same value to the retailer as one spent by a car driver. In the United Kingdom, one-third of all shopping journeys are made by non-car modes as the main mode. The best source of information on shopping spend by different users comes from work undertaken for the Association of London Government (Tyler et al., 2012). Their study found that 'Shopkeepers consistently overestimate the share of their customers coming by car. In some cases, this is by a factor of as much as 400%' (p. 5; see also Mingardo & van Meerkerk, 2012). Importantly however, whilst 'car drivers spend more on a single trip; walkers and bus users spend more over a week or a month. In 2011, in London town centres, walkers spent £147 more per month than those travelling by car. Compared with 2004, spending by public transport users and walkers has risen; spending by car users and cyclists has decreased' (p. 5). The findings need to be seen in context, as London has a very dense network of public transport provision relative to many cities. Some of these findings have been seen also in Graz and Bristol (Sustrans, 2006). Nonetheless, this points to the need for much greater attention and awareness to be given to the changing nature of shopping and of those accessing shopping centres. With increased internet shopping it is no longer necessary to have the car close by to take bulky goods home. The evolution of research on retail parking policy needs to incorporate an understanding of the change in the retail sector and shopping practices.

Discussion

The debate about draconian town centre parking policies is seeking to address the wrong issue. Maximising the strength of retail centres means making them places that people want to go to; however they choose to get there. The evidence from London points to the need for a much broader understanding of the spend by users of all types and for strategies to promote access by car and non-car users alike.

The debate about town centre parking policies is also missing the point for another reason. Whilst I suggest earlier that the cost of parking at out of town centres is bundled with the cost of shopping and is not 'free', it is still a crucial differentiator between town centre and out of town retail which, the evidence suggests, encourages more out of town shopping. Unbundling (as also suggested for residential units) parking price from shopping fees at least provides a clear cue to drivers as to what each element costs. Beyond that, it is not useful to get too drawn in to the politics of out of town versus town centre. Out of town centres are often large pedestrianised areas with high quality (if bland) covered and heated (or cooled) shopping environments. Shoppers are attracted by a diversity of shopping offer and a good environment to shop in. This is where town centres need to compete and to do so needs a coherent parking policy. Weaker centres may need low fees or time restrictions whereas stronger centres not only can, but must levy higher fees in order to manage congestion and make public spaces attractive places to be – and that goes for all users not just car drivers.

WORKPLACE PARKING POLICY

Workplace parking is important for different actors in different ways. A key objective for employers is to maximise their accessibility to employees.

The wider the labour pool, the lower the pressure on wages and the greater the potential to match skilled people to jobs (Laird, 2006). Accessibility needs to be considered by public transport, bike, walk and car, with studies on social exclusion noting that proximity is not always a good indicator that it is easy to access sites by non-car modes (Lucas, 2004). Parking for work also generates the most concentrated pattern of parking over the course of the day with, in the United Kingdom, around 30% of all parking acts during the week occurring before 9:30 am (RAC, 2012). This clearly makes the management of commuter parking a challenge and an important contributor to urban congestion and pollution. Commuter parking acts are, however, only 28% of all parking acts in the United Kingdom (*ibid.*)

Options

Parking is a cost to employers and it may be physically difficult or environmentally undesirable to accommodate the potential demand for parking. Equally, the provision of parking may be seen to be a perk or an 'entitlement' of the job. The demand for workplace parking has been managed in a variety of ways:

1. On-site free parking, where employers provide free parking to employees as part of their employment package. The costs of parking are absorbed by the business and the presumption is that the provision of parking is sufficient to accommodate demand.
2. On-site paid and managed parking is more typically offered by employers where there is a capacity constraint or where the employment is located in a central area and constraints on parking have been required by the local authority.
3. Off-site parking can be provided through rental agreements with private parking suppliers.

There are clearly various variations on these broad classifications. In particular, recent years have seen a number of advances in the sophistication of on-site parking management. These include parking cash-out schemes where employees are offered incentives to use their car less frequently or to surrender their permits and innovations in permit management (Enoch, 2002; Shoup, 1997), where employees can purchase different levels of access to parking spaces (e.g. right to search or a guaranteed place) or where fees are determined according to other criteria such as the environmental performance of vehicle or enrolment in liftsharing schemes (Rye & Ison, 2005).

Interest has also begun to grow in workplace parking levies, which are schemes designed to capture a tax of some sort on the provision of parking at sites of employment, typically above some minimum threshold of employer size. These charges may or may not be passed on to the employees which clearly impacts on their likely effectiveness as a tool to influence mode-choice. Nonetheless, they overcome part of the problem of the provision of parking as a tax free perk. Van Ommeren and Wentink (2012) found, using Dutch data, that free parking at work 'induces welfare losses of about 10% of employer parking resource costs' (p. 965). Chapters 13–15 provide an overview of impacts of the first workplace parking levy schemes to be implemented.

Evidence

It is not possible here to provide a comprehensive overview of all of the evidence on workplace parking. Excellent reviews of the evidence of the impacts of employer parking policies can be found in TCRP (2005) and Shoup (2005). Further examples are provided in Chapter 11 onwards of this book. Nonetheless, some important common messages emerge. One of the main behavioural responses of commuters to parking restrictions is a change in parking location (as duration is typically outside of their control). This is in contrast to those parking for retail where walk time is valued more highly than search time and in-car access time (Axhausen & Polak, 1991; Shiftan, 2002). This means that commuters look to find cheaper or free parking in the vicinity, with some studies reporting walk times of up to 30 minutes (Rye, Cowan, & Ison, 2004). Klementschitz and Stark (2008) found that more than 50% of commuter parkers could avoid parking fees at work and highlighted the importance of the introduction of effective controlled on-street parking in the areas around workplaces with strong parking management.

A further means of avoiding workplace parking prices is to change mode or car share. Shoup's work on parking cash out confirms this to be a significant option with a mix of shift to transit, car share and walk and cycle observed (1997). This points to the need to look at workplace parking policies as a part of a broader set of workplace travel planning policies that are in place (Roby, 2010). Parking restrictions are typically introduced alongside incentives to change mode in order to maintain the accessibility of the workplace. Buehler (2012) examines the role of bicycle parking, cyclist showers, free car parking and transit benefits as determinants of cycling to work in the Washington, DC area. He finds that 'bicycle parking and cyclist showers are related to higher levels of bicycle commuting – even when controlling for other explanatory variables. The odds for cycling to work are greater for employees with access to both cyclist showers and bike parking at work compared to those with just bike parking, but no showers at work. Free car parking at work is associated with 70% smaller odds for bike commuting. Employer provided transit commuter benefits appear to be unrelated to bike commuting' (p. 525). Buehler's is one of few pieces of work directly examining the role of cycle parking provision on mode-choice.

Discussion

There is a section of the working population that will drive to work when given a 'free permit' to do so but who are prepared to surrender that permit and choose other modes when suitably incentivised to do so. Unbundling parking costs from employment packages and charging (or taxing the perk) accordingly provides a more transparent signal. In particular, removing the 'all or nothing' decision about holding a permit and incentivising less frequent usage appears effective.

It has been argued that good parking provision is critical in encouraging employers to relocate into an area (Gerrard, Still, & Jopson, 2001). However, a recent study exploring the role of travel demand restraint policies in economic development has found that employers locating to areas with good accessibility do not expect local authorities to agree to high levels of free parking. Whilst authorities were all able to discuss the potential for employers to locate elsewhere for better parking, none were able to provide examples of when this had happened (Mullen & Marsden, 2014). It appears that other factors such as the availability of skilled employees and proximity to markets are more important in the business location decision (McQuaid, Greig, Smyth, & Cooper, 2004). Once again, however, the evidence base on the more individual level impacts of policies dominates the level of evidence about parking provision and locational choice for businesses of various sorts.

INTEGRATING PARKING POLICY

Having looked at residential, retail and workplace parking separately, it is necessary to consider these policies together and, perhaps more importantly, their role in a broader more integrated transport strategy. Managing parking is fundamental to the effective functioning of cities. This is however somewhat different to using parking policy as a key tool to reduce the overall demand for travel. The former requires effective combinations of spaces, regulation, information and enforcement. The latter requires a vision for the city and the balance between the different modes that will be used to connect the city. This is more than a semantic difference, as applying demand restraint policies in parking without reinforcing these policies through roadspace reallocation, improving alternatives and better land-use planning will be both unpopular and ineffective. Studies on integrated transport policy (May, Shepherd, & Timms, 2000) show that parking pricing and supply adjustments are just one of a series of measures that need to be applied to deliver improvements to congestion, environmental performance and safety.

That is not to suggest that achieving such integration is easy. First, there are real political concerns about the impacts of parking restraint on the local economy, even if the evidence base appears to suggest this is overstated or, in some circumstances wrong (Mullen & Marsden, 2014). Political commitment, local network conditions and organisational capacities are all important in the choice of approach to parking policy (Dijk & Montalvo, 2011). Second, the governance of parking means that the reality of parking management is often far from any economically calculable optimum. The issue of free workplace parking is described above, but even with charged workplace parking there are issues of a complex mix of public and privately owned off-street spaces and on-street provision which can serve to undermine parking policy (Hamer, Young, & Currie, 2012).

This chapter began with a reflection on the importance of parking as a land-use. If parking policy is to work well as part of an overall package of demand restraint, it needs to be applied in conjunction with thinking about land-use planning. In transport terms this means connecting parking policy to non-car accessibility. In areas where non-car accessibility is high, the amount of parking provided should be lower and land-uses which involve significant flows of people should be encouraged. By contrast, where non-car accessibility is low but car access is high, this is better suited to land-uses which are vehicle dependent (such as warehousing) and are unlikely to be successful sites for demand restraint. These principles underlay the thinking behind the Dutch ABC policy, although this was ultimately seen as too prescriptive to be effective (Schwanen, Dijst, & Dieleman, 2004). An alternative application along similar lines from Surrey County Council (2003) in the south east of England is shown in Fig. 1. Here, only particular

	Area 1	Area 2	Area 3	Area 4
Description	Regional or major town centres	Larger town centres and periphery of Area 1 centres	Smaller town centres, urban fringes or inner suburbs	Outer residential areas and isolated built-up areas
Public Transport Accessibility	High – hub for frequent bus and rail services	Good – extensive network of bus routes and possibly suburban rail	Moderate – close proximity to suburban or radial bus or rail corridors	Low – infrequent bus services or long walks to bus stops/rail stations
Parking Reduction % of maximum Standards	0 – 25%	25 – 50%	50 – 75%	75 – 100%
Residential (Density) permitted	high	high/medium	low/medium	low
Large National/Regional Company likely to fit with area	yes			
Medium Urban Function Company likely to fit with area	yes			
Small/Medium Specialised Company likely to fit with area	yes	yes		
Small Localised Function Company likely to fit with area	yes	yes	Yes	

Fig. 1. Matching Parking Standards, Accessibility and Area Type. *Source*: Adapted from Surrey County Council Framework for Parking and Land-Use Development (2003).

types of development are considered permissible in particular places. So, you would permit large national/regional companies to locate in Area type 1 with good public transport services and facilities but not Area type 4. Similarly, Area 1 would not be a good place for low density housing. Where public transport accessibility is good, there is also an expectation that maximum parking standards will be reduced and the land-use and transport access policies work in unison. The table also shows some grey areas where development may be acceptable. These are always matters of judgement but at least it forms the basis of a need to negotiate over the type of development and any remedial measures that may be required to allow the development to proceed.

Putting the right sort of development in the right sort of place is funda-mental to minimising the parking burden and the associated impacts on travel. However, areas are not typically zoned into one use or another but mixed land-use is encouraged to balance housing and local amenities and to provide some local employment opportunities. It is likely that combinations of residential, workplace and retail parking management strategies will need to be brought to bear in some areas. This is where clear and effective management of on-street parking is required to give the right signals. For example, resident parking permits combined with time limited parking to discourage commuter parking in residential areas or short-stay paid parking very close to retail with longer stay facilities for workers slightly further away for town centres (reflecting the relative willingness to walk of the two different user categories). This makes parking a complex task to manage but it is workable provided clear thought is given as to the purpose of the land-uses that are being served and the options that are available.

CONCLUSION

If the overarching land-use and transport accessibility policies are right then there is a greater possibility for other parking management policies to be effectively applied and integrated in broader transport strategies. The statement and analysis above works most easily in a world where land-uses are strictly zoned. The reality is somewhat different, requiring sometimes complex implementation to balance the needs of residents, shoppers and commuters. An optimal parking policy is surely a theoretical construct rather than a practical prospect. Similarly, there is no prospect of a free market for parking and the price of not having some form of regulatory oversight of the parking market would be substantial environmental, congestion and safety externalities (Barter, 2010). That said, intervention has to correct the market whilst effectively working towards the objectives of the city. Vociferous local interests with a short-term outlook can quite easily influence policy for the worse.

Where the costs of parking are unbundled from house ownership or work or shopping, it has a real influence on choices made over vehicle ownership, frequency of parking acts and destination choice. It provides a better level playing field for public transport, cycling or shared mobility services. Current policies appear to lead to an overprovision with a net welfare loss. Minimum parking standards artificially inflate the amount which the private sector would otherwise provide. However, maximum parking standards need to be considered carefully and properly integrated with land-use and wider transport policy to ensure they do not create unwanted spillover effects.

Looking ahead, parking research and parking policy need to adapt quickly to the possibilities that new technologies and changing mobility opportunities provide. Ottosson, Chen, Wang, and Lin (2013) has shown the potential to vary parking prices by time of day within a geographic area and Caicedo (2012) to have pay by the minute parking. In addition, the growing range of mobility services such as car sharing mean that incorporating car share into residential parking standards is now an important issue (Engel-Yan & Passmore, 2013; Shaheen, Cohen, & Elliot, 2010). Should the move towards electrification gather pace then parking policy will be about managing access to energy supply with a far more complex set of issues relating to charge levels, pace of charging and overall grid demands (Ma, Ahmed, & Osama, 2012).

Whilst it is tempting to get drawn in to the web of possibilities that new technology provides, one important element remains constant. It is critical to be clear about what parking policy is for and how it fits in to a broader transport strategy. There has been an overemphasis on the importance of parking pricing to trip frequency, destination and walk times in the literature. This looks at parking policy as a transport problem. It is a transport problem – but a transport problem that needs to serve several masters and many objectives and one which exists because people are typically at one or other end of a trip to do something. My reading of the literature is that there is too much staring down the microscope and not enough looking through the telescope to understand parking policy. Much greater emphasis should be put in to establishing the extent to which parking restraint supports the economy, the environment and social equity. Only then will we be able to develop a consistent policy framing within which good parking management policy can play out and make a long-term difference to travel patterns and the quality of life in our cities.

NOTES

1. A defined amount of parking which must be provided as a minimum for a new development (e.g. a minimum of one space per 25 square metres of floor area).
2. A limit to the amount of parking which can be provided, but not an obligation to provide that amount (e.g. no more than one space per 25 square metres of floor area).

REFERENCES

Al-Fouzan, S. A. (2012). Using car parking requirements to promote sustainable transport development in the Kingdom of Saudi Arabia. *Cities, 29*(3), 201–211.

Axhausen, K. W., & Polak, J. W. (1991). Choice of parking: Stated preference approach. *Transportation, 18*(1), 59–81.

Balcombe, R. J., & York, I. O. (1993). *The future of residential parking.* Project Report 22. Transport Research Laboratory, Crowthorne, Berkshire, UK.

Barter, P. A. (2010). Off-street parking policy without parking requirements: A need for market fostering and regulation. *Transport Reviews, 30*(5), 571–588.

Barter, P. A. (2012). Off-street parking policy surprises in Asian cities. *Cities, 29*(1), 23–31.

Bonsall, P., & Young, W. (2010). Is there a case for replacing parking charges by road user charges? *Transport Policy, 17*(5), 323–334.

Buehler, R. (2012). Determinants of bicycle commuting in the Washington, D.C. region: The role of bicycle parking, cyclist showers, and free car parking at work. *Transportation Research Part D: Transport and Environment, 17*(7), 525–531.

Caicedo, F. (2012). Charging parking by the minute: What to expect from this parking pricing policy? *Transport Policy, 19*(1), 63–68.

Dijk, M., & Montalvo, C. (2011). Policy frames of Park and Ride in Europe. *Journal of Transport Geography, 19*(6), 1106–1119.

Engel-Yan, J., & Passmore, D. (2013). Carsharing and car ownership at the building scale: Examining the potential for flexible parking requirements. *Journal of the American Planning Association, 79*(1), 82–91.

Enoch, M. (2002). UK parking cash out experience, and lessons from California. *Traffic Engineering and Control, 48*(5), 184–187.

Gerrard, B., Still, B., & Jopson, A. (2001). The impact of road pricing and workplace parking levies on the urban economy: Results from a survey of business attitudes. *Environment and Planning A: Environment and Planning, 33*, 1985–2002.

Habib, K. M. N., Morency, C., & Trepanier, M. (2012). Integrating parking behaviour in activity-based travel demand modelling: Investigation of the relationship between parking type choice and activity scheduling process. *Transportation Research Part A: Policy and Practice, 46*(1), 154–166.

Hamer, P., Young, W., & Currie, G. (2012). Do long stay parkers pay the Melbourne congestion levy? *Transport Policy, 21*, 71–84.

Hensher, D. A., & King, J. (2001). Parking demand and responsiveness to supply, pricing and location in the Sydney central business district. *Transportation Research A, 35*(3), 177–196.

IHT. (2005). *Parking strategies and management.* Essex, UK: Institution of Highways and Transportation, HQ Media Services Ltd., ISBN: 0 902933 36 1.

Jia, W., & Wachs, M. (1999, January). *Parking requirements and housing affordability: A case study of San Francisco.* Paper presented at the 78th annual meeting of the Transportation Research Board, Washington, DC.

Kelly, A. J., & Clinch, P. J. (2009). Temporal variance of revealed preference on-street parking price elasticity. *Transport Policy, 16*(4), 193–199.

Klementschitz, R., & Stark, J. (2008, May 22–23). *Shopping centres and car use: Car park regimentations as a potential lever.* In D. Cygas & K. Froehner (Eds.), Proceedings of 7th International Conference on Environmental Engineering, Vilnius, Lithuania.

Kobus, M. B. W., Gutiérrez-i-Puigarnau, E., Rietveld, P., & Van Ommeren, J. N. (2013). The on-street parking premium and car drivers' choice between street and garage parking. *Regional Science and Urban Economics, 43*(2), 395–403.

Laird, J. (2006). *Commuting costs and their impact on wage rates.* Working Paper No. 587. Institute of Transport Studies, University of Leeds, UK. Retrieved from http://eprints.whiterose.ac.uk/2056/. Accessed on September 27, 2013.

Litman, T. (2004). Parking requirement impacts on housing affordability. Retrieved from www.vtpi.org

Lucas, K. (2004). *Running on empty: Transport, social exclusion and environmental justice.* Bristol, UK: Policy Press, ISBN 1 86134 570 4.

Ma, T., Ahmed, M., & Osama, M. (2012, October 7–11). Optimal charging of plug-in electric vehicles for a car park infrastructure. Annual meeting of the IEEE-Industry-Applications-Society (IAS), Las Vegas, NV.

Marsden, G. (2006). The evidence base for parking policies: A review. *Transport Policy, 13*(6), 447–457.

May, A. D., Shepherd, S. P., & Timms, P. M. (2000). Optimal transport strategies for European cities. *Transportation, 27*, 285–315.

McCahill, C. T., & Garrick, N. W. (2010). Influence of parking policy on built environment and travel behavior in two New England cities, 1960 to 2007. *Transportation Research Record, 2187*, 123–130.

McQuaid, R. W., Greig, M., Smyth, A., & Cooper, J. (2004). *The importance of transport in business' location decisions.* Report to Department for Transport, Napier University, Edinburg, UK.

Mingardo, G., & van Meerkerk, J. (2012). Is parking supply related to turnover of shopping areas? The case of the Netherlands. *Journal of Retailing and Consumer Services, 19*(2), 195–201.

Mullen, C., & Marsden, G. (2014). Transport, economic competitiveness and competition: A city perspective, accepted subject to corrections. *Journal of Transport Geography.*

Ottosson, D. B., Chen, C., Wang, T., & Lin, H. (2013). The sensitivity of on-street parking demand in response to price changes: A case study in Seattle, WA. *Transport Policy, 25*, 222–232.

Palevičius, V., Paliulis, G. M., Venckauskaite, J., & Vengrys, B. (2013). Evaluation of the requirement for passenger car parking spaces using multi-criteria methods. *Journal of Civil Engineering and Management, 19*(1), 49–58.

RAC Foundation. (2012). *Spaced out: Perspectives on parking policy.* London: RAC Foundation.

Roby, H. (2010). Workplace travel plans: Past, present and future. *Journal of Transport Geography, 18*(1), 23–30.

Rodriguez, D. A., Aytur, S., Forsyth, A., Oakes, M. J., & Clifton, K. J. (2008). Relation of modifiable neighborhood attributes to walking. *Preventive Medicine, 47*(3), 260–264.

Rye, T., Cowan, T., & Ison, S. (2004, January). *Expansion of a controlled parking zone (CPZ) and its influence on modal split: The case study of Edinburgh, Scotland and its relevance to elsewhere.* Paper presented at the 83rd annual meeting of the Transportation Research Board, Washington, DC.

Rye, T., Hunton, K., Ison, S., & Kozak, N. (2008). The role of market research and consultation in developing parking policy. *Transport Policy, 15*(6), 387–394.

Rye, T., & Ison, S. (2005). Overcoming barriers to the implementation of car parking charges at UK workplaces. *Transport Policy, 12*(1), 57–64.

Schwanen, T., Dijst, M., & Dieleman, F. M. (2004). Policies for urban form and their impact on travel: The Netherlands experience, *Urban Studies*, 41(3), 579–603.

Shaheen, S. A., Cohen, A. P., & Elliot, M. (2010). Carsharing parking policy review of North American practices and San Francisco, California, Bay Area case study. *Transportation Research Record*, *2187*, 146–156.

Shiftan, Y. (2002). The effects of parking pricing and supply on travel patterns to a major business district. In E. Stern, I. Salomon, & P. H. L. Bovy (Eds.), *Travel behaviour: Spatial patterns, congestion and modelling*. Cheltenham, UK: Edward Elgar Publishing.

Shoup, D. C. (1995). An opportunity to reduce minimum parking requirements. *Journal of the American Planning Association*, *61*(1), 14–28.

Shoup, D. C. (2005). *The high cost of free parking*. Chicago, IL: American Planning Association, Planners Press, ISBN: 1-884829-98-8.

Shoup, D. C. (1997). Evaluating the effects of cashing out employer-paid parking: Eight case studies. *Transport Policy*, *4*(4), 201–216.

Shoup, D. C. (2006). Cruising for parking. *Transport Policy*, *13*(6), 479–486.

Surrey County Council. (2003). A parking strategy for Surrey. Supplementary planning guidance.

Sustrans. (2006). Shoppers and how they travel. Liveable Neighbourhoods Information Sheet LNO2. Bristol, UK. Retrieved from www.sustrans.org.uk

TCRP. (2005). Parking prices and fees: Traveler response to transportation system changes, *Transit Cooperative Research Program Report 95*. Washington, DC: Transportation Research Board, Chapter 13.

Tyler, S., Semper, G., Guest, P., & Fieldhouse, B. (2012). The relevance of parking in the success of urban centres, A review for London Councils. Retrieved from http://www.londoncouncils.gov.uk/. Accessed on September 24, 2013.

Van Ommeren, J., & Wentink, D. (2012). The (hidden) cost of employer parking policies. *International Economic Review*, *53*(3), 965–977.

Van Ommeren, J., Wentink, D., & Dekkers, J. (2011). The real price of parking policy. *Journal of Urban Economics*, *70*(1), 25–31.

Weinberger, R. (2012). Death by a thousand curb-cuts: Evidence on the effect of minimum parking requirements on the choice to drive. *Transport Policy*, *20*, 93–102.

Weinberger, R., Seaman, M., & Johnson, C. (2009). Residential off-street parking impacts on car ownership, vehicle miles traveled, and related carbon emissions New York city case study. *Transportation Research Record*, *2118*, 24–30.

Zhan, G. (2013). Residential street parking and car ownership: A study of households with off-street parking in the New York city region. *Journal of the American Planning Association*, *79*(1), 32–48.

CHAPTER 3

PARKING SUPPLY AND URBAN IMPACTS

Christopher McCahill and Norman Garrick

ABSTRACT

Purpose – *This chapter explains the primary factors influencing the growth in parking supply, what the impacts have been in urban areas throughout the United States, efforts that are underway to better manage urban parking supply, and how these findings relate to international cities.*

Methodology/approach – *This chapter offers a review of prior research and literature, and further explores the impacts of parking using historical data from six cities and by focusing on two specific case studies. It also includes a discussion of global implications.*

Findings – *Parking supply has increased by anywhere from 70% to 160% in urban areas throughout the United States, thereby contributing to considerable land consumption and increases in local automobile use. These increases were driven in large part by minimum parking requirements and perceived market demand. Since 1980, parking growth has slowed considerably in cities that have implemented parking limits and parking management strategies.*

Parking: Issues and Policies
Transport and Sustainability, Volume 5, 33–55
Copyright © 2014 by Emerald Group Publishing Limited
All rights of reproduction in any form reserved
ISSN: 2044-9941/doi:10.1108/S2044-994120140000005017

Practical implications — *Parking is typically viewed as a valuable amenity that should be provided indiscriminately. This work outlines the consequences associated with this view and highlights isolated cases in which policies have been successfully implemented to address the negative outcomes of conventional policy approaches.*

Originality/value of paper — *This chapter offers a comprehensive overview of prior research in parking policy and ties the findings to specific outcomes in urban areas throughout the United States. No other study to date has tracked long-term changes in urban parking supply or its impacts. This work provides a valuable perspective on the magnitude of those impacts and the potential to mitigate those impacts thorough policy reform.*

Keywords: Parking policy; urban transportation; land use; travel behavior; history

INTRODUCTION

A century ago, when the earliest automobiles were first introduced into the U.S. market, there were virtually no dedicated parking spaces. Now there are more than 800 million estimated parking spaces in the United States, which amounts to more than three spaces per vehicle (Chester, Horvath, & Madanat, 2010). During this period, the purveyance of parking has transformed the human-built environment more than any other automobile infrastructure, except for maybe freeways in urban areas (Manville & Shoup, 2005), and has raised Americans' expectations of access for automobiles (Robertson, 2007).

Surface parking lots, which are the most common form of parking in the United States, frequently cover more land than the buildings they serve, making them one of the most prominent features of the built landscape (Marshall & Garrick, 2006; Snyder, 1999). This style of development where surface parking dominates has been the primary pattern of growth in formerly non-urbanized areas, but has also contributed to changing land use patterns in urban centers. In some urban areas, parking covers close to one-quarter of the land (Manville & Shoup, 2005; McCahill & Garrick, 2010a). These are typically places that once had far less parking or no designated parking at all, so this change has serious implications for the way those places function and even effects the way people travel.

This chapter explains the primary causes of this growth in parking supply, what its impacts have been in urban areas throughout the United States, and efforts that are underway to better manage urban parking supply. It offers a review of prior research and literature, and further explores the impacts of parking using historical data from six cities and by focusing on two specific case studies. Finally we consider the global implications of these findings by comparing the American cases to international cities.

FACTORS DRIVING PARKING SUPPLY

Two primary factors drive increases in parking supply. The first is that most jurisdictions require a minimum amount of parking with any new development. The second is that developers are often reluctant to provide what they consider to be too little parking to meet market demands. Accompanying these factors is the fact that in many places land is so inexpensive and automobile use so prominent that parking is viewed as a perfectly productive use of land.

Parking Requirements

Ferguson (2004) provides a comprehensive history of parking requirements in the United States. During the first half of the twentieth century, a small number of American cities had begun to incorporate parking requirements into their zoning codes, beginning with larger cities. By the 1970s, however, this group included more than 95% of cities with populations greater than 25,000. Parking requirements remain common in most communities today, though some typically larger cities have revised their policies considerably, as discussed later.

Parking requirements often vary by land use type. For example, municipalities usually specify a certain number of required spaces per dwelling unit, room or bed, for residential uses, and, most commonly, per unit floor area for retail or office uses. These minimum requirements have generally increased over time and now typically fall within the range of three to four spaces per 1,000 square feet of building floor area (Ferguson, 2004; Kusmyak, Weinberger, Pratt, & Levinson, 2003; Shoup, 1995). The purpose of these requirements is primarily to ensure that sufficient parking is provided near destinations to prevent the overflow of parking into nearby facilities (Kusmyak et al., 2003).

As discussed earlier, parking requirements are only one factor driving parking supply. However, they are particularly important because they establish a lower limit on parking supply that is essentially permanent and relatively inflexible. This approach has been criticized because meeting these requirements typically requires large amounts of land (Kusmyak et al., 2003) along with considerable capital and maintenance costs (Shoup, 1999) and because the costs are often hidden, which distorts the market in favor of automobile use (Feitelson & Rotem, 2004; Shoup & Willson, 1992).

Perceived Market Demand

The role that developers and lending agencies play in dictating parking supply is less well understood. In some cases — even when parking requirements are lower — developers are still reluctant to provide parking at this lower level without additional incentives such as greater building intensity allowances (Kusmyak et al., 2003). In other cases, developers fear that not providing ample parking may hurt their ability to compete for tenants or secure funding from lending agencies. Ultimately, these decisions also depend in large part on the value of land and the quality of alternative travel options in the area (Voith, 1998).

In many cases, parking provision is set to match those of nearby or similar developments, regardless of how the demand was determined at those locations. As the following section reveals, however, parking supply typically exceeds demand, even at peak usage. When developers recognize that there is an existing abundance in parking supply and that there are opportunities to provide less, they will often willingly provide the minimum amount required or seek further reductions (Kusmyak et al., 2003; MacMillan, 2013a). The result is that, although parking supply often exceeds minimum requirements, it could also be quite lower, particularly in urban areas.

Estimates of Parking Demand

Tracing the sources of minimum parking requirements can be difficult, but most estimates of parking demand originated from a handful of studies conducted over the past several decades (Ferguson, 2004; Shoup, 1999).

The earliest recommendations for setting parking requirements came from national surveys of parking standards conducted by the Eno Foundation beginning prior to 1950. The Institute of Transportation Engineers (ITE) adopted values from those surveys as recommended practice as early as 1950. Parking generation estimates from observed parking demand data were first published by ITE in 1987 (Ferguson, 2004). A fourth edition of ITE's *Parking Generation* was published in 2010 and includes values for 106 different land uses (Institute of Transportation Engineers, 2010).

Another key study, published by the Urban Land Institute (ULI) in 1982, was the largest of its time to estimate commercial parking demand (Shoup, 1995). The recommendations from that study − which called for more than four spaces per 1,000 square feet of building floor area − are intended to meet parking demand at the 20th busiest hour of the year based on data from 506 sites in the United States and Canada. The ULI publication, *Parking Requirements for Shopping Centers*, serves as a basis for estimating parking demand at shopping centers in many cities; it was updated in 1999 (Urban Land Institute & International Council for Shopping Centers, 1999).

As critics have pointed out, parking demand estimates of the type outlined above are problematic for a number of reasons. Most notably, these estimates typically relate parking demand to building space, despite this relationship being weak in reality (Shoup, 1999). Moreover, these estimates fail to account for the fact that price and supply of parking itself both influence demand (Kusmyak et al., 2003; Shoup, 1995). Donald Shoup − author of *The High Cost of Free Parking* and many research papers on the subject − has argued that parking demand cannot be determined without taking price into account. For example, his research reveals that parking demand is close to 20% lower when employees pay for parking at work (Shoup, 1995).

Most studies of parking supply and demand reveal that existing supply is actually considerably underutilized. Some of the earliest studies in the 1980s and 1990s found that parking facilities are typically only 50−80% occupied (Kusmyak et al., 2003; Snyder, 1999; Willson, 1995). A more recent study by Marshall and Garrick (2006) comparing suburban and urban sites revealed similar findings. That study found that suburban sites providing 79% of required parking were only 50% utilized at peak, while urban sites providing only 45% of required parking (half the supply rates of suburban sites) were 80% occupied at peak.

Research of this kind highlights some of the difficulties in predicting parking demand, particularly in urban areas where there are often a wider variety of transportation options and opportunities for shared parking facilities. A recent study in King County, Washington, considered 100 different factors related to development type, household characteristics, accessibility by different modes, and land use patterns to determine how each influences residential parking demand (Rowe, McCourt, Morse, & Haas, 2013). That work revealed that neighborhood block size, population and job density, and walking and transit access influence parking demand by as much as 50%. The King County study provides precisely the type of information that is needed to develop more accurate estimates of urban parking demand, but studies like this one are cumbersome and scarce.

PARKING IN URBAN AREAS

Judging by the current nationwide supply of parking, the growth rates of parking in the United States during the twentieth century have been staggering. While the largest quantities of parking are often at suburban commercial locations (Davis, Pijanowski, Robinson, & Kidwell, 2010; Marshall & Garrick, 2006; Snyder, 1999), the impact of parking growth in many formerly dense urban areas has been markedly more dramatic in terms of its impact.

To better understand the magnitude of these changes and their impacts, we tracked parking supply in six small U.S. cities over a period of more than forty years. The cities are Arlington, Virginia; Berkeley, California; Cambridge and Lowell, Massachusetts; and Hartford and New Haven, Connecticut. These cities were selected from a database of more than 100 cities because they have populations in the range of 100,000–300,000 people and experienced relatively little population growth over the study period – indicating they were largely built up by 1960 and later adapted to changes in automobile use. While citywide population densities varied somewhat in 1960 – ranging from 2,600 people per square km in Arlington and Lowell to 7,000 in Cambridge – a majority of the population in each city was concentrated in dense, central areas. Automobile ownership rates were all in the range of 0.23–0.36 vehicles per person.

Despite their many similarities prior to 1960, they now represent very different conditions, particularly with regards to automobile use and land use patterns. Using aerial photographs dating back to the 1950s, we estimated the amount of land devoted to off-street parking and determined the total number of parking spaces in each city at twenty-year intervals.

We relied on journey-to-work reports from the U.S. census to determine the number of residents, the number of employees, and commute mode shares for each time period. As reflected below, journey-to-work statistics were not reported for one city, Lowell, in the year 1960.

Of the six cities studied, off-street parking supply increased by anywhere from less than 70% in Berkeley to more than 160% in New Haven. For most of these cities, the growth was most pronounced in the period leading up to 1980, during which time parking supply increased by between 50% and 90%. After 1980 however, while parking growth continued in all of the cities, these increases were only 11% in three of the cities. Even more pronounced are the changes in the number of parking spaces per person (residents and employees), also shown in Fig. 1. Given fluctuations in population and employment, the number of available parking spaces per person actually leveled off or decreased in three of the cities, while continuing to rise in the other three. The implications of these changes are discussed below.

The differences in parking growth among the six cities are linked to a number of factors including the extent of demolition during urban renewal efforts in the 1960s and 1970s, local parking policies and regional development and travel patterns. These differences are best illustrated by the two cities (Cambridge and New Haven) described in case studies below. By linking these changes to specific outcomes, this work casts new light on two key interrelated issues associated with a large supply of parking in urban areas. The first is the physical impact of parking in areas that were historically

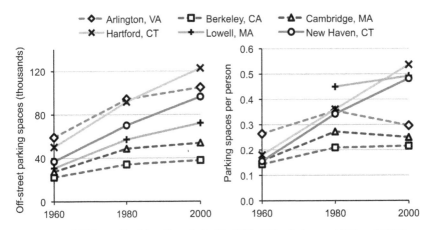

Fig. 1.   Off-Street Parking Supply in Six U.S. Cities between 1960 and 2000.

dense and the second is the effect that these changes have on local travel behavior in cities that predate automobiles. While there has been some speculation regarding the magnitude of these impacts, no other work to date has demonstrated precisely how great these changes have been.

Physical Impacts of Parking

By analyzing 100 parking lots of various sizes and dividing the total lot size by the number of spaces, we determined that an average off-street parking space requires around 30 m^2 of area (including space for maneuvering), which a typical commuter occupies for 8 hours each day. Multiply this by thousands of employees working in any given downtown and one can easily imagine setting aside a substantial portion of a city for storing cars. This fact − often downplayed or overlooked by planners and engineers − has important implications in urban areas with limited land.

The theory of automobile use and land consumption was advanced considerably through the work of Shin, Vuchic, and Bruun (2009). By developing a complex mathematical model of urban land use, they demonstrate that increases in automobile use are linked inseparably to drastic changes to the urban built environment, primarily through the loss of land needed for parking. This finding − later validated with data from McCahill and Garrick (2012) − echoes earlier work reported by Newman and Kenworthy (1999) and by Manville and Shoup (2005). Recent estimates show that parking now accounts for anywhere from 10% to 40% of land in urban central business districts (CBDs) (Akbari, Rose, & Taha, 2003; Marshall & Garrick, 2006; McCahill & Garrick, 2010a). In the 1960s, parking typically accounted for less than 24% of CBD land (Manville & Shoup, 2005).

This sizeable commitment of land for parking is fundamentally at odds with key characteristics that are associated with efficiently functioning urban places − characteristics such as density, mixed-use development and a human-scale environment. Parking often degrades the quality of the urban environment, which discourages walking and undermines the economic success of CBDs (Manville & Shoup, 2005; McCahill & Garrick, 2010b; Mukhija & Shoup, 2006; Voith, 1998; Willson, 1995). Parking also uses up land that could otherwise be invested more productively, thereby inhibiting higher concentrations of activities and lowering land values (Manville & Shoup, 2005; McCahill & Garrick, 2012; Willson, 1995). It has recently been the case that researchers have begun to consider the magnitude of these impacts over longer periods of time.

This recent research only lends more credibility to an idea posed decades earlier by writers such as Jane Jacobs and Lewis Mumford: that cars and cities don't mix. In the early 1960s — when urban renewal efforts were entering their peak — noted urban studies writer Jacobs cautioned, "too much dependence on private automobiles and city concentration of use are incompatible" (Jacobs, 1961). Although Mumford recognized the advantages that modern automobiles offered, he also warned that they would bring, "congestion and frustration, plus a threat of stagnation and blight, to the city" (Mumford, 1963, p. 9). Instead, he argued for the "virtues of concentration" (Mumford, 1963, p. 29) and insisted that cities should be planned primarily around pedestrians and well-served by transit. As it turns out, one of the greatest obstacles to accommodating a lot of cars in cities is finding room for parking without displacing everything else.

Parking and Travel Behavior

Although parking is often considered a necessity for satisfying perceived demand relating to rising levels of automobile use in cities, there are many ways in which it actually contributes to these anticipated increases in driving. Roadway capacity improvements have a similar effect, leading to what is commonly called *induced traffic*. Induced traffic results mainly from changes in travel mode, time of travel, routes, destinations, and from new development due to improved driving conditions (Goodwin & Noland, 2003). Compared to the effects of increased road capacity, parking has received considerably less attention from transportation professionals, but the evidence of its influence on travel behavior is compelling. In fact, parking may be one of the most influential factors affecting decisions to drive when other options are available (Shiftan & Burd-Eden, 2001).

A majority of studies explaining the role that parking plays in affecting travel behavior have focused on the price that employees pay for parking at work. Numerous studies have found that employees are more likely to drive to work when parking is less expensive (Hess, 2001; McCahill & Garrick, 2010a; Shiftan & Burd-Eden, 2001; Shoup & Willson, 1992; Willson, 1995). To illustrate this fact, we analyzed parking policies and employee travel behavior for six major employers in downtown Hartford, Connecticut (McCahill & Garrick, 2010a). At locations where employees were offered free parking, 83–95% of employees drove alone to work. However, at one insurance company where employees paid a monthly fee for optional parking, only 71% of employees drove alone to work. These markedly lower rates of driving by generally high-earning employees in a city where driving is the norm are a profound indication of the influence that parking prices play. Of course, these lower rates of automobile use are only possible because there are alternative options such as carpools and public transit, yet parking is the key differentiating factor.

Parking prices also affect mode choice decisions for non-work trips, but since these trips are often discretionary, there are some concerns that higher travel costs can deter visitors (Marsden, 2006; Shiftan & Burd-Eden, 2001). Overall, however, there doesn't appear to be any evidence linking parking prices to CBD success (Marsden, 2006; Tyler, Semper, Guest, & Fieldhouse, 2012). In fact, it has been argued that priced parking is necessary for managing traffic demand in any successful CBD (Shoup, 2006; Voith, 1998).

Fewer studies have looked at the influence that the *availability* of parking has on driving, but those studies suggest the effects are similar to those of parking prices (Shiftan & Burd-Eden, 2001; Weinberger, Kaehny, & Rufo, 2010). When asked if longer search times for parking would affect their behavior, a majority of survey respondents in Haifa, Israel, said they would change their travel mode or travel at a different time of day (Shiftan & Burd-Eden, 2001). Studies in New York and New Jersey also found that parking availability was a key factor explaining automobile commuting in neighborhoods near transit stations (Chatman, 2013; Weinberger, 2012).

The influence of parking on urban travel behavior is likely to be more complex than any prior research suggests. This is due to the combined effects that parking provision has on both automobile capacity and on the urban built environment. As discussed above, improved automobile access makes driving a more attractive option. However, when combined with the associated loss of urban concentration and degradation of the urban environment, alternatives such as walking, cycling, and to some extent transit also become less attractive (Ewing & Cervero, 2010; McCahill & Garrick, 2010b; Zegras, 2010).

To better understand the potential impacts of these combined effects on travel behavior, we compared changes in parking supply to changes in local automobile use for the six cities described above. We relied on mode share data from U.S. census journey-to-work reports to estimate automobile use and we focused exclusively on commuters that both live and work within each city. This ensures that the data reflect changes in travel mode for shorter trips that can be reasonably made by non-automobile modes, depending to some extent upon the available infrastructure and the quality of those alternatives.

Table 1 shows the twenty-year changes in the six cities. Changes in parking per unit area reflect the impacts of parking on the built environment and changes in parking per person reflect parking availability. There is considerably more variation in changes in parking availability, suggesting it potentially has a greater influence than changes in the built environment; however, both measures are linked fairly consistently to greater increases in local automobile use. Changes in local automobile use range from an 18% decrease in Berkeley to a 30% increase in Hartford.

Other factors such as rapid highway construction also contributed to these marked changes in local automobile use, particularly in the period

Table 1. Twenty-Year Changes in Parking Supply and Local Automobile Use.

	Parking Spaces per sq. km			Percent Change	
	1960	1980	2000	1960–1980	1980–2000
Arlington	878	1,397	1,557	59	11
Berkeley	821	1,246	1,379	52	11
Cambridge	1,481	2,625	2,917	77	11
Hartford	1,074	1,968	2,634	83	34
Lowell	812	1,515	1,909	87	26
New Haven	738	1,402	1,927	90	37

	Parking Spaces per Person			Percent Change	
	1960	1980	2000	1960–1980	1980–2000
Arlington	0.26	0.35	0.30	34	−16
Berkeley	0.14	0.21	0.22	45	3
Cambridge	0.16	0.27	0.25	73	−8
Hartford	0.18	0.36	0.54	99	49
Lowell	–	0.45	0.49	–	10
New Haven	0.16	0.34	0.48	120	41

	Portion of Local Commute Trips by Auto			Percent Change	
	1960	1980	2000	1960–1980	1980–2000
Arlington	0.58	0.64	0.66	11	4
Berkeley	0.51	0.42	0.42	−18	0
Cambridge	0.32	0.31	0.27	−1	15
Hartford	0.45	0.59	0.65	30	11
Lowell	–	0.76	0.83	–	9
New Haven	0.50	0.58	0.62	16	7

Source: Parking estimates from aerial photographs; person and automobile use estimates from U.S. census journey-to-work reports.
Note: "–" represents data not available.

before 1980. Given the prior research on parking's influence, however, the role that parking has played cannot be ignored, particularly in cases where supply has more than doubled. As shown in Fig. 2, which plots the growth in local automobile use against the growth in parking spaces per person from Table 1, the link between parking availability and local automobile use is fairly consistent over the study period. This link is most apparent during those periods where parking growth was the greatest, but it is also worth noting the changes that occurred after 1980, by which time a majority of the highway construction and road capacity improvements were completed. During that time, marked parking growth continued in only three cities, along with increases in local automobile use between 7% and 11%. In the three other cities, parking growth slowed to only 11% and local automobile use rose decidedly less or even decreased. In other words, parking was the only major infrastructural change that can be linked to automobile use during this time and the association between the two is quite clear.

Berkeley presents one notable exception to the trends shown in Fig. 2. This is due mainly to the considerable decrease in local automobile use that the city experienced prior to 1980, despite its growth in parking. This indicates that increased parking supply does not necessarily lead to additional automobile use, when other factors make other modes attractive options. Given the lack of detailed mode share data in 1960 (i.e., rates of walking, cycling, and transit use) it is not clear exactly what contributed to the decline in rates of driving. Between 1980 and 2000, however, both parking supply and local driving rates remained constant.

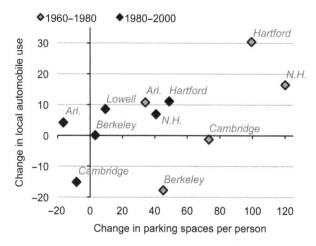

Fig. 2. Twenty-Year Changes in Parking per Person versus Changes in Local Automobile Use.

CASE STUDIES IN PARKING POLICY

In addition to parking requirements, which have been the main focus of this chapter to this point, there are a wider variety of parking regulations aimed not only at better managing existing supply, but also limiting the amount of new parking and even reducing parking supply. Parking management strategies typically offer greater flexibility than conventional minimum requirements and sometimes involve setting maximum allowances; in some cases, they also focus more on the form of parking than on quantity (Engel-Yan & Passmore, 2010). In fact, most large cities impose maximum parking limits in addition to or in place of minimum requirements (Mukhija & Shoup, 2006). Most small- to medium-sized cities still rely heavily on minimum parking requirements to regulate parking, but some have begun implementing parking management strategies, usually in isolated CBD areas.

The six cities we focused on above represent a variety of different policy approaches. For example, Arlington and Berkeley relax their parking requirements near transit stations, while Lowell allows parking spaces to be leased from public facilities or shared among different uses, depending on the time of day that peak demand occurs. Here, we focus specifically on two of the six cities, which, as shown above, were remarkably similar in terms of parking supply and automobile use prior to 1960, but have experienced very different changes since that time. These cities offer an opportunity to understand the differences in their approaches to parking policy – particularly after 1980 – and the prospective impacts of those policies. We also consider one European example, which characterizes a dramatic shift in parking and transportation policy in stark contrast to most examples from the United States.

New Haven and Cambridge

New Haven, Connecticut, and Cambridge, Massachusetts, are coastal New England cities located about 200 km apart. Both are home to respected universities with large student populations living throughout the cities. New Haven is home to Yale University and Cambridge is home to Harvard University and the Massachusetts Institute of Technology (MIT). At their peaks, around 1950, New Haven was home to 150,000 people and Cambridge to 120,000. Although the population in New Haven has since dropped as low as 120,000, it has maintained a dense central business district.

Early in the twentieth century, both cities struggled from losses of industry, metropolitan decentralization, and population decline. Prior to

1960, the city officials began contemplating urban renewal efforts and the two cities faced the prospect of major Interstate highway construction in their centers. In New Haven, these major construction projects were largely realized; in Cambridge, however, reconstruction occurred at a smaller scale and the proposed highways were blocked entirely (McCahill & Garrick, 2010b). Other key differences set these two cities apart, including Cambridge's higher density and its proximity to the region's central city: Boston. Despite their differences, however, these two cases shed important light on the impacts of parking supply and the different roles that parking policy can play in urban centers.

    Prior to 1980, policymakers established minimum parking requirements in both New Haven and Cambridge and focused on off-street parking as a preferred alternative to on-street parking, which was often viewed as an impediment to efficient vehicle movement. Large demolition projects in both cities were viewed as opportunities to construct new off-street parking facilities; however, these proposals were often met with public opposition. In 1967, the City of New Haven agreed to finance the rapid, large-scale construction of additional parking structures, amidst a great deal of opposition from aldermen (Dudar, 1967; Keish, 1967). These efforts continued through the 1970s, despite protests, during which time the director of the city's Parking Authority proposed adding nearly 5,000 parking spaces (an approximate 10% increase based on our estimate of parking supply at the time), which he called, "essential to economic vitality of downtown" ("100 Oppose Audubon St. Garage Plan," 1976, "4,800 Parking Spaces Key To City Resurgence," 1978). Similarly, a 1968 proposal for central Cambridge that included adding 2,000 parking spaces was abandoned after facing public opposition. Nonetheless, the push for parking continued. In 1976, planners in Cambridge recommended additional parking in Harvard Square to serve business owners (Sullivan, 1999).

    At the start of the 1980s, policymakers in New Haven continued to push for additional parking. Upon learning that the city had more downtown parking than any other city in the state, the then Mayor Biagio DiLieto proclaimed, "I am very gratified with this information and I remain strongly committed to maintaining and improving parking facilities for workers, shoppers, and visitors in the downtown area" (Venoit, 1982). As shown in Fig. 1, this pursuit was fruitful; our data reveals that parking supply increased by more than one-third in the following two decades.

    In Cambridge, however, the 1980s marked a substantial shift in parking policy along with much smaller growth in parking supply. In 1981, policymakers first introduced limits on the amount of parking allowed by the city's zoning code (McCahill & Garrick, 2010b). By 1998, these regulations were bolstered through the city's Parking and Transportation Demand Management policy, which limits parking provision further and requires new businesses to outline plans for reducing parking demand (McCahill & Garrick, 2010b).

Currently, both cities enforce minimum parking requirements, but these requirements are considerably more flexible in Cambridge, where there are stringent maximum allowances for common land use types including office, retail and dining. For comparison, we consider the parking regulations for retail land uses in each city.

The parking requirements in New Haven call for a minimum of five parking spaces per 1,000 ft^2 (93 m^2) of retail area for uses totalling more than 600 ft^2 (56 m^2) and 10 spaces per 1,000 ft^2 for uses larger than 5,000 ft^2 (465 m^2). However, the city offers some exemptions and reductions in selected areas located mainly within its CBD. In Cambridge, the highest minimum requirements call for only two parking spaces per 1,000 ft^2 of general retail area (less than half of the requirement in New Haven) or as few as 1.1 spaces per 1,000 ft^2. More importantly, the city does not allow more than four parking spaces per 1,000 ft^2; in some areas the city does not allow more than 1.7 spaces per 1,000 ft^2. In other words, the standard minimum requirements in New Haven are 20% higher than the maximum allowed parking anywhere in Cambridge, representing what are essentially two opposite approaches to parking policy.

In New Haven, parking remains at the center of debate for many proposed development projects. The city has recently attracted considerable growth, but developers insist that inflated parking requirements could deter future development (Bass, 2013). There are a number of documented cases in which the city's requirements were vehemently challenged, with mixed outcomes. One recent proposal to convert a large, vacant building into more than 100 small apartments required nearly a one-third reduction in parking requirements, which developers proposed to meet through an agreement to use existing public parking; their proposal was not opposed (MacMillan, 2013a). In another case, however, a proposed parking supply of 0.6 parking spaces per dwelling unit was deemed too low to allow a 268-unit apartment development project to move forward (MacMillan, 2013b, 2013c). Since developers wishing to provide less than the minimum required amount of parking must engage in a cumbersome appeals process, a majority of new projects will likely add to the city's existing parking supply at nearly the same rate as they have throughout the last 50 years. In contrast, the city of Cambridge relaxed their minimum

requirements early in the 1980s and saw the growth in parking slow considerably, despite maintaining a fairly level number of residents (between
95,000 and 110,000) and experiencing nearly a doubling in its number of
employees since 1960.

Fig. 3 shows the changes in off-street parking provision that occurred in
the centers of Cambridge and New Haven between 1960 and 2000. A large
majority of parking growth in Cambridge was concentrated in areas of

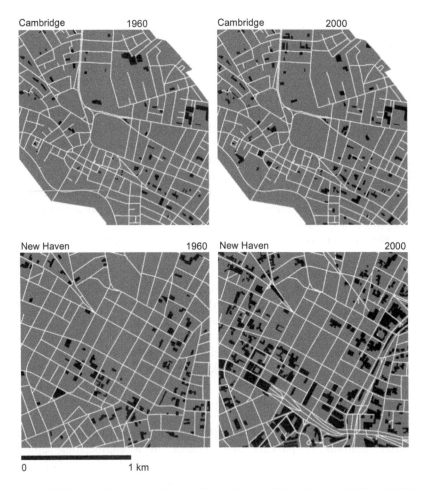

Fig. 3.   Off-Street Parking in Central Cambridge and New Haven, 1960 and 2000.

lower-density development at its fringes, leaving the central parking foot-print virtually unchanged. In New Haven, however, a great deal of new parking was concentrated in the CBD, taking up entire blocks in some cases. The large central blocks absent of parking shown in Fig. 3 represent the New Haven town green and part of the Yale campus.

Not only has this growth in parking consumed large amounts of valuable urban land, but it has also dramatically shifted the transportation system in favor of automobiles – by improving automobile access and by degrading the walking environment. To assess the magnitude of these changes, we estimated changes in the total number of parking spaces available for each person, indicating changes in the relative ease of parking in each city. This number accounts for both residents and employees as reported by the U.S. Census – sometimes referred to as the number of *activities* (Newman & Kenworthy, 1999; Shin et al., 2009). In 1960, both cities had approximately 0.16 off-street parking spaces per person. By 2000, this number had increased to 0.25 in Cambridge (following a slight decline after 1980) and to 0.48 in New Haven. This change in New Haven represents a tripling in the number of parking spaces available per person and a current supply rate that is nearly twice that of Cambridge.

The impacts of improved automobile access on travel behavior are reflected in the marked rise in driving for local commute trips in New Haven – that is, trips that take place entirely in its 50-km^2 area. In 1960, local automobile use was already somewhat higher in New Haven than in Cambridge; 50% of local commuters traveled by automobile in the former, compared to 32% in the latter. Over the next forty years, however, the portion of local commuters driving in New Haven increased to 62%, while in Cambridge this number decreased to 27%. This difference in automobile use for shorter trips (once made entirely by walking, cycling, and public transit) is attributable almost entirely to changes in the local transportation system and built environment. In fact, increases in house-hold income, which are typically useful for explaining rises in automobile ownership and use, were considerably smaller in New Haven than in Cambridge.

GLOBAL IMPLICATIONS

As noted above, the cities included in this study were chosen because they represent older U.S. cities that adapted to rising levels of automobile use over the past century. While Cambridge and New Haven represent two drastically different scenarios, these two cities have much more in common with each other than with many other younger U.S. cities and towns, built with automobiles as the primary mode of transportation. These automobile-oriented cities are typically developed in low-density styles that make any other mode of travel considerably more difficult, even with major retrofits. Nonetheless, there are many compact urban places throughout the United States and around the world that still face decisions similar to those made in Cambridge and New Haven as pressure to accommodate the automobile grows.

As in the United States, many historically compact cities around the world have also taken steps to increase parking supply as automobile use rises and many currently face similar decisions. While some may continue along this path of growing parking supply, as New Haven has for several decades, others have already reversed this trend, as in Cambridge. Two noteworthy examples — one European and one Australian — are discussed below.

The story of parking policy in Zurich, Switzerland, is similar to that of Cambridge. In the 1960s, policymakers in Zurich responded to rising levels of automobile use by adopting minimum parking requirements. In 1989, a few years later than Cambridge, Zurich set maximum allowances on parking. These maximums were more in line with the "city friendly" approach to planning that Zurich enacted a decade earlier. In 1996, policymakers took another contentious step — referred to now as the "historic parking compromise" — by capping citywide parking at 1990s levels and urging parking to be scaled back in locations well-served by transit. Strict limits on parking were ratified by 55% of the city's residents at a public referendum in 2010 and remain in place today.

Zurich now requires roughly 0.75 spaces for each 1,000 ft^2 of space in small retail, which is somewhat less than the number of spaces required in Cambridge and less than one-sixth of the minimum requirements in New Haven. No more than 0.08 spaces per 1,000 ft^2 are allowed in Zurich's city center and no more than 0.50 spaces per 1,000 ft^2 are allowed in surrounding CBDs. This maximum allowance in the city's main center is one-twentieth of the lowest maximum allowances for new construction in Cambridge. Unlike almost any other city, Zurich now maintains a comprehensive inventory of parking supply and carefully tracks changes, in the same way that most cities monitor and manage other transportation infrastructure.[1]

Perth, Australia – a considerably larger city than those above – also took an automobile-oriented policy approach from 1960 until around 1990, during which time parking supply roughly tripled. In the following decade, however, the city implemented a new policy approach incorporating parking and travel demand management. The city's new parking policy, adopted in 1999, includes new licensing fees for all parking facilities and restrictions on the quantity and placement of parking. In the decade since the parking policy was adopted, car traffic has dropped markedly, parking supply decreased by 10%, and all of the parking revenues have been used to fund transit service in the city (Richardson & Merz, 2010).

As these cases demonstrate, the contrasting experiences in Cambridge and New Haven are not necessarily unique to cities in the United States, but reflect common international trends. As some of the earliest world cities to implement parking standards, however, the outcomes in U.S. cities serve as valuable lessons for other compact industrialized cities around the world.

CONCLUSIONS

This chapter provides a general overview of the factors contributing to increases in off-street parking throughout the United States for more than half a century – including minimum parking requirements and perceived market demand. This work also highlights some key issues associated with the conventional approach to parking policy and provision as well as examples of alternative policy approaches.

By focusing on a handful of small cities and tracking the changes in those cities, this chapter offers a unique perspective on the magnitude of the impacts from parking increases with regard to the built environment and travel behavior in urban areas. This work reveals that off-street parking supply increased by anywhere from 70% to 160% over a period of 40 years. In some cities, these increases were fairly constant over the study period. In three cities, parking increases slowed after 1980, despite increases in the combined number of residents and employees. Case studies in Cambridge and New Haven suggest that differences in parking provision are due in large part to differences in policy approaches. Beginning in 1981, Cambridge began to limit new parking and manage existing supply; New Haven still imposes higher minimum parking requirements for new development throughout most of the city.

As the literature suggests, parking increases appear to a have a direct influence on the rates of automobile use within each city. Among cities with the most new parking, automobile use for local trips increased by as much as 45%. Among cities with the least new parking, automobile use for local trips decreased by 16% or more. This is attributable to both improved accessibility for drivers and degraded conditions for non-automobile modes, due to off-street parking.

The often-overlooked impacts of parking provision have important implications for transportation policy in urban areas around the world. These impacts can be addressed through policies that treat parking as one integral component of a multimodal transportation system and that aim to better manage existing supply in conjunction with other transportation infrastructure, rather than continually increasing the supply to meet demand. Cities that implemented parking demand management strategies − including international examples − have experienced a decrease in driving and performed exceedingly well in terms of growth and development. More work is still needed to better understand the factors affecting parking demand in different contexts, including internationally. However, the examples above should serve as evidence that parking caps and management strategies can be implemented successfully and that they can actually be mechanisms for mitigating the negative impacts of parking on land consumption and excessive automobile use in urban areas.

NOTE

1. Norman Garrick's findings from Zurich were originally reported in *The Atlantic Cities* and can be viewed online at http://www.theatlanticcities.com/commute/2012/08/lessons-zurichs-parking-revolution/2874/

ACKNOWLEDGMENTS

We thank the many researchers who contributed to the parking assessments included in this chapter and Bryan Blanc, in particular, for his in-depth study of New Haven. We also thank the Center for Transportation and Livable Systems (CTLS) at the University of Connecticut and the University Transportation Centers (UTC) for funding a portion of this work.

REFERENCES

100 Oppose Audubon St. Garage plan. (1976, July 27). *New Haven Register*. New Haven, CT.

4,800 Parking spaces key to city resurgence. (1978, November 5). *New Haven Register* (p. A18). New Haven, CT.

Akbari, H., Rose, L. S., & Taha, H. (2003). Analyzing the land cover of an urban environment using high-resolution orthophotos. *Landscape and Urban Planning, 63*(1), 1–14.

Bass, P. (2013, March 13). Parking? That's so last century. *New Haven Independent*. New Haven, CT. Retrieved from http://www.newhavenindependent.org/index.php/archives/entry/parking_thats_so_last_century/

Chatman, D. G. (2013). Does TOD need the T? *Journal of the American Planning Association, 79*(1), 17–31.

Chester, M., Horvath, A., & Madanat, S. (2010). Parking infrastructure: Energy, emissions, and automobile life-cycle environmental accounting. *Environmental Research Letters, 5*, 1–8.

Davis, A. Y., Pijanowski, B. C., Robinson, K. D., & Kidwell, P. B. (2010). Estimating parking lot footprints in the Upper Great Lakes Region of the USA. *Landscape and Urban Planning, 96*(2), 68–77.

Dudar, W. (1967, October 15). Garage to be built despite some protests. *New Haven Register* (p. 1). New Haven, CT.

Engel-Yan, J., & Passmore, D. (2010). Assessing alternative approaches to setting parking requirements. *ITE Journal, 80*(12), 30–34.

Ewing, R., & Cervero, R. (2010). Travel and the built environment. *Journal of the American Planning Association, 76*(3), 265–294.

Feitelson, E., & Rotem, O. (2004). The case for taxing surface parking. *Transportation Research Part D: Transport and Environment, 9*, 319–333.

Ferguson, E. (2004). Zoning for parking as policy process: A historical review. *Transport Reviews, 24*(2), 177–194.

Goodwin, P., & Noland, R. B. (2003). Building new roads really does create extra traffic: A response to Prakash et al. *Applied Economics, 35*(13), 1451–1457.

Hess, D. B. (2001). Effect of free parking on commuter mode choice: Evidence from travel diary data. *Transportation Research Record: Journal of the Transportation Research Board, 1753*, 35–42.

Insitute of Transportation Engineers. (2010). *Parking generation* (4th ed.). K. G. Hooper (Ed.). Washington, DC: ITE. Retrieved from http://trid.trb.org/view.aspx?id=1104498

Jacobs, J. (1961). *The death and life of great American cities*. New York, NY: Random House.

Keish, W. E. (1967, February 20). City would tap budget to pay garage bonds. *New Haven Register* (p. 1). New Haven, CT.

Kusmyak, J. R., Weinberger, R., Pratt, R. H., & Levinson, H. S. (2003). Parking management and supply. In *TCRP Report 95: Traveler response to transportation system changes*. Washington, DC: Transportation Research Board.

MacMillan, T. (2013a, May 15). Downtown developer pitches parking plan. *New Haven Independent*. New Haven, CT. Retrieved from http://www.newhavenindependent.org/index.php/archives/entry/parking_plan_pitched_for_new_apartment_tower/

MacMillan, T. (2013b, March 5). Neighbors question star supply plan. *New Haven Independent*. New Haven, CT. Retrieved from http://www.newhavenindependent.org/index.php/archives/entry/star_supply_plan_draws_scrutiny/

MacMillan, T. (2013c, April 10). Star supply plan squashed. New Haven, CT. Retrieved from http://www.newhavenindependent.org/index.php/archives/entry/star_supply_plan_squashed/

Manville, M., & Shoup, D. (2005). Parking, people, and cities. *Journal of the American Planning Association, 131*(4), 233–246.

Marsden, G. (2006). The evidence base for parking policies: A review. *Transport Policy, 13*, 447–457.

Marshall, W. E., & Garrick, N. W. (2006). Parking at mixed-use centers in small cities. *Transportation Research Record: Journal of the Transportation Research Board, 1977*, 164–171.

McCahill, C., & Garrick, N. W. (2010a). Losing Hartford: Transportation policy and the decline of an American city. *18th Annual Meeting of the Congress for the New Urbanism*, Atlanta, GA.

McCahill, C., & Garrick, N. W. (2010b). Influence of parking policy on built environment and travel behavior in two New England cities, 1960 to 2007. *Transportation Research Record: Journal of the Transportation Research Board, 2187*, 123–130.

McCahill, C., & Garrick, N. W. (2012). Automobile use and land consumption: Empirical evidence from 12 cities. *Urban Design International, 17*(3), 221–227.

Mukhija, V., & Shoup, D. (2006). Quantity versus quality in off-street parking requirements. *Journal of the American Planning Association, 72*(3), 296–307.

Mumford, L. (1963). *The highay and the city*. New York, NY: Harcourt Brace Jovanovich.

Newman, P., & Kenworthy, J. (1999). *Sustainability and cities: Overcoming automobile dependence*. Washington, DC: Island Press.

Richardson, E., & Merz, S. K. (2010). Extracting maximum benefit from parking policy: 10 years experience in Perth, Australia. *European Transport Conference*, Glasgow, Scotland, UK.

Robertson, K. (2007). The psychology of downtown parking. *Urban Land, 66*(4), 125–127.

Rowe, D., McCourt, R. S., Morse, S., & Haas, P. (2013). Do land use, transit, and walk access affect residential parking demand? *ITE Journal*, (February), 24–28.

Shiftan, Y., & Burd-Eden, R. (2001). Modeling response to parking policy. *Transportation Research Record: Journal of the Transportation Research Board, 1765*, 27–34.

Shin, Y. E., Vuchic, V. R., & Bruun, E. C. (2009). Land consumption impacts of a transportation system on a city. *Transportation Research Record: Journal of the Transportation Research Board, 2110*, 69–77.

Shoup, D. C. (1995). An opportunity to reduce minimum parking requirements. *APA Journal, (Winter)*, 14–28.

Shoup, D. C. (1999). The trouble with minimum parking requirements. *Transportation Research Part A: Policy and Practice, 33*, 549–574.

Shoup, D. C. (2006). Cruising for parking. *Transport Policy, 13*, 479–486.

Shoup, D. C., & Willson, R. W. (1992). Commuting, congestion and pollution: The employer-paid parking connnection. *Congeston Pricing Symposiam*, Arlington, VA.

Snyder, M. C. (1999). A study of parking supply and utilization in neighborhood commercial centers in the Puget Sound Region, Washington state. *World Parking Symposium II*, Banff, Alberta, Canada.

Sullivan, C. M. (1999). Harvard square history and development. Retrieved from http://www2.cambridgema.gov/Historic/hsqhistory1.html. Accessed on August 23, 2013.

Tyler, S., Semper, G., Guest, P., & Fieldhouse, B. (2012). *The relevance of parking in the success of urban centres: A review for London Councils.* Retrieved from http://www.londoncouncils.gov.uk/policylobbying/transport/parkinginlondon/parkingurban.htm

Urban Land Institute, & International Council for Shopping Centers. (1999). Parking requirements for shopping centers (2nd ed., p. 81). Retrieved from http://www.amazon.com/Parking-Requirements-Shopping-Centers-Institute/dp/0874208289

Venoit, S. J. (1982, December 9). City has most parking of five largest in state. *New Haven Register* (p. 56). New Haven, CT.

Voith, R. (1998). The downtown parking syndrome: Does curing the illness kill the patient? *Business Review (Federal Reserve Bank of Philadelphia)*, (January–February), 3–14.

Weinberger, R. (2012). Death by a thousand curb-cuts: Evidence on the effect of minimum parking requirements on the choice to drive. *Transport Policy, 20*, 93–102.

Weinberger, R., Kaehny, J., & Rufo, M. (2010). U.S. parking policies: An overview of management strategies. Retrieved from http://www.itdp.org/documents/ITDP_US_Parking_Report.pdf

Willson, R. W. (1995). Suburban parking requirements. *Journal of the American Planning Association, 61*(1), 29–42.

Zegras, C. (2010). The built environment and motor vehicle ownership and use: Evidence from Santiago de Chile. *Urban Studies, 47*(8), 1793–1817.

CHAPTER 4

PARKING DEMAND

John Bates

ABSTRACT

Purpose − *This chapter examines the primary factors affecting the demand for parking, distinguishing between residential demands and parking at other destinations. The demand for parking relates not only to where people may want to park, but also at what time and for how long.*

Methodology/approach − *This chapter is largely based on an analysis of the Great Britain National Travel Survey (NTS), over the period 2002−2010. While data on residential parking is straightforward to obtain, extracting data for non-residential parking involves 'following' successive trips made by the same vehicle and deriving the duration of parking, using the NTS 7-day trip diary.*

Findings − *At the home end, the main variations in parking demand are related to housing type and residential density: the issues associated with residential parking are essentially an urban problem. At the destination end, commuting parking dominates because (a) it is the largest single purpose category; (b) with the minor exception of Holiday parking, it has the greatest duration; and (c) the onset of working time is more concentrated than that for other purposes. Nonetheless, at the peak of*

Parking: Issues and Policies

Transport and Sustainability, Volume 5, 57−86

ISSN: 2044-9941/doi:10.1108/S2044-994120140000005010

destination parking activity (around 12 noon), other purposes add about 44% to the base demand due to workplace parking.

The analysis also reveals that only a small percentage of destination parking acts make any payment, and that for those that do, the average is under £2 per stay. On an annual basis, it is suggested that parking consumes about 3% of motoring expenditure but 97% of motoring time (on average).

Practical implications − Residential Parking is only a significant problem at higher densities (above 45 ppHa, say) where the housing types required to support the population density result in competition for on-street parking. For non-residential parking, the dominance of commuter parking causes particular problems both in terms of space provision and its impact on mode choice. Neither form of parking capacity appears to be well managed by current pricing policy, at least on the basis of the British evidence.

Originality/value of paper − To the author's knowledge, diary travel surveys have not previously been analysed to investigate parking demand. While the technique is most relevant to multiple-day diaries like NTS, the approach opens up the possibility of more extensive analysis of other surveys to reveal the patterns of parking, and duration in particular.

Keywords: Duration; purpose; density; charges; on-street; dwelling type

INTRODUCTION

It is a truism that each car journey involves a parking act at both ends (with the minor exception of journeys made purely to pick up or drop off persons or objects). However, the full implications of this are rarely taken into account, either by transport planners or transport modellers. There is a sense in which parking is taken for granted, and only managed or regulated when problems are apparent. In fact, as we shall see, the average car spends most of its life stationary (i.e. parked), while the concentration of transport analysts is on the movement of cars.

Nonetheless, the provision and regulation of parking are important for transport policy, and to make progress on these we need to know the demand for parking. While the mode and destination choice components of standard transport models imply the location of parking, the time of arrival and duration of parking are also central to an understanding of parking demand. In other words, we need to know where, when and for how long, parking acts occur. Previous modelling efforts devoted to parking have been reported (e.g. Bates, Skinner, Scholefield, & Bradley, 1997; Hunt, 1988), but they have not been integrated into the mainstream transport models.

Investigations into the demand for parking are bedevilled by data issues. Much parking is essentially informal, even when it takes place on the public highway, and surveying it is tedious and expensive. For example, one of the most detailed attempts to survey parking in London (MVA, 2000) involved a carefully designed series of observations over about 5% of the total area of Greater London, but when this was updated 5 years later (MVA, 2005), the area sampled was reduced by a factor of 6, on grounds of cost.

More detailed information – especially about duration – may be available from car park operators, but this is usually of restricted quality and subject to commercial confidentiality. While electronic detection of number plates on both entry and exit is becoming more common, such data is primarily used for charging purposes and would not normally be made available for research purposes.

The lack of readily available data on a consistent basis has meant that parking policy remains of essentially local concern, and generally has the quality of 'fire-fighting'. Schemes for controlling residents' parking are only introduced when serious capacity concerns arise, and any associated attempts to charge for on-street parking are resented. Parking restrictions have usually been designed primarily with traffic flow conditions in mind, and are seldom reviewed once implemented. And when serious attempts are made, at the local level, to develop parking policies, these may often be subject to 'competitive response' from neighbouring localities, typically leading to a zero-sum game which is to no one's advantage.

In this chapter we show how large scale travel surveys (and in particular, the British National Travel Survey – NTS) can be analysed to provide useful secondary data relating to parking, revealing both the pattern and the duration of demand. The work reported here makes use of research carried out by the author on behalf of the RAC Foundation (Bates & Leibling, 2012).

In the following section, we provide a brief description of the NTS. This is then followed by two major sections based on analysis of this survey: the third section discusses the more readily available data on parking at the home, while the fourth section demonstrates the potential of such surveys to provide information on 'destination parking' (i.e. at locations away from home). The chapter ends with a discussion relating both to policy and the need for further data.

THE BRITISH NATIONAL TRAVEL SURVEY

National Travel Survey (NTS) is a continuous survey providing up-to-date and regular information about personal travel within Great Britain and monitoring trends in travel behaviour. While earlier surveys were commissioned on an ad hoc basis, fieldwork has been conducted on a monthly basis since July 1988, and since 2002 the annual sample size has been increased to about 15,000 addresses. It is based on a stratified two-stage random probability sample of private households in Great Britain,[1] firstly by selecting the Primary Sampling Units (PSUs) based on postcode sectors, and then by selecting addresses within PSUs.

In the course of the survey, individuals in sampled households are interviewed face-to-face to collect personal information, such as age, gender, working status, car access and driving licence holding. They are also asked to complete a seven-day travel diary and provide details of trips undertaken, including purpose, method of travel, time of day and trip length. For more information, the Technical Reports[2] should be consulted.

The NTS datasets contain several hierarchical levels of records, in particular:

- PSU
- Household
- Individual
- Trip
- Stage
- Vehicle

A subset of the data is made available for research purposes by the UK Data Archive at the University of Essex, and additional variables have been provided on request by the Department for Transport (DfT): the author is grateful for all assistance provided. The basic research, as carried out for the RAC Foundation, covers the years 2002–2008, but a small amount of additional research has been carried out for the years 2009–2010. No warranty is given by the DfT as to the accuracy and comprehensiveness of either the data or the analysis, and the author alone is responsible for the analysis and any possible errors.

The questions about residential parking are straightforward to administer and analyse. By contrast, collating the data on what we refer to as 'destination parking' – which occurs when the car is actually used to convey people to another location to carry out various activities – is much more complex. It thus makes sense to discuss the two kinds of parking separately, even though, as noted, they may to some extent be in competition.

OVERNIGHT PARKING AT HOME

In respect of each household vehicle, the following question is asked in NTS:

Where is the VEHICLE usually parked overnight? Is it ...

1. *... in the garage (at this address),*
2. *not garaged but still on the property of this address,*
3. *on the street or public highway,*
4. *or, elsewhere (at or near your home)? (Specify)*
5. *(DOES NOT USUALLY PARK AT/NEAR HOME)*

This question was not asked in the years 2004–2006, so the data below relates only to the years 2002, 2003, 2007–2010.

Some of the vehicles are not cars, but the majority of these (e.g. vans, land-rovers) require the same sort of parking as cars.

Overall, the total number of vehicles parked in each type of location, appropriately weighted for representativity,[3] are given in Table 1. Between the first two years (2002–2003), the two years (2007–2008) and the last two (2009–2010) there has been a consistent trend of some reallocation between the first two categories, with the proportion in garages falling (from 21.5% to 16.4% to 15.1%). This reduction in the use of garages can be considered to be due to four factors:

- garages are increasingly used for storage of other items besides cars;
- modern cars tend to be larger and do not fit into the garages of older houses;[4]
- modern cars are more reliable, with better corrosion protection, and can be stored in the open with the confidence that they will start; they also have better theft protection;
- there has been a growth in multi-car households – the extra cars cannot be parked in the garage.

Table 1.   Location of Overnight Parking.

Parking Location (V145)	Sample (Re-Weighted for Representativity)[a]	% Proportion (of Respondents)
Garage	12,687.14	17.27
Private property (not garaged)	40,511.83	55.15
Street	17,870.82	24.33
Other	2,031.06	2.77
Not near home	354.81	0.48
Total responding vehicles	73,455.7	

Source: NTS data 2002–2003, 2007–2010.
[a]See Note 3.

However, there has been no overall change in the proportions parked on-street or in the residual categories.

Thus nationally, only about a quarter of vehicles is parked on-street. However, this varies strongly with the type of area and the type of dwelling, and these two factors themselves are of course related. As the best indicator of area type – relating to urban/rural status, we have used the local residential density in persons per hectare (ppHa). In NTS this relates to the sample area (PSU[5]), which is based on postcode delivery points. The PSU density is a much better indicator for street parking than the more conventional 'type of urban area' variable, since even relatively small urban areas can still have an appreciable amount of population at high densities, and this has the expected effect on parking, in that less space is available to accommodate cars off-street.

Table 2 gives some key information by population density. The effect of density on on-street parking is very clear, rising to nearly 70% at the highest density (>75 persons per hectare). At the same time, the average level of cars per household falls regularly with increasing density. Although some of this effect is due to smaller households in the more urbanised areas, the pattern mainly reflects the greater cost (due to parking) and reduced utility (because of the availability of other modes and shorter distances to opportunities) of car ownership. This lower car ownership to some extent offsets the increased tendency to park on-street shown clearly in the last column. However, even with the lower urban car ownership, the propensity *per household* for a vehicle to be parked on-street in the most urban areas is double that in the most rural areas.

The distribution of households according to the NTS is shown in Fig. 1, based on Table 2. The central upward-sloping graph shows the cumulative

Table 2. On-Street Parking by Housing Density.

Population Density (ppHa)	Approximate % of Households Living at this Density	Average Cars per Household	% of Vehicles Parked On-Street
Less than 1	9	1.45	13
1–5	16	1.37	17
5–10	10	1.26	19
10–20	16	1.15	23
20–30	15	1.10	25
30–40	11	1.08	27
40–60	13	0.93	38
Over 60	10	0.64	58
All	100	1.12	25

Source: NTS data 2002–2010 (last column excludes period 2004–2006); author's analysis.

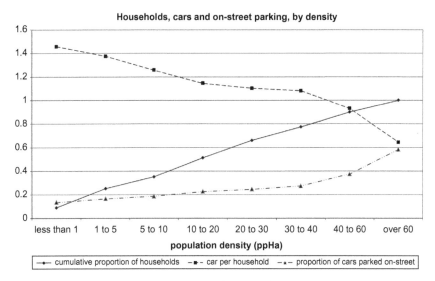

Fig. 1. Key Indicators, by Population Density (Persons per Hectare).

proportion of households living at densities below the value on the *X*-axis. This is based on *all* responding households in all years 2002–2010. About 10% of all households live in the most rural areas (less than 1 ppHA), and another 10% in the most urban areas (greater than 60 ppHA).

In the most rural areas, most of the houses are detached, while in the most urban there are virtually no detached houses and most people live in terraces or flats. In Inner London, about 83% of households are in areas with density greater than 60 ppHA: for Outer London, the corresponding figure is about 20% and for conurbations built-up areas and other urban areas with more than 250,000 population, it is about 10%.

In addition, the downward-sloping curve on the graph notes how average car ownership (here measured as cars per household) falls with increasing population density, from nearly 1.5 at the lowest density to less than 0.7 at the highest. The bottom rising graph shows how the proportion of on-street parking rises with density, with the increase particularly noticeable above 40 ppHa.

Note that within the period 2002–2008 there has been a general increase in cars per household, although this is not evident at the highest densities, as shown in Fig. 2.

However, the latest data, for 2009–2010, shows virtually no change from the 2005–2008 position.

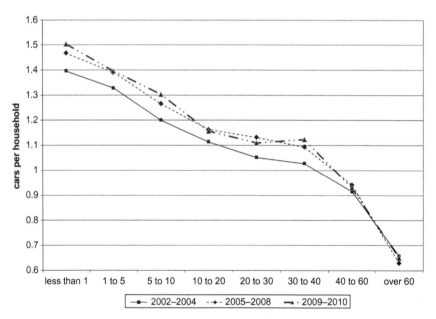

Fig. 2. Changes in Cars per Household over Time, by Population Density.

Table 3. Location of Overnight Parking According to Residential Density.

PSU Density (ppHa)	Responding Vehicles (Weighted Sample)	% Parked in				
		Garage	Private Property (Not Garaged)	Street	Other	Not Near Home
Under 1	8,621.03	21.96	60.74	13.48	3.29	0.53
1–4.99	14,016.41	19.87	60.23	16.58	2.83	0.48
5–9.99	8,104.612	19.40	59.00	18.61	2.35	0.64
10–14.99	6,097.616	17.79	56.14	23.27	2.48	0.32
15–19.99	6,034.527	19.07	55.68	22.04	2.84	0.38
20–24.99	5,409.8	17.38	55.70	24.17	2.36	0.40
25–29.99	5,419.15	16.31	55.62	24.99	2.62	0.46
30–34.99	3,958.863	13.94	57.30	25.58	2.84	0.34
35–39.99	4,167.107	15.47	51.98	28.97	3.08	0.50
40–44.99	2,752.01	12.27	50.36	34.42	2.52	0.44
45–49.99	2,388.614	12.23	47.45	37.74	2.20	0.37
50–59.99	2,226.625	10.05	46.05	41.07	2.45	0.39
60–74.99	2,121.383	8.55	36.76	51.45	2.53	0.71
75 and over	2,137.91	6.83	22.52	65.09	4.55	1.01

Source: NTS data 2002–2003, 2009–2010; author's analysis.

There are different patterns in parking location according to density, as Table 3 shows.

There is a regular pattern whereby Street Parking increases at the expense of the two other main categories (Garage and Private Property) as density increases. While there is some evidence that for multi-car households, the primary vehicle has a higher chance of being parked in a garage, there is no strong indication that secondary vehicles are more likely to be parked on the street.

As far as dwelling type is concerned, the results for the main categories are shown in Fig. 3. The percentage figures indicate the percentage of all vehicles occurring in each dwelling type.

The parking pattern is as one would expect, with over 50% of vehicles in terraced houses or non-purpose-built flats being kept on the street. About 26% of all vehicles are owned by households living in these housing types.

Nonetheless, there are separate effects arising from dwelling type and density on the proportions parking on-street. Even within the dwelling types, the on-street proportion still increases with density, as Fig. 4 shows. In this figure, the two types of flat/maisonette categories have been

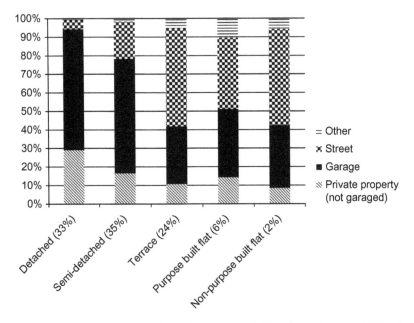

Fig. 3. Where Cars are Parked by Type of Housing. *Source*: NTS data
2002–2003, 2007–2008; authors' analysis.

combined for reasons of sample size; however, at higher densities, there is a
tendency for non-purpose-built flats to have more on-street parking.

Thus, the proportion of vehicles parked overnight on the street is most
affected by housing type and the degree of urbanness, best represented by the
PSU density. In terms of the most common housing type, detached houses
dominate at densities below 10 ppHA, semi-detached houses dominate
between 10 and 50 ppHA, and thereafter terraced housing. Flats and
maisonettes only achieve a share of more than 10% for densities above
45 ppHA, but thereafter rise steadily.

It is not surprising that residential parking is essentially an urban problem, but the analysis shows how both concentration of persons (density)
and the type of dwelling play a role. Since parking anywhere other than at
or near street level involves specialised equipment and/or building arrangements, there is a critical density beyond which it is hardly possible to provide further space for vehicle storage while at the same time maintaining
access to the vehicle and vehicular access to the road system. This makes
the system extremely vulnerable to further increases in car ownership

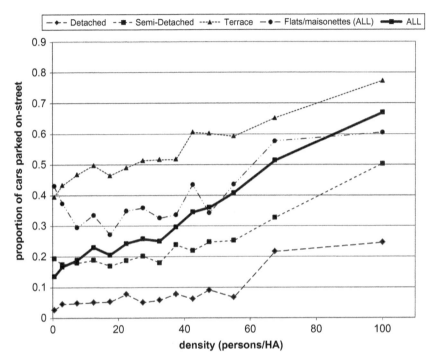

Fig. 4. Proportion Parking On-Street by Dwelling Type and Density. *Source*: NTS data 2002–2003, 2007–2008; authors' analysis.

(though, as we have seen, NTS data suggests that the level of car ownership at the highest densities has hardly changed over 10 years).

The NTS does not ask questions about residents' parking arrangements in terms of whether they have to pay for on-street parking, and there does not appear to be any central register of such schemes, which are operated by local authorities. The research for the RAC suggested that charges for such schemes are low, and their main aim is to 'protect' parking for residents, especially those nearest urban centres, from competition with parking for non-residents. Of course, as we shall see in the next section, there is potential scope for 'shared use', where residents who use their cars for commuting free up spaces during the course of the working day.

In May 2009 the DfT published the results of questions asked in December 2008 about parking on the regular monthly Office for National Statistics (ONS) omnibus survey of around 1,100 individuals in Great

Britain (DfT, 2009). Nearly one in ten (9%) of those who had availability of on-street parking outside their house required a parking permit if they wished to park there. Of these who required a permit, 53% did not have to pay for it, but a quarter had to pay £81 or more a year (it should be noted that the sample was small).

What remains unclear is how far the parking problem in urban areas actually has an impact in suppressing car ownership. Given that the charges are low, any such impact is likely to be associated with the general difficulty of finding a space. There is room for further research here, and this would also be of importance in deciding an appropriate pricing structure.

More detailed evidence on changes in car ownership in London is available from other sources. Comparing the 2001 census with the averages of the three years of the London Travel Demand Surveys (LTDS) shows that while the population of London increased by about 600,000 and the number of households by over 200,000 the number of cars fell by over 100,000 (see Table 4).

The drop in car ownership is spread between the inner and outer boroughs − 50,000 in inner boroughs and 66,000 in outer. All but five boroughs showed a drop, the largest being in Southwark (14,000), but Ealing, Kensington and Chelsea, Richmond and Waltham Forest all experienced a drop of 8,000 or more. The boroughs which increased were Greenwich (by 8,000), Westminster (6,000), Tower Hamlets (4,000), Havering (3,000) and Camden (1,000), despite Camden and Westminster having particularly rigorous parking controls. This shows that parking availability is only one of a number of factors affecting car ownership.

Transport for London (TfL)'s own modelling shows that the following factors explain the level of car ownership at a detailed geographical level:

- household structure
- household income
- tenure

Table 4. Changes in Car Ownership in London in the Context of Other Demographic Changes (Thousands).

	2001 Census	LTDS 2007−2008 to 2009−2010	Absolute Change	% Change
Population	6,993	7,596	+603	+8.6
Households	3,016	3,232	+217	+7.2
Cars	2,693	2,575	−117	−4.3

Source: 2001 census/LTDS.

- nationality
- parking availability
- public transport accessibility
- access to employment and services
- up-front and ongoing costs

Work for TfL by Whelan, Crockett, and Vitouladiti (2010) on car owner-ship at a much finer level of detail concludes that '… parking control, public transport levels of service, and walk/cycle accessibility to key attractions were all statistically significant and had parameter estimates of a plausible sign and magnitude. Findings from a recent study by the DfT on sensitiv-ities to car costs allowed the model to respond to variables that varied in a temporal as opposed to spatial dimension'. However, they point out that the information on parking controls for different areas is very incomplete.

DESTINATION PARKING

In order to produce the figures in this section, a substantial analysis has been carried out of the car driver trips in the NTS diary data set. While NTS is a survey of travel rather than parking, the start and end times of each journey are noted. This allows the parking duration to be calculated by following successive trips through the day and calculating the elapsed time between the end of one trip and the start of the next. In some cases, there are intervening trips by other modes while the car is left parked. However, the nature of the seven-day travel 'diary' makes this a more or less unique source for parking activity of all kinds.

The analytical approach has been to re-form the diary data as home-based tours (a series of car driver trips beginning and ending at the home). In a small number of cases, errors of sequence have been found (e.g. where the end location of one trip does not correspond with the start location of the following, or where the time of arrival is not recorded): these have been discarded. Detailed addresses of destinations are not available, and the best description of the destination location is that according to the NTS 'urban area classification' (the PSU residential density is only available for the home location). With the exception of the data relating to where the vehicle was parked (this question was not asked in the years 2007–2008[6]), all data in this section relates to the sample for 2002–2008.

Note that we have only worked with data where car is the main mode of the trip. This means that journeys (and associated parking) where the car is only used as access to a public transport mode (for example) are excluded. While these may be significant in the context of rail commuting to London, they are a small proportion of all car journeys.

Of the total car driver records, approximately 93.5% could be classified into tours, yielding 529,485 parking 'acts' at locations other than the home. These constitute the evidence on which the following tables are based. However, some of these are not in fact parking events, since the next trip begins immediately, so that they are either collecting or dropping off persons or goods. 7.7% of the parking 'acts' fall into this category.

Of the 397,230 tours compiled, the great majority (80%) were simple 'out and return' (2-leg) tours, though a few tours were found with 25 or more 'legs'. 97.3% of tours had fewer than 5 legs. The Tables 5 and 7−11 below have been weighted for representativity.[7]

Analysis of Parking by Duration and Purpose

As would be expected, the incidence of parking acts is reduced at weekends, shown in Table 5.

The following two figures give a general overview of the time at which parking events start, and the variation in their duration. However, as we shall see, there is considerable variation between weekends and weekdays because of the different purpose mix.

Fig. 5 shows that only 10% of all parking events begin before 0800 hours and only 10% begin after 1830 hours. Of the remainder, 20% occur between 0800 and 0930, with the greatest activity between 0830 and 0900:

Table 5. Incidence of Parking Acts by Day of Week.

Days	Parking Acts in Sample (Re-Weighted for Representativity)[a]	Percentage
Sunday	56,703.72	9.99
Monday	83,192.4	14.65
Tuesday	87,761.02	15.46
Wednesday	88,797.23	15.64
Thursday	89,324.89	15.73
Friday	89,584.97	15.78
Saturday	72,483.72	12.76
All	567,847.9	100.00

Source: NTS data 2002−2008.
[a]See Note 7.

Fig. 5. Onset of Parking Act by Time of Day.

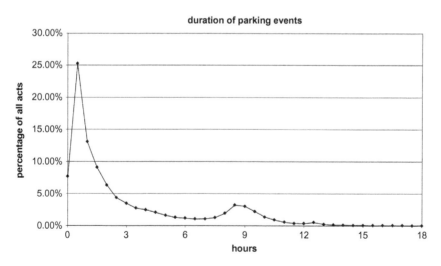

Fig. 6. Distribution of Duration of Parking Acts.

thereafter the pattern is more or less constant throughout the day, but with a declining tendency.

Fig. 6 shows the highly skewed duration of most parking acts. After the 7.8% that do not park at all, there is a further 38.2% which park for less than 1 hour. Nearly 70% of all parking acts are for less than 3 hours, and

72

JOHN BATES

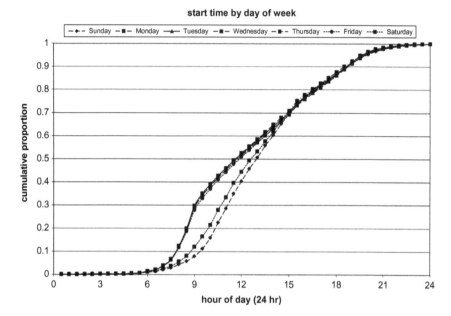

Fig. 7. Cumulative Distribution of Start Times.

nearly 90% are for less than 8½ hours. The secondary 'peak' around durations of between 8 and 9 hours is, of course, associated with commuting.

If we investigate how the cumulative profile of the start time varies by
day of week, we see, as expected, that the pattern is different at weekends,
but that all the weekdays are very similar, as shown in Fig. 7.

Given this, we will concentrate on the weekday data, and not make any
further distinctions by day of week.

The NTS allows for 22 categories of location purpose outside the home.
We have grouped them into more conventional categories according to
Table 6. Note that we have chosen not to represent the separate purposes
associated with escort trips.

For the weekday data, the proportion of parking acts associated with
each purpose, together with the average duration of parking, is given in
Table 7.

The overall average of 3.5 hours is strongly influenced by the commuters
('Work'). If we omit them, the average falls sharply to 1.3 hours.

An important aspect of parking analysis is the level of occupancy over
time – in other words, how many cars are parked at any moment, and

Table 6. Classification of Journey Purpose Associated with Parking Acts.

NTS Purpose Definition	Classification
Work	Work
In_course_of_work	Employers' business
Education	Education
Food_shopping(from_98)	Shopping
Non_food_shopping(inc._food_shopping_before_98)	Shopping
Personal_business_medical	Personal business
Personal_business_eat/drink_(from_95)	Personal business
Personal_business_other	Personal business
Eat/_drink_with_friends_(inc._pers._bus._eat/drink_pre-1995)	Social/recreational
Visit_friends	Visit friends (VFR)
Other_social	Social/recreational
Entertain/_public_activity	Social/recreational
Sport:_participate	Social/recreational
Holiday:_base	Holiday
Day_trip/_just_walk	Social/recreational
Other_non-escort	Social/recreational
Escort_home	Escort
Escort_work	Escort
Escort_in_course_of_work	Escort
Escort_education	Escort
Escort_shopping/pers._business	Escort
Other_escort	Escort

Table 7. Weekday Parking Acts by Purpose.

Purpose Category	% of Parking Acts	Average Duration (Hours)
Work	28.33	7.63
Employers' Business (EB)	6.30	3.48
Education (Ed)	0.59	5.21
Personal Business (PB)	8.53	1.51
Shop	17.32	1.48
Social/recreation (Soc/rec)	9.76	2.49
Holiday	0.41	12.24
Visiting Friends and Relatives (VFR)	8.38	3.05
Escort	20.38	0.81
All purposes	100	3.5

Source: NTS data 2002–2008 (weekdays only).

what is the composition in terms of journey purpose. By taking the starting time of each parking event, and allowing for its duration, we can construct a profile of parking 'activity', showing the level of parked vehicles at any time in the day. We refer to this as the parking 'accumulation' and analyse the data separately by purpose category.

It is obvious that, during working hours, the accumulation pattern is dominated by parking associated with the workplace. This is shown in Fig. 8 where, for legibility, we have combined all the other purposes. There are three reasons for this dominance: (a) as shown in Table 7, workplace parking is the largest single category; (b) with the minor exception of Holiday parking, workplace parking has the greatest duration; and (c) the onset of working time is more concentrated than that for other purposes.

In order to see the pattern of the other purposes more clearly, we include a second version of the figure, omitting the workplace parking, and changing the vertical scale, in Fig. 9. Note the later peaks for VFR and Social/ Recreational purposes.

If we put all these together as in Fig. 10, we can see the cumulative effect of the various purposes on the total demand for parking spaces throughout the day, where the same data is plotted but adding on the spaces for each purpose. The highest demand for parking spaces is at 1200 hours. At this time, the non-workplace parking demands add about 44% to the base demand due to workplace parking.

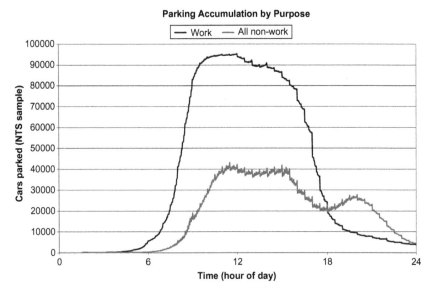

Fig. 8.   The Accumulation of Parking for Work and Non-Work Purposes.

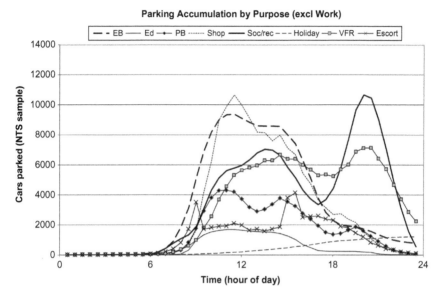

Fig. 9. The Accumulation of Parking for Individual Non-Work Purposes.

Fig. 10. Implied Overall Parking Profile by Time of Day.

Analysis of Parking by Location and Purpose

As well as the duration and temporal profile, a further important issue is where the parking takes place, both in terms of the area (urban, rural, etc.) and whether on the street, in a garage, etc. Fig. 11 and Tables 8–10 provide general information about this.

In the first place, there is very little variation by purpose in the proportion of parking in each type of area, as Fig. 11 shows (the only obvious outliers – Education and Holiday – are based on small samples). In other words, the breakdown of parking acts by purpose is more or less independent of the type of area where the parking occurs.

However, journey purpose does have an important effect on the kind of parking location that is used, as Table 8 shows (this is based on the years 2002–2006 only, as the question on where the vehicle was parked was not asked in the last two years).

The types of locations 'Firm/work car park', Public Car Park, and Street together account for 86% of all parking acts, but public car parks are especially used by Shoppers and those travelling for social and recreational activities, while firms' car parks are heavily used by people travelling

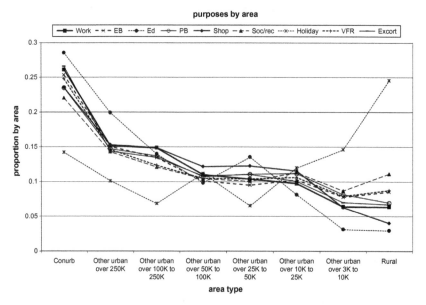

Fig. 11.   Proportion of Parking by Area, for Each Purpose.

Table 8. Parking Location Proportions According to Journey Purpose.

	Work (%)	EB (%)	Ed (%)	PB (%)	Shop (%)	Soc/rec (%)	Holiday (%)	VFR (%)	Escort (%)	All (%)
On own/friends premises	1.18	6.05	1.17	3.44	0.43	2.09	29.78	36.67	4.97	5.50
Firm/work car park	74.19	20.44	0.00	0.01	0.01	0.02	0.00	0.00	0.70	22.40
Other private car park	0.84	7.59	3.92	2.97	0.65	4.37	7.66	1.52	1.05	1.88
Park & Ride car park	0.02	0.01	0.16	0.01	0.04	0.02	0.00	0.00	0.00	0.02
Public car park	12.79	31.50	74.34	55.71	80.42	70.59	39.27	4.65	21.18	36.46
Street	10.68	33.18	20.20	33.70	16.58	20.87	21.83	56.98	44.24	26.94
Not parked	0.11	0.40	0.21	3.86	1.83	1.20	0.26	0.12	27.79	6.57
Other	0.19	0.83	0.00	0.30	0.04	0.83	1.19	0.06	0.08	0.24
All parking locations	100	100	100	100	100	100	100	100	100	100

Source: NTS data 2002–2006 (weekdays only).

to work, with a lower use by Employers' Business trips. Note that 28% of escort trips do not park at all (in other words, they are 'pick-up' or 'drop-off'). The use of Park & Ride by all purposes is very low, though the exclusion of journeys where the car is not the main mode should be borne in mind. Park & Ride is dealt with in more detail in Chapter 9.

Table 8 shows the proportion of the different parking locations used, separately for each purpose. However, it is also instructive to view the data another way, taking each parking type separately and analysing the proportionate use by each purpose. In this case we get the results in Table 9.

So 94% of parking acts in firms' car parks are by travellers going to their workplace, and only 5.6% by travellers on Employers' Business. The Park & Ride sample is too small to give a reliable breakdown by purpose.

It turns out that there is very little variation in the pattern of parking location by purpose in respect of the type of urban area, apart from a slight tendency for greater use of street parking in conurbations and the largest urban areas. The only clear exception to this is for the VFR trips where the balance switches from mainly 'On own/friends' premises' in the most rural areas to mainly on-street in the most urbanised areas: this reflects the housing pattern.

Since the pattern of purpose for parking varies little by type of area, and the types of location used for parking by purpose are also generally regular across area types (with the minor exceptions just noticed), it follows that there is little variation in the proportionate use of different types of parking by the type of area. This is demonstrated in Table 10.

Thus, the composition of parking both by purpose and type of parking location is only marginally dependent on the type of area. The key issue which impacts on the type of parking area is the overall level of parking activity relative to parking capacity.

The Cost of Parking

It is highly noteworthy that 94% of all parking acts in the NTS record no charge.[8] Of the remaining 6% that do pay something, over 82% pay less than £3 per parking act, and almost half pay less than £1, as Fig. 12 shows. There is some tendency in reporting to round to the nearest pound. Of course, there is also a need to take account of parking location and duration.

Table 9. Journey Purpose Proportions According to Parking Location.

	Work (%)	EB (%)	Ed (%)	PB (%)	Shop (%)	Soc/rec (%)	Holiday (%)	VFR (%)	Escort (%)	All Purposes (%)
On own/friends premises	6.07	6.80	0.13	5.32	1.37	3.61	2.02	**56.03**	18.66	100
Firm/work car park	**93.70**	5.64	0.00	0.00	0.01	0.01	0.00	0.00	0.64	100
Other private car park	12.55	24.91	1.23	13.44	6.03	22.01	1.52	6.77	11.55	100
Park & Ride car park	–	–	–	–	–	–	–	–	–	
Public car park	9.93	5.34	1.20	13.01	38.72	18.34	0.40	1.07	11.99	100
Street	11.22	7.61	0.44	10.65	10.81	7.34	0.30	17.76	33.88	100
Not parked	0.47	0.37	0.02	5.01	4.90	1.74	0.01	0.15	**87.33**	100
Other	21.83	21.17	0.00	10.60	3.05	32.71	1.85	2.05	6.73	100
All	28.29	6.18	0.59	8.51	17.56	9.47	0.37	8.40	20.63	100

Source: NTS data 2002–2006 (weekdays only).
Note: The values greater than 50% are in **bold**.

Table 10. Differential Use of Parking Locations by Type of Urban Area (Rows Add to 100%).

	On Own/Friends Premises (%)	Firm/Work Car Park (%)	Other Private Car Park (%)	Park & Ride Car Park (%)	Public Car Park (%)	Street (%)	Not Parked (%)	Other (%)
All built-up conurbations	4.25	22.17	1.61	0.01	33.59	31.32	6.91	0.13
Other urban over 250K	4.47	22.75	1.77	0.02	37.09	27.57	6.19	0.13
Other urban over 100–250K	4.53	24.68	1.91	0.04	37.43	24.76	6.51	0.15
Other urban over 50–100K	5.54	23.02	1.91	0.03	38.91	24.24	6.15	0.20
Other urban over 25–50K	5.53	21.52	1.54	0.02	39.45	24.37	7.44	0.14
Other urban over 10–25K	6.48	21.47	2.12	0.01	38.08	25.13	6.39	0.33
Other urban over 3–10K	8.45	20.71	2.34	0.00	36.00	26.03	6.05	0.43
Rural	11.23	20.89	3.10	0.00	30.93	26.37	6.23	1.25
All	5.50	22.39	1.88	0.02	36.47	26.94	6.57	0.24

Source: NTS data 2002–2006 (weekdays only).

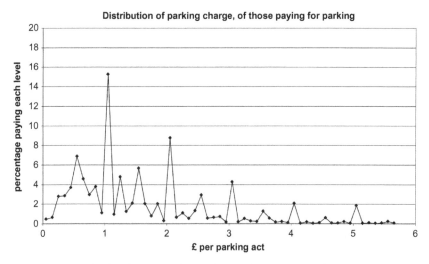

Fig. 12. Distribution of Parking Charges, for those Making a Payment.

Table 11. Percentage Paying and Average Fee Paid, by Type of Parking.

	Total	% Not Paying	Average Paid
On own/friends premises	17,112.53	99.75	–
Firm/work car park	69,732.72	98.82	£1.48
Other private car park	5,862.13	97.75	£2.16
Park & ride car park	–	–	–
Public car park	113,502.30	87.84	£1.91
Street	83,873.53	98.63	£1.91
Not parked	20,438.92	99.98	–
Other	–	–	–

Source: NTS data 2002–2006 (weekdays only).

Table 11 shows, for each parking category, the total number of parking acts, the percentage not paying any charge, and, for those who do pay, the average charge paid.

In the case of the first three categories, it is perhaps not surprising that payments are not required. In the case of street parking, it may be that for VFR and escort purposes, parking is often covered by Visitors' permits under a Residents' Parking scheme – the resident may have to pay for this, though the charge would not usually be passed on to the Visitor. However, even in public car parks, the vast majority of people apparently do not pay. This does seem odd. There is a slight tendency for the proportion not paying to decrease, and the average amount paid to increase, with increasing duration of stay, but given the small numbers of people actually paying, the figures cannot be given with any reliability.

Paying for parking is an emotive subject, as motorists often feel that they should not pay for parking on the street, it being seen as common property for which they have already paid through taxation. The same emotive argument applies to road user charging. Furthermore, paying for parking is a nuisance, involving either finding small change for machines or paying by credit card over the phone.

Nevertheless, the evidence produced here shows that personal expenditure on parking is actually very low. Overall, the analysis suggests that, *excluding* any charges for residential parking, the average annual parking cost is about £41.50 per vehicle, and, with an average of 1.14 cars per household (NTS, 2008/2009), this translates to about £47 per household p.a. As discussed below, these figures are in line with other sources, and show that despite the outcry in the local press which has often accompanied changes in fees for local authority car parks, the average parking costs cannot be considered significant.

Other information is available from the Living Costs and Food Survey (formerly the Expenditure and Food Survey, and before that the Family Expenditure Survey). This shows that the average household spends £42 per year on 'Parking fees, tolls, and permits (excluding motoring fines)'. Since the average expenditure on motoring fines, which will include speeding and other offences, is small (£5 per year averaged over all households), virtually all of the £42 must be parking – either tickets, permits or penalties. The proportion of households recording some expenditure each week on personal (as opposed to public) transport is 74%, but only 28% of these households record any expenditure on parking. Of course, these figures *include* residential parking charges (though, as noted earlier, only about 2% of households have to pay more than £81 per year for these).

Hence, while it is difficult to pinpoint the average annual household expenditure on parking with any certainty, it seems certain to be less than £50. As usual, of course, such averages hide considerable variation: parking at an airport for a few days can easily cost in excess of £50. But in terms of overall car use, these are relatively rare events. By contrast the annual amount spent on fuel alone is about £1,600 per vehicle (based on an average kilometrage of 13,500 p.a., and a fuel cost of about 12p per km).

DISCUSSION

Based on published figures (TSGB, 2009,[9] Table 1.4), the average number of journeys per individual made as car driver per year is about 410, and with a population of around 60 million, this equates to about 25 billion car trips per year. With some 27 million cars, this suggests an average of just under 18 trips per car every week. Analysis shows that the duration of the average car trip is about 20 minutes, implying that the average car is only on the move for 6 hours in the week: for the remaining 162 hours it is stationary – parked.

Using the NTS diary to compare the time travelling as car driver with the time the car is parked away from home, the latter is about 4.6 times the former, suggesting that on average the car is parked away from home for about 28 hours a week. Of course, this conceals much variation, especially between those who drive to work and those who do not. Nonetheless, the average car is parked at home for about 80% of the time, parked elsewhere for about 16.5% of the time, and only actually used for the remaining 3.5 %, as the following 'pie chart' illustrates (Fig. 13).

This pattern of allocation is completely different to the amount paid, where – even if we only consider *fuel* costs in relation to car travel – the amount spent on parking is about 3–4% of the amount spent on travel. Thus to caricature the situation, parking consumes about 3% of motoring expenditure but 97% of motoring time (on average).

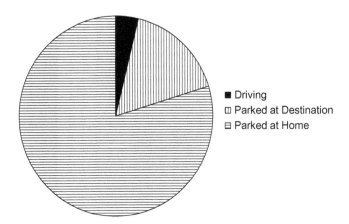

Fig. 13. Time Spent by Car in Different Activities.

The Policy issues relating to the demand for car parking are essentially a function of activity relative to capacity, and this applies whether we speak of parking at home or destination parking, though the options for these two types of parking are different. Undoubtedly the most obvious source of growth in the demand for parking is increased car ownership (though restricted parking availability may itself reduce car ownership). While it can be noted that the growth had slackened in recent years (at least partly for reasons associated with the economic climate), there is plenty of 'latent' demand, and official forecasts expect further growth, partly fuelled by continuing reductions in household size and increasing population. Even if there is some suggestion from the London data that the highest density areas may be 'choking off' further increases in car ownership, there is likely to be increased stress on residential parking.

On the other hand, there could be a shift in the pattern of destination parking, depending on the development of the labour market. Commuting is the dominant component of destination parking, both in terms of the volume of parking acts and the duration. If the proportion of those economically active falls (as expected with an ageing population), then the balance of demand may shift somewhat towards short-term parking. More flexible work patterns, including home-working, could also contribute to this. If this process was well managed, then the required increase in non-residential parking supply could be lessened.

Given what appears to be a considerable divergence between current charges and 'efficient' or market-based prices, any proposed move towards the latter will need to be introduced gradually. It should also be introduced in a way which minimises the general inconvenience associated with most current parking arrangements (such as poorly functioning machinery, restricted payment opportunities, machines not delivering change, disproportionate penalties for overstaying and so on), as well as promoting clarity of pricing structure.

Finally, it may be noted that the modelling tools for testing parking policies have not developed in the last ten years, possibly because of the attention paid to other kinds of transport policies. Although parking options are often seen as somewhat blunt instruments (in comparison to sophisticated road user charging measures, for example), they do have the advantage of practicality. There needs to be something of a renaissance of interest in both the theory and practice of models of parking provision and charging.

NOTES

1. As of 1 January 2013, the NTS no longer covers Scotland and Wales.

2. Available at https://www.gov.uk/transport-statistics-notes-and-guidance-national-travel-survey

3. As recommended in the NTS User Guide provided by the Data Archive, all tables in this section, being based on the Vehicle sample, are weighted with the Interview sample household weight (W3).

4. The average width of a new car sold in the United Kingdom is 2011 was 6 ft 1 in (1.85 m). The Ford Escort was 5 ft 2 in (1.57 m) wide in 1968 and its replacement, the Focus, is now 6 ft 1 in wide (1.85 m). This also causes problems where bays are marked out in public car parks, as the DfT recommended width is 5 ft 11 in (1.80 m) (*Sunday Times*, 19 February 2012).

5. There are 8,571 PSUs in Great Britain (7239 in England, 471 in Wales and 861 in Scotland), and although they are defined differently, they can be compared with the Census output areas, of which there are 7193 MSOAs in England and Wales and while in Scotland there are 1,235 areas in the 'intermediate Geography'. So as a rough guide one could conclude that the PSUs are slightly smaller than MSOAs in England and Wales, but rather larger than the 'intermediate Geography' in Scotland.

6. This was also true of the years 2009−2010.

7. As recommended in the NTS User Guide provided by the Data Archive, all tables in this section, being based on the Journey sample, are weighted with the trip/stage weight (W5), except for individual-based data, where W2 is used (Diary sample household weight). Since the work is only concerned with car trips, no corrections for short walks have been necessary.

8. We again remind the reader that journeys where the car is not the main mode have been excluded from the analysis.

9. Transport Statistics for Great Britain, available at https://www.gov.uk/government/organisations/department-for-transport/series/transport-statistics-great-britain

ACKNOWLEDGEMENTS

The assistance of David Leibling, co-author of the RAC Foundation Report 'Spaced Out: Perspectives on Parking Policy', is gratefully acknowledged, as is the RAC Foundation for funding the study on which much of this work is based. In addition, the provision of the NTS data from the ESDS (Economic and Social Data Service) archive, together with additional variables and advice provided by the DfT, is gratefully acknowledged. The data processing and conclusions remain nevertheless the author's responsibility: no warranty is given by the DfT as to the accuracy and comprehensiveness of the data.

REFERENCES

Bates, J., & Leibling, D. (2012, July). *Spaced out: Perspectives on parking policy*. Report for RAC Foundation, London.

Bates, J., Skinner, A., Scholefield, G., & Bradley, R. (1997). Study of parking and traffic demand: 2. A traffic restraint analysis model (TRAM). *Traffic Engineering and Control, 38*(3), 135–141.

Department for Transport. (2009). *Public experiences of and attitudes towards parking.* Retrieved from http://www2.dft.gov.uk/pgr/statistics/datatablespublications/trsnstatsatt/parking.html. Accessed on January 2012.

Hunt, J. D. (1988). *Modelling commuter parking location choice and its influence on mode choice.* Ph.D. Dissertation. University of Cambridge, UK (approved on November 15, 1988).

MVA. (2000, July). London parking supply study. Main Report (in Association with Data Collection Ltd). Prepared for Government Office for London (GOL).

MVA. (2005). Update of London parking supply study MVA for TfL, Transport for London. Unpublished.

NTS. (2008/2009). [Transport Statistics Great Britain] (2010), Table NTS 9902. Department for Transport.

Whelan, G., Crockett, J., & Vitouladiti, S. (2010). A new model of car ownership in London: Geo-spatial analysis of policy interventions. Transport for London, MVA Consultancy. Unpublished.

CHAPTER 5

THE HIGH COST OF MINIMUM PARKING REQUIREMENTS

Donald Shoup

ABSTRACT

Purpose – *This chapter estimates how minimum parking requirements increase the cost of constructing housing, office buildings, and shopping centers. It also explains proposed legislation to limit how much parking cities can require in transit-rich districts.*

Methodology – *I assembled data on the cost of constructing office buildings, shopping centers, and parking spaces in eight American cities, and data on the minimum parking requirements in these cities. I then combined the parking construction costs with the number of required parking spaces for each land use to estimate how the minimum parking requirements increase development costs for office buildings and shopping centers.*

Findings – *Minimum parking requirements increase the cost of constructing a shopping center by up to 67 percent if the parking is in an above-ground structure and by up to 93 percent if the parking is underground.*

In suburban Seattle, parking requirements force developers to spend between $10,000 and $14,000 per dwelling to provide unused parking spaces.

Parking: Issues and Policies
Transport and Sustainability, Volume 5, 87–113
Copyright © 2014 by Emerald Group Publishing Limited
All rights of reproduction in any form reserved
ISSN: 2044-9941/doi:10.1108/S2044-994120140000005011

On a typical construction site in Los Angeles, parking requirements reduce the number of units in an apartment building by 13 percent.

Practical implications – *To mitigate the high costs imposed by minimum parking requirements, California is considering legislation to set an upper limit on how much parking cities can require in transit-rich districts: no more than one space per dwelling unit or two spaces per 1,000 square feet (93 square meters) of commercial space. This legislation would limit parking requirements, but it would not limit the parking supply because developers can always provide more than the required number of spaces if they think demand justifies the added cost.*

Value of the chapter – *This chapter measures how minimum parking requirements increase the cost of housing, office buildings, and shopping centers in order to subsidize parking. Urban historians often say that cars have changed the city, but urban planning has also changed the city to favor cars.*

Keywords: Parking; parking requirements; real estate; infill development; housing

INTRODUCTION

A city can be friendly to people or it can be friendly to cars, but it can't be both.

– Enrique Peñalosa

City planners are put in a difficult position when asked to set the minimum parking requirements in zoning ordinances, largely because they must rely on guesswork. Planners do not know the parking demand at every site, or how much the required parking spaces cost, or how the requirements increase the cost of urban development. Nevertheless, planners have managed to set parking requirements for hundreds of land uses in thousands of cities – the Ten Thousand Commandments for off-street parking.

Critics of minimum parking requirements argue that these regulations subsidize cars, increase traffic congestion and carbon emissions, pollute the air and water, encourage sprawl, raise housing costs, damage the economy, degrade urban design, reduce walkability, and exclude poor people. To my knowledge, no city planner has argued that parking requirements do *not* have these harmful effects.

In *Parking Reform Made Easy*, Richard Willson (2013a) recommends analytical and practical ways for planners to justify reducing or eliminating parking requirements. As Willson says, "All the land-use plans, design reviews, and streetscape renderings in the world will not produce desired outcomes if we do not reform parking requirements" (Willson, 2013b, p. 30). But planners must first *want* to reform before anything will happen.

To show the need for reform, this chapter examines how parking requirements can dramatically increase the cost of constructing new buildings. After all, if planners do not know how much required parking spaces cost, they cannot know how much the parking requirements increase the cost of development. So how much do the required spaces cost, and how much do they increase the cost of urban development? I will answer these questions, and will then use the answers to make the case for reducing or removing off-street parking requirements.

THE COST OF REQUIRED PARKING SPACES

Because construction costs vary by location, there is no single measure of how much a parking space costs. But we can estimate the price tag in different locations by using published estimates of local construction costs. Rider Levett Bucknall (RLB), an international consulting firm that specializes in estimating real estate construction costs, publishes quarterly cost estimates for several real estate categories in cities around the world, including 12 cities in the United States.[1] Table 1 presents RLB's estimates of the average cost of parking spaces in these 12 American cities in 2012. Even within the same city, the cost can vary according to the soil conditions, the height of the water table, the shape of the site, and many other factors. RLB therefore reports both a low and a high construction cost; for simplicity; I have used the average of these two costs for each city.

Columns 1 and 2 show the average cost per square foot to build underground and aboveground parking structures. The average parking space, including the access aisles, occupies about 330 square feet (31 square meters). Given this size, Column 3 shows the cost per parking space for an underground garage. For example, the average cost of constructing an underground garage in Boston is $95 per square foot, and the average space occupies 330 square feet, so the average cost of a parking space is $31,000 ($95 × 330). Across the 12 cities, the average cost per space ranges from a low of $26,000 in Phoenix to a high of $48,000 in Honolulu, with an overall

Table 1. The Construction Cost of a Parking Space.

City	Construction Cost per Sq Ft		Construction Cost per Space	
	Underground $/sq ft (1)	Aboveground $/sq ft (2)	Underground $/space $(3) = (1) \times 330$	Aboveground $/space $(4) = (2) \times 330$
Boston	95	75	31,000	25,000
Chicago	110	88	36,000	29,000
Denver	78	55	26,000	18,000
Honolulu	145	75	48,000	25,000
Las Vegas	105	68	35,000	22,000
Los Angeles	108	83	35,000	27,000
New York	105	85	35,000	28,000
Phoenix	80	53	26,000	17,000
Portland	105	78	35,000	26,000
San Francisco	115	88	38,000	29,000
Seattle	105	75	35,000	25,000
Washington, DC	88	68	29,000	22,000
Average	103	74	34,000	24,000

Source: Rider Levett Bucknall, *Quarterly Construction Cost Report, Third Quarter* (2012).

average of $34,000 per space. For an aboveground garage, the cost per space ranges from $17,000 in Phoenix to $29,000 in Chicago and San Francisco, with an average of $24,000.

These estimates refer to the cost of *constructing* a parking space. For an aboveground garage, the land beneath the garage is another cost. Underground garages also occupy space that could be used for other purposes, such as storage and mechanical equipment, and the opportunity cost of this space has been called the underground land value.[2] Because numbers in Table 1 do not include the cost of land, they underestimate the total cost of parking spaces.[3]

To put the cost of parking spaces in perspective, we can compare this cost with the value of the vehicles parked in them. In 2009, the U.S. Department of Commerce estimated that the total value of the nation's 246 million motor vehicles was $1.3 trillion. The average value of a motor vehicle was therefore only $5,200.[4] (This average value seems low because the median age of the fleet was 10.3 years in 2009.) Because the average cost of an underground parking space is $34,000, the average vehicle is therefore worth about 15 percent of this cost ($5,200 ÷ $34,000). And because the average cost of an aboveground garage space is $24,000, the average vehicle is worth about 22 percent of this cost ($5,200 ÷ $24,000).

A parking space can cost much more than the value of the car parked in it, and there are also several parking spaces for every car. Using aerial photographs of all the off-street parking lots in Illinois, Indiana, Michigan, and Wisconsin, Davis et al. (2010) found between 2.5 and 3 off-street surface parking spaces per vehicle registered in these states. In addition, Zhan Guo and Luis Schloeter (2013) estimated that suburban streets alone contain more than enough on-street parking spaces to park all the passenger cars in the United States.

Parking spaces outnumber cars, and each space can cost much more than a car parked in it, but planners continue to set parking requirements without considering this cost. If I buy the average American car for $5,200, cities require someone else to pay many times more than that to ensure that parking spaces will be waiting for me whenever and wherever I drive. Minimum parking requirements amount to an Affordable Parking Act. They make parking more affordable by raising the costs for everything else. So who does pay for all these required parking spaces?

THE COST OF PARKING REQUIREMENTS FOR OFFICE BUILDINGS

Most cities require parking in proportion to the size of a building, such as 4 spaces per 1,000 square feet of building area. We can use the RLB data on the cost of parking spaces to show how parking requirements increase construction costs. Eight of the 12 cities in Table 1 require parking in direct proportion to the size of an office building.[5] We can calculate the cost of required parking per 1,000 square feet of building area in these eight cities by combining the parking requirements with the cost of constructing a parking space.

Table 2 shows how the cost of satisfying the parking requirement increases the total cost of constructing an office building. Column 1 shows the minimum parking requirement in each city, although certain areas of the city may have higher or lower requirements according to their specific area plans. Las Vegas, for example, requires 3.3 spaces per 1,000 square feet. Because the average size of a parking space is 330 square feet, this translates to 1,100 square feet of parking per 1,000 square feet of office building (Column 3). Thus, Las Vegas requires parking structures that are bigger than the buildings they serve.

Columns 4 and 5 show the RLB data on the cost per square foot for an office building and an underground garage.[6] Column 6 shows the cost of

Table 2. The Cost of Parking Requirements for Office Buildings – Underground Parking Structure.

City	Parking Requirement	Building Area	Parking Area	Construction Cost		Building Cost	Parking Cost	Cost Increase
				Building $/sq ft	Parking $/sq ft			
	Spaces/1,000 sq ft	Sq ft	Sq ft	$/sq ft	$/sq ft	$	$	%
	(1)	(2)	(3) = (1) × (2) × 0.33	(4)	(5)	(6) = (2) × (4)	(7) = (3) × (5)	(8) = (7)/(6)
Las Vegas	3.3	1,000	1,100	148	105	148,000	116,000	78
Phoenix	3.3	1,000	1,100	128	80	128,000	88,000	69
Honolulu	2.5	1,000	825	233	145	233,000	120,000	52
Portland	2.0	1,000	660	138	105	138,000	69,000	50
Los Angeles	2.0	1,000	660	158	108	158,000	71,000	45
Denver	2.0	1,000	660	125	78	125,000	51,000	41
Seattle	1.0	1,000	330	138	105	138,000	35,000	25
New York	1.0	1,000	330	225	105	225,000	35,000	16
Average	2.1	1,000	708	161	104	161,625	73,125	47

Source: Rider Levett Bucknall, *Quarterly Construction Cost Report, Third Quarter* (2012).

constructing 1,000 square feet of an office building, and Column 7 shows the cost of constructing the required parking. Finally, Column 8 shows that the required parking increases the cost of an office building in Las Vegas by 78 percent. Because most developers will provide some parking even if the city does not require it, the parking requirements are not responsible for all the money spent on parking. Nevertheless, Columns 7 and 8 show the minimum cost of the required parking for buildings with underground garages.

The high cost of structured parking gives developers a strong incentive to build in low density areas where cheaper land allows surface parking, thus encouraging sprawl. Surface lots cost developers less money but they cost the city more land that could have better and more profitable uses.

Table 2 ranks cities by how much the required parking increases the cost of office buildings (Column 8), which turns out to be the same ranking as by the size of the parking requirement (Column 1). Las Vegas and Phoenix have the highest parking requirements (3.3 spaces per 1,000 square feet) and the highest cost increases (78 percent and 69 percent). Seattle and New York have the lowest parking requirements (1 space per 1,000 square feet) and the lowest cost increases (25 percent and 16 percent). The last row shows that the required parking increases the average cost of an office building by 47 percent.

Table 2 shows the results for underground parking. Table 3 shows the same calculations for an aboveground garage. On average, the cost of providing the required parking in an aboveground structure adds 30 percent to the cost of an office building. Fig. 1 compares these results from Tables 2 and 3. The higher the parking requirement, the more it costs to construct an office building.

The average parking requirement for office buildings in these eight cities is only 2.1 spaces per 1,000 square feet, which is lower than in most American cities. One survey of 117 cities, for example, found that the median parking requirement for office buildings was 4 spaces per 1,000 square feet, which is almost double the average requirement in Tables 2 and 3. Some planners call this requirement of 4 parking spaces per 1,000 square feet for office buildings the "golden rule" or "magic number" (Shoup, 2011, pp. 612–613).

All this required parking takes up a lot of space. Fig. 2 compares the area of parking required for a 100,000-square-foot office building with the area of the buildings themselves in 45 American cities. While the parking lots look large in proportion to the buildings, most of these cities have atypically low parking requirements. Only one city in Fig. 2

Table 3. The Cost of Parking Requirements for Office Buildings — Aboveground Parking Structure.

City	Parking Requirement Space/1,000 sq ft (1)	Building Area Sq ft (2)	Parking Area Sq ft (3)=(1)×(2)×0.33	Construction Cost Building $/sq ft (4)	Construction Cost Parking $/sq ft (5)	Building Cost $ (6)=(2)×(4)	Parking Cost $ (7)=(3)×(5)	Cost Increase % (8)=(7)/(6)
Las Vegas	3.3	1,000	1,100	148	68	148,000	74,000	50
Phoenix	3.3	1,000	1,100	128	53	128,000	58,000	45
Portland	2.0	1,000	660	138	75	138,000	50,000	36
Los Angeles	2.0	1,000	660	158	78	158,000	51,000	32
Honolulu	2.5	1,000	825	233	83	233,000	68,000	29
Denver	2.0	1,000	660	125	55	125,000	36,000	29
Seattle	1.0	1,000	330	138	75	138,000	25,000	18
New York	1.0	1,000	330	225	85	225,000	28,000	12
Average	2.1	1,000	708	161	71	161,625	48,750	30

Source: Rider Levett Bucknall, *Quarterly Construction Cost Report Third Quarter* (2012).

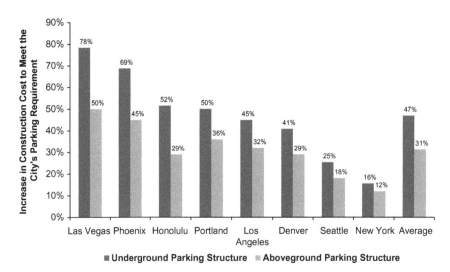

Fig. 1. How Parking Requirements Increase the Cost of Constructing Office Buildings.

Fig. 2. Graphing the Parking Requirements for Office Buildings in 45 American Cities. *Source*: Reproduced from *Graphing Parking*, with permission from Seth Goodman (2013).

(San Jose) requires the common number of 4 spaces per 1,000 square feet of an office building.

THE COST OF PARKING REQUIREMENTS FOR SHOPPING CENTERS

Because RLB also provides data on the cost of shopping centers, we can use the method described above to estimate how parking requirements increase the cost of building a shopping center. Tables 4 and 5 and Fig. 3 show these estimates for underground and aboveground parking structures.

Cities usually require more parking for shopping centers than for office buildings. Los Angeles's requirement of 4 spaces per 1,000 square feet, for example, leads to parking lots that are 32 percent larger than the shopping centers they serve. For underground parking, this requirement increases the cost of building a shopping center by 93 percent; for an aboveground garage the cost increase is 67 percent. In contrast, New York City's requirement of 1 space per 1,000 square feet increases the cost of a shopping center by only 18 percent for underground parking and 14 percent for an aboveground garage. On average, the required off-street parking increases construction costs by 53 percent if underground and by 37 percent if aboveground.

The average parking requirement for shopping centers in these eight cities is only 2.8 spaces per 1,000 square feet, which is lower than in most American cities. The Urban Land Institute recommends at least 4 spaces per 1,000 square feet for small shopping centers, and 5 spaces per 1,000 square feet for large shopping centers (Shoup, 2011, pp. 84–87). Five parking spaces per 1,000 square feet would increase the average cost of constructing a large shopping center by 95 percent if underground, and by 66 percent if aboveground.

Parking requirements would do no harm, of course, if they did not force developers to provide more parking than they would supply voluntarily. But research has repeatedly found that developers usually provide only the required number of parking spaces, which strongly suggests that the requirements drive the parking supply. Most recently, using data on 9,279 properties in Los Angeles County, Cutter and Franco (2012, Table 8) found that developers provided almost exactly the number of parking spaces that cities require for office buildings. In their study, the average parking requirement was 3.02 spaces per 1,000 square feet, and the average parking supply was 3.03 spaces per 1,000 square feet.

Table 4. The Cost of Parking Requirements for Shopping Centers – Underground Parking Structure.

City	Parking Requirement	Building Area	Parking Area	Construction Cost		Building Cost	Parking Cost	Cost Increase
	Space/1,000 sq ft	Sq ft	Sq ft	Building $/sq ft	Parking $/sq ft	$	$	%
	(1)	(2)	(3)=(1)×(2)×0.33	(4)	(5)	(6)=(2)×(4)	(7)=(3)×(5)	(8)=(7)/(6)
Los Angeles	4.0	1,000	1,320	153	108	153,000	142,000	93
Phoenix	3.3	1,000	1,100	135	80	135,000	88,000	65
Honolulu	3.3	1,000	1,100	255	145	255,000	160,000	63
Denver	2.5	1,000	825	105	78	105,000	64,000	61
Las Vegas	4.0	1,000	1,320	298	105	298,000	139,000	47
Portland	2.0	1,000	660	153	105	153,000	69,000	45
Seattle	2.0	1,000	660	158	105	158,000	69,000	44
New York	1.0	1,000	330	195	105	195,000	35,000	18
Average	2.8	1,000	914	181	104	181,500	95,750	53

Source: Rider Levett Bucknall, *Quarterly Construction Cost Report, Third Quarter* (2012).

Table 5. The Cost of Parking Requirements for Shopping Centers – Aboveground Parking Structure.

City	Parking Requirement	Building Area	Parking Area	Construction Cost		Building Cost	Parking Cost	Cost Increase
	Space/1,000 sq ft	Sq ft	Sq ft	Building $/sq ft	Parking $/sq ft	$	$	%
	(1)	(2)	(3)=(1)×(2)×0.33	(4)	(5)	(6)=(2)×(4)	(7)=(3)×(5)	(8)=(7)/(6)
Los Angeles	4	1,000	1,320	153	78	1,53,000	1,02,000	67
Phoenix	3.3	1,000	1,100	135	53	1,35,000	58,000	43
Denver	2.5	1,000	825	105	55	1,05,000	45,000	43
Honolulu	3.3	1,000	1,100	255	83	2,55,000	91,000	36
Portland	2.0	1,000	660	153	75	1,53,000	50,000	33
Seattle	2.0	1,000	660	158	75	1,58,000	50,000	32
Las Vegas	4.0	1,000	1,320	298	68	2,98,000	89,000	30
New York	1.0	1,000	330	195	85	1,95,000	28,000	14
Average	2.8	1,000	914	181	71	1,81,500	64,125	37

Source: Rider Levett Bucknall, *Quarterly Construction Cost Report, Third Quarter* (2012).

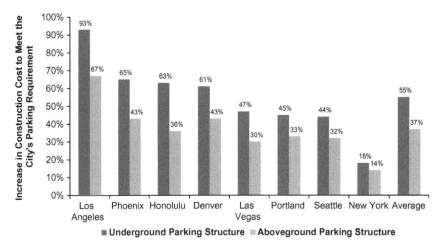

Fig. 3. How Parking Requirements Increase the Cost of Constructing Shopping Centers.

Cutter and Franco (Table 10) also estimated how much an additional parking space adds to a building's value. For retail service buildings with high parking requirements such as restaurants, the last parking space cost $14,700 more than it added to the building's value.[7] High parking requirements thus force developers to provide parking spaces that lose money. In effect, parking requirements tax buildings to subsidize parking. Cutter and Franco (2012, p. 919) conclude, "minimum parking requirements lower site density, increase land consumption, oversupply parking and reduce profits per unit of covered land."

THE COST OF PARKING REQUIREMENTS FOR APARTMENT BUILDINGS

City planners cannot predict how many parking spaces an apartment needs any more than they can predict how many cars a family needs. But the parking requirements for apartments help to predict how many cars a family will own. Even when planners try to measure the "need" for parking by observing the number of cars parked at existing buildings, they often require too much. Seattle's Right Size Parking Project, for instance, surveyed occupancy at over 200 apartment buildings in the region in 2012. The parking requirements in suburban Seattle were, on average, 0.4 spaces per dwelling unit greater than the observed parking occupancy (King County Metro, 2013, p. 11). Table 1 shows that underground parking costs $35,000 per space in Seattle, and aboveground parking costs $25,000 per space. These figures suggest that the parking requirements in suburban Seattle require developers to spend between $10,000 (0.4 × $25,000) and $14,000 (0.4 × $35,000) per apartment to provide unused parking spaces.

The typical requirement of two spaces per apartment forces developers to spend at least $70,000 per dwelling unit for parking if the spaces are underground, or $50,000 per dwelling unit if the spaces are in an aboveground structure. These estimates refer to the *average* cost of building a parking space. The *marginal* cost of a parking space, however, can be far higher due to natural break points in the cost of building a parking structure. For example, a dramatic break point occurs with the construction of a second level of underground parking because it requires removing several spaces on the first level to provide a ramp to the lower level. Therefore, the marginal cost of the first space on the second level can be far higher than the average cost of the spaces on the first level. This high marginal cost of excavating a second parking level severely limits what developers can build on a site.

To demonstrate how break points in the cost of building a garage affect development decisions, Fig. 4 shows a four-story apartment building in Los Angeles on a typical lot that is 50 feet (15 meters) wide and 130 feet

Fig. 4.   Seven-Unit Apartment Building on a 50 × 130 Foot Lot (47 Units per Acre).

Fig. 5. Tandem Compact Parking Space in Underground Garage.

(40 meters) deep. The city's R3 zoning allows eight apartments on the site, and the city's parking requirement is 2.25 spaces per unit. Eight apartments would therefore require 18 parking spaces (8 × 2.25), but only 16 spaces could be squeezed onto one level of underground parking (Fig. 5 shows how tightly the spaces are packed).[8] In response, the developer built only seven apartments on the site, rather than excavate a second level of parking to provide two additional spaces for the eighth apartment.

In this case, the parking requirement, not the density allowed by zoning, constrained the number of apartments. If the city had allowed the developer to provide only two parking spaces per apartment, the developer could have built eight apartments and 16 parking spaces. The prohibitively high *marginal* cost of two more spaces on a second underground level, however, reduced the feasible number of dwellings from eight to seven, or by 13 percent.

Repealing or reducing a city's parking requirement does *not* mean that developers won't provide parking. Even without parking requirements, the developer in the example above would probably have built a garage with 16 spaces, because the site told the developer that 16 spaces were feasible. With parking requirements, however, the garage told the developer that only seven apartments were feasible. More parking for cars means less housing for people.

By increasing the cost of development, parking requirements can reduce the supply and increase the price of real estate in two ways. First, parking requirements can reduce the density of what gets built, as in the 13 percent reduction in apartments in the example above. Parking requirements increase the density of cars but reduce the density of people (Manville, Beata, & Shoup, 2013). Because parking requirements reduce the supply of apartments, they increase the price of housing. On some days, planners think about housing affordability, but on most days they think about parking and forget about housing affordability.

Second, parking requirements not only reduce the density on sites that are developed, but also reduce the number of sites that are developed. If the required parking spaces increase the cost of constructing a building by more than they increase the market value of the building, they will reduce the residual value of land. Residual land value is defined as the market value of the most profitable development that could be constructed on a site minus the cost of constructing it.[9] For example, if the best choice for development on a site would cost $750,000 to construct and would have a market value of $1 million, the residual value for the land is $250,000. If $250,000 is not enough to pay for buying and demolishing an existing building on the site, redevelopment won't happen. The residual land value of a site for redevelopment must be greater than the value of the existing building on the site before a developer can buy the building, clear the site, and make a profit on a new development. Therefore, if minimum parking requirements reduce residual land values, they make redevelopment less likely.

In their analysis of parking requirements for retail services, Cutter and Franco (2012) found that the last parking space adds $14,700 more to a building's cost than it adds to the building's value. Requiring one more parking space at a proposed restaurant thus reduces the residual land value of the site by $14,700. Where parking requirements reduce residual land values, they will reduce infill redevelopment. This reduction in the supply of real estate drives up the price of everything except parking and shifts the cost of parking from drivers onto all economic activity in the city.

THE COST OF PARKING REQUIREMENTS FOR HISTORIC BUILDINGS

Cornell professor Michael Manville (2013) showed how parking requirements can reduce the supply of housing by preventing the reuse of historic buildings. He examined what happened after Los Angeles adopted its Adaptive Reuse Ordinance (ARO), which allows developers to convert economically distressed or historically significant office buildings into new residential units – with no new parking spaces required.

Parking requirements often make reusing historic buildings difficult or impossible, because old buildings rarely have all the parking spaces cities require for new uses. Downtown Los Angeles is a prime example. It has the nation's largest collection of intact office buildings built between 1900 and 1930. Starting in the 1960s, the city's urban renewal program created a new office district on Bunker Hill and left many splendid Art Deco and Beaux Arts buildings in the old office district on Spring Street (once known as the Wall Street of the West) vacant except for retail uses on the ground floor.

Before Los Angeles adopted the ARO in 1999, the city required at least two parking spaces per condominium unit in downtown. In the 30 years between 1970 and 2000, only 4,300 housing units were added in downtown. In the nine years after the ARO was adopted, developers created 7,300 new housing units in 56 historic office buildings. All these office buildings had been vacant for at least five years, and many had been vacant much longer.

Developers provided, on average, only 1.3 spaces per apartment, with 0.9 spaces on-site and 0.4 off-site, often by renting spaces in nearby lots or garages. If the city had not adopted the ARO, it would have required at least two *on-site* spaces for every condo unit, or more than twice as many as developers provided. Deregulating the quantity and the location of parking for the new housing was a key factor in restoring and converting the office buildings.

Removing the parking requirements also produced other benefits. It allowed the restoration and conversion of many historic buildings that had been vacant for years and might have been demolished if parking requirements had been maintained. Historic buildings are a scarce resource in a city, and the evidence shows that parking requirements stood in the way of preservation. Not only did removing the parking requirements preserve individual buildings, it also helped revitalize an entire historic district. The ARO applied only to downtown when it was adopted in 1999, but its benefits were so quickly apparent that the city council extended the ARO to several other historic parts of the city in 2003.

Parking requirements prevent many good things from happening in cities, but usually we cannot see the good things that parking requirements are preventing. Nevertheless, the beautifully restored buildings on Spring Street unveil what parking requirements had been holding back. Many wonderful buildings were restored and reinhabited only after the city removed the minimum parking requirements for these buildings (Fig. 6).

Fig. 6.   Office Building Converted to Housing with No New Parking.

Cities also discourage historic preservation if they require additional parking when a rental apartment building is converted to condominium ownership. Los Angeles requires at least 1.5 spaces per unit before an apartment building can be converted to owner-occupancy (Shoup, 2011, p. 157). Because most old buildings do not have 1.5 parking spaces per apartment, the solution is often to reduce the number of apartments to match the number of parking spaces available, either by combining small apartments to create fewer but larger and more expensive ones, or by demolishing some apartments and converting the land to parking. More commonly, developers demolish the rental apartment house and build a new condominium with all the required parking (see Fig. 4). Many residents of historic buildings would prefer to own rather than to rent their apartments, but parking requirements preclude this opportunity. In practice, the law discriminates against tenants who would like to own their housing but have only one car.

CIRCULAR PARKING REQUIREMENTS

Off-street parking requirements are a strong planning intervention based on scant, unreliable evidence. Because planners do not know how many cars every family needs, they cannot know how many parking spaces every residence needs. And because the number of available parking spaces affects the number of cars a family will own, the number of cars a family owns cannot predict the number of parking spaces to require. Minimum parking requirements increase the demand for cars, and then the number of cars increases the minimum parking requirements. It's like requiring closet space in every residence based on how much stuff planners think people will want to store, and then using the amount of stuff stored in the required closets to set the minimum closet requirements.

Because city planners and elected officials don't know how much it costs to construct a parking space, they can't take this cost into consideration when deciding how many spaces to require. Instead, they often use the occupancy of parking spaces at existing buildings to estimate the "need" for parking spaces at new buildings, as though the cost of a space was irrelevant. Since most drivers park free at existing buildings, parking requirements based on existing occupancy at sites with free parking will therefore reflect the demand for *free* parking, no matter how much the required spaces cost. To use a familiar analogy, if pizza were free, would there ever be enough pizza? Charging drivers a price for parking that is high enough to cover the cost of constructing and operating a garage would reduce the occupancy rates that planners use to estimate parking requirements.

PUTTING A CAP ON PARKING REQUIREMENTS

I thought the time to reform parking requirements had finally arrived when Assembly Bill 904 (The Sustainable Minimum Parking Requirements Act of 2012) was introduced in the California Legislature. AB 904 would set an upper limit on how much parking cities can require in transit-rich districts: no more than one space per dwelling unit or two spaces per 1,000 square feet of commercial space. The bill defined these districts as areas within a quarter-mile of transit lines that run every 15 minutes or better. AB 904 would limit how much parking cities can require, but it would not limit the parking supply because developers can always provide more than the required number of spaces if they think demand justifies the cost.

Minimum Parking Requirements in Transit-Rich Areas

Why would state officials want to limit parking requirements in areas with good transit service? The federal and state governments give cities billions of dollars every year to build and operate mass transit systems, yet most cities require ample parking based on the assumption that almost everyone will drive almost everywhere. Los Angeles, for example, is building its "subway to the sea" under Wilshire Boulevard, which already has the city's most frequent bus service. Nevertheless, along parts of Wilshire, the city requires at least 2.5 parking spaces for each dwelling unit, regardless of the number of habitable rooms.[10] If every one-bedroom apartment has 2.5 parking spaces, how many residents will ride public transit?

Los Angeles also requires *free* off-street parking along parts of Wilshire Boulevard: "For office and other commercial uses there shall be at least three parking spaces provided for each 1,000 square feet of gross floor area available at no charge to all patrons and employees of those uses."[11] If all commuters and shoppers can park free, fewer will leave their cars at home and ride the bus or subway to work or shop on Wilshire.

Close to Wilshire Boulevard in Westwood, 20 public transit lines serve the UCLA campus, with 119 buses per hour arriving during the morning peak (7–9 am). Nevertheless, across the street from campus, Los Angeles requires 3.5 parking spaces for every apartment that contains more than four habitable rooms, and even a kitchen counts as a habitable room.

On another stretch of Wilshire, Beverly Hills requires 22 parking spaces per 1,000 square feet for restaurants, which means the parking lot is seven times larger than the restaurant. Public transit in this parking environment is as superfluous as a Gideon Bible at the Ritz.

The Rationale for a Statewide Limit on Minimum Parking Requirements

Cities get money from states and the federal government to build transit systems, and then require developers to provide parking spaces that undermine these transit systems. We would own fewer cars, and use them more sparingly, if drivers instead paid prices for parking that covered the cost of constructing the parking spaces. Parking requirements are policy choices, and choices have consequences.

The rationale for a statewide limit on parking requirements in transit-rich districts is the same as the rationale for most city planning: the uncoordinated actions of many individuals can add up to a collective result that most people don't like. In this case, the uncoordinated parking requirements of many cities can add up to an asphalt wasteland that blights the environment and compels people to drive. Reducing the parking requirements in transit-rich neighborhoods can reduce this blight by making redevelopment at higher density more feasible near transit stations.

The United Kingdom's guidance on parking policy provides a precedent for national action to manage local parking requirements. In 2001, the U.K. Department for Communities and Local Government (2001, pp. 51–52) published a guidance document stating that cities should "not require developers to provide more spaces than they themselves wish. ... There should be no minimum [parking] standards for development, other than parking for disabled people." Following this guidance, the Greater London Authority (2004) required its 33 boroughs to set a maximum number of parking spaces allowed, with no minimum number required. For apartment buildings that are near public transit or are within a ten-minute walk of a town center, for example, the maximum number of parking spaces allowed is now one space per dwelling unit.

Zhan Guo and Shuai Ren at New York University studied the results of London's shift from minimum parking requirements with no maximum, to maximum parking limits with no minimum. Using a sample of developments completed before and after the reform, they found that the supply of parking after the reform was only 68 percent of the maximum allowed, and only 52 percent of the previous minimum required. If, after the reform, developers provided only 52 percent of the parking spaces previously required, and rarely provided as many parking spaces as allowed, the result implies that the previous minimum parking requirement almost *doubled* the number of parking spaces that developers would have voluntarily provided on their own. Summarizing their results, Guo and Ren (2013, p. 1193) say,

> It is clear that, with the minimum standard but no maximum, most developments do not provide more than the minimum required. With the maximum standard but no minimum, most developments provide less than the maximum allowed.

They concluded that removing the minimum parking requirement caused 98 percent of the reduction in parking spaces, while imposing the maximum standard caused only 2 percent.

London's *maximum* of one parking space per unit everywhere is the same as California's proposed cap on *minimum* parking requirements in transit-rich districts. And even if California does limit how much parking cities can require, developers could always provide more.

National and regional governments guide local parking policies in the United Kingdom, but planning for parking is solely a local responsibility in the United States. As a result, American parking policies are parochial. Because sales taxes are an important source of local public revenue in California, cities are under terrific pressure to attract retail sales. Fierce competition for sales tax revenue puts cities in a race to offer ample free parking for all potential customers. This battle is an expensive negative-sum game within a region because more parking everywhere consumes valuable land and capital, without increasing total regional sales.

Beyond competing for sales tax revenue, cities have another incentive to set high parking requirements. Everyone wants to park free, and parking requirements allow elected officials to provide free parking at someone else's expense. The required parking spaces cost a lot, but the cost is hidden in higher prices for everything else.

Opposition from the California Chapter of the American Planning Association

To my dismay, the California Chapter of the American Planning Association lobbied against the proposed legislation. The California APA (2012, p. 1) argued that AB 904 "would restrict local agencies' ability to require parking in excess of statewide ratios for transit intensive areas unless the local agency makes certain findings and adopts an ordinance to opt out of the requirement."

According to the California APA, all cities should have the right to require abundant parking in transit-rich districts without presenting any findings to show that a high parking requirement is justified. That is, cities can tell property owners what to do, but the state cannot tell cities what to do. The California APA wants cities to require parking without being subject to any statewide planning.

City planners must, of course, take direction from local elected officials, but the American Planning Association represents the planning profession, not cities. AB 904 gave the planning profession an opportunity to recommend a reform that would coordinate parking requirements with public transportation, but instead the California APA insisted on retaining local control over parking requirements regardless of any wider concerns.[12]

Planning for parking is an ad hoc skill learned on the job, and it is more a political than a professional or technical activity. Most city planning textbooks do not even mention minimum parking requirements. Despite their lack of professional training, planners in every city must set parking requirements for every land use, and they have adopted a veneer of professional language to justify the requirements. Simply put, planners are winging it when it comes to parking requirements, which are, at best, the outcome of simple tinkering. City planners do not have the omniscience to predict the need for parking at every restaurant, apartment house, church, and nail salon. Instead of reasoning about parking requirements, planners usually rationalize them. Minimum parking requirements result from complicated political and economic forces, but city planners enable these requirements and even oppose efforts to reform them. The public bears the high cost of this pseudoscience.

Suppose the automobile and oil industries have asked you to devise planning policies that will increase the demand for cars and fuel. Consider three promising policies that will make cars essential for most trips. First, segregating land uses (housing here, jobs there, and shopping somewhere else) will increase travel demand. Second, limiting development density will spread the city and further increase travel demand. Third, minimum parking requirements will ensure that drivers can park free at the beginning and end of almost every automobile trip. American cities have unwisely embraced each of these three planning policies.[13] Zoning ordinances that segregate land uses, limit density, and require parking will create sprawled, drivable cities and prohibit compact, walkable neighborhoods. Urban historians often say that cars have changed the city, but urban planning has also changed the city to favor cars.

MINIMAL PARKING REQUIREMENTS

Many people believe that America freely chose its love affair with the car, but I think there was an arranged marriage. By recommending minimum parking requirements in zoning ordinances, the planning profession was both a matchmaker and a leading member of the wedding party.

Unfortunately, however, planners failed to provide a good prenuptial agreement. Now, city planners should become marriage counselors or divorce lawyers. By working to reform minimum parking requirements, planners can help to secure a fair and friendly settlement between people and cars where the relationship no longer works well.

Minimum parking requirements limit urban development. They often force developers to provide more parking than necessary, or to construct smaller buildings than the zoning allows. Parking requirements promote an unsustainable city. If cities require ample off-street parking everywhere, most people will continue to drive everywhere, even if Santa Claus delivers a great transit system. Cities get the traffic they plan for and the behavior they subsidize.

The California Legislature has delayed action on the bill to cap parking requirements in transit-rich areas. Nevertheless, the proposal has already fomented debate within the planning profession. Should cities have minimum parking requirements with no maximums, like Los Angeles? Or should they have maximum parking limits with no minimums, like London? Or neither? And should state or national governments limit how much parking cities can require? Parking is an important policy issue and not merely a regulatory detail.

City planners should begin to consider minimal, not minimum, parking requirements. "Minimal" means barely adequate, or the smallest possible number, depending on the context. A minimal parking requirement would thus require planners to estimate an adequate number of parking spaces, after taking all the costs into account. For example, can the adjacent roads handle all the additional traffic caused by the cars that will park in the required spaces? Can the city's air safely absorb all the additional vehicle emissions? Can the earth's atmosphere safely absorb all the additional carbon emissions? How will the required parking spaces increase the cost of housing and all other real estate? And who will pay for all the required parking spaces?

If they are faced with the impossible task of calculating the costs and benefits of parking spaces required for every building in every location, planners may appreciate the idea of going Dutch on parking: Each driver can pay for his or her own parking, and planners should abandon the idea of parking requirements. If you pay for your parking and I pay for mine, someone who does not own a car will not pay for parking.

Most cities will not want to abandon parking requirements altogether, but perhaps they can start by reducing the minimum number of spaces required until they reach a minimal number that seems reasonable.

Eventually, they might reinterpret this to mean the maximum number of spaces allowed, not the minimum number required. With only a slight change in terminology, cities can require developers to provide no more than an adequate number of parking spaces. But as Guo and Ren found in London, simply removing the minimum parking requirements will greatly reduce the supply of new parking spaces, even without imposing any maximum parking limit. Removing a minimum parking requirement can be far more important than imposing a maximum parking limit, and politically easier. If cities do impose maximum parking limits, however, they can offer developers the option to pay per-space fees if they want to exceed the maximum number of spaces allowed, just as cities already offer developers the option to pay in-lieu fees if they want to provide fewer than the minimum number of parking spaces required.

CONCLUSION

I hope the information I have provided about the high cost of minimum parking requirements will encourage transportation and land use planners to examine how these requirements affect cities, the economy, and the environment. The politics that produce minimum parking requirements are understandable, but their high costs are indefensible. Irrefutable evidence on the health cost of smoking eventually led many people to kick their addiction to tobacco. I hope evidence about the high cost of required parking spaces will eventually lead cities to kick their addiction to minimum parking requirements.

NOTES

1. Rider Levett Bucknall, *Quarterly Construction Report, Third Quarter* (2012).
2. Pasqual and Riera (2005) explain the theory of underground land values.
3. These estimates probably come from building a garage with several hundred spaces, taking advantage of economies of scale in construction. Where parking requirements mandate only 10 or 20 spaces, there will be no economies of scale and the spaces will be much more expensive.
4. See Tables 723 and 1096 in the 2012 Statistical Abstract of the United States.
5. The other four cities exempt small buildings from parking requirements. Washington, DC, for example, exempts the first 3,000 square feet of building area from parking requirements; Chicago exempts the first 4,000 square feet; and San Francisco exempts the first 5,000 square feet.

6. RLB provides cost estimates for two categories of office buildings, Prime (the most expensive) and Grade A or Secondary. I have used the cost estimates for Grade A office buildings.

7. Shoup (2011, pp. 698–699) uses the data in Cutter and Franco's Table 10 to calculate the marginal value and marginal cost of the required parking spaces.

8. Shoup (2008) explains this example in greater detail.

9. Adams (1994, pp. 26–27) explains residual land values. Shoup (1970) explains the optimal timing of redevelopment.

10. City of Los Angeles, Park Mile Specific Plan (Ordinance No. 162530), Section 6.B.1.

11. City of Los Angeles, Park Mile Specific Plan (Ordinance No. 162530), Section 6.B.2.

12. Letters about AB 904 from mayors, planning academics, planning practitioners, and the California Chapter of the American Planning Association are available at http://shoup.bol.ucla.edu/LettersAboutAssemblyBill904.pdf

13. Cities have also adopted other policies that increase the demand for cars and fuel, such as free on-street parking and street-width requirements. For example, Section 1805 of the California Streets and Highways Code states, "The width of all city streets, except state highways, bridges, alleys, and trails, shall be at least 40 feet." On a 40-foot wide residential street, with two 12-foot-wide travel lanes and two 8-foot-wide parking lanes, curb parking takes up 40 percent of the roadspace. The U.S. Department of Commerce estimates that the value of roads is 36 percent of the value of all state and local public infrastructure, which also includes schools, sewers, water supply, residential buildings, equipment, hospitals, and parks (Shoup, 2011, p. 206). Because curb parking occupies a large share of road space, it is a substantial share of all state and local public infrastructure. Free curb parking may be the most costly subsidy that American cities provide for most of their citizens. Guo and Schloeter (2013) explain how minimum street-width requirements are a de facto on-street free parking policy.

REFERENCES

Adams, D. (1994). *Urban planning and the development process*. London: UCL Press.

California Assembly Bill 904. (2012). The Sustainable Minimum Parking Requirements Act of 2012. Retrieved from http://shoup.bol.ucla.edu/AssemblyBill904.pdf

California Chapter of the American Planning Association. (2012, June 20). Memo to Assembly Member Nancy Skinner.

Cutter, W., & Franco, S. (2012). Do parking requirements significantly increase the area dedicated to parking? A test of the effect of parking requirements values in Los Angeles County. *Transportation Research Part A, 46*, 901–925.

Davis, A. Y., Pijanowski, B. C., Robinson, K. D., & Kidwell, P. B. (2010). Estimating parking lot footprints in the Upper Great Lakes region of the USA. *Landscape and Urban Planning, 96*, 68–77.

Goodman, S. (2013). Parking requirements for office buildings. *Graphing Parking*. Retrieved from http://graphingparking.com/2013/05/17/parking-requirements-for-office-buildings

Greater London Authority. (2004). *The London plan: Spatial development strategy for greater London.* Annex 4: Parking Standards (pp. A19–A29). Retrieved from http://tinyurl.com/kr9vdjh

Guo, Z., & Ren, S. (2013). From minimum to maximum: Impact of the London parking reform on residential parking supply from 2004 to 2010? *Urban Studies, 50*(6), 1183–1200.

Guo, Z., & Schloeter, L. (2013). Street standards as parking policy: Rethinking the provision of residential street parking in American suburbs. *Journal of Planning Education and Research, 33*(4), 456–470.

King County Metro. (2013, July 12). King County parking requirements and utilization gap analysis. Retrieved from http://metro.kingcounty.gov/up/projects/right-size-parking/pdf/gap-analysis-7-12-13.pdf

Manville, M. (2013). Parking requirements and housing development: Regulation and reform in Los Angeles. *Journal of the American Planning Association, 79*(1), 49–66.

Manville, M., Beata, A., & Shoup, D. (2013). Turning housing into driving: Parking requirements and density in Los Angeles and New York. *Housing Policy Debate, 23*(2), 350–375.

Rider Levett Bucknall. (2012). *Quarterly construction report, third quarter 2012.* Retrieved from https://dl.dropboxusercontent.com/u/35546513/rlb-usa-report-third-quarter-2012-1.pdf

Pasqual, J., & Riera, P. (2005). Underground land values. *Land Use Policy, 22,* 322–330.

Shoup, D. (1970). The optimal timing of urban land development. *Papers of the Regional Science Association, 25,* 33–44.

Shoup, D. (2008). Graduated density zoning. *Journal of Planning Education and Research, 28*(2), 161–179.

Shoup, D. (2011). *The high cost of free parking.* Chicago, IL: Planners Press.

United Kingdom Department for Communities and Local Government. (2001). *Planning policy guidance 13: Transport.* Retrieved from http://webarchive.nationalarchives.gov.uk/20120919132719/http://www.communities.gov.uk/documents/planningandbuilding/pdf/155634.pdf

Willson, R. (2013a). *Parking reform made easy.* Washington, DC: Island Press.

Willson, R. (2013b). Parking reform made easy. *Access, 43,* 29–34.

CHAPTER 6

PARKING CHOICE

Sarah Brooke, Stephen Ison and Mohammed Quddus

ABSTRACT

Purpose – *Parking choice involves an individual selecting a parking place based upon various inter-related factors. This chapter examines the factors that influence parking choice decisions.*

Methodology – *A review of the literature on parking choice has been undertaken. The influence of various factors on parking choice and recommendations for future parking policy will be outlined.*

Findings – *Most often it is a combination of several factors which influence individuals' choice of parking place.*

Practical and social implications – *Increased knowledge of the factors which influence parking-search behaviour will inform urban parking policy applications with associated environmental and economic benefits.*

Keywords: Parking choice; influencing factors; area-wide factors; individual characteristics; parking policy implications

Parking: Issues and Policies
Transport and Sustainability, Volume 5, 115–135
Copyright © 2014 by Emerald Group Publishing Limited
All rights of reproduction in any form reserved
ISSN: 2044-9941/doi:10.1108/S2044-994120140000005018

INTRODUCTION

Upon arrival at a destination, car-drivers select a parking place from a variety of options that fulfil their particular requirements on a specific parking occasion. Parking choice decisions are linked to wider parking and traffic management as choice leads drivers to search for a preferred parking place based on a combination of factors, comprising time-related and price-related, area-wide traffic network and parking policy, physical parking (built environment) and individual characteristics (Table 1). This creates a problem in urban areas in terms of the impact on the traffic network of additional vehicle miles travelled by drivers searching for a parking space. The environmental and economic impact can be quantified in terms of increased emissions, congestion and time delays both for individuals who are searching and for other drivers delayed by the slower vehicle speeds of searching drivers. This chapter discusses the factors that influence parking choice. The factors included in this chapter are not exhaustive but can be seen to influence parking choice behaviour. The aim is to outline how an individual's choice of parking place in urban areas involves decisions comprising several different but often inter-related factors.

Table 1. Parking Choice Influencing Factors.

Category	Factor
Area-wide traffic network policy	• PGI systems
Area-wide parking policy	• Illegal parking control and enforcement
	• Requirement for parking permits
Time-related	• Search, access and egress
	• Queuing and waiting
Price-related	• Parking charges
	• Willingness-to-pay
Physical parking (built environment) characteristics	• Parking provision type
	• Parking supply
	• Parking capacity
	• Occupancy and turnover
	• Times of operation
Individual characteristics	• Trip-related
	• Personal factors and preferences
	• Socio-demographic
	• Socio-economic

AREA-WIDE TRAFFIC NETWORK POLICY

Network characteristics such as traffic congestion may impact on parking choice through drivers changing routes in order to avoid more congested areas and associated time delays. Alternative routes will lead motorists to encounter different parking places to those initially sought when the driver set out from a point of origin. Dynamic Parking Guidance Information (PGI) influences individuals' parking choice by presenting drivers with real-time information about changing traffic and parking conditions in order to divert motorists from congested routes and parking facilities, encourage utilisation of unsaturated car-parks (Polak, Hilton, & Axhausen, 1989; Thompson, Takada, & Kobayakawa, 1998), reduce parking-search times and traffic congestion (Polak et al., 1989). PGI is most effective when off-street parking demand approximately equals supply (DfT, 2003). PGI research has focused on effectiveness in achieving these aims however results highlighted differing levels of effectiveness between user groups. Wide variation in PGI awareness and usage among different driver groups (Thompson & Bonsall, 1997; Thompson et al., 1998) and an overall low response to PGI was found (Thompson & Bonsall, 1997). Similarly, Axhausen, Polak, Boltze, and Puzicha (1994) and Chatterjee and McDonald (2004) found high awareness but low usage of PGI, while Polak et al. (1989) identified that PGI, despite being recognised by a majority of urban drivers, was used by a minority who were mostly unfamiliar with an area. Axhausen et al. (1994) identified how PGI was not used in an initial parking strategy but was utilised if a first-choice of parking place was unavailable. In contrast, Liu, Deng, and Pan (2011) found higher PGI usage although drivers with greater familiarity of a local area were less likely to follow PGI. Furthermore, PGI had limited impact on travel time; reducing total travel time by 0.1−1.0% in a network simulation parking choice model (Waterson, Hounsell, & Chatterjee, 2001). Hounsell, Chatterjee, Bonsall, and Firmin (1998) found scope for increasing utilisation of variable-message signs through providing information about unpredictable incidents; this being positively viewed by drivers. In Nottingham (United Kingdom), PGI was disseminated through radio broadcasts, accompanied by parking location information distributed through leaflets. Findings indicated drivers' car-park knowledge and utilisation of Park-and-Ride increased (Khattak & Polak, 1993). Caicedo (2009) suggested PGI has implications for parking choice and reducing unnecessary travel to already full car-parks by determining the occupancy level at which PGI should describe a parking facility as 'full' and transmitting information about parking space availability within specific facilities. With a similar aim of reducing travel time, Thompson, Takada, and Kobayakawa (2001) suggested distributing excess demand across parking facilities having spare capacity in order to minimise parking queues (waiting-time) and diverting drivers from centrally located parking towards car-parks closer to travel origin.

AREA-WIDE PARKING POLICY

The control and enforcement of illegal parking involves imposing fines on individuals who have parked in opposition to stated regulations in a particular locality, for example, overstaying a time restriction, parking in areas where parking is not permitted, or not paying a required fee. Parking enforcement in some areas of the United Kingdom involves clamping or towing-away of vehicles, for which drivers must pay to release or retrieve vehicles. Parking control represents an additional cost for motorists; therefore, likelihood of enforcement is an influencing factor in parking choice. This decision-making process was identified by Hess and Polak (2004) who observed higher parking fees created more disutility than an expected fine for illegal parking; drivers were more likely to park illegally if parking fees were high. Similarly, Van der Waerden, Oppewal, and Timmermans (1993) found the probability of illegal parking decreased when likelihood of receiving a parking fine increased. Likely enforcement was a factor for drivers in Athens (Greece); occasional fines for illegal parking resulted in drivers parking illegally when accompanied by reduced walk-time (Tsamboulas, 2001). Likewise, in Haarlem (Netherlands), visitors made little distinction between illegal or legal on-street parking preference (Van der Goot, 1982). Simulation by Saltzman (1994) of the effect that increased parking enforcement would have on discouraging illegal parking and by Gur and Beimborn (1984) found as the parking fine increased, long-duration parkers were more likely to change from an illegal to a legal parking choice. The effect of wheel-clamping was investigated by May and Turvey (1984), who found the number of central London vacant on-street meter-spaces increased, indicating that enforcement improved on-street parking availability.

Parking choice may be restricted to specific user groups (such as residents, employees or persons with a disability) who have been issued with a permit for a designated parking place. Employer-provided parking typically offers employees access to a privately owned car-park from which a parking space can be selected; residential and disability parking spaces are likely to be publicly owned, with the exception of allocated disability parking within private businesses (food-retail outlets, for example). Regulations differ for each permit scheme, with some schemes subject to specific times of operation or restricted durations; others being more flexible. For employees possessing a parking permit for an employer-provided car-park, choice of parking becomes unnecessary, as the permit offers a guaranteed parking place; hence no further parking decisions need to be made unless an employee chooses an alternative non−employer-provided parking facility for reasons of personal preference, or is unable to locate an available space within the permit-users' car-park (Gillen, 1977). Users of residential or disability permits are typically given a choice of parking spaces within an allocated area but have no guarantee of finding an available space at a desired time and location, resulting in increased parking search.

Park and Ride (P&R) facilities are intermodal transfer facilities. 'They provide a staging location for travellers to transfer between the auto mode and transit or between the single occupant vehicle (SOV) and other higher occupancy vehicle (HOV or carpools)' (Spillar, 1997). These are typically located on the outskirts of urban areas, the aim being to discourage motorists from travelling into city centres in order to reduce traffic congestion and associated air and noise pollution (Meek, Ison, & Enoch, 2008). Despite this aim, Parkhurst (2000) found that P&R generated more traffic outside the urban area than was avoided within the central cores; the conclusion being that P&R schemes redistribute, rather than reduce, traffic. However, P&R offers an alternative parking choice to motorists; the benefits and dis-benefits of which will be evaluated alongside other factors by drivers considering a parking place (See chapter 9 by Parkhurst and Meek for more detail on Park and Ride).

TIME-RELATED

The influence of search-time (time taken to locate a parking space upon arrival at a destination), access-time (travel from point of origin to parking place) and egress-time (walking-time from parking place to final destination) on parking choice has been investigated. Hess and Polak (2004) found significant differences in respondents' valuation of each travel-time component; while Axhausen and Polak (1991) found high absolute time-cost values and relatively similar search-time and egress-time values for respondents in

Karlsruhe (Germany) and Birmingham (United Kingdom). As early as 1969 the uncertainty of parking decisions and the influence of uncertainty on choice were investigated by Lambe (1969). Decades later, possibility theory was applied to model uncertainty in parking choice and the influence of access-time, search-time and egress-time were investigated (Dell'Orco, Ottomanelli, & Sassanelli, 2003; Ottomanelli, Dell'Orco, & Sassanelli, 2011). Tsamboulas (2001) estimated drivers' behaviour change from an already-chosen parking location, based on a combination of increased/ decreased walking-time and higher/lower parking charges, and found that more expensive parking choice was considered if associated with reduced walking-time. Sattayhatewa and Smith (2003) incorporated parking cost alongside access-time and egress-time in an investigation into factors influencing event-specific parking choice. Findings indicated the influence of egress-time in car-park first-choice preference, and of access-time, which was statistically significant in parking choice.

The influence of egress-time alongside parking charges on parking choice has been investigated. Findings indicated walking-distance influenced parking choice; drivers chose between increased walking-distances and lower parking fees, or paying more for parking to reduce walking-distances (Yun, Lao, Ma, & Yang, 2008). Similarly, Harmatuck (2007) found parking charges and walking-distances among university employees to be highly negatively significant. While Lam, Li, Huang, and Wong (2006a, 2006b) indicated the influence of walking-distance on parking choice behaviour; with parking charges and car-park capacity also identified as influencing factors. Meanwhile, Van der Goot (1982) found walking-time had greater influence on parking choice among visitors to Haarlem (Netherlands) than did parking charges or car-park occupancy levels. Ergun (1971) found individuals chose increased walk-time to avoid higher parking charges; interestingly, walk-time was not reduced by higher income levels, as indicated in other studies (Harmatuck, 2007; Yun et al., 2008). Similar to Ergun (1971) and Lambe (1969) indicated Central Business District employees chose to walk longer distances to reduce parking cost. Meanwhile Hunt and Teply (1993) found egress-time to be one of several factors influencing parking choice; other factors being parking charges and likelihood of search- and/or waiting-times. Golias, Yannis, and Harvatis (2002) investigated factors influencing individuals' choice of on- or off-street parking places and found increasing search-time for on-street parking enhanced off-street parking's attractiveness, where greater likelihood of finding a parking space may have been perceived. However, longer walk-times between off-street parking and destination encouraged drivers to choose alternative (not off-street) parking types (Golias et al., 2002).

Waiting-time occurs when an individual, having reached a preferred parking place, must wait for a parking space to become available. Parking choice may therefore be influenced by perceived waiting-time, which is affected by factors such as car-park capacity, parking occupancy and vehicle turnover. The influence of queuing/waiting-times on parking choice were investigated by Lau, Poon, Tong, and Wong (2005) who found egress-time to have greater influence than search- or waiting-time; while Teknomo and Hokao (1997) found waiting-time to be one of several factors influencing parking choice; other factors being parking space availability, trip purpose, parking charges, search- and egress-time. Hunt and Teply (1993) and Thompson and Richardson (1998) focused on car-park disutility as affecting individual parking choice; observing how waiting-time becomes one cost aspect affecting car-park disutility, against which other parking factors and alternative parking places would be compared and evaluated. Van der Waerden et al. (1993) researched the influence of perceived waiting-time on individuals' parking behaviour when faced with a fully occupied first-choice parking facility. Findings indicated the likelihood of waiting decreased with anticipated length of waiting-time, with a higher number of waiting cars, or when having already visited an increasing number of alternative parking places.

PRICE-RELATED

The price of parking varies according to duration and parking type and influences parking choice through its inter-relationship with other factors, for instance an individual's willingness-to-pay or personal income level. Kelly and Clinch (2006) found drivers with different trip purposes were influenced by a parking charge increase; business-travellers stated they would be less affected than did drivers making non-business trips. This difference became more pronounced with higher parking charges; an effect identified by Clinch and Kelly (2004), finding increasing price sensitivity between trip purposes and rising parking pricing. Similarly, Simicevic, Milosavljević, Maletić, and Kaplanović (2012) found greater inelasticity of parking demand for users having business/commuting purposes, indicated by lower sensitivity to parking price increases; while shopping/leisure parkers were more affected by higher prices. Likewise, Hensher and King (2001) found individuals on business trips were more likely to park in a CBD, while drivers who paid for their own parking chose to park outside a CBD where fees were lower, leading them to suggest that parking pricing is effective for controlling demand. Clinch and Kelly (2004) examined parking choice sensitivity and found relocation to an alternative parking facility was the most likely driver response to parking charge increases. Contrastingly, Chalermpong and Kittiwangchai (2008) found lower price elasticity for non-commuters' parking choice. In investigating temporal variance in price elasticity of demand following a parking price increase, Kelly and Clinch (2009) found the time period experiencing highest traffic volume was most responsive to increased parking charges. It was suggested that parking pricing can be used to target different market-segments, to attract or deter different trip purpose users. Tsamboulas (2001) investigated parking choice through combinations of parking charge and walking-distance, assessing the potential for increasing parking charges to change individuals' parking location choice. Other research has focused on pricing of on- and off-street parking and choice; Shoup (2006) found individuals were more likely to drive around searching for parking if on-street parking was priced lower than off-street alternatives. Similarly, Golias et al. (2002) found parking cost to be the main influencing factor for individuals' parking choice, observing how off-street parking price increases led to decreasing off-street parking occupancy. In contrast, Guan, Sun, Liu, and Liu (2005) found parking cost was not a factor influencing parking choice, due to vehicles owned by private organisations or government agencies resulting in parking charges not being paid by individual drivers. Willingness-to-pay is a parking choice influencing factor as individuals expressing lower willingness-to-pay for parking would be more likely to select a free of charge parking space or a low-priced car-park. Research found drivers exhibited greater sensitivity to parking price increases if parking for longer durations (Kobus, Puigarnau, Rietveld, & van Ommeren, 2013), which could be expected due to higher total cost if parking for longer; while older respondents, individuals on lower incomes and non-university educated respondents were less willing to pay (Anastasiadou et al., 2009). Barata, Cruz, and Ferreira (2011) found greater willingness-to-pay for a reserved parking space on a university campus among higher income individuals and among female respondents.

PHYSICAL PARKING (BUILT ENVIRONMENT) CHARACTERISTICS

Parking types can be categorised as 'on-street', 'off-street', 'multi-storey', 'underground' and 'illegal' parking places. Within each type, variations exist according to private or public ownership and usage, payment and permit requirements, times of operation, accessibility, size and other factors. Many individuals may not state a particular parking type preference; others select a parking place based initially on a specific type. For instance, Hunt and Teply (1993) found on-street parking spaces were preferred to off-street parking facilities due to convenience and easier access, although employer-provided parking was preferred to on-street parking, possibly due to having guaranteed space availability. These findings contrasted with Teknomo and Hokao (1997) who found lowest usage of on-street parking compared to off-street or multi-storey facilities, although the reason could be higher availability of spaces in the latter two facilities. A different focus on parking type was investigated by Nurul-Habib, Morency, and Trépanier (2012), who found parking type choice was important to travel activity scheduling (activity start time, duration and location).

A factor influencing parking choice is the supply of different parking types in any given area. The significance of parking supply in meeting demand was highlighted by Shang, Lin, and Huang (2007) who found parking supply shortage created overspill on-street parking. Strategic parking management was informed by investigating existing parking supply and predicting future parking demand (Lam, Fung, Wong, & Tong, 1998; Lau et al., 2005); by modelling parking supply and demand interaction under stochastic spatial and temporal networks (Li, Lam, Wong, Huang, & Zhu, 2008); and by simulating supply and demand of different parking types (Bifulco, 1993; Coppola, 2002). The need to make optimal use of parking supply to fulfil demand was examined by Dirickx and Jennergren (1975), who modelled driver assignment to specific parking types to optimise utilisation of parking facilities. Parking capacity is related to supply by determining the amount of available parking; larger car-parks possess increased capacity, which may be an influencing factor for parking choice. Van der Waerden et al. (1993) found 74% of respondents in Eindhoven (Netherlands) city-centre were not influenced by car-park size when choosing a parking place, as indicated by a significant negative result for car-parks possessing a larger number of parking spaces (Van der Waerden, Borgers, & Timmermans, 1998). This contrasts with the finding that an increasing number of parking spaces (found in larger car-parks) increased parking utility (Van der Waerden, Borgers, & Timmermans, 2008, 2010); a finding supported by Lambe (1969) in that car-parks having smaller capacity (<50 cars) were less attractive to employees than larger parking facilities.

Parking occupancy is '*the number of parking places occupied*' (Barata et al., 2011) in a specific parking facility or on-street area. Some facilities experience high occupancy levels, frequent saturation of vacant spaces and increased driver search- and wait-times. Parking turnover relates to inflow and outflow of vehicles entering or leaving a parking place over a set time period (Shang et al., 2007). High turnover, as occurs in short-stay parking, increases the number of drivers parking over a set period, but simultaneously increases the volume of traffic entering/exiting a facility and may lead to congestion in the wider network locality. Occupancy and turnover influence parking choice through (un)availability of parking spaces upon an individual's arrival at a parking place. Additional search-time and overall journey time from encountering a saturated car-park was observed by Van der Goot (1982); while the influence on search-time of car-park occupancy relative to capacity was modelled by Balijepalli, Shepherd, and Kant (2009). Car-park occupancy levels are an uncertainty when individuals embark on a trip and whether or not a parking space will be available upon reaching a destination remains unknown up to the time of arrival (Ottomanelli et al., 2011). It is therefore not possible for an individual to plan to park in a particular parking place and be certain of having that expectation fulfilled. This uncertainty highlights how first-choice of parking place cannot be guaranteed; necessitating further parking decisions to be taken which incorporate individual preference and other parking factors.

Different on-street parking places and off-street car-parks present various times of operation during which drivers may park a vehicle, varying from limited times of day up to and including 24-hour availability. Thus, times of operation may influence parking choice with regards to an individual needing to find a parking place with times to suit their particular requirements on a specific parking occasion. Time restrictions and parking charges were investigated as attributes evaluated by drivers in combination with parking duration, search- and walk-time, whereby the choice set from alternative options judged by the individual to fulfil their particular utility would be selected (Coppola, 2002).

INDIVIDUAL TRIP CHARACTERISTICS

Different trip purposes (for example, commuting or shopping) are an influencing factor on parking choice as time constraints may be more significant for certain trip purposes than for others, leading to less willingness for individuals to spend time searching for a parking space and greater demand for parking places close to desired destinations. Some studies have shown parking type choice to be related to trip purpose (Mo, Zhang, & Yan, 2008; Teknomo & Hokao, 1997; Yun et al., 2008); while Van der Goot (1982) found the significance of different parking choice influencing factors varied according to trip purpose. Meanwhile, Chalermpong and Kittiwangchai (2008) found different trip purposes affected the likelihood of changing parking behaviour given parking charge increases. However, Golias et al. (2002) did not find trip purpose to be a parking choice influencing factor. Thompson et al. (1998) found PGI utilisation varied according to trip purpose; commuters requiring less information on waiting-times and car-park locations, compared to shoppers who needed both types of information and business-users who required parking directions. Tourists were the most likely trip purpose users of PGI influencing parking choice (Thompson & Bonsall, 1997), particularly if possessing limited knowledge of parking options and having no specific destination.

Parking duration is the length of time for which individuals intend to park on any one specific trip and is an influencing factor for parking choice. Parking duration was investigated alongside parking charges, search- and egress-time in individual's preference for on- or off-street parking (Golias et al., 2002); findings indicated preference for off-street car-parking increased as parking duration lengthened, which was explained by more favourable off-street parking charges and heightened security measures. Kobus et al. (2013) examined the hypothetical influence of parking duration for on- or off-street (multi-storey) parking choice and found where on- and off-street parking was equally priced parking duration did not influence choice. However, where on-street parking was free or lower priced than off-street parking, individuals wanting to park for longer durations reacted more strongly to price changes than those parking for shorter durations. Similar findings by Tsamboulas (2001) indicated that longer-duration parkers reacted negatively to increased parking charges due to a higher total parking cost for longer parking duration. Parking duration in relation to search-time for on-street parking spaces has been investigated, with the finding that longer-duration parking requirements increased search-times for on-street parking (Shoup, 2006; Van Ommeren, Wentink, & Rietveld, 2012).

Two under-researched parking choice influencing factors are the number of previously visited car-parks (per trip occurrence) and perceived travel time to alternative parking facilities. The number of previously visited car-parks is important to parking choice research as this factor highlights how drivers evaluate car-parks according to relatively strict criteria which not all encountered car-parks are able to fulfil. Perceived travel time to alternative parking places indicates the significance of a further time-related factor in choice of parking place, in addition to factors such as search-time and walk-time. Van der Waerden et al. (1993) found individuals showed decreasing likelihood of waiting and searching for parking with an increasing number of previously visited car-parks. By contrast, travel time to parking alternatives had less significance on parking choice, waiting- and search-time (Van der Waerden et al., 1993). Individuals' immediately preceding route-choice determined the order in which parking facilities were encountered, depending on the proximity of different parking places to an individual's trip origin, from which individuals evaluated car-parks' (dis)utility based on individual parking preference. This was demonstrated by Bonsall and Palmer (2004), who included immediately preceding route-choice as an influencing factor, thereby improving the performance of a parking choice simulation model.

SOCIO-DEMOGRAPHIC CHARACTERISTICS

The influence of individuals' sex on parking choice has been highlighted by Salomon (1986), who found differences between males and females in parking choice for duration, search-time and illegal parking. This contrasted with Golias et al. (2002) who found individuals' sex did not influence parking choice. Meanwhile, other literature has reported differences in parking choice behaviour attributed to individuals' sex. Tsamboulas (2001) found males were more likely to accept a parking charge increase than were females; a finding supported by Mo et al. (2008) that females were more likely than males to consider parking charges as one of the most important factors in choice of parking place; possibly implying a greater sensitivity among females to parking price. Mo et al. (2008) additionally found males were more likely to park for short durations (<1 hour) than were females, although both sexes parked most frequently for 1-3 hours. Meanwhile, Fletcher (1995) found males were significantly more likely to illegally park in spaces reserved for disabled-users. Regarding PGI awareness, understanding and usage, wide variation according to individuals' sex has been found (Liu et al., 2011; Thompson & Bonsall, 1997; Thompson et al., 1998). Inconsistent findings involving individuals' age and parking pricing have highlighted the challenge in establishing age as a reliable parking choice factor. This is shown by findings indicating different age groups demonstrated behaviour distinct from other age groups when facing increased parking charges (Tsamboulas, 2001), and older respondents being less willing to pay for parking (Anastasiadou et al., 2009). Illegal parking in spaces reserved for disabled-users was also found to be significantly related to age (Fletcher, 1995); while Teknomo and Hokao (1997) found younger drivers preferred multi-storey car-parks over other parking facility types. In contrast, Golias et al. (2002) did not find age to be a parking choice influencing factor. However, as occurred for individuals' sex, wide variation according to a person's age was found in PGI awareness, understanding and usage (Thompson & Bonsall, 1997; Thompson et al., 1998); with PGI awareness increasing with age (Liu et al., 2011). The impact of individuals' ethnicity on parking choice has been a little-researched factor, with the exception of Fletcher (1995), who investigated the significance of race, alongside sex and age, in occurrences of illegal parking. Findings showed non-white drivers as more likely to park illegally in spaces reserved for persons with disabilities, particularly if no enforcement existed for parking infringement. Further research on ethnicity and parking choice is necessary to establish the potential significance of ethnicity as an influencing factor.

SOCIO-ECONOMIC CHARACTERISTICS

Income is a factor which influences parking choice through individuals' willingness-to-pay and the level of parking charge personally considered acceptable to access a parking place. Increasing willingness-to-pay for parking with rising income has been shown (Anastasiadou et al., 2009; Gillen, 1977; Kuppam, Pendyala, & Gollakoti, 1998; Shiftan & Burd-Eden, 2000; Tsamboulas, 2001). Income has been investigated alongside egress-time; finding that commuters chose to pay more for parking to reduce walk-time to destination (Lambe, 1969), higher income individuals preferred to park nearer to their destination to reduce walk-time (Gillen, 1977), and lower income employees indicated less sensitivity to increased walking-distances (Harmatuck, 2007). Studies have examined the influence on parking choice of income alongside other factors; for instance, Teknomo and Hokao (1997) found no difference in income level and parking type choice, while Cools, van der Waerden, and Janssens (2013) showed income to be related to increasing familiarity with local parking facilities. However, Golias et al. (2002) did not find income influenced parking choice, although it is noted this factor and individuals' sex and age may be incorporated within other parking cost and time factors.

The influence of individuals' education level on parking choice was investigated by Anastasiadou et al. (2009), who found university-graduates were willing to pay on average higher parking charges than non-university educated individuals. Additionally, Salomon (1986) found a negative correlation between individuals' education and parking-search time; it was suggested this may arise from highly educated individuals having greater personal values of time. This explanation supported the positive finding of Anastasiadou et al. (2009) of higher education level and willingness-to-pay for parking as higher parking charges may be associated with reduced search-times. Individuals' employment status is a factor that has received little attention in terms of potential to influence parking choice. While employed individuals may reveal different parking choices to those individuals who are unemployed, it may be that such preferences are influenced by factors related to employment, such as income, willingness-to-pay for parking and time constraints; factors which have been investigated in parking choice research and have been earlier outlined in this chapter.

INDIVIDUAL PERSONAL CHARACTERISTICS

Parking habits formed after repeat visits to areas may reduce the influence of other parking choice factors. Initially important factors may be sub-consciously replaced; instead of thinking rationally about the utility/disutility of specific parking places or trip decisions, drivers act automatically following previous behaviour (Aarts, Verplanken, & van Knippenberg, 1997; Verplanken, Aarts, van Knippenberg, & Moonen, 1998). By including driver parking choice on previous visits (parking habit) Bonsall and Palmer (2004) found model performance improved, as indicated by the finding that drivers possessing familiarity with the local area and parking options frequently chose to park in a car-park used for previous trips. A further parking choice influencing factor is drivers' familiarity with a local area and parking places. Constructed from past experience, familiarity gives individuals a knowledge-base from which to evaluate attributes and (dis)utility of parking options (Khattak & Polak, 1993). Contrastingly, Thompson and Richardson (1998) found the effect of parking experience from repeated journeys did not significantly influence parking choice; although, due to increased knowledge of parking availability and vehicle departure rates, waiting-times reduced considerably. Despite drivers' familiarity with a locality, parking awareness may remain limited to a few parking facilities, as shown by findings in Edinburgh (Scotland), in which 33% of respondents were unable to give the number of city-centre car-parks; only 3% correctly identified all nineteen (Rye, Hunton, Ison, & Kocak, 2008). Similarly, Cools et al. (2013) investigated drivers' parking familiarity in the locality of a shopping-centre in Hasselt (Belgium) and found differing levels of parking place familiarity among user groups. Meanwhile, Bonsall and Palmer (2004) incorporated varying levels of driver familiarity and local knowledge into a parking choice model and found absence of familiarity with the locality and parking places created random individual pre-trip and route-choice parking decisions (Bonsall & Palmer, 2004). Similarly, Waterson et al. (2001) incorporated drivers' network familiarity as a factor and demonstrated a difference in PGI utilisation between drivers who were familiar (or unfamiliar) with the local road network; unfamiliar drivers placed greater importance on PGI. The number of occasions an individual may be required to travel to and park within a particular area may influence initial and subsequent parking choice. This may be a result of increasing familiarity with perceived parking availability or due to rising accumulative parking costs over repeat visits. Research conducted on trip- and/or parking-frequency found frequent car-use increased familiarity with free of charge car-parks (Cools et al., 2013); however, Golias et al. (2002) found trip frequency did not affect parking choice. PGI, meanwhile, was less utilised by frequent travellers to an area; instead drivers used parking knowledge gathered from prior trip experience (Thompson & Bonsall, 1997). Similarly, Thompson et al. (1998) found high frequency travellers to an area were less likely to require information on waiting-times and car-park locations. Furthermore, frequent visitors were less likely to change parking behaviour when parking charges were introduced (Van der Waerden, Borgers, & Timmermans, 2006); similarly, high frequency travellers would accept parking price increases out of necessity of having to travel to a destination (Tsamboulas, 2001).

Individual perception of personal safety and vehicle security as a parking choice influencing factor has been investigated; for instance, Caicedo, Robuste, and Lopez-Pita (2006) found 60% of respondents (79% of female respondents) considered safety and security when deciding on which level to park within a multi-storey parking facility. Extending from the micro-scale of a single parking facility, Ji, Deng, Wang, and Liu (2007) found safety to be the second most important parking choice influencing factor after egress-distance from a car-park to desired destination; underground car-parking being perceived as most safe. Meanwhile, Teknomo and Hokao (1997) found differences in the importance of security by users of on-street or off-street/multi-storey car-parks; off-street facility users highlighted security as the most important factor. Personal value-of-time is difficult to measure with any level of certainty but can influence parking choice through an individual's willingness to spend time searching or waiting for parking. To take into account imprecise values of time which may not be perceived as the same by each individual but to recognise the importance of this factor, personal value-of-time was specified as a fuzzy number within a parking choice model (Dell'Orco et al., 2003; Ottomanelli et al., 2011). Similarly, where values of time are unknown Anastasiadou et al. (2009) suggested applying contingent valuation methodology to assess willingness-to-pay for parking. Shoup (2006) meanwhile, predicted individuals would be more likely to search for parking if individuals placed low value on personal value-of-time. By expressing value-of-time as a monetary value, Ergun (1971) found individuals would walk further from a parking place to a destination if savings were greater than personal value-of-time.

CONCLUSIONS AND POLICY IMPLICATIONS

Individuals' parking choice decisions are complex and multi-faceted, with often contradictory findings revealed among the factors influencing choice of parking place. This has created a need for further research in order to establish the influence and significance of specific factors on parking choice; this despite the apparently large number of studies that have investigated this topic. Parking choice has wider implications for parking and traffic policy, particularly in the area of parking management as an element of broader transport demand management strategy. Awareness of parking choice as an important aspect of travel behaviour enables implementation of measures to address some of the issues created by individuals searching for preferred parking places. However, the complexity of parking choice, and management of this issue, may result in policy implementation that creates further problems for wider traffic management. As parking choice is influenced by numerous inter-related factors, which vary according to the individual concerned, the scale of issues created by parking choice is unclear. The complexity of individual differences comprises factors such as: trip purpose, which influences parking choice through time constraints and various end destinations; varying levels of driver knowledge regarding familiarity with a locality and available parking options; and utilisation of information technology such as Internet parking websites, satellite navigation systems or dynamic PGI signage. In a spatial context, parking choice is location specific; varying between larger urban cities compared to smaller market towns, and between similar-sized cities or towns that have implemented different parking management strategies which may limit or alternatively expand the parking choices available to motorists. Temporal complexity arises from the changing significance over time of parking choice as an issue affecting urban areas, as car-use remains a preferred transport mode for a large element of the population. Through wider application of parking management strategies involving controlled parking supply and demand regulation, in addition to technology designed to ease parking choice decision making, parking choice may become less of a challenge for individual drivers to negotiate and for urban policy makers to control. The large number of potential influencing factors, in addition to the spatial and temporal complexity of parking choice, has created a challenging area, which is in need of further research.

REFERENCES

Aarts, H., Verplanken, B., & van Knippenberg, A. (1997). Habit and information use in travel-mode choices. *Acta Psychologica, 96*, 1–14.

Anastasiadou, M., Dimitriou, D. J., Fredianakis, A., Lagoudakis, E., Traxanatzi, G., & Tsagarakis, K. P. (2009). Determining the parking-fee using the contingent-valuation methodology. *Journal of Urban Planning and Development, 135*(3), 116–124.

Axhausen, K. W., & Polak, J. W. (1991). Choice of parking: Stated-preference approach. *Transportation, 18*(1), 59–81.

Axhausen, K. W., Polak, J. W., Boltze, M., & Puzicha, J. (1994). Effectiveness of the parking-guidance-system in Frankfurt/Main. *Traffic Engineering and Control, 35*(5), 304–309.

Balijepalli, N. C., Shepherd, S. P., & Kant, P. (2009). Integrating car-park location choice with equilibrium-assignment. *Transportation Research Board 88th Annual Meeting* (09-0527). Transportation Research Board of the National Academies, Washington, DC.

Barata, E., Cruz, L., & Ferreira, J. P. (2011). Parking at the UC campus: Problems and solutions. *Cities, 28*(5), 406–413.

Bifulco, G. N. (1993). A stochastic user equilibrium-assignment model for the evaluation of parking policies. *European Journal of Operational Research, 71*(2), 269–287.

Bonsall, P., & Palmer, I. (2004). Modelling drivers' car parking behaviour using data from a travel-choice simulator. *Transportation Research Part C: Emerging Technologies, 12*(5), 321–347.

Caicedo, F. (2009). The use of space availability information in 'PARC' systems to reduce search-times in parking-facilities. *Transportation Research Part C: Emerging Technologies, 17*(1), 56–68.

Caicedo, F., Robuste, F., & Lopez-Pita, A. (2006). Parking management and modeling of car-park patron behavior in underground-facilities. *Transportation Research Record: Journal of the Transportation Research Board, 1956*, 60–67.

Chalermpong, S., & Kittiwangchai, K. (2008). Effects of parking policy on travel demand in Bangkok's commercial district. *Transportation Research Board 87th Annual Meeting* (08-1679). Transportation Research Board of the National Academies, Washington, DC.

Chatterjee, K., & Mcdonald, M. (2004). Effectiveness of using variable-message signs to disseminate dynamic traffic information: Evidence from field trials in European cities. *Transport Reviews, 24*(5), 559−585.

Clinch, J. P., & Kelly, J. A. (2004). Temporal variance of revealed-preference on. *83rd Annual Meeting of Transportation Research Board.* Transportation Research Board of the National Academies, Washington, DC.

Cools, M., van der Waerden, P. J. H. J., & Janssens, D. (2013). Investigation of the determinants of travellers' mental knowledge of public parking-facilities. *Transportation Research Board 92nd Annual Meeting.* Transportation Research Board of the National Academies, Washington, DC.

Coppola, P. (2002). A joint model of mode/parking choice with elastic parking demand. *Transportation Planning, 64,* 85−104.

Dell'Orco, M., Ottomanelli, M., & Sassanelli, D. (2003). Modelling uncertainty in parking-choice behaviour. *82nd Annual Meeting of the Transportation Research Board.* Transportation Research Board of the National Academies, Washington, DC.

Department for Transport. (2003). *Parking guidance and information* (No. 4). Department for Transport, London, UK.

Dirickx, Y. M. I., & Jennergren, L. P. (1975). An analysis of the parking situation in the downtown-area of West Berlin. *Transportation Research, 9*(1), 1−11.

Ergun, G. (1971). Development of a downtown-parking model. *Highway Research Record, 369,* 118−134.

Fletcher, D. (1995). A five-year study of effects of fines, gender, race, and age on illegal-parking in spaces reserved for people with disabilities. *Rehabilitation Psychology, 40*(3), 203−210.

Gillen, D. W. (1977). Estimation and specification of the effects of parking-costs on urban transport-mode choice. *Journal of Urban Economics, 4*(2), 186−199.

Golias, J., Yannis, G., & Harvatis, M. (2002). Off-street parking-choice sensitivity. *Transportation Planning and Technology, 25*(4), 333−348.

Guan, H., Sun, X., Liu, X., & Liu, L. (2005). Modeling parking-behavior for better control and pricing: A case-study from one of the busiest retail-shopping areas in Beijing, China. *84th Annual Meeting of the Transportation Research Board.* Transportation Research Board of the National Academies, Washington, DC.

Gur, Y. J., & Beimborn, E. A. (1984). Analysis of parking in urban-centers: Equilibrium-assignment approach. *Transportation Research Record, 957,* 55−62.

Harmatuck, D. J. (2007). Revealed-parking choices and the value of time. *Transportation Research Record: Journal of the Transportation Research Board, 2010*(1), 26−34.

Hensher, D. A., & King, J. (2001). Parking demand and responsiveness to supply, pricing and location in the Sydney central-business district. *Transportation Research Part A: Policy and Practice, 35*(3), 177−196.

Hess, S., & Polak, J. W. (2004). Mixed-logit estimation of parking-type choice. *83rd Annual Meeting of the Transportation Research Board.* Transportation Research Board of the National Academies, Washington, DC.

Hounsell, N. B., Chatterjee, K., Bonsall, P. W., & Firmin, P. E. (1998). Variable message signs in London: Evaluation in CLEOPATRA. *Road Transport Information and Control, 454,* 217−221.

Hunt, J. D., & Teply, S. (1993). A nested-logit model of parking-location choice. *Transportation Research Part B: Methodological, 27*(4), 253–265.

Ji, Y., Deng, W., Wang, W., & Liu, G. (2007). Two-phased parking-choice model for pre-trip parking-guidance system. *Transportation Research Board 86th Annual Meeting* (07-1403). Transportation Research Board of the National Academies, Washington, DC.

Kelly, J. A., & Clinch, J. P. (2006). Influence of varied parking-tariffs on parking-occupancy levels by trip purpose. *Transport Policy, 13*(6), 487–495.

Kelly, J. A., & Clinch, J. P. (2009). Temporal variance of revealed-preference on-street parking-price elasticity. *Transport Policy, 16*(4), 193–199.

Khattak, A., & Polak, J. W. (1993). Effect of parking-information on travelers' knowledge and behavior. *Transportation, 20*(4), 373–393.

Kobus, M., Puigarnau, E. G., Rietveld, P., & van Ommeren, J. N. (2013). The on-street parking-premium and car-drivers' choice between street- and garage-parking. *Regional Science and Urban Economics, 43*(2), 395–403.

Kuppam, A. R., Pendyala, R. M., & Gollakoti, M. A. V. (1998). Stated-response analysis of the effectiveness of parking-pricing strategies for transportation control. *Transportation Research Record*, (1649), 39–46.

Lam, W. C. H., Fung, R. Y. C., Wong, S. C., & Tong, C. O. (1998). The Hong Kong parking-demand study. Proceedings of the institution of civil engineers. *Transport, 129*(4), 218–227.

Lam, W. H. K., Li, Z. C., Huang, H. J., & Wong, S. C. (2006a). Modeling time-dependent travel-choice problems in road-networks with multiple-user classes and multiple-parking-facilities. *Transportation Research Part B: Methodological, 40*(5), 368–395.

Lam, W. H. K., Li, Z. C., Huang, H. J., & Wong, S. C. (2006b). Optimization of time-varying parking-charges and parking-supplies in networks with multiple-user classes and various parking-facilities. *Transportation Research Board Annual Meeting*. Transportation Research Board of the National Academies, Washington, DC.

Lambe, T. A. (1969). The choice of parking-location by workers in the central-business district. *Traffic Quarterly, 23*(3), 397–411.

Lau, W. W. T., Poon, P. S. T., Tong, C. O., & Wong, S. C. (2005). The Hong Kong second parking-demand study. Proceedings of the Institution of Civil Engineers. *Transport, 158*(1), 53–59.

Li, Z. C., Lam, W. H. K., Wong, S. C., Huang, H. J., & Zhu, D. L. (2008). Reliability evaluation for stochastic and time-dependent networks with multiple-parking-facilities. *Networks and Spatial Economics, 8*(4), 355–381.

Liu, Z., Deng, W., & Pan, D. (2011). Driver response to parking-guidance and information systems in Nanjing. *ICCTP: Towards Sustainable Transportation Systems*, 689–698. American Society of Civil Engineering (ASCE) 2011.

May, A. D., & Turvey, I. G. (1984). *The effects of wheel-clamps in central London: Comparison of before-and-after studies* (No.184). Institute for Transport Studies, University of Leeds, UK.

Meek, S., Ison, S., & Enoch, M. (2008). Role of bus-based Park and Ride in the UK: A temporal and evaluative review. *Transport Reviews, 28*(6), 781–803.

Mo, Y., Zhang, B., & Yan, K. (2008). A study of parking-behavior and parking-information requirements in Shanghai CBD. *Seventh International Conference of Chinese Transportation Professionals (ICCTP)*. American Society of Civil Engineering (ASCE) (2008), Reston, VA.

Nurul-Habib, K. M., Morency, C., & Trépanier, M. (2012). Integrating parking-behaviour in activity-based travel demand modelling: Investigation of the relationship between parking-type choice and activity-scheduling process. *Transportation Research Part A: Policy and Practice, 46*(1), 154–166.

Ottomanelli, M., Dell'Orco, M., & Sassanelli, D. (2011). Modelling parking-choice behaviour using possibility theory. *Transportation Planning and Technology, 34*(7), 647–667.

Parkhurst, G. (2000). Influence of bus-based Park and Ride facilities on users' car traffic. *Transport Policy, 7*, 159–172.

Polak, J. W., Hilton, I. C., & Axhausen, K. W. (1989). *A review of parking-guidance and information systems* (No.480). Transport Studies Unit, Oxford University, UK.

Rye, T., Hunton, K., Ison, S., & Kocak, N. (2008). The role of market-research and consultation in developing parking policy. *Transport Policy, 15*(6), 387–394.

Salomon, I. (1986). Towards a behavioural approach to city-centre parking: The case of Jerusalem's CBD. *Cities, 3*(3), 200–208.

Saltzman, R. M. (1994). Three proposals for improving short-term on-street parking. *Socio-Economic Planning Sciences, 28*(2), 85–100.

Sattayhatewa, P., & Smith, R. L., Jr. (2003). Development of parking-choice models for special events. *Transportation Research Record, 1858*, 31–38.

Shang, H., Lin, W., & Huang, H. J. (2007). Empirical study of parking problem on university-campus. *Journal of Transportation Systems Engineering and Information Technology, 7*(2), 135–140.

Shiftan, Y., & Burd-Eden, R. (2000). Modeling the response to parking policy. *Transportation Research Board 80th Annual Meeting*. Transportation Research Board of the National Academies, Washington, DC.

Shoup, D. C. (2006). Cruising for parking. *Transport Policy, 13*(6), 479–486.

Simicevic, J., Milosavljević, N., Maletić, G., & Kaplanović, S. (2012). Defining parking-price based on users' attitudes. *Transport Policy, 23*, 70–78.

Spillar, R. J. (1997). *Park-and-Ride planning and design guidelines.* New York, NY: Parsons Brinckerhoff Inc.

Teknomo, K., & Hokao, K. (1997). Parking-behavior in central-business district: A study case of Surabaya, Indonesia. *Easts Journal, 2*(2), 551–570.

Thompson, R. G., & Bonsall, P. (1997). Drivers' response to parking-guidance and information systems. *Transport Reviews, 17*(2), 89–104.

Thompson, R. G., & Richardson, A. J. (1998). A parking-search model. *Transportation Research Part A: Policy and Practice, 32*(3), 159–170.

Thompson, R. G., Takada, K., & Kobayakawa, S. (1998). Understanding the demand for access-information. *Transportation Research Part C: Emerging Technologies, 6*(4), 231–245.

Thompson, R. G., Takada, K., & Kobayakawa, S. (2001). Optimisation of parking-guidance and information systems display configurations. *Transportation Research Part C: Emerging Technologies, 9*(1), 69–85.

Tsamboulas, D. A. (2001). Parking-fare thresholds: A policy tool. *Transport Policy, 8*(2), 115–124.

Van der Goot, D. (1982). A model to describe the choice of parking-places. *Transportation Research Part A: General, 16*(2), 109–115.

Van der Waerden, P. J. H. J., Borgers, A., & Timmermans, H. J. P. (1998). The impact of the parking situation in shopping-centres on store-choice behaviour. *Geojournal, 45*(4), 309–315.

Van der Waerden, P. J. H. J., Borgers, A., & Timmermans, H. J. P. (2006). Attitudes and behavioral responses to parking measures. *European Journal of Transport and Infrastructure Research, 6*(4), 301–312.

Van der Waerden, P. J. H. J., Borgers, A., & Timmermans, H. J. P. (2008). Modeling parking-choice behavior in business-areas. *Transportation Research Board 87th Annual Meeting* (08-1539). Transportation Research Board of the National Academies, Washington, DC.

Van der Waerden, P. J. H. J., Borgers, A., & Timmermans, H. J. P. (2010). Modeling the combined choice of entrance and parking in enclosed business areas. *12th WCTR*, July 11–15, 2010. Lisbon, Portugal.

Van der Waerden, P. J. H. J., Oppewal, H., & Timmermans, H. J. P. (1993). Adaptive-choice behaviour of motorists in congested shopping-centre parking-lots. *Transportation, 20*(4), 395–408.

Van Ommeren, J. N., Wentink, D., & Rietveld, P. (2012). Empirical evidence on cruising for parking. *Transportation Research Part A: Policy and Practice, 46*(1), 123–130.

Verplanken, B., Aarts, H., van Knippenberg, A., & Moonen, A. (1998). Habit versus planned behaviour: A field study. *British Journal of Social Psychology, 37*(1), 111–128.

Waterson, B. J., Hounsell, N. B., & Chatterjee, K. (2001). Quantifying the potential savings in travel-time resulting from parking-guidance systems: A simulation case-study. *Journal of the Operational Research Society, 52*, 1067–1077.

Yun, M., Lao, Y., Ma, Y., & Yang, X. (2008). Optimization-model on scale of public parking-lot considering parking-behavior. *Logistics: The emerging frontiers of transportation and development in China* (pp. 2692–2699). Reston, VA: American Society of Civil Engineering (ASCE).

CHAPTER 7

PARKING PRICING

Michael Manville

ABSTRACT

Purpose − *Drawing primarily on examples from the United States, this chapter explains how cities often misprice street parking, and the consequences that flow from that mispricing. The chapter then discusses progress toward charging market prices for street parking. In particular I examine equity- and fairness-based objections to market prices and find that most of these objections do not withstand scrutiny*

Methodology/approach − *I present street parking as an example of price controls, and use a sample of American cities to show that many street parking regimes exhibit the four hallmark consequences of price ceilings: shortages, misallocation, search costs, and shadow markets.*

Findings − *Most parking in American cities is free or underpriced (relative to nearby off-street parking), which creates the conditions for cruising and the justification for minimum parking requirements. Contrary to perceptions, off-street parking in US downtowns is usually available − most garages have at least 20 percent vacancy. Lastly, on-street parking charges are often lower than round-trip transit fares, even though drivers are on average more affluent than transit riders.*

Practical implications − *The chapter demonstrates the logical inconsistency of keeping street parking free, as well as the practical problems*

Parking: Issues and Policies
Transport and Sustainability, Volume 5, 137−155
ISSN: 2044-9941/doi:10.1108/S2044-994120140000005019

that arise by doing so. It also addresses the common concerns that dense areas have insufficient parking, and that accurately priced street parking would burden low-income people.

Originality/value of paper – *By using the price control framework, the chapter provides a novel way to think about parking pricing, one that emphasizes the distortions created by governments' refusal to price their valuable street space. The chapter also provides new evidence about the relative prices of on- and off-street parking, and the burdens of parking charges relative to charges for transit.*

Keywords: Parking; pricing; land use; public finance; markets; cruising

The history of parking pricing in the United States, and indeed most of the world, is one of price controls, or no prices at all. In this chapter I focus on the United States, but the broad picture I paint applies to most cities around the globe, although the details of course change. Suppose you drive into Manhattan and park on 116th Street near Morningside Drive. This is not the most expensive part of New York, but it is nevertheless home to Columbia University, a bustling park, and many businesses and residents. The area's property values reflect its wide variety of people and activities. In the Census tract where you are parked, the median value of an owner-occupied home is almost $835,000. The average apartment rent is $1,700 per month.

Now suppose a few days earlier you had parked on Main Street in downtown Bozeman, Montana. Bozeman is beautiful. Yet while it offers some amenities New York lacks (mountain air, moose sightings, fly-fishing), on balance a person in Bozeman has access to fewer opportunities than a person in New York. As such, the demand to live in Bozeman is lower, and so too are housing costs: the median home value is $269,000, while average rent is $826. Perhaps none of this is surprising: the way a property's surroundings determine its value – "location, location, location" – is now a tired cliché. Prices rise with access to destinations.

Yet not all real estate adheres to this rule-of-thumb. If location matters, your Manhattan parking space should cost more than your Bozeman space. The world outside your car door on Morningside Drive is bigger and faster than the world on Bozeman's Main Street. But New York City offers you this Manhattan space, which has a vastly greater *value* than the Bozeman space, for exactly the same *price*, and that price is zero. One-hundred-seventy square feet of New York real estate is yours for nothing, so long as you bring a car. Nor is that all. The price of parking on both Morningside Drive and Main Street is never *not* zero, even though the value of each space undoubtedly fluctuates by day and by hour.[1] In Manhattan and Bozeman alike, a parking space offers access to more opportunities at midday than midnight, and on a weekday than a weekend. Anyone who doubts this can simply watch prices rise and fall in private off-street garages, with their early-bird specials, evening and weekend rates, and higher prices during special events. The price on the street, however, doesn't change.

Were we to price other forms of real estate this way – if housing in New York and Bozeman were always and everywhere free, or if its price never changed – chaos would ensue. Of course this couldn't happen. Many different people own housing, and good luck convincing any of them – let alone all of them – to give it away. In the world of parking, however, the most convenient, ground floor real estate – the curb – is owned by single monopoly providers: city governments. And these governments overwhelmingly give this real estate away for free. Even when they don't, they often charge prices based on the amount of revenue they hope to collect, not on a desire to effectively manage street spaces and deliver a high-quality service to drivers. The resulting system serves neither drivers nor residents nor city governments well, and it has consequences that reverberate throughout the urban economy.

Again perhaps this is not surprising. Anyone who has suffered through an economics class has learned (or at least been told) that bad things happen when governments divorce price from value. Policies that hold down prices yield four predictable results: shortages, misallocation, high search costs, and shadow markets (the cost of the unpriced good end up in the price of other goods). The canonical examples are Soviet breadlines, America's gasoline price controls of the 1970s, and rent controlled housing, especially in New York City. Certainly these examples fit the bill. But they are also rather exotic, and students reading about them might wonder if price controls even exist anymore. The Soviet Union and the 1970s are both long gone. Rent control, for better or worse, is a dinosaur lumbering toward extinction. Fewer than two percent of US local governments have any sort of rent control, and even in New York City, where almost 2/3 of the housing stock is subject to rent regulation, only two percent of the housing stock has an actual hard price ceiling (Arnott, 1995).

By contrast, *every* city in the country, *right now*, keeps most of its street parking free or underpriced. (Every city also keeps it streets and roads free, which is a related and highly relevant topic but best reserved for another essay). Gasoline price controls were a temporary response to a temporary crisis, and they badly distorted driver incentives. Parking price controls are an ongoing policy, enacted in response to no crisis, that also badly distorts driver incentives. Rent controlled housing might be on its way out, but the United States, and in fact most of the world, operates a large rent control program for cars, with textbook results. First, when demand is high, curb parking spaces rapidly fill up (shortages). Second, drivers who urgently need spaces and who would pay high prices to park for just moments cannot do so, while people who place little value on spaces can luck into them and remain parked for hours (misallocation). Third, drivers who arrive to find no vacancies often choose not to pay for the more-expensive, uncontrolled off-street spaces, and instead circle the block in the hope that someone leaves. This behavior results in extra driving, extra congestion, and increased pollution (high search costs). Fourth, cities, faced with these problems, force all new developments to provide off-street parking. In essence, cities create problems by refusing to manage parking on their public streets and then react and create more problems by forcing developers to provide parking on private property. The costs of the controlled good spill into the uncontrolled sector. The price of development rises to keep the price of parking low, and people pay for street parking in the price of housing and other goods (shadow markets).

Several scholars have described street parking as a tragedy of the commons (Epstein, 2002; Guo & Xu, 2012; Shoup, 2006). I don't disagree with that interpretation, and my argument here is compatible with it. Street parking spaces are rival but not excludable, and left unpriced they can be overused. But suggesting that street parking is a commons risks lending it a complexity it doesn't deserve. Commons problems are difficult to solve when property rights are hard to establish. But unlike the air or the oceans (or the fish in the oceans), parking spaces are visible, tangible, immobile, and controlled by a single jurisdiction. I use the lens of price controls because I want to emphasize that governments have *chosen*, even if only through inaction, to keep curb spaces free or cheap. Efforts to price roads and parking spaces are often met by protests about unjust government interference. Yet the decision to keep a public service free is a decision. Sometimes this decision is warranted, sometimes not. In the case of parking it has caused no end of trouble.

THE SCARCITY OF PAID PARKING

Why is most curb parking free? It's a good question. Parking spaces are land, and most land isn't free to users, but most parking spaces are. One could argue that parking spaces are a particular kind of land − public infrastructure, a utility − but most utilities aren't free either. Water and electricity and fuel are all metered, while most street parking isn't. Perhaps parking is more akin to libraries than utilities. Certainly cities treat some parking spaces like library books: the government supplies them at no charge, and asks users only to give them up after a reasonable period, or else pay a fine. But free libraries encourage the accumulation of knowledge, making society as a whole better off. Free parking encourages more driving, which makes some drivers better off but leaves society − through congestion and pollution − worse. And of course many street parking spaces are neither priced nor time-limited. To be sure, some street spaces are free because free is the right price: in places where few people want to park, pricing makes little sense. Yet this does not describe many streets in cities large and small, where people often complain about congestion at the curb.[2]

At the simplest level, cities keep curb parking free because it has been free for a long time, because most voters are drivers, and most drivers like the status quo of free street parking. This explanation, while doubtless valid, only raises the question of why parking has been free for a long time. After all, most voters are water and power users as well, but no one revolts against water meters. To my knowledge no systematic examination of this topic exists, but I can speculate. I think parking meters have occupied an unusual place in both public opinion and public finance, and this position has led their pricing astray. Most utility charges are collected quietly (the water meter is in the basement, not mounted in the shower, and the bill only comes once a month), and often by government agencies that finance themselves exclusively via those collections. The charges are not salient, and even when they are, users often understand that the money they pay finances the utility itself. No one therefore has strong incentives to reduce or cease pricing. In contrast, drivers directly feed parking meters, often with cash, every time they park, and the revenue disappears into the city's general fund. Voters are thus both more aware of parking charges and more likely to resent them, and elected officials more likely to see meters as sources of revenue rather than instruments of allocation.

This last mistake − seeing metered parking primarily as a path to revenue − is costly. Parking charges are rent for using space, and the economic benefits of rent come from collecting it, not in how its revenue is used. Housing rents allocate housing units, regardless of how landlords spend the proceeds. Water companies don't meter because (or entirely because) they need to cover costs.[3] They meter to prevent people from turning on the tap and then leaving for hours without turning it off. Collecting the rent yields social benefits; the revenue is a byproduct of the socially beneficial activity. With parking, somewhere this distinction got lost. Because cities and voters alike see parking meters as revenue tools, it has always been tempting to defer rate increases, or to think that removing prices would do users a favor. It is hard to imagine an electric utility, in anticipation of a record heat wave, announcing that all electricity will be free. Yet during the holiday shopping season many city councils declare "meter holidays" in their downtowns, eliminating parking prices and inviting shoppers to experience a shortage.[4]

Just how much curb parking is free or underpriced? Table 1 shows, for 20 American cities, the number of paid street spaces, the number of centerline miles of street, and the ratio of paid street spaces to centerline mile. Interpreting these ratios is difficult. A centerline mile of street is what it sounds like — the linear distance of street as measured from the middle of the road. A street parking space is typically 20 feet long, so if every foot of centerline was part of parking space, and every street had parking on both sides, then the maximum ratio of paid spaces to centerline mile would be 528 ($5,280 \times 2 \div 20$). As the table's third column shows, no city comes remotely close to this ratio. The average number of paid spaces per centerline mile is 6.5; even San Francisco, which stands out for having 35 paid street spaces per centerline mile (over 5 times the sample mean), still prices less than one-fifteenth of its street spaces.

The denominator in this calculation, however, is not realistic. Many centerline miles of street cannot or do not hold parking spaces. Street-miles are interrupted by intersections, driveways, curb cuts, bus stops and loading zones. Some streets are too narrow to hold parking on one or both sides, and many cities ban parking on some wide streets to prioritize vehicle flow.[5] So what is the correct denominator — what share of street-miles hold parking spaces? The only American city for which we can answer that question is San Francisco, because San Francisco completed a parking census in 2010. The census found that the city had 280,000 on-street spaces, or 329 spaces per centerline mile. Thus the city's actual count of parking spaces was about 62 percent of its theoretical maximum, and the city priced about 11 percent of its street spaces ($35.3 \div 329$). In other words, even after

Table 1. Incidence and Distribution of Paid Parking, Select US Cities (2013).

City	Paid Street Parking Spaces	Centerline Street-Miles	Paid Spaces/ Centerline Mile	Percent Parking Priced	Max. Hours Paid Parking	Max. Days Paid Parking
Atlanta	2,500	1215	2.1	0.8	12	6
Boston	7,000	785	8.9	3.4	12	6
Charlotte	1,100	2,400	0.5	0.2	24	7
Chicago	36,000	4,000	9.0	3.4	24	7
Cincinnati	4,979	985	5.1	1.9	11	6
Columbus	4,215	2,053	2.1	0.8	13	6
Dallas	4,513	3,538	1.3	0.5	12	6
Denver	6,300	1,860	3.4	1.3	24	6
Houston	7,000	5,700	1.2	0.5	11	6
Indianapolis	3,700	3,000	1.2	0.5	14	6
Los Angeles	40,000	6,500	6.2	2.3	12	6
Miami	9,300	663	14.0	5.3	12	7
Minneapolis	7,000	1,081	6.5	2.5	18	7
New York	85,000	6,300	13.5	5.1	14	6
Philadelphia	9,843	2,525	3.9	1.5	12	6
Phoenix	2,300	4,837	0.5	0.2	8	5
Pittsburgh	9,000	1,031	8.7	3.3	10	6
Portland	9,700	2,062	4.7	1.8	11	7
San Diego	5,200	2,800	1.9	0.7	10	6
San Francisco	30,000	850	35.3	13.4	13	7
San Jose	2,600	3,334	0.8	0.3	13	7
Seattle	13,000	1,677	7.8	2.9	12	6
Washington, DC	17,000	1,392	12.2	4.6	15	6
Mean			6.5	2.5	13.8	6.3

Source: Author's research. "Percent parking priced" assumes that half of a city's centerline miles are street parking spaces.

adjusting the data, the city with the *most* paid parking nevertheless kept almost 90 percent of its street spaces free.

Can we assume San Francisco's denominator applies to all cities? On the one hand, San Francisco is unlike other cities: with its density and older street grid, it probably has more transit stops and intersections than most other municipalities. Yet these characteristics might be cancelled out if San Francisco also has fewer curb cuts and driveways, since fewer of its buildings have off-street parking. Further, cities that have plentiful off-street parking, such as Phoenix, may be more likely to ban street parking on major arterials.

Because there are no data to help answer this question, I will be conservative and simply cut the theoretical maximum in half, and use that to (roughly) estimate the share of street parking that cities price. Thus in the fourth column of Table 1 I assume cities can have a maximum of 217 spaces per centerline mile, and then derive the share of street spaces that are priced. I emphasize again that this estimate is crude, but the results are nevertheless astonishing. On average, the cities price only *2.5 percent* of their street spaces. After San Francisco, the cities that price the greatest share of their street spaces are New York and Miami, at 5 percent each. Nine cities price fewer than 1 percent of their street spaces; Phoenix prices two-tenths of one percent of its street parking.

Even the priced spaces are not priced all the time. Sometimes these spaces are free because there is no demand for them, or because parking isn't allowed overnight. But many cities turn off their meters on weekends regardless of demand, and charge no evening prices in neighborhoods full of restaurants, theaters, and nightclubs. Columns 6 and 7 show the maximum number of hours per day, and days of the week, that the city charges for street parking. Note that this is the maximum and not the mode: in most places parking is priced for fewer hours, and sometimes on fewer days. For example, parking is priced all day every day in Chicago's Loop (the densest part of the Central Business District), but most of the city's parking is priced only ten hours a day. Likewise Charlotte maintains 24-hour pricing only on South Boulevard: everywhere else it prices parking 5 days a week, from 7 a.m. to 6 p.m. Yet even using these inflated figures, in 12 of the 25 cities priced spaces are free at least half the day, and in 20 cities priced spaces are free on Sundays. Since these estimates are biased upward, it is reasonable to conclude that most street parking spaces are not priced, and that most priced spaces are still free most of the time.

THE CONSEQUENCES OF LOW OR NO PRICES

Street parking is the ground floor real estate of parking. Because it offers the best proximity to most destinations (and the greatest ease of arrival and departure), it should command the highest price per hour. As such, most people should therefore consume street parking in relatively small increments of time. Cities should see rapid turnover in higher-rent street spaces, and longer parking durations in off-street spaces where per-hour rates are lower. When cities price parking below its market value, however, they upset this logic, because the more valuable street spaces become cheaper than the less valuable garage spots. At this point the unfortunate chain of events I described earlier begins: more people want spaces, for longer periods of time, than there are spaces to sell for those durations. A shortage results, and the shortage is compounded by misallocation. Drivers arriving to find a full street almost always have the option of pulling into an off-street lot, but the off-street parking is not price-controlled and therefore comparatively expensive, while the street parking – though unavailable – is cheap or free. To drivers, the price of the less-desirable off-street parking seems too high, when in fact the problem is that the price of the more-desirable on-street parking is too low.

This imbalance between on- and off-street prices leads drivers to skip garages and circle the block in search of street parking, a behavior called cruising. Table 2 illustrates cruising's benefits for drivers. The table shows, for the CBDs of 25 American cities, the highest price for one hour of street parking, and then the low, median, and high prices for one hour of off-street structured parking. (I gathered the on-street data; the off-street rates are from Collier's International (Cook & Simonson, 2012).) The on-street prices are the highest the city charges at any time – thus the $5 for New York represents a Friday night in Greenwich Village, not the lower rates that prevail in most places most of the week, and the $6.50 in Chicago represents the peak time and place as well. Yet even biasing the street parking price upward in this way, in over half the cities the *lowest* price in an off-street CBD structure is higher than the *highest* CBD price at the curb. In *every* city the highest on-street price is lower than the median off-street price.

The median return to cruising for someone who parks for an hour is the highest on-street price subtracted from the median off-street price. It ranges from 42 cents in Little Rock to $14 in New York City; across all cities in the table returns to cruising average just over $4. Thus a driver in downtown Philadelphia knows the least he will pay is $9.50 for an hour in an off-street structure, while in half the garages he will pay $13 or more. If he keeps circling the block, however, he could get lucky and pay only $2.00. His median return to cruising is approximately $11.00 an hour.[6] For many people in this situation, cruising is entirely rational.

A series of rational actions, however, can add up to a profoundly irrational outcome. Many drivers circling the block for even short periods can generate vast amounts of excess travel and congestion. Shoup (2006)

Table 2.   Returns to Cruising in American CBDs (2012).

City	Highest Meter Rate ($/Hr)	CBD Hourly Off-Street Parking Rates			Median Return to Cruising	CBD Off-Street Occupancy (%)
		Low	Median	High		
Atlanta	2.00	$1.00	$4.00	$8.00	$2.00	60−80
Boston	1.25	$6.00	$12.00	$26.00	$10.75	60−80
Charleston	1.00	$1.00	$2.00	$4.00	$1.00	>80
Chicago	6.50	$10.00	$19.00	$28.00	$12.50	60−80
Cincinnati	2.00	$1.00	$3.50	$6.50	$1.50	60−80
Columbus	1.00	$1.00	$3.00	$8.00	$2.00	60−80
Dallas	1.50	$1.00	$4.60	$10.00	$3.10	60−80
Denver	1.00	$2.00	$8.00	$10.00	$7.00	60−80
Hartford	1.00	$2.00	$3.00	$5.00	$2.00	<60
Houston	2.00	$3.00	$4.50	$13.00	$2.50	>80
Indianapolis	1.50	$1.00	$5.00	$13.00	$3.50	>80
Little Rock	1.00	$1.09	$1.42	$1.50	$0.42	>80
Los Angeles	6.00	$1.00	$12.50	$25.00	$6.50	60−80
Miami	1.50	$3.00	$5.00	$6.00	$3.50	60−80
Minneapolis	2.50	$2.00	$4.00	$8.00	$1.50	60−80
New York	5.00	$7.00	$19.00	$40.00	$14.00	60−80
Oakland	2.00	$2.25	$4.00	$6.00	$2.00	60−80
Philadelphia	2.00	$9.50	$13.00	$17.00	$11.00	60−80
Phoenix	1.50	$2.00	$3.00	$3.00	$1.50	60−80
Portland	1.60	$1.50	$5.00	$12.00	$3.40	60−80
San Diego	1.25	$6.00	$8.00	$10.00	$6.75	>80
San Francisco	5.50	$2.50	$10.00	$18.00	$4.50	60−80
San Jose	2.00	$2.25	$3.00	$3.75	$1.00	60−80
Seattle	4.00	$5.00	$9.00	$13.00	$5.00	60−80
Washington, DC	2.00	$9.00	$11.00	$12.00	$9.00	60−80
Average	2.34	$3.32	$7.06	$12.27	$4.72	

Sources: Author's research and Cook and Simonson (2013).

estimated that in the Westwood Village neighborhood of Los Angeles, drivers cruised for an average of just over three minutes each, and traveled about a half mile − but this cruising added up to 260 hours of excess travel and 3,500 excess vehicle miles driven per day. Most of this travel is pure social waste. Travel is valuable to society when people get where they need to go − to school or work or other activities. Cruisers, however, are not going anywhere. They have already arrived, and are just searching for a place to park.[7] Because they are searching while driving, cruisers are also distracted: they move slowly, start and stop, hover between lanes, watch the curb instead of the road, and hold up the traffic behind them (including transit vehicles).

Often these drivers' frustrations are needless: they are circling neighborhoods where parking is plentiful. The final column of the table shows, for each city, the average occupancy in CBD parking structures. In 20 of the 25 CBDs, the structures are usually less than 80 percent full. Thus mispricing leads drivers to orbit empty garages while complaining about a shortage of parking.

If cities priced street parking correctly, many circling vehicles would find homes in these structures. Cities, however, have adopted a different solution for cruising: minimum parking requirements. Much has been written about these laws, including a full chapter in this volume, so I won't belabor them here. There is by now ample evidence that places with higher parking requirements have higher vehicle densities and lower housing densities (Manville, Beata, & Shoup, 2013); that parking requirements increase both vehicle ownership and driving (Guo, 2012, 2013; Weinberger, 2012); and that they limit infill development, prevent the reuse of older buildings, and make lower-priced housing difficult to construct (Manville, 2013). There is no need for me to retread these arguments here.

I will make only two points. First, there is little evidence that minimum parking requirements accomplish their nominal purpose, which is to decongest the curb. So long as street spaces are free, many people will want them; only after street spaces are full will drivers migrate toward off-street parking. We see evidence of this in the vacant CBD garage spaces in Table 2. Guo and Xu (2012) discuss residents of New York City (of all places!) who have garages but nevertheless jockey for street space, because it is more convenient, and lets them use their garages to store household goods.

The second, related point is that for all the damage they do, minimum parking requirements are not the core problem of urban parking. They are instead a poor solution to the core problem. Minimum parking requirements are cities' response to a different problem they have caused – mispriced, and therefore congested, street parking. Mispricing on the street is the central problem of urban parking; it is the original distortion from which the other distortions flow. When cities price street parking correctly, no one will have an incentive to search for cheap or free curb space. Curb spaces will be available, but they will be available precisely because they *aren't* free. And when a few curb spaces are always available, the justification for minimum parking requirements will disappear. Thus to solve the problem at its source, cities must charge the right price for street parking.

TOWARD MARKET PRICES FOR CURB PARKING

Researchers generally recommend that cities price their curb parking so that one to two spaces are always available on a block. At this price an arriving driver can always finds a space, but most spaces are occupied most of the time. If we think of parking as a commodity, the right price is one where any willing buyer finds a seller and sellers are not saddled with excess inventory — a few spaces are always open but most are full. One might argue in response that parking should not be a commodity. I will not fully address this objection; certainly markets are not the proper allocation mechanism for everything. But the harms from not pricing parking are large, and philosophers who argue against market allocation often do so for goods with long time horizons and considerable uncertainty, like human organs or votes or health care. Parking spaces do not meet these criteria. Indeed, there is already a vibrant market in off-street parking, which few people object to. Lastly, not charging people money for parking often means charging people in time. Money has the advantage of being fungible. Cities can reinvest the revenue from parking charges, even return some of it to drivers. Time, once spent, is gone forever.

Certainly voters like free parking and dislike the idea of paid parking. But experience with congestion charges on roads suggests that voters who initially dislike pricing grow to appreciate it once it is in place, because it works: congestion does in fact decline (i.e., Harsmann & Quigley, 2010; Santos, 2008). Drivers pay, but they get something in return: reliable travel on uncongested roads. In principle, the same should be true of market-priced parking. The challenge, therefore, lies in initial implementation: how to win approval for performance pricing? Shoup (2005) argues that cities can win acceptance for priced street parking through astute use of the revenue. He proposes that cities dedicate parking revenue to the neighbor-hoods where the meters are located, and use it to finance public services that neighborhoods value. Thus while revenue is not the economic purpose of metering (allocation is), cities can use revenue to build political support for pricing. Market-priced parking that finances public improvements can let cities deliver excellent service to people driving *to* neighborhoods and people who live and work *in* neighborhoods.

Market prices should be dynamic: rates should change with the time of day, day of week, and time of year. Cities planning to charge market prices must therefore upgrade their meters. Meters now accept credit and debit cards as well as municipal "smart parking" cards (a sort of local debit card that can, among other things, let cities charge residents less to park on their own streets, which helps local build support for more meters). Almost all new meters let drivers pay via mobile phone. Meter pay stations can accept payment for up to 20 parking spaces, allowing cities to price parking in places that lack room for many single-space meters, or in places – such as historic districts – where people think meters are aesthetically inappropriate. Some meters are solar powered, and there are even "mobile" meters, like E-Z passes, that drivers can load with money and simply hang from their rearview mirrors. All these meters rarely break down, and when they do they communicate with central servers to alert municipal officials. Cities can also deploy these meters in conjunction with sensors embedded in the pavement below parking spaces. The sensors track occupancy and can help cities determine the correct prices for different neighborhoods at different times, and can also make parking enforcement more efficient, by identifying areas where many vehicles are parked but few are paying.

Despite this technological progress, many medium-sized and smaller American downtowns continue to use older coin-operated devices, for the simple reason that newer machines are expensive. Pay station kiosks, for instance, cost between $7,000 and $8,000 apiece. Because each kiosk replaces five or six regular meters, and lasts about ten years, they should pay themselves back, at least in cities of some size. But many cities lack the money upfront to invest in them. These cities continue with older meters that break easily, require coins, and cannot charge different prices at different times.

In the past decade large cities have begun modernizing their meter stocks, in three ways. Some have invested their own funds, others – most notably Los Angeles and San Francisco – have buttressed their own spending with grants from the federal government, and two others (Chicago and Indianapolis) have privatized their meters. In 2008 Chicago leased its spaces to a private consortium for 75 years. The consortium agreed to install modern meters and pay the city about $1 billion upfront. In return, the consortium is entitled to all the revenue from the meters over the 75-year period. At the end of the 75 years, the consortium returns the meters to the city. In Chicago's wake, Sacramento, Cincinnati, and some smaller cities have also considered meter privatization.

Chicago's lease has been controversial, largely because critics believe the city negotiated poorly: over the course of 75 years, the consortium is expected to net $9 billion, for an initial investment of $1 billion plus the meter upgrade. To critics, this amounts to a massive giveaway. I am inclined to agree with that assessment, but there is nothing about privatization that says cities must negotiate poorly – Indianapolis, for example, seems to have driven a harder bargain than Chicago. My concerns about meter leases are different. My first worry is that these leases confuse markets with privatization; one needn't imply the other. Granted, a private firm may have more motivation to charge market prices, and privatization can give cities political cover if drivers grow angry over higher prices. For the next six decades, Chicago politicians can shrug helplessly when voters become irate about parking prices, and blame their predecessors who signed a binding contract from which they cannot escape. (This is not, I should emphasize, a small advantage). But a public agency can harness market forces. A city willing to take the plunge can charge market prices for its parking; it needs no help from the private sector do so.

Second, a publicly run market in parking might work better than a privately run market for the simple reason that the socially optimal parking charge might be different from the profit-maximizing charge. The goal of a private operator is to maximize revenue; the goal of a city operator is (or should be) to maximize *performance* − to ensure that spaces are available for drivers. Consider the difference between Chicago's pricing structure and that of *SFpark*, San Francisco's municipal experiment in market-priced parking run by the city government. When Chicago signed its lease in 2008, it agreed to pre-set rate increases for years going forward. The 2008 agreement, for instance, called for meter rates in the Loop to rise to $6.50 per hour in 2013. These increases would occur regardless of actual demand. In San Francisco, by contrast, the city regularly evaluates occupancy rates and changes prices every two months based on the observed occupancy. It would be impossible for *SFpark* officials to know, as Chicago officials do, what the price in a given neighborhood will be 5 or 15 years hence. Yet this sort of demand-responsive pricing is possible because maintaining vacancy, not maximizing revenue, is the program's goal.

PRICED PARKING AND FAIRNESS

Is it fair to charge prices, and potentially high prices, for a public resource? This concern takes two forms. First, people sometimes object that priced parking is a form of "double-taxation"; voters have already paid for spaces with their property taxes, so forcing them to pay each time they use a space is unfair. Second, voters object that the regressive nature of priced parking will harm low-income people.

The double-taxation argument confuses the provision of a good with its allocation. While it is true that cities use property taxes (and most likely grants from higher levels of government as well) to construct parking spaces, the cost of constructing and maintaining spaces is wholly different from the price needed to manage demand for them. A house built in Bozeman sells for less than an identical one in New York, simply because more people want to live in New York than Bozeman. Similarly, cities use a combination of taxes, grants, and fees to construct water treatment facilities, sewer pipes, and power plants and power lines. Yet few people argue that water, gas, or electric meters are instruments of double-taxation. Nor do these services regularly disappoint. Roads and street parking spaces are the only forms of public infrastructure that fail from overuse multiple times a day. They are also the only form of public infrastructure we leave largely unpriced.

That said, we cannot simply dismiss the idea of double-taxation. The logic above has a surprising implication, which is that the double-taxation argument carries some weight if the city is charging a below-market price. If metering is justified because it allocates space properly and eliminates congestion, then the meter price must be high enough to actually accomplish those goals, or else drivers are not getting a service in return for their money. When parking prices are set to ensure some vacancy at all times, the meter price is a fee-for-service; the driver pays the city, and the city delivers an open space. When the price is too low but not zero, the driver gets the worst of both worlds – a fee with bad service. Drivers circle the block and are charged for their trouble. In these circumstances drivers can be forgiven for thinking they get nothing for something.

Increasing the price to the market rate can eliminate these concerns, although it does not remove the concern that parking prices might harm the poor. A parking charge is regressive (its burden falls proportionally more on people with lower incomes) so it would appear to violate horizontal and vertical notions of equity. At the same time, however, one pays a parking charge only if one in fact uses a parking space, so market-priced parking adheres to the "benefits received" or "user pays" principle of equity. Moreover, to the extent a parking charge is a pure fee-for-service, its regressivity is meaningless with respect to the distribution of income (Fischel, 2002). Suppose a person pays a private vendor the going rate for a parking space; most people would consider this a market transaction and think little of its equity impact. If the city took over the garage and charged the same price, would the transaction suddenly become a regressive tax? If so, then a transaction can become a regressive tax based on nothing but the identity of the revenue collector. This idea is incoherent. In the name of fairness, cities could privatize their meters, transforming regressive taxes into market exchanges simply by transferring ownership. If a parking charge is a fee-for-service, it makes no more sense to call it regressive than it does to call purchasing a gallon of gasoline, or indeed purchasing a vehicle, regressive.

Even if we accept that a parking charge is regressive, it is regressive through the *driving* population, not the population at large. The poorest people tend not to drive at all (often they are on buses, being slowed down by people cruising), and richer people drive more than poorer people. Thus while free street parking gives some poor people some benefits, it gives affluent people much larger benefits. If we want to alter across-the-board prices to make travel less expensive for the poor, we would be better off increasing transit subsidies. Transit fares are also regressive, and transit riders are much more likely than drivers to have low incomes. Table 3 shows, for 20 American cities, the highest hourly rate for curb parking and lowest transit fare (for cities that have rail systems, it is the lowest one-way rail fare, for other cities it is the lowest one-way bus fare). Although the average maximum one-hour parking price is 45 cents more than the average minimum transit fare, the parking price mean is biased upward by a handful of cities with expensive downtown parking. In 11 cities, the highest one-hour parking price is less than the lowest one-way transit fare. In 16 of the 20 cities, the highest one-hour parking price is lower than *two* one-way transit fares. These disparities exist even though, as the final four columns of the table demonstrate, solo drivers are twice as likely as transit riders to earn more than $75,000 a year, and less than half as likely to be poor.[8] Further, it is worth considering what the parking charge and the transit fare can buy. In New York City, for example, a driver paying $5 can occupy 170 square feet of land in Greenwich Village for an hour on a Friday night. A transit rider who pays the same amount gets a seat (and sometimes not even that) on two subway trips that could be as short as five minutes.

None of these points means that low-income people would never be burdened by market-priced street parking. The discussion does suggest, however, that the number of vulnerable people harmed might be small, and some further reflection suggests that the problem would be neither unique nor unsolvable. Water, heat, and electricity are certainly more important than curb parking, and some low-income people cannot afford them. Yet we rarely look at this problem and decide that all water and heat prices are too high; we conclude instead that some people's incomes are too low. Rather than slash rates across-the-board, or keep all utilities free so the poorest can afford them, we identify vulnerable people and give them targeted assistance. I see no reason governments cannot do the same for street parking. Cities with smart meters could distribute special debit cards

Table 3. Parking Charges, Transit Fares, and Economic Characteristics by Commute Mode.

City	Highest Meter Rate ($/Hr)	Lowest One-Way Transit Fare	Workers Earning Over $75k		Workers in Poverty	
			Drive Alone (%)	Transit (%)	Drive Alone (%)	Transit (%)
Atlanta	2.00	$2.50	26	6	7	22
Boston	1.25	$2.00	24	12	6	11
Charlotte	1.00	$2.00	17	9	6	21
Chicago	6.50	$2.25	17	15	6	12
Cincinnati	2.00	$1.75	14	3	10	29
Columbus	1.00	$2.00	6	2	10	27
Dallas	1.50	$2.50	10	4	8	23
Denver	1.00	$2.25	15	5	9	22
Hartford	1.00	$1.30	18	11	8	16
Houston	2.00	$1.25	7	2	9	22
Indianapolis	1.50	$1.75	16	7	9	24
Los Angeles	6.00	$1.50	11	3	8	22
Miami	1.50	$2.00	18	3	7	22
Minneapolis	2.50	$1.75	11	2	10	27
New York	5.00	$2.75	18	8	8	19
Philadelphia	2.00	$2.25	22	18	4	8
Phoenix	1.50	$2.00	12	7	6	13
Pittsburgh	3.00	$2.50	14	6	7	17
Portland	1.60	$1.25	17	9	8	11
Raleigh	1.00	$1.00	17	4	7	23
San Francisco	5.50	$2.00	35	27	3	7
San Diego	1.25	$2.50	23	6	6	23
San Jose	2.00	$2.00	29	18	5	14
Seattle	4.00	$2.00	27	20	5	8
Washington, DC	2.00	$1.25	36	26	3	6
Average	2.38	$1.93	18	9	7	18

Sources: Parking and transit data gathered by author; earnings and poverty data from American Community Survey (2009–2011).

to low-income residents to help them pay. Better still, governments could provide low-income people with a more general transportation allowance that could be used for parking, gas, transit, bicycles or even walking shoes. A cash allowance would give the poor more choices and treat all modes equally. Such an allowance would not punish low-income people who drive, but would reward those who chose other modes, since they would have more cash remaining at the end of each month.

CONCLUSION

Local governments around the world commit what Shoup (2005) calls a "sin of omission": they fail to accurately price street spaces. The consequences that flow from this decision – and it is a decision – are negative and substantial. I have sought, in this chapter, to highlight not only the extent of underpricing and the severity of its consequences, but also its logical incoherence. It is neither uncommon nor unjust for cities to charge accurate prices for their resources. Pricing parking at its market value does not require cities to become private sector mercenaries, nor ignore the needs of their most vulnerable residents, nor become "anti-car." Cities that charge the right price for parking are no more anti-car than Starbucks is anti-coffee. To the contrary, cities that price street parking accurately can deliver a high-quality service to drivers, finance other services for residents, and offer protection from the market for low-income residents who need it. There are legitimate debates to be had about the extent of markets in public life. But those difficult and necessary discussions do not include parking spaces. Parking spaces are valuable land, and cities should not give their valuable land away.

NOTES

1. New York City does not meter its residential streets. Bozeman does not meter any streets.
2. For instance, a perfunctory online search can yield newspaper articles about curb parking shortages in New York City (population 8 million), Amherst, NY (population 122,000) and Ithaca, NY (population 30,000) (see Santora, 2012; Tan, 2013; Lechtenberg, 2000).
3. Water companies often use two-part pricing to simultaneously cover fixed costs and allocate use. I don't mean to imply in this discussion that water companies and other utilities are models of efficiency; only that compared to street parking, these utilities are much more comprehensively priced.
4. Hardin (1968) first noted the counterproductive nature of meter holidays. Fischel (2005) argues that such holidays are actually efficient, although he bases that conclusion on rather strong assumptions.
5. Some cities have neighborhoods where only residents with permits can park on the street. While these spaces are not metered, they are not always free. However, the price is often negligible. An overnight parking permit in Beverly Hills, California costs $111 a year, or 30 cents a day. Resident permits in Boston are free.
6. The return is approximate because cruising is not costless; it consumes time and fuel. Thus, drivers with lower values of time are more likely to cruise longer.

7. See Pierce and Shoup (2013) for estimates of the incidence of cruising.

8. Commuting data are not synonymous with travel data, that is, some people with vehicles may take transit to work. Commute data are, however, the most readily available travel data at the city level.

REFERENCES

Arnott, R. (1995). Time for revisionism on rent control? *Journal of Economic Perspectives*, 9(1), 99–120.

Cook, J., & Simonson, J. (2012). Parking rate survey. *Collier's International*. Available at http://www.colliers.com/~/media/files/marketresearch/unitedstates/colliers_2012_na_parking_survey.pdf

Epstein, R. (2002). The allocation of the commons: Parking on public roads. *Journal of Legal Studies*, 31, S515.

Fischel, W. (2002). *The homevoter hypothesis*. Cambridge, MA: Harvard University Press.

Fischel, W. (2005). *Free parking at Christmas is not a tragedy of the commons*. Working Paper. Dartmouth Economics, Hanover, NH. Available at http://www.dartmouth.edu/~wfischel/Papers/Fischel_Parking_apr05.pdf

Guo, Z. (2012). Home parking convenience, household car storage, and implications to residential parking policies. *Transport Policy*, 29, 97–106.

Guo, Z. (2013). Does residential parking supply affect household car ownership? *Transport Geography*, 26, 18–28.

Guo, Z., & Xu, P. (2012). The duet of the commons. *Journal of Planning Education and Research*, 33(1), 34–48.

Hardin, G. (1968). The tragedy of the commons. *Science*, 62, 1243–1248.

Harsmann, B., & Quigley, J. (2010). Political and public acceptability of congestion pricing: Ideology and self interest. *Journal of Policy Analysis and Management*, 29(4), 854–874.

Lechtenberg, D. (2000, September 4). City tries to improve collegetown parking. *Cornell Daily Sun*. Retrieved from http://cornellsun.com/blog/2000/09/04/city-tries-to-improve-college town-parking/

Manville, M. (2013). Parking requirements and housing development. *Journal of the American Planning Association*, 79(1), 49–66.

Manville, M., Beata, A., & Shoup, D. (2013). Turning housing into driving: Parking requirements and density in Los Angeles and New York. *Housing Policy Debate*, 23(2), 350–375.

Pierce, G., & Shoup, D. (2013). Getting the prices right: An evaluation of pricing parking by demand in San Francisco. *Journal of the American Planning Association*, 79(1), 67–81.

Santora, M. (2012, February 3). Can't park? Blame a Condo. *New York Times*, RE1.

Santos, G. (2008). London congestion charging. *Brookings-Wharton Papers on Urban Affairs*, 177–233.

Shoup, D. (2005). *The high cost of free parking*. Chicago, IL: Planner's Press.

Shoup, D. (2006). Cruising for parking. *Transport Policy*, 13, 479–486.

Tan, S. (2013, March 5). Amherst aims to block Daemen-area street parking by students. *Buffalo News*. Available at http://www.buffalonews.com/20130305/amherst_aims_to_block_daemen_area_street_parking_by_students.html

Weinberger, R. (2012). Death by a thousand curb cuts. *Transport Policy*, 20, 93–102.

CHAPTER 8

PARKING MANAGEMENT

Tom Rye and Till Koglin

ABSTRACT

Purpose — *This chapter explains how and why local parking policies are developed, the sometimes conflicting relationship between parking, revenue raising and economic development and the circumstances in which it may be appropriate to use parking policy as a demand management tool.*

Methodology/approach — *This chapter offers a review of prior research and literature on the topic parking management and further explores the impacts and difficulties of parking management. Moreover, empirical data in this chapter comes from the authors' own survey study of southern, eastern and southeastern European cities about their parking problems and policies.*

Findings — *The findings of this chapter show that there is a need to consider what parking solutions cities may choose and what solutions might work for them. It is difficult to say that very different solutions will suit cities of different sizes, but rather that the level of implementation of the solutions must be related to the scale of the problem in each city, and its citizens' demands. In addition, each city must work within its particular legislative context, which is why certain solutions might not work in some cities.*

Parking: Issues and Policies

Transport and Sustainability, Volume 5, 157–184

Copyright © 2014 by Emerald Group Publishing Limited

All rights of reproduction in any form reserved

ISSN: 2044-9941/doi:10.1108/S2044-994120140000005027

Practical implications — *Parking policy and parking management are key to urban mobility and to managing its negative effects. It is possible to develop a car parking policy that will manage the negative impacts of urban car use whilst also supporting business and the economy; but this is a balancing act, which is why it is important to learn from the experience of other places, as we have shown in this chapter. Parking demand and the response of different cities to it are very important when considering the rise of car use in Europe and other parts of the world. Future solutions for parking problems are detailed at the end of this chapter.*

Originality/value of the chapter — *This chapter offers a comprehensive overview of prior research in parking management and connects this overview to findings of the authors own survey in south, eastern and southeastern European cities. Very few studies have made similar connections and provided in-depth insights into parking management in European cities. Moreover, the research provides useful information for planners and professionals dealing with parking issues and what solutions might work in their city.*

Keywords: Parking demand; parking policy; parking management; land-use planning

INTRODUCTION

The availability and cost of a parking space is an important determinant of whether or not people choose to drive to a particular destination, and also whether they choose to own a car at all — it is likely that the relatively lower levels of car ownership in many inner cities (in spite of their greater wealth relative to other areas) are partly a result of the lack of on-street parking (so nowhere to put a car), as well as the above average levels of public transport accessibility.

Local authorities have direct control over the use of kerb space (other than on national roads) in their areas, and therefore of the supply and price of on-street parking. Many authorities own public off-street car parks, over whose use and price they also have control (although the extent to which they are the provider of public off-street parking varies from locality to locality). Through the development control process, they also have some control over the level of parking that is provided in new developments.

Whilst parking controls and prices are rarely popular with the public, they are a policy option that is relatively well-known and, certainly in larger towns and cities, accepted – if there is an obvious shortage of parking spaces then many people may accept that there is a need for parking controls. Parking controls and pricing are the transport demand management measure that is most frequently implemented by local authorities, yet little of the academic literature deals with experience of this policy, preferring instead to concentrate on the 'sexier' topic of congestion charging. This chapter attempts to redress that balance a little. By the time you have finished reading it, you should (better) understand:

- how and why local parking policies are developed, and be able to critically apply your understanding to a case study
- the sometimes conflicting relationship between parking, revenue raising and economic development
- the circumstances in which it may be appropriate to use parking policy as a demand management tool.

Car parking is an issue of significance both at the local and at the strategic level of planning. Parking policy and supply play a major role in the management of transportation systems in dense urban areas. In order for parking policy decisions to be well founded, the analysis of parking behaviour and the effect of parking policies should be fully integrated with the other elements of the transport planning process (Coombe, Guest, Bates, & Le Masurier, 1997).

PARKING: SOME BASIC CONCEPTS

Parking Demand

Users of parking facilities constitute more than half the population and this proportion is growing: the EUROSTAT online transport statistics database shows that the number of cars per 1,000 population in the EEA30 countries rose from 321 in 1995 to 411 in 2009 (a rise of 30%). The car is the dominant mode of transport accounting for 84% of all surface passenger kilometres in the EEA30. However, these figures mask considerable variations: whilst growth rates in car ownership per 1,000 people were around 20% in most northern and western European countries during this period, in southern and eastern European countries they were closer to and in some cases (e.g. Lithuania) well over 100%. This means that, for example, Slovenia and Cyprus now have more cars per 1,000 people than the United Kingdom or Sweden. These huge growth rates have put enormous pressure on existing formal and informal parking stock in these countries. They also may make parking management less acceptable than in countries and cities with lower rates of car ownership. For example, car ownership in the City of Copenhagen in 2010 was 236 cars per 1,000 people (Koglin, 2013) – with car owners clearly in the minority, this may make it politically easier to manage parking.

In 2009 there were more than 242 million cars in the EEA30, up from over 177 million in 1995 (European Environment Agency, 2010). There are only two places where these vehicles can be found: they are either on-street or off-street. If they are on-street, they can be considered to be parked, searching for parking or in transit. Almost all cars that are off-street will be parked. Estimates show that cars spend more than 95% of their lives parked (RAC, 2005).

In transport terms, demand is usually measured by observing activity: for example, traffic flows along a route, or parking acts at a site. In 'uncontested' conditions, where the space available equals or exceeds the demand, then demand is equal to the observed consumption. In 'contested' conditions, where there is competition for space, the observed activity or consumption is constrained; it does not measure the potential demand because some drivers have either been priced out of the market or physically excluded by a shortage of space. It is in this second contested context that controls must most often be introduced.

Types of Parking

There are four main types of parking – places that you can park a car (TRL, 2010). These are:

- On-street. As its name suggests, a parking space on the public road.
- Public off-street. A car park not on the public road, in which any member of the public can park their car, subject to complying with any regulations (e.g. maximum stay (in hours), or paying a fee). This kind of car park may be owned and/or operated by the public and/or private sector.
- Private non-residential off-street. This is car parking that is associated with a particular building or land use – parking for a shopping centre, or an office-building. Only people who are connected with that building or land use should, in theory, be able to use the parking, and the land-

owner has control over this use (within legal constraints in the member-state concerned).

- Private residential parking – off-street parking associated with houses or flats. In theory, only the residents of these houses or flats should be able to use the parking.

The pattern of parking supply in our towns and cities in recent years has been in a state of continuous evolution as parking demand has increased. From the outset, this has been influenced by the public and private organisations involved in providing parking infrastructure. It is worth remembering the basic types of parking and the degree to which local authorities have control over them. The major distinction when considering parking supply is that between parking provided on-street and that provided off-street as shown in Table 1.

Table 1. Parking Type and the Sector Controlling and/or Supplying it.

Location	On-Street				Off-Street				
Use	Public				Private	Public			
Owned	Public				Private	Private	Public		
Operated	Public or private				Private	Private	Private	Public	
Type	Free	Priced	Permit	Duration Control	Free	Priced	Priced	Free	Priced

On-Street Parking

On-street parking is all publicly owned and is provided by local authorities in Europe, often under the general guidance and legal framework set by central government. Local authorities determine which restrictions should apply in specified streets, within central government guidelines, taking into account the national and local pressures for road safety, traffic flow, public transport provision and movement, the functioning of the local economy, the needs of residents and access for emergency services. In many countries, they must involve the local community in the process of introducing parking restrictions, and communicate the changes effectively to local road users; we return to this topic later in the chapter when we consider how to build acceptance for parking policy changes.

Off-Street Parking

Off-street parking will, in the average European medium to large-sized city, provide the majority of the parking space available in and around the city centre. Most local authorities will require a certain amount of off-street parking to be built for the users of all new developments in their area – this topic is discussed further later in the chapter. In addition, all are likely to try to provide some public off-street parking, open to all users, sometimes at a charge. However, the construction of new off-street parking can be extremely expensive. Excluding land costs, the following figures are typical:

- Surface space, asphalted, with drainage and lighting – €3,000.
- Space in a parking structure (multi-storey car park) – €15,000–€20,000.
- Underground space – €40,000.

In addition, there is a maintenance and security charge for each space, which can easily be €150–€450 per year (Mingardo, 2008a).

The degree of public sector control over public off-street parking depends very much on how much of it they own. In the United Kingdom, this varies considerably: in one city (e.g. Edinburgh) the local authority may own virtually none of this kind of parking; in another (e.g. Nottingham) it may own the majority of spaces. Where local authority transport spending is limited, they may be unable to afford to build new car parks. In southern Europe, it is understood that municipalities play a much bigger role in the provision of public off-street parking, and so are better able to influence how it is priced, and thus how it is used, and by whom (Ferilli, 2009).

PARKING MANAGEMENT PROBLEMS AND OBJECTIVES FOR PARKING POLICY

Parking management should be implemented to address parking problems. The authors have worked with parking professionals in 10 different EU countries and it is remarkable that, regardless of different national contexts, similar categories of problem are cited:

Operational problems – The financing of controlled parking zones in primarily residential areas may be problematic because there is insufficient parking turnover and demand for paid parking to generate the income to pay for enforcement. Other problems related to existing parking controls may include poor enforcement, difficulty of payment, poor image of the operation, and collection of fees and fines; and specific problems in parking large vehicles. There is a need for innovative approaches to parking management operations in order to resolve these issues.

Externalities of parking — congestion and pollution caused by circulating traffic searching for a parking space in popular areas; conflicts between different parking users (residents and commuters competing for parking, for example); or safety and pedestrian accessibility problems caused by poorly parked vehicles; similar problems for buses on narrow streets.

Spatially concentrated demand — leading to perceptions of insufficient parking in some areas (and calls for more parking to support economic activity), yet under-used parking in other nearby areas.

Insufficient kerb space — insufficient kerb space to park the vehicles of all the car-owning residents in some residential areas, such as older high density suburbs and some peripheral high rise housing areas, both built with little off-street parking. This problem is particularly acute in southern and eastern European cities built at very high densities and now in some cases with higher car ownership levels than in northern and Western Europe.

The problems mentioned above are frequently experienced in cities and are of similar importance for city officials to deal with. Their relative importance varies from city to city, but as one descends the list above, longer term approaches are required to resolve them.

It is clear from the literature that parking can have a significant impact on people's choice of travel mode (see, e.g. Feeney, 1989; NEDO, 1991; Shoup & Willson, 1992; DfT, 1996; Kelly & Clinch, 2009; Litman, 2008). This, and the problems above, suggest that parking policy should best be situated in the context of a more integrated urban mobility plan (such as a Local Transport Plan in England, or PDU in France), which can help to situate parking management in relation to the strategic objectives that it can help to achieve. For example, the mobility plan may include objectives on reducing congestion, and enhancing economic development, and parking management should proceed from the point of how it can support such objectives.

In practice, objectives for parking policy tend to be rather reactive and operational (Mingardo, Van Wee and Rye, forthcoming), driven primarily by the need to 'keep people happy' — especially residents living in areas where other parkers compete with them for parking space, and especially local retailers who almost always perceive parking on-street outside their shop to be far more crucial to their economic wellbeing than it in fact is (for more data on this see Sustrans, 2003). Parking is also often seen as, and often is in fact, an important source of local authority revenue.

There are also many conflicts within parking policy. For example, policy objectives may include reducing congestion caused by private cars and reducing CO_2 emissions, but also improving the local economy. This latter may mean favouring short stay shoppers in place of longer stay commuters. However, this may generate more vehicle miles as one space will be used by a greater number of cars per day for shopping than for commuting. A main concern of a private operator of an off-street car park will be to maximise profits, but a local authority may have a range of other objectives. They may wish to provide public off-street parking, simply to make sure that visitors to their town or city have somewhere to park. They may also wish to control the price of such parking – perhaps to make it relatively more expensive for long-stay commuters (to reduce peak hour traffic) but cheaper for shoppers, who tend to travel in the off-peak. The revenue-raising objective may also conflict with policies to reduce car traffic to city centres when on-street parking, controlled by the local authority, is considered. Parking policy objectives at the level of the individual street ('maximise supply') may conflict with those at the city level ('preferential parking for certain user groups') and at the regional level ('parking policy should support sustainable land use planning'). Parking policy cannot fully resolve these conflicts but it should at least set out a rationale for choosing one policy option over another.

APPROACHES TO PARKING MANAGEMENT

Regulating On-Street Parking

In almost all Western European countries, the local authority decides on the parking regulations on-street. There is a general tendency for on-street parking regulations to become more stringent (restrictive), the closer that one goes to the centre of towns and cities – because these are the areas of greatest demand. The vast majority of on-street spaces in a given member-state remain unregulated in any way, because there is little or no demand for them. But, as demand increases, then typical restrictions that might be found include the following (with the first group tending to be introduced prior to the second):

Traffic flow and safety related

- No parking at any time around the mouths of junctions in order to ensure sightlines for vehicles, and safety and access for pedestrians crossing.
- Parking restrictions on main roads at peak hours to facilitate traffic flow.
- Parking restrictions on one side of a narrow road to permit two-way traffic flow.

Restrictions to target space at particular categories of user

- Time limited on-street parking in order to facilitate the turnover of parking spaces — usually to ensure that short-term parkers (e.g. shoppers) can get a space.
- Parking restrictions in certain areas to provide kerb space so that commercial vehicles can load and unload to service shops and offices alongside the road.
- Time limits around stations (e.g. no parking 13.00−14.00 weekdays) to stop informal park and ride.

The extent to which unregulated kerb space is used for parking is determined by the demand of the area and the availability of off-street alternatives. Local authority restrictions will generally only apply when supply is exceeded by demand in a particular area (Balcombe & York, 1993), or where safety problems are caused by parking (e.g. sightlines at junctions are restricted). Those restrictions are not always appreciated by car drivers. However, in order to make road space safer, to increase the accessibility both for shoppers and goods transported to the shops, cafés etc. and to prevent chaotic situations on the urban road space, these regulations are very important.

Pricing On-Street Parking

The introduction of area wide controls — a controlled parking zone (CPZ), also called a blue zone in continental Europe — usually involves some non-essential users such as commuters being given lower priority in preference to users such as residents, shoppers and short-term business parkers. Short-term parkers must pay a charge per hour whilst residents must buy a permit. A CPZ or blue zone will normally include:

- Parking spaces for residents only (or sometimes shared with visitors, in the next category).
- Paid public parking — Whilst in the last century parkers were forced to estimate the length of time that they would stay in the space, and buy a ticket from a machine by the use of cash for that length of time, as soon as they parked, and display it in their car, this model is being superseded by mobile phone payment and use of number plates rather than tickets to show that a driver has paid their fee.
- Space for loading people and goods to/from vehicles, but not parking.
- Space where no parking or loading is allowed (e.g. around junctions, at bus stops).

On-street parking charges should if possible be higher than off-street charges as this will act as an incentive to people to park off-street, rather than drive round and round looking for a cheaper (as well as a more convenient) on-street space — although in practice the opposite is usually the case, due to the low infrastructure costs for on-street parking and because prices are set politically rather than economically (Shoup, 2006; authors' own survey of southern, eastern and southeastern European cities, 2013). Problems from these controlled areas may arise if the displaced users continue to park, but just outside the controlled area; this may result in parking pressure near the boundary of the zone.

Central governments set the legal framework in terms of the traffic code (signs and lines) and the legal process required for CPZs to be set up and operated. However, central government may also set operational restrictions that can constrain the local authority's flexibility and the effectiveness of the CPZ: for example, maximum fines (as in France), or maximum daily charges for on-street parking (as in Poland).

How Much Does it Cost to Park on-street in Different Countries in the EU?
First of all, it is worth noting that residents who live in CPZs are usually provided with a permit at a preferential (cheap) rate. For example, in the centre of the City of Edinburgh in the United Kingdom, for someone to park all day for the whole year in a public parking bay on-street would cost around about €6,000 (if there were no time limit), and a similar price for parking in a public off-street car-park. A resident living in that area obtains a permit providing the same service but for €280 per year and in many EU cities, permits for residents to park on-street are much cheaper still. In those countries where municipalities have been active in building and operating off-street car parks, they may also offer their residents preferential rates in these — €120 per month for a space in central Lyon, for example.

With regard to public on-street parking rates, which are normally set by local authorities, some examples are shown in Fig. 1.

Experiences of Parking Price Changes and Zoning in Town Centres
Still and Simmonds (2000) confirm that there is an increasing trend amongst local authorities that have control of a reasonable proportion of the off-street public parking in their areas to change the pricing structure to deter all-day parkers in order to free up parking spaces for shorter stay shopping and business parkers. Such policies have been adopted by many cities, such as Munich, Vienna, Freiburg and Lyon, amongst many others. In the United Kingdom, Healey and Baker (1998) surveyed 123 local

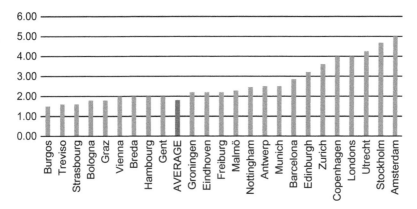

Fig. 1. On-Street Parking Tariffs per Hour, Various Central Cities (2011–2013).
Sources: City of Gent (2013); ITDP (2011).

authorities and found that, at that time, 25% were planning to cut the number of parking spaces in their urban centres, with more than 50% increasing parking charges in real terms.

However, there has been little evaluation of the effects of such policies, with the exception of Canterbury's (United Kingdom) policy of reducing city centre parking and replacing it with park and ride. This has been successful in reducing city centre traffic levels without negatively impacting on city centre trade (Valleley, 1997). Kelly and Clinch (2009) found an elasticity of −0.29 in response to a 50% price rise in on-street parking charges in Dublin; whilst COST 342 (2006) cites the implementation of parking pricing on-street in districts 5–9 of Vienna leading to a 30% reduction in trips by car to the areas affected.

Enforcement
If parking regulations are to be effective, they must be enforced − otherwise, they will fall into disrepute. The fine must also be in proportion to the cost of hourly parking − if it is not, parkers will risk the very low fine rather than paying proportionately higher hourly parking charges (this is a significant problem in France, where the fine is set by the national government.) In some cases, as noted in COST 342 (2006, p. 30), and by the LEDA project, local authorities are, at least partially, dependent on the police for enforcing parking regulations. Increasingly, though, countries have changed their legal framework such that the role of the police and judiciary is partly or wholly removed from parking enforcement (including setting fines). In all

cases, this has significantly enhanced the quality of enforcement, and in the United Kingdom it has also generated considerable income for some local authorities – leading to some public resentment (RAC, 2005; University of Birmingham, 2005).

The quality of enforcement of decriminalised (or, as it is now known in the United Kingdom, civil) parking arrangements in comparison to police enforcement, is illustrated by the example of the City of Newcastle in the United Kingdom, which in 2008 applied to national government for permission to take over the enforcement of waiting restrictions on its main roads from the police. At that time, the municipality enforced residents' parking bays and off-street car parks only. The police selected the level of enforcement for other locations, and issued around 10,000 fines per year on main roads, compared to 60,000 issued by the municipality's 60 parking attendants in residents' parking areas. The addition of 10 further enforcement staff to work on main road enforcement was anticipated to increase fines issued on main roads from 10,000 to 30,000 per year. (Newcastle City Council, 2008)

The UK example is an interesting one to consider. Under the 1991 Road Traffic Act, local authorities became able to take over responsibility for on-street parking enforcement in their areas from the police, but such Special Parking Areas (SPAs) must be self-funding, with operating costs paid for from fines. If a parker contravenes any of the regulations, the local authority (or its contracting company) can levy a fine. This varies greatly from place to place – in Edinburgh, United Kingdom, it is currently €90, dropping to €45 if the fine is paid within two weeks. The fine is the same, whatever the contravention (e.g. staying 35 minutes when you have paid for 30 minutes gets the same fine as parking your car illegally in a bus lane and blocking all the buses). In contrast, in many English cities, where legislation from 2004 applies, there is a higher penalty for more obstructive parking, and a lower penalty charge for, for example, overstaying on a metered bay. The purpose of this difference is to improve the acceptability of parking enforcement, which is a problematic (political) issue for many cities.

Park and Ride

Towns and cities often adopt park and ride as part of their strategy to tackle traffic congestion, in the main on routes into town and city centres (although there are examples of park and ride sites that serve major workplaces outside city centres). COST342 estimates that, between 1970 and 1990, the number of cities in Europe with park and ride sites increased by a factor of three, to around 76, and the number of parking spaces available by 337%.

Park and Ride works by diverting city centre-bound trips into a car park *en route* and taking the drivers onwards from there by public transport. For park and ride to be successful, it is vital that:

- The public transport route is fast, frequent and reliable. If it is faster, including interchange and wait time, than the corresponding car journey, its market will not be limited only to those who have no (free) parking available in the city centre.
- The frequency of an urban park and ride service should be every 10 minutes or, if possible, less, with real time information at stops.
- The (perceived) cost of using the site should be lower than the fuel and parking cost of driving into the city centre. Depending on the target market for the park and ride, it may be desirable to price the park and ride ticket for a car full of people (i.e. one person pays the same as a family travelling together).
- Over time, the amount of parking – both PNR and public parking – in the town centre should be reduced, and it should be more expensive than the park and ride.
- There should be easy access from the main road network to the park and ride and, preferably, segregated exits from the park and ride for public transport vehicles (if they run on the road).
- Capacity should be great enough to cater for demand; but not so great that walking distances from the furthest parts of the car park are excessive. This may entail a parking structure (multi-storey) if demand increases beyond a certain point.
- Security for passengers and their cars at the site should be very high – CCTV and, preferably, a staff presence, will increase users' confidence in the service.

COST342 cites Madrid, Spain; Bern, Switzerland and Oxford, United Kingdom, as places with highly effective park and ride services. Madrid's services are based primarily on suburban rail and metro. Bern has a combination of rail and tram to serve its park and ride. Oxford's five sites are all served by bus only (24 hours per day). The effects of such park and ride can be significant, but this depends on the factors listed above being in place. A few examples of the effects of park and ride on traffic are listed below (from COST 342, 2006)

- In Vienna – park and ride captures 12% of city centre-bound car traffic.
- In Chester, United Kingdom the corresponding figure is 20%.

- Madrid's park and ride sites have 20,000 users per day, while there are 12,000 in Barcelona and 10,000 in Hanover.
- In Strasbourg park and ride has been a key element in the success of its two tram lines. Some 43% of motorised trips now made by public transport.
- In Oxford, United Kingdom, park and ride sites are estimated to have led to a 3—9% reduction in city centre-bound car traffic.

It should be noted, however, that there are some park and ride sites whose costs far outweigh their benefits (including even environmental factors), and that even the best planned park and ride is likely — where new public transport services are implemented to serve it — to attract users who previously made their entire trip by public transport, but who switch to park and ride because it is quicker and/or cheaper (Parkhurst, 2000). COST342 estimates that these can account for up to one-third of users of a new park and ride. Another perverse effect can occur where a park and ride site is built in one location but users drive to another (and make use of informal parking opportunities, for example, on-street around a station) because the public transport service level at the second location is much better. See chapter 9 by Parkhurst and Meek for more detail on Park and Ride.

Company Parking Space Management
Large employers with an accessibility, congestion or staff mobility-related problem will sometimes choose to implement mobility management at their site(s). Sometimes, this will include management of the employer's parking spaces — especially where these are limited in relation to the number of staff and/or visitors. The rationing, of or charging for, parking spaces at work is not an enormously popular policy with staff — especially in the planning stages. To make it more acceptable, the following steps and conditions should be satisfied (based on Rye & Ison, 2005):

- A problem is identified and parking management is a solution to that problem. For example, some hospitals in the United Kingdom have suffered from parked cars blocking routes for ambulances. Clearly, here, parking management is required.
- There are alternatives available to driving to work for those staff who do not qualify for a permit and/or do not wish to pay a charge.
- Widespread consultation is carried out with staff. This should cover a number of important issues, including:
- How should permits and (if appropriate) actual parking spaces be allocated — what criteria should be used, and how many different types of parking space should be defined?

- What should the charge be (if a charge is planned), and should it be income-related?
- How should a charge be paid? Daily, monthly, annually – and via a ticket machine, or through salary, for example?
- How senior staff should be treated – acceptance increases if these staff are perceived to be treated as fairly as everyone else.
- Legal requirements, with regard to employment contracts, are properly dealt with. These vary from country to country.
- It is clear how the money raised will be used. Acceptance is likely to be increased if at least some of the income is used to fund improvements in car parking and car park security; and some used to improve or reduce the price of alternatives to driving.

For examples of companies that have implemented parking management, how they dealt with the points above, and the effects of this, see Rye and Ison (2005). The Department for Transport (DfT) published a series of case studies of employers with travel plans (site mobility management plans) in place in 2002. This showed clearly that the most effective travel plans are those that include some form of effective parking management – either rationing or pricing of spaces (DfT, 2002). Experience from the United States, cited in Pratt (2003) supports this conclusion.

Parking and Land-Use Planning – Parking in New Developments
One area in which it might be imagined that these links might be made more explicit is land use, and in particular, the amount of parking that is permitted in new developments. However, and once again according to COST 342 (2006), although there is guidance in most countries on this issue, its strength/force varies from country to country. In addition, and importantly, such guidance will only act to restrain car use where it stipulates a *maximum* number of parking spaces that should be permitted in different types of development. There is some move away from minimum standards, towards maxima, but the degree to which this has occurred in different countries is by no means clear – the LEDA project implies that in most EU countries, there is still considerable emphasis on providing a *minimum* number of parking spaces with new development, or not regulating this issue at all. But, as COST 342 (2006) says (p. 52):

- Parking standards should be set as maximums.
- In more attractive, densely developed areas, parking standards should be lower, in combination with park and ride.

- It is important to allow the combined use of parking spaces, to avoid too much parking being provided.

In general, it would appear that those areas that have had most success in linking parking controls and standards with their planning objectives are historic (university) cities such as York, Chester, Oxford and Cambridge. Oxford's 'Balanced Transport Policy' has been in place since 1973 and has combined a reduction in city centre on- and off-street parking (both public and privately controlled) with the provision of improved cycle and pedestrian facilities, bus priority and the United Kingdom's most successful park and ride system. This policy can be seen to have achieved its objectives in that the number of vehicles entering the city centre every year over the past 40 years has been kept constant, it is crucial to note that this success has been achieved by the consistent application of a policy over a long period of time. Some evaluation of the impacts of Oxford's policy is available in the Oxfordshire Local Transport Plan's annual progress report (Oxfordshire County Council, 2005).

Maximum parking standards − as opposed to minima, over and above which developers are free to build as much as they think is required for their development − were first advocated in UK central government guidance in the 1994 version of PPG13. There is a sound theoretical basis for applying maximum standards, as it should, in the long term, limit parking supply and therefore influence travel demand. It will also lead to higher density development that is conducive to walking and cycling. Further, it reduces the opportunity cost of the land that is used for parking. And, finally, there is considerable evidence from the United States − where parking minima are very much the norm − that an excess of parking will be provided, over and above actual demand (Pratt, 2003). It is still the case that most European cities use minimum standards also, at least outside their city centres (ITDP, 2011). Also see chapter 7 by Manville in relation to minimum parking requirements.

However, local authorities in the United Kingdom had been relatively slow to adopt maximum standards, perhaps because central government took its time to set recommended national maxima, finally providing for local authorities a national benchmark beyond which other authorities could find it difficult to go. The former English national maximum standards are shown in summary below:

- Food retail 1 space per 14 m^2
- Non-food retail 1 space per 20 m^2
- Cinemas and conference facilities 1 space per 5 seats
- B1 including offices 1 space per $30m^2$ = 1 space per 2−3 staff

- Higher and further education − 1 space per 2 staff + 1 space per 15 students
- Stadia 1 space per 15 seats
- Residential (PPG3) max (average) 1.5 spaces/house or flat

Until this national benchmark was set, authorities may have been fearful that, in setting their own maxima, they would simply encourage development to relocate to areas with less stringent standards − a constantly recurring theme in parking policy. (Although evidence that this competition actually occurs in practice is, however, weak or contradictory (Marsden & Mullen, 2012).) However, after a short period in Great Britain with national maximum parking standards for larger developments and for residential development, new national planning guidance (PPS4 in England; SPP in Scotland) in 2010 abandoned them (England), or made them only advisory (Scotland). This is related to the belief that a less prescriptive planning system is associated with greater economic success.

Emerging Problems in Parking Management
'Typical' parking policies have tended to see a gradual increase in controls on on-street parking, starting in the city centre and spreading out from there, in order to deal with competition between commuters and residents for on-street parking, and to prioritise certain types of parkers whilst encouraging others to change mode. In southern European cities this has been accompanied by the construction of underground car parks in central areas and inner suburbs (Ferilli, 2009), whilst in northern Europe the trend has been more towards the construction of park and ride, and the pricing of existing inner city car parks to discourage long-stay parkers. However, with growing car ownership in most EU member states, particular problems have begun to emerge in recent years that the conventional parking policy responses have difficulty dealing with. These include the following.

Firstly, on-street parking demand from residents is outstripping available parking supply in areas where off-street parking supply is lower than car ownership, unavailable or not used. Many older medium and high density inner suburbs were constructed before mass car ownership and therefore before off-street parking was required to be provided in new buildings. With perhaps 4−6 on-street parking spaces outside a building housing 10−20 households, kerbside parking is insufficient for unrestrained demand. Even more acute residential parking problems occur in more peripheral high rise developments in the outer suburbs of former socialist cities, where mass car ownership was never envisaged at the time the buildings were constructed. In other areas in southern and Eastern Europe off-street parking was constructed in newer residential buildings but is then either converted to further dwelling space or rented out for other activities, such as small businesses.

In such situations, new off-street parking may appear to be the solution, but the cost of construction and limits on public borrowing make it problematic for local authorities to finance such investments. If the investment is private, the parking charges required to provide a return on the investment are prohibitively high for long-term residential parkers, who will seek out a space on-street or on any spare open ground rather than pay commercial charges.

There is limited evidence that even in high density areas with high car ownership, introducing CPZs will lead to a significant reduction in parking demand. Table 2 shows data from the London Borough of Camden, in England (London Borough of Camden, 2007), and the percentage reductions in parked vehicles achieved after introducing CPZs. It is particularly

Table 2. Percentage Reduction in Parked Vehicles in Newly Introduced CPZs in Camden, London.

Zone		Reduction in Parked Vehicles (%)	
		Daytime	Evening
	CPZs with 'standard control hours'		
	8.30 am−6.00 pm or longer		
CA-J	Primrose Hill	45	33
CA-L	West Kentish Town (Outer)	60	43
CA-M	East Kentish Town	45	27
CA-N	Camden Square	57	29
CA-P (a)/(b)	Fortune Green	27	24
CA-Q	Kilburn	38	40
CA-R	Swiss Cottage	31	33
Average		43	33
	CPZs with 2-hour controls		
CA-P (c)	Fortune Green	40	28
CA-L	West Kentish Town (Inner)	47	41
CA-S	Redington/Frognal	58	34
CA-U	Highgate	32	18
Average		44	30

Source: LB Camden (2007, p. 36).

interesting to note that parking demand fell even outside the hours that parking controls are in operation.

However, there are public acceptability issues that make the introduction of further controls problematic, and the economics of a purely residential on-street parking operation are not particularly attractive if manual enforcement is to be used, since parking violations and ticket income are likely to be too low to finance the enforcement operation (City of Edinburgh, 2011). If this is the case, one alternative is to use automatic enforcement as implemented with success in Utrecht, Netherlands in the EU CIVITAS MIMOSA project (CIVITAS MIMOSA, 2012). This uses a 'scan car' equipped with cameras to check the registration numbers of parked cars. Since paid and residents' parking is based on registration numbers, the onboard computer in the car can quickly check whether a car is parked legally and, if not, enforcers can be dispatched. This reduces the number of enforcement staff required.

Alternatively, car clubs can be promoted as a substitute to conventional car ownership. One car club car is reported to replace up to 10 private cars, so the potential to reduce on-street parking problems is significant. The difficulty however is to increase membership to a level where it is sufficient to make a difference to on-street parking demand; in Great Britain, currently, for example, only around 0.25% of the adult population are in a car club (although this is the second highest level in Europe, MOMO EU Project, 2010).

RELATIONSHIP BETWEEN PARKING AND ECONOMIC DEVELOPMENT

There is an inherent tension in parking policy between three key objectives for local authorities: local economic development (preserving economic vitality); raising revenue from parking charges; and travel demand management. The latter two objectives imply a need to reduce the number of parking spaces and/or charge for their use; the former is often seen to imply that as much parking space as possible should be provided, in order to ensure that no car borne trade or inward investment is deterred from the area in question.

COST 342 (2006, pp. 47, 48) reports some interesting experiences about attempts to use parking policy to stimulate local economic development. Because of political pressures from retailers in particular, several cities have tried relaxing their parking restrictions in order to stimulate greater trade. These include:

In *Oslo*, weekend parking was made free. Instead of attracting lots of additional shoppers, fewer people parked for longer (and some of those were shopkeepers!). Occupancy rose to almost 100%, parking duration by 30% and so there was less turnover, and it became more difficult for people to park. Most retailers were negative about the experiment and it was abandoned in 2000.

In *Herford*, Germany, the first half hour of parking was made free. This increased occupancy, encouraged more short-term visitors into town, but also led to a deterioration in the traffic environment.

In *Appeldoorn*, Netherlands, parking fees were increased at the same time as a cheap public transport ticket was introduced. The latter brought an increase in people coming into town, whilst parking occupancy remained as it was before. However, the view of most retailers was that people were choosing where to shop mainly on grounds of the quality of the shops, not the parking opportunities.

On the other hand, a Dutch study, also cited by COST 342 (2006, p. 48), on regional parking policy, argued that:

• On the one hand, cities and towns with unique quality/features can implement restrictive parking policies with little effect on their retail sector.
• On the other, where there are a number of quite similar competing towns and cities, with little to choose between them, then parking policy can be a deciding factor for people in where to go and shop.
• Therefore, a regional parking policy can be helpful in that it can help to maintain the relative positions of existing centres within the region, and also (in theory) help to prevent the development of new, competing centres (but this depends on the planning system at a regional level).

In spite of the significance of the issue of parking and economic development, very few studies have in fact been carried out to better understand the links between parking availability, economic vitality and inward investment. Early work by Kamali and Potter (1997) concluded (p. 420) that there is 'no evidence that a relaxed attitude to parking improves economic performance'. Sanderson (1997, p. 56) comments that 'Other, much more important variables than parking provision are likely to be responsible for the differences in economic variability between London's centres'.

More recent work by Mingardo (2008a and b), analysing the performance of retail centres in the Netherlands in relation to their parking provision and pricing, was unable to find any strong relationship. A similar study by the author for 25 shopping centres in Britain and their off-street parking supply and price came to a similar conclusion (Rye for City of Edinburgh, 2006): public off-street parking spaces per 100 sq metres of retail floor area, and off-street parking price per hour, were plotted against the Experian retail ranking for the shopping centre in question (most large shopping centres in the ranking list are city centres as opposed to stand along malls). There was no relationship for parking availability, and a slightly negative relationship for price, suggesting that parking costs more in the more popular centres. A study on the wider parking policy (in particular, restraint based parking standards for new development) and economic performance of four larger European cities (Martens, 2005) was also unable to find a link between the level of parking restraint and the economy of the city – as he notes (p5):

'The cities and city centers show an ongoing economic vitality after the introduction of the restrictive parking norms' and

'The city centers remain the dominant office location in all case study cities'.

In terms of inward investment by employment uses, there is anecdotal evidence that parking availability has an impact on choice of location, but this has not been backed up by more rigorous empirical studies. Faber Maunsell (2002) note from interviews with the development sector that parking availability is unlikely to play a role in the inward investment process until the decision is at the level of choices between competing locations at the local level; thus, it could influence a firm's decision as to whether to locate in Vienna or in nearby Wiener Neustadt, for example. Work carried out for the UK Department for Transport during the consultation on abandoning national maximum parking standards in England drew similar conclusions (DfT, 2008).

The Politics of Introducing Parking Policies: Gaining Acceptance

Parking is always a controversial matter. Incremental (step by step) change is likely to be more accepted than a large sudden change. But the public must be 'carried along' with the changes, and whether they are or not will depend to a large degree on the *communication* that has been carried out. Effective communication involves broad participation of those with an interest in parking in the change process; a monitoring process, so that people know what the effects of parking changes are, as those changes are introduced; management of complaints, as part of communication; and the use of new forms of communication (e.g. special meetings between politicians and 'key stakeholders').

The public's acceptance of parking policy changes will also depend on whether a number of factors are in place, as follows (after COST 342, 2006, pp. 68–70) that:

- they know and understand the measures.
- they perceive that there will be a benefit, in terms of the solution of a problem – and that parking fees and other regulations are related to the scale of this problem.
- there are alternatives to parking (in the controlled area), such as park and ride, or better public transport services.
- the revenue will be allocated fairly and transparently (people know where it has gone).
- the parking regulations will be enforced consistently and fairly, and that fines will not be excessive (and, ideally, that the fines are related to the seriousness of the offence – for example, overstaying on a parking meter would be a lesser offence than parking illegally in a bus lane).

There are many things to take into account when changing parking policy. However, if they are not taken into account then the parking planner risks a situation where measures may have to be removed and regulations rescinded when a change is made, without sufficient communication, and therefore without user acceptance.

A CASE STUDY

In order to illustrate how the foregoing discussion is relevant to the reality of parking in an actual city, we briefly discuss here the case of Utrecht, Netherlands, a city at the forefront in Europe of the use of new technology to tackle problems that are still in many ways similar to those outlined earlier in this chapter. This helps to show how parking management may move forward in the next decade, in Europe at least. The source of the information on Utrecht is from CIVITAS (2012) and City of Gent (2013).

Utrecht is a city of 330,000 people in the densely populated Randstad region in the west of the Netherlands, with about 21,000 parking spaces controlled by the municipality, the majority of which are on-street. There are three official park and ride sites, covering all main approaches to the city, where a ticket combining parking and unlimited daily public transport travel for up to 5 people travelling together currently costs €4.50 per day. One site is connected to the city by bus, one by busway, and the third by rail. In comparison to on-street parking costs in town (over €4.00 per hour), the park and rides offer good value, but their use remains limited and so the city is trying to improve the quality of the park and ride offer further (City of Gent, 2013).

Residents qualify for one or two permits per household at a heavily discounted rate, whilst visitors must pay per hour for parking (residents' visitors pay less per hour). The number of residents' permits available in different areas of the city is capped, and in some areas there is a waiting list for people who have moved in and want a permit; the total number issued is just under 24,000. In terms of mobility patterns, about 50% of trips by residents are made by car and the rest by cycling or public transport, and car ownership lies at an average of 0.97 per household, with a third of households having no car. This places Utrecht at around 500 cars per 1,000 population, or towards the higher end of the EU average.

Car parking policy is seen by the municipality as a key element in improving the liveability and attractiveness of the city; there are also policy objectives to reduce local and global pollution from transport, but of course at the same time political pressure to ensure that the city (centre) remains perceived to be accessible. Operationally, there are pressures to reduce the unit costs of the parking operation (in part, so that it can be extended in scope, and in part because of general pressures on city budgets); and to make it more user-friendly. Thus, Utrecht's parking related problems and objectives are typical of many cities, but the way in which it is dealing with them gives some pointers as to future opportunities within the field.

The main change that the City of Utrecht has implemented within its parking operation in the recent past is the full digitalisation of on-street parking payment and enforcement, together with an increase in the controlled area. The digitalisation was carried out within the framework of the CIVITAS MIMOSA project 2008–2012 (CIVITAS MIMOSA, 2012). On 1 January 2008, shortly but not as part of CIVITAS, the city took over parking enforcement from the local police, and a year prior to that, significantly raised parking charges.

The installation of 530 digital parking machines during 2010 and 2011, together with digital enforcement, improved the efficiency of the operation. For political and legal reasons, visitors are not obliged to enter their licence plate number into the machine when parking, and all must still therefore display a paper ticket issued by the machine. Residents and their visitors must provide a licence plate number. Mobile phone parking was introduced at the same time (no ticket needs to be displayed, and billing is monthly in arrears) and around 20% of visitors now pay in this manner. A vehicle carrying number plate recognition cameras is able to alert enforcement staff to those parked cars not registered on the payment database, and appropriate enforcement action can then be taken. The introduction of digital parking was accompanied by a major publicity campaign and a re-vamp of the city's parking information website. Whilst the extent of the controlled area increased by around 14% during the project period, the number of enforcement officers fell from 63 to 45, but compliance with regulations (based on the number of tickets sold, and fines issued) improved. User satisfaction with parking in Utrecht was therefore also deemed to have improved.

Utrecht could of course go further in using new technology to address its parking problems and objectives. User-friendliness of the system could be improved by introducing real time monitoring of on-street parking occupancy and guidance via signage or GPS to less occupied areas of parking. This could be complemented by pay-per-minute parking and/or regular adjustments in parking pricing in different areas (there are currently only three zones of different parking prices) in order to 'fine-tune' occupancy in relation to demand. The challenge in so doing would in part be one of communication, since the system would become more complex and therefore potentially more difficult to understand. It is also not certain that the investment costs would be outweighed by measurable benefits; digital parking as it has been introduced so far offers, in contrast, some very clear benefits. Utrecht nonetheless remains an inspiring example as it has implemented innovative payment and in particular enforcement systems to improve its parking operation, and done so in a very short time period. For those cities that currently do not have any system of charging for parking, some of the technological solutions implemented by Utrecht offer the opportunity to avoid investment in 'old-tech' (e.g. ticket machines) and jump straight to a more advanced and user-friendly system.

CONCLUSIONS

In order to summarise the findings of this chapter it is helpful to refer back to the list of common problems that were identified at the start of the chapter and to consider what solutions cities may choose to deal with them. It is difficult to say that very different solutions will suit cities of different sizes, but rather that the level of implementation of the solutions must be related to the scale of the problem in each city, and its citizens' demands. In addition, each city must work within its particular legislative context (as the example of Utrecht shows, where paper tickets are still required because there is no obligation to provide registration plate information) (Table 3).

Table 3. Parking Problems and Some (Future) Solutions.

Problem	Possible Solutions
Operational problems	Decriminalisation of parking enforcement Creation of separate parking departments within city administrations Digital parking payment and enforcement
Externalities of parking	Self-enforcing measures (bollards, kerb build-outs) to deter obstructive parking Controlled parking zones and improved enforcement Parking guidance systems (static or real time; linked to occupancy) to reduce parking search Differential pricing to encourage use of off-street and under-used on-street parking Park and ride coupled with management and higher pricing of city centre parking Differential parking tariffs depending on environmental characteristics of vehicles
Spatially concentrated demand	Differential pricing to encourage use of off-street and under-used on-street parking Improved publicity of existing under-used parking Improve accessibility by other means of transport
Insufficient kerb space for residents' cars	Controlled parking zones and improved enforcement Car clubs Reduced parking standards for new non-residential developments Limited or no availability of on-street parking permits, particularly for new residential developments

This chapter has aimed to show that parking policy and parking management are key to urban mobility and to managing its negative effects. As car ownership grows, so demand for parking will grow, and most towns and cities will have to deal with many of the issues that have been outlined in this chapter. It is possible to develop a car parking policy that will manage the negative impacts of urban car use whilst also supporting business and the economy; but this is a careful balancing act, which is why it is important to learn from the experience of other places, as we have shown in this chapter. Parking demand and the response by the cities are very important, when considering the rise of car use in Europe and other parts of the world. If a sustainable transport system is the goal, balanced parking policies and the tackling of parking problems becomes even more important. This chapter has shown both problems and solutions for parking demand. It is vital that transport planners and city officials deal with parking properly in order to take a further step towards sustainable and attractive cities.

REFERENCES

Balcombe, R. J., & York, I. O. (1993). *The future of residential parking.* Project Report 22, Transport Research Laboratory, Crowthorne, Berkshire, UK.

Camden, L. B. (2007). *Annual parking and enforcement report.* London Borough of Camden, Euston, London.

City of Edinburgh. (2011, August 2). *Priority parking: Various areas, Edinburgh. Transport, infrastructure and environment committee.* Retrieved from www.edinburgh.gov.uk

City of Gent. (2013). *Parkeerplan Gent 2020.* Research Report: Part 2, Benchmarking. City of Gent, Belgium.

CIVITAS MIMOSA. (2012). *Measure evaluation results.* Report UTR3.1 Innovation of the system of parking permits and rates. European Commission, Utrecht.

Coombe, D., Guest, P., Bates, J., & Le Masurier, P. (1997). Study of parking and traffic demand. *Traffic Engineering & Control, 38*(2), 62–75.

COST 342. (2006). *Parking policy and the effects on economy and mobility.* REPORT on COST Action 342, August, 2005, Technical Committee on Transport, European Commission.

DfT. (1996). *Parking perspectives.* Report by MVA for DfT Department for Transport, London, UK.

DfT. (2002). *Making travel plans work.* London: UK DfT.

DfT. (2008). *Research into the use and effectiveness of maximum parking standards.* Report by Atkins to DfT, London.

European Environment Agency. (2010). Passenger car ownership in the EEA. Retrieved from http://www.eea.europa.eu/data-and-maps/figures/passenger-car-ownership-in-the-eea. Accessed on January 6, 2014.

Faber Maunsell. (2002). *The effect of maximum car parking standards including inward investment implications.* Report to Scottish Executive. Retrieved from http://www.scotland. gov.uk/Publications/2002/04/14550/3200

Feeney, B. P. (1989). A review of the impact of parking policy measures on travel demand. *Transportation Planning and Technology, 13*, 229–234.

Ferilli, G. (2009). *An analysis of the city centre car parking market: The supply side point of view.* PhD, Edinburgh Napier University, Edinburgh, UK.

Healey and Baker (Chartered Surveyors). (1998). *Town centre accessibility.* London: Healey and Baker.

ITDP. (2011). *Europe's parking U-Turn: from accommodation to regulation.* Retrieved from http://www.itdp.org/documents/European_Parking_U-Turn.pdf

Kamali, F., & Potter, H. (1997). *Do parking policies meet their objectives?* Paper presented at the European Transport Forum Annual Meeting, London.

Kelly, J. A., & Clinch, P. (2009). Temporal variance of revealed preference on-street parking price elasticity. *Transport Policy, 16*(4), 193–199.

Koglin, T. (2013). *Vélomobility: A critical analysis of planning and space.* Doctoral dissertation, Lund University, Department of Technology and society, Traffic and Roads, Bulletin, 284.

Litman, T. (2008). *Parking management: Strategies, evaluation and planning.* Victoria, Canada: Victoria Transport Policy Institute. Retrieved from www.vtpi.org

Marsden G., & Mullen C. (2012). *How does competition between cities influence demand management?* Paper to 44th Annual Universities Transport Study Group conference, Aberdeen, UK.

Martens, K. (2005). *The effects of restrictive parking policy on the development of city centers.* Report for the Israeli Ministry of Transport, Tel Aviv, Israel.

Mingardo, G. (2008a, March). Parkeren als schakel voor mobiliteit en leefbaarheid [Parking as the link between mobility and livability]. *Verkeer in Beeld, 2.*

Mingardo, G. (2008b, September). Parkeren heeft weinig invloed op winkelomzet [Parking has little influence on retail sales]. VExpansie 2, pp. 16–19.

Mingardo, G., Van Wee, B., & Rye, T. (forthcoming). *Urban parking policy: a conceptualization of past and possible future trends.* Paper submitted for publication.

MOMO EU. Project. (2010, June). *The state of European car-sharing.* Final Report D 2.4 Work Package 2. Bundesverband CarSharing e. V., Willi Loose.

National Economic Development Office. (1991). *Company car parking.* London: NEDO.

Newcastle City Council. (2008). Application for Decriminalised Parking Enforcement (DPE), Planning & Transportation Strategy Committee 27 July, City of Newcastle.

Oxfordshire County Council. (2005). *Local Transport Plan 2001–2006: Annual Progress Report.* Retrieved from http://portal.oxfordshire.gov.uk/content/publicnet/council_services/roads_transport/plans_policies/local_transport_plan/apr5.pdf, Accessed on March 12, 2013.

Parkhurst, G. (2000). Influence of bus-based park and ride facilities on users' car traffic. *Transport Policy, 7*(2), 159–172.

Pratt, R. (2003). *Parking management and supply: Traveler response to transportation system changes,* Transit Cooperative Research Program Report 95, Chapter 18, Transportation Research Board, Washington, DC.

RAC Foundation. (2005). *Motoring towards 2050: Parking in transport policy.* London: RAC Foundation.

Rye, T. (2006). Unpublished analysis of public off-street parking and retail performance in UK cities. Edinburgh, UK.

Rye, T., & Ison, S. (2005). Overcoming barriers to the implementation of car parking charges at UK workplaces. *Transport Policy, 12*(1), 57–64.

Sanderson, J. (1997). A response to SACTRA's consultation: Transport investment, transport intensity and economic growth. London Planning Advisory Committee, London, UK.

Shoup, D. (2006). Cruising for parking. *Transport Policy, 13*(6), 479–486.

Shoup, D., & Willson, R. (1992). Employer-paid parking: The problem and proposed solutions. Working Paper No. 119. *UC Transportation Research Centre, University of California, Berkeley, CA.*

Still, B., & Simmonds, D. (2000). Parking restraint policy and urban vitality. *Transport Reviews, 20*(3), 291–316.

Sustrans. (2003). *Traffic restraint and retail vitality.* Bristol, UK: Sustrans.

184   TOM RYE AND TILL KOGLIN

TRL (2010). *Parking measures and policies research review.* London UK: Prepared for DfT.
University of Birmingham Institute of Local Government Studies, School of Public Policy.
(2005). *Local authority parking enforcement defining quality-raising standards.* Report to
British Parking Association, Birmingham.
Valleley, M. (1997). *Parking perspectives.* London: Landor.

CHAPTER 9

THE EFFECTIVENESS OF PARK-AND-RIDE AS A POLICY MEASURE FOR MORE SUSTAINABLE MOBILITY

Graham Parkhurst and Stuart Meek

ABSTRACT

Purpose — *The chapter provides a* general review *of the policy debate around the provision of formal Park-and-Ride (P&R) facilities and the empirical research evidence about travellers' responses to the opportunities they present, drawing on evidence from the United Kingdom and the Netherlands. The effects of the schemes on road traffic and car dependence are considered.*

Design/methodology/approach — *The different ways in which private vehicles and public transport are combined during journeys are reviewed. The position of P&R is considered as a modal variant within a 'socio-technical system' competing with the more established journey options of fully private and fully public transport. Scenarios which can maximise the traffic reduction and sustainable development potential of P&R are examined.*

Parking: Issues and Policies
Transport and Sustainability, Volume 5, 185–211
ISSN: 2044-9941/doi:10.1108/S2044-994120140000005020

Findings — *The review of the policy context establishes that a range of policy objectives are conceived for P&R depending on different professional and citizen perspectives. There is partial understanding amongst local authorities about the effectiveness with which P&R addresses the range of objectives in practice. The key travel behavioural findings are that only a portion of P&R users' car trips are shortened. Hence, overall increases in car use occur, combined with overall reductions in public transport use, and in some cases less active travel. Where dedicated public transport services are operated, these are also a further source of additional traffic.*

Practical implications — *P&R implementations are generally successful where they are explicitly for providing more parking for economic growth or traffic management reasons, rather than to enhance sustainable mobility. The essential conditions for traffic reduction to occur in future are a strategic subregional integrated parking and public transport strategy which achieves interception of car trips early and ensures public transport services remain attractive for a range of access modes.*

Originality/value — *The chapter provides a synthesis of work by a number of leading authors on the topic and includes elements of originality in the combination of the established knowledge, the addition of novel insights, and in overall interpretation.*

Keywords: Park-and-ride; strategic transport planning; public transport; parking; automobility; sustainable mobility

INTRODUCTION

In its most simple terms, a park-and-ride (P&R) journey occurs when a private vehicle, normally a car, is parked at a public transport node, to enable the use of a public transport service for part of the journey. The modal interchange is made either because the traveller wishes to use the public transport service as the primary mode for the journey, but a private car is judged the most effective way to access the public transport network, or, conversely, the car is the preferred primary mode for the journey, but advantages are perceived if the final part of the journey is made by public transport.

Within this broad description, a range of P&R phenomena exist, but the most common kinds are parking at rail stations and dedicated bus P&R.

Rail P&R itself is a diverse phenomenon, serving journeys of a range of lengths, from local to intercity. Depending on network configuration and service patterns, a specific station car park may be oriented towards opening up a whole network of destinations or towards a particular city. Moreover, the interchange may occur at various points in the journey. Where it is early, the car acts as a station access mode; where it is very late, the railway is in effect a shuttle service within the destination area. When it provides this latter function, rail P&R operates in a similar mode to most bus P&R schemes, which are oriented towards local or regional demand for travel to a core city and typified by interchange relatively late in the overall trip. One key difference, however, is that rail P&R is typically an add-on to an existing public transport service, whereas bus P&R usually involves a dedicated car park on the periphery of the urban area and a dedicated shuttle bus service which is additional to the existing bus network.

The current chapter focusses on P&R facilities with a subregional function, as this type of scheme features more intense and direct interactions with the urban parking market. Within this focus there is an emphasis on the empirical evidence about the effects of P&R policies. As much of this evidence relates to bus-based schemes there is a further pragmatic focus on that mode.

The chapter will begin by examining P&R as a transport planning practice, through two sections which first consider interchange capacity provision as being variants of a sociotechnical system and then examine the different policy perspectives which can motivate formal P&R policy implementation. The third and fourth sections in turn then consider the empirical evidence on the behavioural effects of P&R systems and the implications of that evidence for the wider sustainable development context, including how P&R might be delivered in ways which achieve enhanced accessibility benefits whilst also reducing total traffic. The chapter concludes by noting that the main contributions of P&R policy to date have been in the economic and traffic management domains, and by emphasising the key strategic transport planning requirements if P&R is to make a sustainable mobility contribution.

P&R PROVISION AS A SOCIOTECHNICAL SYSTEM

As in the case of parking in general, accurate censuses of P&R supply are hard to conduct, as the facilities are promoted by multiple agencies, are often introduced and then expanded, and may not be formally recognised as P&R, but simply as 'station parking'. However, summary statistics are provided here for two European states to give an indication of scale.

Mingardo (2013) reviewed the development of P&R in the Netherlands; one of the leading European proponents. The first official P&R was introduced in 1979 in Schagen, north of Amsterdam. By the end of the 1980s, more than 50 official P&R facilities were in use and, in 2003, 386 P&R facilities were in operation in the country.

For the United Kingdom, Pickett and Gray (1993) estimated that 85,000 official parking spaces throughout the southeast of England potentially served Central London, including those at London Underground stations. However, P&R trips from those spaces were estimated to account for just 2% of commuter trips from within Greater London and 8.5% of those originating outside. Since then policy has increased this supply and parking fees have become an important revenue stream in the operation of UK rail franchises. Many of these journeys are of an inter-regional nature and enable London to function as a megacity: the concentration of commercial and administrative activity in the relatively compact area of Central London would not be possible without a public transport-dominated modal split.

More generally, Clayton, Ben-Elia, Parkhurst, and Ricci (2014) record that the United Kingdom was one of the countries that pioneered the use of bus-based P&R in the early 1970s, with substantial investment having resulted in P&R becoming an important feature of many local transport policies. By 2000 there were 70 sites established and by 2007 there were more than 130 P&R sites operating in Great Britain, together serving approximately 60 towns and cities across the country. Overall, this capacity is estimated to provide 70,000 parking spaces and to utilise more than 400 buses daily. Annually, bus P&R has been found to account for 46 million passenger journeys in the United Kingdom and to generate revenues of £40m (TAS Partnership, 2007).

The case of Oxford, one of the UK cities with both extensive bus P&R capacity and restraints on city centre car use, provides an indication of the local significance of this aggregate picture. By 2001 there were approximately 5,000 spaces in five sites and P&R was the most celebrated feature of local transport policy. The system was providing for around 7% of trips to the city centre (Parkhurst & Dudley, 2004, Fig. 1). Whilst not being an insignificant contribution, in practical rather than symbolic terms P&R was a minor mode, as conventional buses were delivering one-third of travellers and approaching half used private cars.

Moreover, most cities have little or no P&R capacity. In this context the current scale of supply in the United Kingdom is low in overall terms, and there may therefore be considerable potential to promote interchange as a sustainable transport policy.

Within the broad introductory definition of P&R, there are multiple criteria which distinguish different types of P&R 'system'. These are:

- the relative distance of the modal transfer point from the final destination;
- the mode of transport which is transferred to, with the most common options being bus, light rail, urban/commuter rail and inter-city rail;
- the exclusive or integrated nature of the public transport service, that is, whether it is solely used by travellers making P&R trips (which may arise either because it is hard to access the public transport using any other feeder mode or because travellers not arriving by car are deterred as a matter of policy);
- whether the parking capacity is reserved for interchange passengers or shared with other types of parking demand (either simultaneously or at different times);
- the basis for charging for the P&R facility, which typically amounts to whether the car parking is free or charged, but can involve integration with the public transport user fares. Most important is the relative cost of P&R use compared with the cost and ease of accessing the destination by car and parking there. These relative costs are variously determined by a mix of public and private sector providers seeking to maximise return on assets or achieve public policy objectives through regulation and price mechanisms.

To expand on the issue of transfer point, Mingardo (2013) takes a strategic spatial-locational focus, categorising the most common P&R systems in the Dutch context as being:

- *remote*, located in suburban residential areas and oriented towards the early interception of commuter trips;
- *peripheral*, edge of town facilities, with a destination-oriented function, whose aim is to intercept drivers just before their final destinations;
- *local*, with a 'field function' to intercept drivers on main transport corridors at intermediate points between origin and destination.

A fundamental influence on the decision to change mode, and where that transfer occurs, is the availability of parking.[1] Here it is important to note that proactive P&R supply policies interact with innovative individual travel behaviour, with P&R demand and supply showing both formal and informal development. Using a before and after methodology, Heggie and Papoulias (Papoulias and Heggie, 1976; Heggie and Papoulias, 1976) found that 13% of users of Oxford's first formal bus P&R were already parking near a bus stop to catch a general-purpose bus service not conceived or marketed as providing a modal interchange offer. On-street parking near suburban railway and metro stations is a widespread phenomenon; generally ignored or tolerated until it conflicts with other parking demands.[2] Indeed, formal P&R provision policy is strongly driven by the need to dedicate P&R parking capacity to avoid such conflicts. Travel to work is a common P&R journey purpose. In unregulated conditions early-arriving commuters might be expected to occupy, throughout the day, the on-street parking facilities also sought by shoppers. Conversely, where P&R is being promoted as a policy, there is a need to ensure the capacity provided, often at public expense, is used to facilitate the desired behaviour, and not used as additional parking for activities which happen to be near the public transport node. In a few cases, where P&R has been promoted through the provision of a public transport journey at a lower fare than the equivalent journey on the public transport system, but accessed on foot, policymakers have sometimes perceived a need to ensure the users of the public transport have in fact arrived by car.

Given that decisions about parking provision and cost can have a significant influence on motorists' choices, studies have sought to identify the theoretically optimal location for P&R facilities. Horner and Groves (2007), considering rail P&R in the United States, summarise the challenge as seeking to maximise the interception of cars but also intercepting them as early as possible in order to boost rail patronage and traffic reduction, whilst, where possible, achieving secondary socioeconomic objectives, such as locating the facilities at commercial centres which might benefit from the interchange traffic. However, individual travellers may not share these societal benefits. Travellers are more likely to interchange early in the journey if the public transport mode offers an attractive journey time or reliability advantages; attributes often associated with rail systems. Conversely, if the main incentives for P&R use are scarce or expensive parking at the final destination then travellers may be more oriented towards interchanging late in the journey. As well as city centres, airports provide good examples of the latter market mechanisms, with travellers often being provided with a range of short and long-stay parking and P&R options, with price declining with distance from the terminal.

Where P&R is provided on a rail network, travellers are often presented with multiple P&R options, sometimes on different lines, and have a choice of interchanging early or late, as well as not at all. In the United Kingdom, dedicated 'parkway' stations on main lines outside of urban centres served by high frequency express trains and with large parking facilities have been successful at attracting a car-dependent patronage. However, concerns that such facilities could encourage 'railheading' — encouraging motorists to interchange late in order to take advantage of a higher quality rail service but at the expense of extra road traffic — led the authority Transport for London to adopt a policy presumption against P&R development on the rail networks within the London area (Buxton & Parkhurst, 2005).

Therefore, P&R provision is not simply defined by explicit policies on capacity provision and regulations about use, but represents a number of travel practices, influenced by infrastructure provision and social expectation, as well as space-time economics. Considered in terms of a sociotechnical transition, the development of a new P&R service presents challenges greater than the sum of those associated with the modes being integrated (Parkhurst, Kemp, Dijk, & Sherwin, 2012). In most developed country contexts, the dominant mobility 'regime' is that of car use, which is generally the most straightforward and obvious mode to use. Car travel requires the lowest cognitive effort for the majority of citizens which are car-oriented, and most transport planners and engineers have traditionally emphasised professional skills and experience in providing for the car. Other transport modes are more likely to be novel and require greater cognitive and physical effort. They exhibit more complexity, have less extensive networks (in both the transport and social senses) and information about the practice and custom of using them is less diffuse. In the case of public transport services, knowledge of custom and practice tends to lie within a parallel, separate sociotechnical culture constituted by providers, mainly public transport operators, and the subgroup of citizens who are their significant users. This knowledge includes procedures and practices ranging from logistical aspects such as how timetables are read, interconnections made, and the purchase and validity of tickets, through to subtle cultural practices, such as whether it is socially acceptable to eat on a vehicle, talk to fellow passengers, and which seat to occupy on a partially full vehicle.

P&R as a form of intermodality seeks to link these different sociotechnical systems in order to offer the benefits of each, but in doing so potentially faces barriers of acceptance from each. The hard engineering aspects can be relatively easy to address, through capital investments in dedicated interchanges, reducing tangible barriers such as physical accessibility. However, the cultural practices of the niche require users to seek and acquire new knowledge and those practices may need to evolve to meet user expectations, to overcome incompatibilities between the regimes. For example, local authorities have needed to respond to the expectation that overnight parking be permitted at P&R sites, when they were originally intended for day-long trips; that public transport fares for P&R users travelling in groups should be charged at or close to the individual rate (mirroring the marginal cost of an additional passenger in a car); that high frequency shuttle services should be available into the evening, despite tapering demand. Nonetheless, notwithstanding the apparent complexities presented to the novel user, P&R is generally simpler to understand and more oriented to the perspective of the habitual motorist than the typical bus network. For all but the smallest towns, the latter generally has a greater variety of routes and often many destinations served from a single bus stop, and often a wider range of fares.

Where P&R schemes have been most successful, they have generally functioned by adding P&R capacity to high-status, well-resourced modes such as commuter rail, or by 'mutating' the public transport offer through dedicated bus provision so it delivers a level of service much closer to that of the private car than typically available in that locality. This is generally only possible through the allocation of public subsidy to the operations. Moreover, considerable public sector costs and professional efforts are involved to align and coordinate interests and resources, in order to deliver the infrastructure and services. Such policy construction requires a sharp and distinct policy 'frame', or way of encapsulating a problem and proposed solution (Schön & Rein, 1994). The narratives developed from these frames tend to present strong beliefs and expectations about the potential benefits of P&R investment and subsidy, typically in the domains of economic promotion or environmental protection. As is often the case when a particular sociotechnical practice such as P&R is promoted as a revolutionary solution to long-standing problems, rival perspectives drawing on different evidence or interpretations emerge. Combined with a complex policy implementation context, with varied and diverse behavioural responses and outcome consequences, P&R can be a challenging policy measure to assess. The following section considers further these different perspectives.

DIFFERENT PERSPECTIVES ON THE ROLE OF P&R

As noted in the previous sections, the individual traveller's perspective on P&R can be characterised as perceiving P&R as an opportunity to:

- avoid constrained parking near the destination, due to scarcity or price,

- avoid unattractive driving conditions en route, as a result of congestion, distance fatigue or complex navigational requirements,
- retain the benefits of private car use for the first leg of the journey, the origin of which may not be immediately accessible by public transport.

Such perceptions generally occur in the context of a highly automobile society.

The policymaker's perspective is more complex. Indeed there are multiple perspectives which tend to reflect professional orientation:

- A transport planner will emphasise the potential of P&R to have direct influence on traffic and/or congestion, with the expectation that each of these should reduce. Indirectly, positive consequences for exhaust emissions will be assumed. Successful achievement of traffic reduction may enable the reallocation of road space and land used for parking to other purposes. Due to the potential to influence air quality, environmental health professionals can be expected to take an interest in these outcomes, whilst not necessarily being in a position to influence policy strongly themselves (Olowoporoku, Hayes, Longhurst, & Parkhurst, 2012).
- An economic development professional will regard P&R as one means of providing and advertising more attractive conditions for car users, to encourage retail customers and other commerce to locate in the city centre. Generally, there will be a preference for P&R capacity to be in addition to, rather than instead of, city centre parking. Flexibility can however be shown towards the relocation of parking capacity in particular contexts where P&R is seen to be supporting a strongly business-oriented city centre access and public realm strategy (Parkhurst & Dudley, 2004).
- The transport operator's perspective will depend on the regulatory regime, but will generally be favourable where P&R is seen to simplify operations by focussing demand at specific nodes, and to be a means of attracting or retaining customers. Road public transport operators may expect reduced traffic to improve operating conditions for all services.
- Professionals with a specific remit to assess and reduce climate change emissions might be expected to take a more strategic view, examining the system-wide effects, and considering indirect and long-term implications.

Individual perspectives can be assumed to vary according to the spatial extent of competence and responsibility each actor has. A transport planner with a clear remit for a particular urban area may have little professional regard for any traffic overspill consequences, provided objectives within the city are met. Similarly local economic development professionals will have a remit to focus on city or subregional performance, rather than total national productivity or the needs of other neighbouring cities. Importantly, some of the objectives of the different professionals will coincide, but some will be in conflict.

Dijk and Montalvo (2011) examined the pattern of P&R adoption in Europe, finding that a quarter of cities were strongly engaged in P&R development and a half moderately engaged. Engagement was stronger to the north and west of the continent compared with the south and east. Overall the spatial pattern of adoption was found to be uneven, despite the fact that the incidence of urban transport problems shows a high degree of consistency across the continent. Based on linear regression analysis the authors argued that the variation reflected the wide diversity of policy frames justifying P&R development. The most important factors in whether city governments chose to engage in P&R development or not were found to be: the presence of economic objectives, the extent of citizen demand, and the readiness of organisational learning capabilities. However, overall, these factors explained only around 40% of the variance. Support for P&R emerged as qualified; often being the 'second best' choice by administrations, with other measures seen as being more effective in improving accessibility and liveability and P&R regarded as playing a supporting role within a package of measures.

More recently, in a repeat survey study involving the same cities, Dijk, de Haes, and Montalvo (2013) identified similar findings. However, a higher degree of variance in extent of engagement (65%) was explained by the factors of: perceived community pressures for P&R, economic implications, and organisational capabilities. The authors suggested that greater awareness about the environmental problems associated with transport had encouraged the pressure from citizens. However, local authorities continued to take a less optimistic view of the capabilities of P&R, with 69% believing that other transport measures would be more effective in addressing environmental issues.

At the UK national level, Meek, Ison, and Enoch (2008) found that P&R has been subject to a series of distinct phases and these have broadly followed the changing sentiments in overall transport policy. The late-1990s saw positive encouragement of P&R given the UK Government's 'Pragmatic Multimodalism' (Shaw & Walton, 2001); trying to manage congestion and emissions whilst not appearing to favour particular transport-sector interests. The attention in national policy was relatively short-lived and national policy towards local transport has more recently emphasised decentralisation, with P&R being one of many measures which authorities can include in applications for national funding for local transport capital investment and travel management packages.

Meek, Ison, and Enoch (2010) examined why bus-based P&R was popular amongst UK local authority officers and councillors through a survey which revealed that a primary motivation for its introduction was that it is identified as a positive 'carrot' policy measure, which presents the authority to the electorate as tackling traffic congestion whilst encouraging the economy; two objectives which are often conflicting in transport policy. A perception was identified amongst policymakers that P&R is an effective measure for reducing car use. Indeed, P&R was ranked fifth out of 18 local transport measures for both effectiveness in reducing car use and public acceptability. The evidence about effectiveness in reducing car use will be critically examined in the next section. The initial political appeal of P&R, at least in its bus-based form, was reinforced by its ability to be in the exclusive control of local authorities, sometimes one individual authority.

Indeed, the desire or need to avoid negotiating with other neighbouring authorities is one constraint external to transport policy considerations which encourages the siting of P&R facilities very close to cities, or indeed within their urban extent, on land under direct planning control and/or ownership by the authority.[3] It is also the case that, in the context of a largely deregulated and privatised bus industry in Great Britain (except for London), P&R services were one of a very few ways in which authorities could continue to exert an element of direct control on urban bus networks.[4]

EVIDENCE ON THE EFFECTS OF P&R

Given that P&R is a complex sociotechnical system, with diverse implementation types, and subject to a wide range of potential policy objectives for implemented schemes, it is important for evidence-led transport planning to be clear about the extent to which the different types of P&R achieve those policy objectives.

In the case of the United Kingdom, by the early 2000s, Parkhurst and Richardson (2002) had concluded, from a review of studies, that the belief that it contributed to overall car traffic reduction was generally contradicted, and that, for the urban areas downstream of P&R sites, the evidence was variable in terms of the direction of change, and arguably modest in magnitude where a reduction was achieved. Fig. 1 indicates these net changes for the eight cities for which extensive data were collected as part of a study for the United Kingdom Government (Harris, Cooper, & Whitfield, 1998).[5] These data were subject to further analysis by Parkhurst (2000a). One

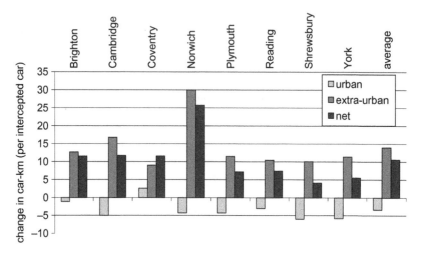

Fig. 1. Changes in Traffic Arising from P&R Implementations for Eight UK Cities. *Source*: Data from Parkhurst (2000a, Table 8).

notable addition to the analysis was the inclusion of the bus traffic generated by the dedicated P&R service. This was achieved by applying a factor of 2.5 car-km per bus-km operated, to reflect the higher traffic and environmental impacts of buses over cars, but not taking into account the spatial distribution of congestion or emissions.

Meek, Ison, and Enoch (2011) subsequently re-examined the case of Cambridge, following further development of its P&R facilities, using a higher factor of 3 for bus traffic relative to car traffic, and accounting for the implied alternative travel behaviour of users in more detail. For example, where the alternative was public transport it was assumed that these trips might involve travellers being given lifts to the access point. These refinements produced a lower estimate (5.9 km) compared to that of Parkhurst (2000a) (8.8 km), although the P&R system for Cambridge had changed substantially over the decade between the two studies.

The principal reasons for the findings that bus P&R overall increased traffic in the United Kingdom were that:

- Nearly all of the schemes examined relied on novel bus services. Therefore, in appraising traffic changes these additional bus movements represent an important offset to the traffic reduction due to car interception.
- Some users choose not to use the P&R facility which is optimally located for interception, or do not have access to a facility which would shorten

their car journeys, and therefore they detour to reach a facility, adding traffic (Parkhurst, 2000a).

- Some P&R users reduce their public transport use and increase their car use as a result of using P&R, because they did not access the urban area by car before, either walking to public transport or interchanging from car much earlier in the journey (Parkhurst, 1996). A review of perceived alternative modes amongst P&R users by Meek et al. (2011) showed a range of 9–41% of P&R trips would have used public transport in any case, although with important differences between weekday and weekend travel. In terms of magnitude, this effect is important in the overall traffic implications, as the extra-urban public transport journey legs which would provide the alternative option were long with respect to the P&R public transport legs undertaken within the city (Parkhurst, 2000a). Recent spatial analysis for the city of Bath, United Kingdom demonstrates well how public transport 'all the way', interchanging at P&R sites and driving to the city centre can be substitute journey options (Clayton et al., 2014). Ninety per cent of P&R users had origins within the area shown in Fig. 2a and 80% of car park users originated in the area shown in Fig. 2b. Therefore, most users were arriving from locations within 20km of Bath. Many of the origins, and particularly in the case of P&R, were in urban areas which are served by interurban bus services and in some cases rail services as well.

- There was also more tentative evidence that travel rates increase as a result of P&R, because it was offered at a whole-trip cost lower than any of the existing car-based or public transport-based options. Parkhurst (1996) summarised studies which found P&R users to report a high frequency of visiting the P&R host city, but it was not clear if these were entirely new or redirected trips. Similarly, both Parkhurst (1996) and Meek et al. (2011) reviewed studies reporting a wide range (1–28%) in the share of users who had indicated they would not come to the city in the absence of P&R, although given the hypothetical nature of the survey questions it cannot be certain that all these trips would be lost in the absence of P&R, and whether they would be reduced or redirected.

Mingardo (2013) notes two other kinds of 'unintended effect' of P&R provision. The first of these is a reduction in bicycle use in the Netherlands and Germany and is likely to be a feature in contexts with a high level of cycling. In the United Kingdom some local authorities have sought to integrate P&R and cycling policies by encouraging travellers for whom a

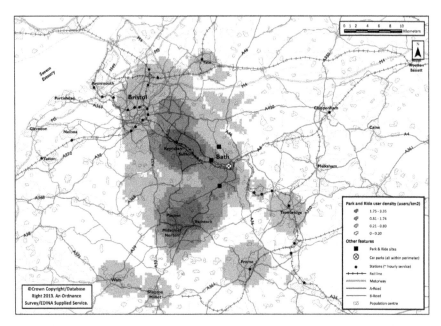

Fig. 2a.   Distribution of Bath P&R Users' Origins.

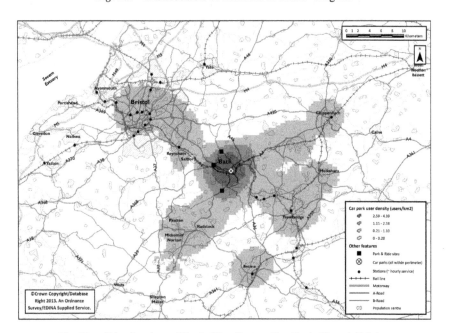

Fig. 2b.   Distribution of Bath City Centre Car Park Users' Origins.

cycle trip all the way to the city centre would be too long to instead park cycles rather than cars at the P&R node. Car-bike trips, whereby a cycle is carried to the P&R site by car for use on the final journey leg in preference to the P&R service have also generally been tolerated. The second of Mingardo's findings was the identification of P&R facilities being used as conventional car parks for journeys completed on foot to destinations nearby. In fact anecdotal evidence of overlapping uses exists from a range of national contexts and is generally unwanted by policymakers, although P&R has at times been used as a means of enhancing the patronage of poorly used car parks and the sharing of parking activities can occur by intention, for example sports stadia car parks in peripheral locations with high weekend and evening use may be used as weekday commuter P&R facilities.

To date, most of the empirical studies of P&R effects have been focussed on bus-based systems (and most of these in Europe) rather than the outcomes of providing P&R on rail public transport systems. A number of factors may explain this lower profile, including that

- rail systems are often complex, spatially extensive networks serving multiple destinations,
- the parking capacity has often been added incrementally to railway lines (which themselves predated the rise of car ownership),
- and the fact that rail systems are generally designed to attract access trips by a range of modes.

Bus P&R, instead, is most often delivered as a novel system of integrated and dedicated parking and public transport services, and has therefore raised more questions about the effects, and effectiveness, of resources specifically allocated to promote interchange.

However, an exception in terms of a study examining local rail P&R behaviour is that by Mingardo (2013), which surveyed users of nine rail-based P&R facilities located around the cities of Rotterdam and The Hague in The Netherlands in 2008 and 2009. Given the long-established nature of the facilities, Mingardo found many travellers using the Rotterdam facilities reported that the only alternative to P&R would be not to travel, as in many cases they had always used the P&R, and so had no 'previous' mode to offer as a potential substitute. Notably, Parkhurst and Stokes (1994) had identified a similar effect in Oxford, surveying bus-based facilities which had been present for 20 years, and these phenomena underline the methodological difficulties with retrospective studies. Table 1 summarises Mingardo's findings, with two other points of note being, in the

Table 1. Alternative Travel Behaviour of Rail P&R Travellers to
Rotterdam and The Hague (%).

	Rotterdam	The Hague
No alternative mode/wouldn't travel	39	2
Car origin to destination	23	19
Public transport near origin to destination	31	37
Cycle origin to destination	4	5
Informal P&R near PT node	–	20
Cycle to PT node	–	17

Data source: Mingardo (2013).

case of The Hague, further evidence of the significant potential for informal P&R but also a further mechanism by which cycling can be abstracted; providing attractive station car parking reduces the incentive to cycle to the station. Moreover, it is striking that, in both cases as few as a fifth of respondents saw the alternative for the trip to be a car journey from origin to destination.

Applying a similar methodology to the UK bus-based studies, Mingardo considered the traffic and emissions implications of the two rail P&R systems, finding that vehicle-km avoided amounted to only a third of the vehicle-km added for the Rotterdam case, but that around a tenth more were avoided than added in the case of The Hague. Importantly, the key reason for The Hague system resulting in a net reduction was that it was functioning as a 'remote' facility, intercepting travellers from near their destinations, and so reducing the absolute importance of the unintended effects.

In summary, the empirical evidence on the effects of P&R is limited in terms of the contexts and modes it covers, but is unanimous in confirming that the behavioural responses are much more varied and complex than simply the expected one of intercepting established car trips and thereby shortening them. The outcome that traffic is avoided in the urban area can often, but not always, arise, and where it does occur, the extent of this avoidance may be much lower than might have been assumed, particularly where additional road public transport is operated to provide the P&R service. Considering system-wide effects, traffic increased overall with only one important exception: rail-based P&R in The Hague, where travellers interchanged early onto an established, not dedicated, public transport service. This finding will be returned to in the final section, considering future policy and planning options for P&R.

FUTURE ROLE FOR P&R IN STRATEGIC SUSTAINABLE DEVELOPMENT POLICY

The growth of P&R provision in line with rising use demonstrates that P&R is a deliverable policy, and attractive to some travellers. However, the behavioural responses discussed above indicate that the outcomes have a closer fit in practice with some of the professional sectorial perspectives than they do with others. Most obviously, P&R meets the objectives of the local economic development frame, as users report greater willingness to travel and a sense of dependence on P&R schemes once introduced. In contrast, evidence presents the greatest challenge to the climate change mitigation perspective, given that traffic is generally increased, and that virtually all the vehicles are powered by fossil-fuelled internal combustion engines. The transport operator may perceive the benefits of operating new high-profile services which can attract more 'discretionary' passengers with cars available. However, the evidence suggests system-wide public transport use, considered in terms of passenger-km rather than passenger-trips, may reduce. If the operator is in a commercial environment and has a focus on profitability rather than total patronage, then the relative simplicity and passenger density of P&R operations may minimise this concern, as may any additional revenues from parking.

The transport and spatial planning perspective requires discussion at greater length. The introduction of P&R capacity is rarely matched with a reduction in city centre capacity (Dijk & Parkhurst, 2014), so it generally brings an increase in the total parking stock of host cities. Subject to the regulation and pricing of that parking, other things being equal, greater supply will tend to increase the attractiveness of car accessibility of the city centre. As well as increasing competitiveness with other urban centres, there may also be a relative enhancement of city centre business at the expense of neighbouring centres when future business location decisions are made. Similarly, where dedicated P&R public transport services are offered, a transfer of demand from existing public transport services may occur, which may decrease the viability of those bus and rail routes which lose patronage, and ultimately the business and social communities which depend on them. Ultimately, as suggested in the analysis of effects above, P&R-dependent spatial forms may be designed or may emerge, so that users would be unable to sustain their established mobility patterns in the absence of P&R capacity, and spatial forms which would not otherwise be functional are permitted. In addition to the spatial economic concept of the most accessible land being that most desired by commerce, a more practical planning conflict is that P&R facilities compete for the same space around suburban stations that would otherwise be particularly attractive for the 'transit-oriented development' sought by integrated transport and spatial planning initiatives (Duncan, 2010). Such facilities can also create urban design and environmental impact conflicts through consequences including increased rainwater run-off from the hard surfaces, light intrusion and loss of undeveloped space, and the physical extent of P&R car parks is often a factor in exacerbating such effects.

Therefore, P&R emerges as having considerable potential influence on travel demand and spatial development. The key policy challenge emerges as to whether it is possible to achieve the outcomes from implementations that support the wider sustainable development agenda, that is, shortening car trips, supporting overall patronage growth on public transport networks, enhancing low-carbon accessibility, whilst at the same time avoiding the negative effects of stimulating additional traffic, including as a result of attracting users from travel behaviours with lower environmental impacts, and minimising impacts local to the site. Various commentators have identified the need for remote location of the facilities as being central to promoting sustainable interchange facilities (Meek et al., 2011; Mingardo, 2013; Parkhurst, 1995; Topp, 1995). Parkhurst (2000b) and Meek et al. (2011) have also identified the operation of dedicated bus services as a key factor influencing sustainability in the UK context.

Parkhurst (2000b) promoted the 'link and ride' (L&R) concept for interchange strategy as involving:

- the location of car-bus interchanges relatively far from the final destinations of travellers, meaning that they would need to be located at various spatial ranges,
- the given level of parking capacity to be provided in relatively numerous but small sites to enable proximity to users and minimise environmental impacts, which in turn would be expected to reduce difficulties in site procurement linked to scale,
- the P&R offer to be on public transport services realistically accessible on foot and by cycle, and
- special subsidies for car users to be avoided, through ensuring users covered the full costs of the P&R sites and any additional services, and also that the 'market rate' for P&R should not be lower than the travel alternatives using public transport, walking and cycling.

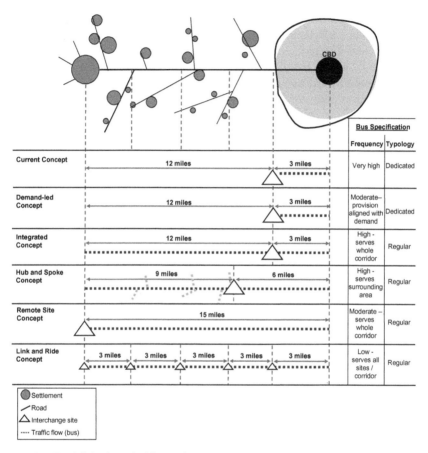

Fig. 3. Established and Alternative Concepts for Bus P&R Implementation.
Source: Meek et al. (2011, Fig. 1, with minor amendment).

Meek et al. (2011) further operationalised this approach considering five implementation variants illustrated in Fig. 3 and summarised below:

- Demand-led public transport supply: the service frequency is reduced to 20 minutes between 10:00 and 16:00, to reflect lower demand rather than operating at 10-minute intervals all day, resulting in an increase in wait time and therefore deterring some users, but also increasing mean load factors on the P&R service and avoiding some bus traffic.

- Integrated concept: uses conventional public transport services routed via a single P&R facility near the destination, thereby facilitating higher load factors and reducing public transport abstraction.
- Hub and Spoke (H&S): has similarities with the integrated concept in using general-purpose public transport services and a single P&R facility, but proposes additional feeder services to the site running on a 20-minute frequency using smaller vehicles, and with the P&R located intermediately with respect to origins and destinations, with the intention of minimising public transport abstraction and stimulating overall use. The feeders are assumed to be routed so that nearly 40% of users are within walking range.
- Remote site: maximises the leg of the trip undertaken on the public transport mode whilst reducing the access distance for a particular cluster of user origins. A medium-frequency (20 minute) bus service is assumed.
- L&R: similar to the concept proposed by Parkhurst (2000b) with a chain of sites at approximately 1.5 km intervals, to reflect the presence of clusters of user origins, and linked by one existing public transport route (Fig. 4).

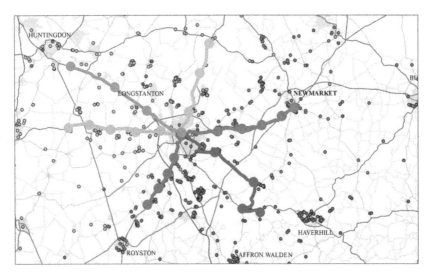

Fig. 4. Link-and-Ride Scenario Applied to Cambridge. *Source*: Meek et al. (2011, Fig. 7).

The five future scenarios were then subjected to GIS modelling analysis drawing on data relating to the existing P&R implementations for Cambridge, United Kingdom, assuming buses provided the services. A fixed matrix demand, car occupancy and alternative behaviour were assumed, except where P&R would be added to existing services in the case of L&R. In the latter case overall demand was assumed to be lower, car occupancy lower, and car used on its own much more likely to be the alternative mode to the interchange trip. The buses used in this scenario were also expected to be smaller, and having a lower environmental impact. The estimated traffic effects are shown in Table 2.

In summary, the findings showed that reducing bus supply in the demand-led scenario had only a minor effect on traffic changes given the importance of car traffic in the overall analysis, and this not allowing for a likely loss of patronage in response to the reduced level of service. The Integrated and H&S approaches did indicate lower traffic increases, with the main limitation on the H&S option being the additional bus traffic created in operating the feeders. These two scenarios could be improved by somewhat reducing bus frequency on the main P&R service. Moreover, if a level of patronage growth is assumed as a result of the enhanced public transport service offer in the wider network then the H&S variant indicated the potential to achieve traffic reduction.

Despite the long bus routes, the Remote Site option indicated the second-lowest level of traffic generation, and a modest reduction in bus frequency had the potential to produce a small traffic reduction. However, it emerged as very user-location dependent as the scenario assumed users would be loyal to using a P&R site located in the same corridor, so some P&R users living near the city would possibly be travelling away from the destination city and/or further than the current P&R implementation, in order to access the site. In the Cambridge case, the relatively long car journey legs of the established P&R users meant this effect was not important. In other contexts the Remote Site approach might potentially generate a more significant level of deviation from shortest path to the city.

Lastly, the L&R concept, with somewhat different modelling assumptions to reflect the higher degree of integration with existing public transport, was the only case to show significant traffic reduction per user. The salient points in this scenario leading to this reduction were, first, the possibility, as the sites are multiple, to fine-tune the site location with respect to user-origins, so radically reducing the length of access trips, and second, the possibility to increase the patronage on existing bus services to a significant degree, without generating new bus traffic.

Table 2. Modelled Traffic Effects of Current and Alternative Interchange Concepts (Miles).

Technical Characteristics	Current Concept	Demand-Led Concept	Integrated Concept	Hub & Spoke Concept	Remote Site Concept	Link & Ride Concept
Access VMT[a] (mean)	24.3	24.3	22.1	16.8	18.9	3.3
Bus VMT (mean)	2.1	1.6	3.64	8.8	6	9.5
Site–centre distance (mean)	3.26	3.26	3.26	3.26	10.6	8.7
Daily site usage	809	809	809	809	809	479
Alternative behaviour						
Car (% of users)	50%	50%	50%	50%	50%	86%
Car occupancy (mean)	1.3	1.3	1.3	1.3	1.3	1.1
Public transport (% of users)	30%	30%	30%	30%	30%	5%
Car equivalent factor applied to buses	2.5	2.5	2.5	2.5	2.5	2.5
Green mode (% of users)	4%	4%	4%	4%	4%	0%
Generated trips (% of users)	9%	9%	9%	9%	9%	9%
P&R use behaviour						
Car-equivalent factor applied to buses	3	3	3	3	3	2.49
Arrived by car						
% of users	96%	96%	76%	56%	75%	90%
Car occupancy (mean)	1.3	1.3	1.3	1.3	1.3	1.1
Arrived by green mode						
% of users	4%	4%	3%	3%	18%	0%
Arrived by bus						
% of users	0%	0%	21%	41%	7%	10%
VMT change (mean)						
Base scenario	3.68	3.16	2.54	2.4	1.67	−7.75
Reduced frequency (15 min)	–	–	1.46	1.97	−0.14	–
Plus 27.4 pax p/h per site	2.50	–	1.41	−0.41	−0.22	–

[a]VMT, vehicle-miles travelled.

CONCLUSION

Following the first detailed analyses of the traffic reduction benefits of P&R schemes in the United Kingdom in the 1990s, further studies have continued to confirm the broad findings that, P&R facilities are often well patronised, but many schemes actually result in a net traffic increase, with evidence recently emerging that some rail-based schemes have similar effects to the bus-based schemes. Hence, they are most likely to be regarded as a success where the objective is not to reduce car use by shortening car trips, but to provide parking where it can more easily and cheaply be made available: on the periphery of a city or at remote railway stations. However, this amounts to an economic strategy to promote further growth within successful cities such as the major commercial centres with intense competition for space and attractive historic cities with protected built environments rather than a sustainable mobility strategy. In addition, formal P&R policy may sometimes be necessary as a traffic management measure to regularise informal parking, such as around railway stations.

Related to the traffic-environmental findings, there is some evidence that the enthusiasm for P&R amongst local authorities in Europe as a whole has been tempered by the realisation that it has limited traffic reduction benefits, and often has a secondary function to support a wider traffic restraint strategy by providing an additional option to travellers. Moreover, the sociotechnical theoretical approach emphasises that, to the extent that P&R seeks to 'make life easy for the motorist' by providing attractive, frequent, subsidised, 'last-mile' transfers onto priority public transport, the policy will contribute to further developing an automobile culture. Indeed, hitherto, the dominant forms of P&R have reflected the wider development of transport and land use systems which embody the aspirations and needs of motorists and run counter to the promotion of active travel, transit-oriented development and reducing climate-warming emissions.

However, the chapter has confirmed that many car users are open to considering alternative trip-making practices including modal interchange. Considerable potential to achieve genuine traffic reduction and more sustainable mobility does exist, provided a number of criteria are met:

- the overall access and interchange strategy needs to be formulated at a subregional or regional level to ensure the needs of different city economies are considered;

- the strategy should not prioritise car access over other modes, notably the active travel modes and public transport, but seek to involve the car as part of an integrated transport system, with some motorists encouraged to switch from car altogether;
- it should seek to encourage early interchange to the more sustainable modes, so that the traffic and environmental costs of any additional public transport services which are necessary are offset by many motorists making much shorter journeys.

In summary, P&R needs to be part of a policy package which gradually reforms the regime of automobility towards one of an effective mobility mix, with each mode contributing according to, but not beyond, its particular advantages in sustainable mobility terms.

NOTES

1. Except in the case of the variant of P&R referred to as 'Kiss and Ride' which obviates the need for parking by the traveller being given a lift to the P&R facility. In this case the key requirement is effective car access to the vicinity of the public transport node.
2. Another example of the importance of informal interchange arises from the practice of 'Park and Share' (P&S), which has similarities with P&R. P&S involves the pre-arranged meeting of private car drivers at mutually convenient locations in order to carpool, so leaving one or more private cars at the meeting point. The practice has generally been informal and user-arranged, making use of motorway service station car parks and P&R facilities as well as more ad hoc facilities, such as the kerbside. However, UK local authorities such as Hertfordshire County Council now offer formal coordination and others such as the City and County of Swansea, as well as the Northern Ireland Executive, have provided dedicated car parks. In principle many of the debates around P&R would also apply to P&S; however, empirical evidence on its effects of park and share is very limited, and it is therefore beyond the scope of this chapter.
3. Such was the case in Oxford in the early 1970s. Oxford City Council had very limited location options for the first two P&R sites as its transport planning responsibilities ended at an administrative border closely following the extent of urban development. The subregional authority responsible for the surrounding territory, Oxfordshire County Council, was not cooperative in respect of P&R policy in the early years of its development. Similarly, the subregional Avon County Council had led the development of P&R in the cities of Bristol and Bath. Since the abolition of that tier of governance in the 1990s, Bath and Northeast Somerset Council, which controls the territory outside of the urban area of Bath has been able to propose additional sites. In contrast, Bristol City Council, which does not even control the entire urban area of the city, has struggled to identify suitable and deliverable additional P&R site options to the northeast of the city, from which orientation travel demand is highest.

4. The UK's 1985 Transport Act empowers local authorities to plan and procure bus services which have not been offered on a commercial basis. In practice the service gaps have essentially been in rural areas and at evenings and weekends. P&R services have generally been a weekday urban exception as they are mostly not commercially viable without local authority support. Operating from a local authority-owned P&R site does not prohibit a bus operator from registering a commercial service, and this does happen, but in practice a greater degree of informal cooperation is required between operator and authority in order for the service to be attractive to potential users, and therefore viable. Local authorities can impose access charges on commercial bus services using P&R sites, and they have the choice to impose parking charges on site users. Generally local authorities have sought to recover user contributions from a bus fare rather than by imposing parking charges, as the former are zero-rated for Value Added Tax, whereas parking attracts a standard rate of 20%, paid to central government. Applying parking charges rather than bus fares in order to raise a given level of revenue for local purposes therefore has a higher charge for the traveller. However, a combination of public sector spending cuts and the introduction of free bus travel for citizens of pensionable age has resulted in authorities with high-capacity P&R schemes (Oxford, York and Cambridge) introducing parking charges in addition to bus fares in order to improve financial performance.

5. The study team reports case-study selection as arising from a process of assessing 15 candidate cities against 41 transport sector criteria and more pragmatic factors such as context data availability and willingness to participate, with a view to reflecting a range of P&R experience and type of city in the selected cases.

REFERENCES

Buxton, S., & Parkhurst, G. (2005, July 5–6). Towards a truly strategic appraisal process for evaluating park and ride schemes: The development of an assessment framework for London. In *Proceedings of the 3rd UK Transport Practitioners Meeting*, Aston University, Birmingham, PTRC, London.

Clayton, B., Ben-Elia, E., Parkhurst, G., & Ricci, M. (2014). Where to park? A behavioural comparison of bus park and ride and city centre car park usage in Bath, UK. *Journal of Transport Geography*, *36*, 124–133.

Dijk, M., & Montalvo, C. (2011). Policy frames of Park-and-Ride in Europe. *Journal of Transport Geography*, *19*, 1106–1119.

Dijk, M., de Haes, J., & Montalvo, C. (2013). Park-and-Ride motivations and air quality norms in Europe. *Journal of Transport Geography*, *30*, 149–160.

Dijk, M., & Parkhurst, G. (2014). Understanding the mobility-transformative qualities of urban park and ride polices in the UK and the Netherlands. *International Journal of Automotive Technology and Management, Special Issue on Sustainable Urban Mobility in Comparison*, *14*(3/4).

Duncan, M. (2010). To park or to develop: Trade-off in rail transit passenger demand. *Journal of Planning Education and Research*, *30*, 162–181.

Harris, C., Cooper, B., & Whitfield, S. (1998). *The travel effects of Park and Ride. Report for United Kingdom Government Department of Environment, Transport and the Regions.* Epsom, UK: WS Atkins Planning Consultants.

Heggie, I. G., & Papoulias, D. (1976). *Operational performance of Park-and-Ride: Objectives and achievements in Oxford.* Working Paper No. 23. Transport Studies Unit, University of Oxford.

Horner, M. W., & Groves, S. (2007). Network flow-based strategies for identifying rail park-and-ride facility locations. *Socio-Economic Planning Sciences, 41,* 255–268.

Meek, S., Ison, S., & Enoch, M. (2008). Role of bus-based Park and Ride in the UK: A temporal and evaluative review. *Transport Reviews, 28*(6), 781–803.

Meek, S., Ison, S., & Enoch, M. (2010). UK local authority attitudes to Park and Ride. *Journal of Transport Geography, 18,* 372–381.

Meek, S., Ison, S., & Enoch, M. (2011). Evaluating alternative concepts of bus-based park and ride. *Transport Policy, 18*(2), 456–467.

Mingardo, G. (2013). Transport and environmental effects of rail-based Park and Ride: Evidence from the Netherlands. *Journal of Transport Geography, 30,* 7–16.

Olowoporoku, D., Hayes, E., Longhurst, J., & Parkhurst, G. (2012). The rhetoric and realities of integrating air quality into local transport planning process in English local authorities. *Journal of Environmental Management, 101,* 23–32.

Papoulias, D., & Heggie, I. G. (1976). *A comparative evaluation of forecast and use of Park and Ride in Oxford.* Working Paper No. 22. Transport Studies Unit, University of Oxford.

Parkhurst, G. (1995). Park and Ride: Could it lead to an increase in car traffic? *Transport Policy, 2*(1), 15–23.

Parkhurst, G. (1996). *The economic and modal-split impacts of short-range Park and Ride schemes: Evidence from nine UK cities.* Report 1996/29. ESRC Transport Studies Unit, UCL, London, UK.

Parkhurst, G. (2000a). Influence of bus-based Park and Ride facilities on users' car traffic. *Transport Policy, 7*(2), 159–172.

Parkhurst, G. (2000b). Link-and-Ride: A longer-range strategy for car-bus interchange. *Traffic Engineering and Control, 41*(8), 319–324.

Parkhurst, G., & Dudley, G. (2004). Bussing between hegemonies: The dominant frame in Oxford's transport policies. *Transport Policy, 11*(1), 1–16.

Parkhurst, G., Kemp, R., Dijk, M., & Sherwin, H. (2012). Intermodal personal mobility: A niche caught between two regimes. In F. Geels, R. Kemp, G. Dudley, G. Lyons, (Eds.), *Automobility in transition? A socio-technical analysis of sustainable transport* (Chapter 15). Routledge Studies in Sustainability Transitions. New York, USA and London, UK: Routledge.

Parkhurst, G., & Richardson, J. (2002). Modal integration of bus and car in UK local transport policy: The case for strategic environmental assessment. *Journal of Transport Geography, 10*(3), 195–206.

Parkhurst, G. P., & Stokes, G. (1994). *Park and Ride in Oxford and York: Report of surveys (1994).* Working Paper No. 797. Transport Studies Unit, University of Oxford.

Pickett, M. W., & Gray, S. M. (1993). *Informal Park and Ride behaviour in London.* Project Report No. 51. Transport Research Laboratory, Crowthorne, UK.

Schön, D. A., & Rein, M. (1994). *Frame reflection: Toward the resolution of intractable policy controversies.* New York, NY: Basic Books.

Shaw, J., & Walton, W. (2001). Labour's new trunk-roads policy for England: An emerging Pragmatic Multimodalism? *Environment and Planning, 33*(6), 1031–1056.

TAS Partnership. (2007). *Park & Ride Great Britain* (4th ed.). Skipton, UK: TAS Partnership.

Topp, H. H. (1995). A critical review of current illusions in traffic management and control. *Transport Policy, 2*(1), 33–42.

CHAPTER 10

CARFREE AND LOW-CAR DEVELOPMENT

Steven Melia

ABSTRACT

Purpose — *This chapter defines and describes the different types of carfree and low-car development found in the United Kingdom and continental Europe, analysing the benefits and problems they bring and their implications for parking policy.*

Methodology/approach — *The chapter draws on the literature on UK and European carfree developments, including primary research conducted by the author into the potential for carfree development in the United Kingdom. It is also informed by a series of observational visits to some of the principal carfree developments around Europe.*

Findings — *The UK concepts of car-free and low-car housing are limited in scope, defined by the absence or reduced level of parking. The European concept of carfree development is broader, bringing greater benefits to the immediate residents. All have led to lower traffic generation. European carfree developments bring other benefits to their residents such as more socialisation between neighbours and earlier independence for children. The potential demand for car-free and low-car housing is greatest in the inner areas of larger cities. These are also the*

Parking: Issues and Policies
Transport and Sustainability, Volume 5, 213–233
ISSN: 2044-9941/doi:10.1108/S2044-994120140000005012

places which offer the most suitable development locations. The most common problems encountered relate to parking and/or management of vehicular access. To avoid overspill problems, parking needs to be controlled on the streets surrounding carfree or low-car developments.

Practical implications − *The benefits of carfree development are greatest in urban areas where road capacity and/or parking are under the greatest pressure. Thus carfree development is a useful tool for cities undergoing urban intensification.*

Originality/value of paper − *The chapter is the first to analyse carfree and low-car development from a parking perspective and to demonstrate their implications for parking policy.*

Keywords: Carfree development; low-car development; parking restraint; controlled parking

INTRODUCTION

The terms 'carfree' or 'car-free'[1] have been used in several different ways to describe quite different forms of housing or new developments. In UK planning policies (e.g. DETR, 2001) and discourse the term 'car-free housing' usually refers solely to the absence of parking, whereas several carfree developments in continental Europe were conceived with a range of broader aims. Nearly all of them involve some degree of compromise with vehicular access and storage, including some limited peripheral parking, so the term 'carfree' is something of a misnomer. 'Traffic free' might be a more accurate term, but as these initiatives spawned an international carfree movement, the term has been widely used in the literature.

Based on examples from around Western Europe Melia, Parkhurst, and Barton (2010) define carfree development as residential or mixed-use developments which:

- Provide a traffic free or nearly traffic free immediate environment,
- Are designed to facilitate movement by non-car means, and
- Offer no parking for residents or limited parking separated from the dwellings.

The second point also typically encompasses provision of car club vehicles for occasional needs.

The sole defining criterion for the UK car-free housing developments is that they offer no parking for residents. They may be designed to facilitate movement by non-car means or may simply be located in places which are already reasonably adapted to living without a car. A third category, 'low-car development' may be defined as residential or mixed-use developments which offer limited parking and are designed to reduce car use by residents. Thus it can be seen that all three categories have implications for parking policy and rely on different forms of parking management.

There are several reasons why carfree developments were proposed in different European countries. In some cases, the proposals were initiated by local authorities seeking to redevelop in areas where road capacity was limited. In other cases, the impetus came from groups of citizens. A carfree movement began in the 1990s in Germany and Austria, led by people with idealistic aims, seeking a better urban environment for people willing to make a positive decision to live without owning a vehicle. Apart from the environmental problems caused by motor traffic, two key claims made by proponents of carfree development relate to social equity and freedom of choice (see Crawford, 2000). People without cars, who typically include those on low incomes and residents of dense inner urban areas suffer some of the worst consequences of pollution and severance caused by others driving through their areas. The progress made in several European countries encouraged the more disparate World Carfree Network to adopt the spread of carfree development as one of its aims. This network did not achieve the impact it had hoped for and by the second decade of this century, it had become dormant (World Carfree Network, 2013). Some of the carfree developments described below have been internationally influential, however, and as this chapter argues, the concept remains relevant as a means of addressing a range of urban planning and transport problems, including some related to parking.

In some of the cases described below, there was evidence of tension between the different actors over the purpose and objectives of European carfree developments. For the United Kingdom, car-free and low-car housing, the purposes have been generally clearer. They have been initiated by local authorities with the aim of reducing traffic generation and/or addressing parking problems in urban areas where these are perceived to be problems.

As there is no agreed set of objectives against which to assess the benefits of carfree developments, the analysis in this chapter will start with their observable characteristics. Underlying the various definitions of carfree development and car-free housing are the two principles of the exclusion of traffic and the non-ownership of vehicles.

The British concept of car-free housing follows only the second of those principles; European carfree development follows both, though a small minority of residents may still own cars. Low-car development also follows the second principle and may or may not follow the first. It may be considered self-evident that a policy which reduces car ownership and use would help to alleviate the problems caused by car use in urban areas. The relationship is far from being direct, however, as illustrated in Fig. 1.

The indirect relationship shown between the Exclusion of Vehicles and Less Car Use illustrates the effects of making parking less convenient and

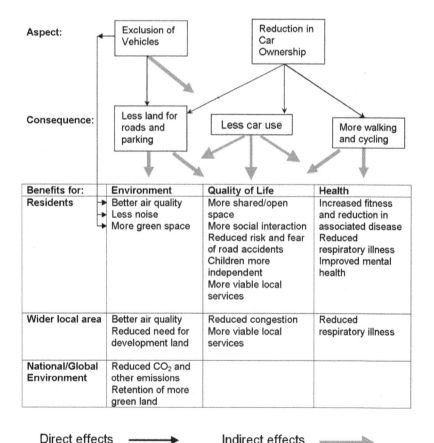

Fig. 1. Benefits of Carfree Development.

increasing the advantages of walking for short distances. Indirect effects on health may be imputed, though they have never been measured directly.

The next section will examine the European experience of carfree development and the UK experience of car-free housing and low-car development. The third section will examine the benefits and problems of each. The final section will draw conclusions for transport, planning and parking policy.

CARFREE DEVELOPMENT IN EUROPE AND THE UNITED KINGDOM

There are many areas of the world where people have always lived without cars because no road access is possible, or none has been provided. In developed countries these include islands and some historic neighbourhoods or settlements, the largest example being Venice with a population of around 70,000. The term carfree development implies a physical change, however, either new building or changes to an existing built area. The literature on carfree development refers almost exclusively to European examples, even in articles written in the context of developing countries (e.g. Wright, 2005). There is as yet no comprehensive list of carfree developments worldwide. An online list was begun a few years ago by Joel Crawford, author of Carfree Cities (Crawford, 2000). This list was subsequently transferred to Wikipedia, where it has grown with few verifiable sources.

Within Germany and Austria a number of groups started more or less spontaneously in different cities during the 1990s. Representatives of these groups were interviewed during study visits made by the author to several European carfree developments during 2006 and 2008 reported in Melia (2009). *Autofreies Wohnen* in Hamburg was one of the first of these groups, started in the early 1990s by activists who described their aim as 'purist': seeking to provide a carfree living environment for people who choose not to own a car. Their campaign eventually persuaded the municipality to provide land for two of the carfree developments described below.

Scheurer (2001) provides the broadest study of European carfree developments and refers to seven carfree developments (as well as some others which would not be considered carfree, as defined here) of which the first five were sufficiently advanced. Some of these developments were studied more recently by Nobis (2003), Bouvier (2005) and Ornetzeder, Hertwich,

Hubacek, Korytarova, and Haas (2008). This section draws on those studies and the observational visits made by the author. Based on these observations, Melia et al. (2010) classified carfree developments found around
Europe into three categories: the Vauban (stellplatzfrei) model, the
'Limited Access' model and pedestrianised centres with significant residential populations.

The Vauban Model

Vauban, in Freiburg, Germany has a population of just over 5,000. Unlike
the other examples discussed here, it has no physical barriers to the
penetration of motor vehicles into the residential areas. The catalyst for its
creation was the acquisition of a former military base by the municipality
and the formation of Forum Vauban by a group of local activists. The
Forum persuaded the municipality to create a neighbourhood for non-car
owners, with opportunities for groups of individuals (*Baugruppen*) to
collectively build their own homes. Car owners would not be excluded but
parking and traffic would be separated from the residential area.

   Although the term *autofrei* (carfree) is sometimes used in connection with
Vauban, this is not how most residents would describe it. The City Council
prefers the term *stellplatzfrei* – literally 'free from parking spaces' – to
describe the majority of streets where this rule applies. Vehicles are allowed
down these streets at walking pace to pick up and deliver but not to park,
although there are frequent infringements. Residents of the *stellplatzfrei*
areas must sign an annual declaration stating whether they own a car or
not. Car owners must purchase a place in one of the multi-storey car parks
on the periphery, run by a council-owned company. The cost of these
spaces – € 17,500 in 2006, plus a monthly fee – acts as a disincentive to car
ownership.

   The planned parking capacity – 0.5 per dwelling – was higher than
other examples described below. At early stages of its construction,
Scheurer (2001) and Nobis (2003) found just over half of households owned
a car, but many of the parking spaces were unused. There have been no
more recent surveys but parking levels suggest a substantial majority of
households do not own cars there.

   Some metered parking is available on the main Vaubanallee access
road. Like most of the larger carfree developments, some parking spaces
are allocated for car club vehicles, which provide an important service
for occasional use, although their contribution to overall modal share is

Fig. 2. Stellplatzfrei Street, Vauban, Freiburg, Germany.

relatively small. Nobis (2003) found 39% of households surveyed in Vauban belonged to Freiburg's car club. Ten vehicles were stationed there in 2006, the largest concentration of car club vehicles in the city.

Although vehicles are physically able to drive down the residential streets, and the no-parking rules are not effectively enforced, in practice, vehicles are rarely seen moving on the *stellplatzfrei* streets. Signs emphasise that children are allowed to play everywhere, and in the absence of moving traffic, children are more evident (Fig. 2) than in the more conventional home zones and traffic-calmed streets common elsewhere in Freiburg.

Limited Access Model

Unlike Vauban, most of the other carfree developments described in the literature physically restrict the access of motor vehicles to the residential areas in different ways. These arrangements have been described as the Limited Access Model (Melia et al., 2010).

Saarlandstrasse and Kornweg in Hamburg are relatively small, with 111 and 64 dwellings respectively. In these cases, a few parking spaces (ratios

0.15 and 0.2) intended for visitors and deliveries are close to the housing, surrounded by semi-private space where vehicles cannot penetrate. These small developments are able to provide a traffic-free environment because of their particular situations – the Saarlandstrasse site is partly surrounded by water and Kornweg is effectively a traffic-free cul-de-sac.

GWL Terrein in Amsterdam and Stellwerk 60 in Cologne are both larger: around 600 and 400 dwellings respectively. Stellwerk 60 includes some houses as well as apartment blocks, with pedestrianised streets between them. Removable bollards restrict access to the core of the site. A residents' organisation controls these bollards which are removed for a limited range of vehicles such as removal vans and emergency vehicles, but not for general deliveries which are done by hand, sometimes using trolleys or cycle trailers (Fig. 3).

In GWL Terrein, blocks of up to 8 storeys high have been built around semi-private space where vehicles cannot penetrate (Fig. 4). Entrances to the blocks are all fairly close to the perimeter, where some time-limited parking is available. Peripheral parking, mainly in multi-storey blocks is provided at a ratio of around 0.2 on both sites, allocated by ballot in GWL Terrein, and separately sold in Stellwerk 60.

Fig. 3.   Access to Stellwerk 60, Cologne.

Fig. 4. GWL Terrein, Amsterdam.

Pedestrianised Centres with Significant Residential Populations

Pedestrianised city, town and neighbourhood centres are widespread across most of Europe, most of which are mainly commercial in nature although some also include residential accommodation. There is long-standing evidence on the traffic impacts of pedestrianisation (e.g. Hass-Klau, 1993; Parkhurst, 2003) although relatively few studies have been published in recent years. Whereas the carfree developments in the previous section were newly built, most pedestrianised city, town and district centres have been retro-fitted. Pedestrianised centres may be considered carfree developments where they include a significant number of car-free residents, due to new residential development within the centres or because these centres already included dwellings when they were pedestrianised.

Groningen, a city in the North of the Netherlands is an example of a city with an unusually large residential population within a mainly traffic-free centre (16,551: Gemeente Groningen, 2008). The total population of the city is 181,000, including about 46,000 students (City of Groningen 2007, cited in: Pucher & Buelher, 2007). The original decision to restrict through traffic was implemented in 1977 (Tsubohara, 2007). Since then, the process has continued incrementally, with its city centre, an area of roughly a square kilometre having nearly half of its streets now pedestrianised and entirely closed to through traffic (although some of them allowing bicycles) with several car parks accessible on an 'in and out' basis.

Parking for non-residents has been progressively restricted to car parks towards the edge of the centre. In 2008 a total of 2,340 parking spaces (900 on-road) are reserved for the residents, amongst whom car ownership (28.7 per 100 households) was roughly half the city average and a third of the national average (Gemeente Groningen, 2008). The strategy of road closures and pedestrianisation contributed to a progressive fall in motor traffic within the city. The modal share for the car was just 33% of trips by city residents in 2003 (Gemeente Groningen, 2008).

Car-free Housing

Some London boroughs with extensive Controlled Parking Zones, define car-free housing by a planning condition precluding occupants from applying for a residents' parking permit. Unlike European carfree developments, the main aim of these boroughs relates to area-wide traffic restraint through lower car ownership rather than quality of life for the residents of the car-free housing, who gain no direct benefit. The London Borough of Camden, which pioneered the approach, granted 'car-free or car capped' planning permissions covering 2,416 dwellings between 2000/1 and 2010/11 (Camden, 2012 p.62). Nearly all the Borough is covered by a Controlled Parking Zone and, as the cost of metered or off-street parking in Central London is prohibitively expensive, this planning condition effectively prevents most affected residents from owning a vehicle.

This planning strategy appears to have contributed to the achievement of its goal to restrain traffic through lower car ownership. Between the 2001 and 2011 Censuses, the population of Camden grew substantially but the number of households owning cars fell in absolute and relative terms. Commuting by car, already very low, fell further over the decade. Several other policies, including the introduction of the Congestion Charge in London in 2003 would also have influenced these trends (Table 1).

Melia, Barton, and Parkhurst (2013) surveyed residents in two wards within Camden with particularly low-car ownership. When asked why they did not own a car, cost was not the main reason: most respondents could have afforded a car if necessary. The most common reason, cited by just under half, was 'I have no need for a car'. Lack of parking was rarely the main reason but a secondary reason for just over a third of respondents.

Table 1. London Borough of Camden: Trends in Car Ownership and Commuting (ONS, 2013).

	2001	2011	Change
Population	220,338	198,022	+11.3%
Households	97,534	91,603	+ 6.5%
Households with a car	40,657	37,939	−6.7%
Households with a car (%)	44.4%	38.9%	−12.4%
Driving to work as usual mode	14.9%	10.0%	−32.9%

Some other British Cities such as Brighton and Glasgow have planning policies which specifically allow for car-free housing (Brighton & Hove City Council, 2005; Glasgow City Council, 2009). In other cities, including Bristol and Exeter, car-free housing has been built without specific policy support in pedestrianised locations which do not allow direct vehicular access. Princesshay in Exeter was built as an extension and redevelopment of the pedestrianised shopping area and was completed in 2007. One hundred and twenty-two flats were included in the redevelopment for which a total of 23 car parking spaces were provided. The absence of parking did not appear to hinder the sale of flats in what was considered a desirable city centre location. Buyers queued in the street overnight before the release of the first phase of the development which had no allocated parking (BBC News Online, 2007).

Low-Car Developments

As with carfree development there is no agreed definition of low-car developments. Melia et al. (2010) define them as residential or mixed-use developments which offer limited parking, and are designed to reduce car use by residents. The term 'limited' requires a judgement which varies according to context. The principle is that parking controls and limited provision constrain the level of car ownership: if more parking were available, higher levels of car ownership, more typical of the surrounding area would result.

Six developments which may be considered 'low car' were reviewed in a study for the United Kingdom's Department for Transport (DfT, 2005). The parking ratios were considerably higher than the carfree developments described above − varying from 0.7 to 1.5 spaces per dwelling. 1.5 was the national maximum parking standard in the United Kingdom at that time (DETR, 2000), although the national standards were not uniformly applied and were subsequently abandoned (CLG, 2006). The developments in the DfT study combined these parking standards with residential travel plans, designed to encourage modal shift amongst the residents. Most of the case studies had yet to begin construction at that time. Melia (2009) surveyed one of these – Poole Quarter in Dorset, England – during 2007. The findings support the view that low-car developments that were well sited in respect to public transport and local services can reduce car use and increase active travel compared to conventional developments. However, there was little evidence of the beneficial changes to the local environment observed in the European carfree developments.

Poole Quarter was a new development of low-rise flats and town houses near the centre of a town with a population of 139,000. The dwellings completed at the time of the survey each had one parking space. The travel plan aimed to promote sustainable movement through information and incentives such as discounts on public transport. 81% of surveyed residents owned a car but multiple car ownership was lower than the surrounding area: only 15% owned more than one car. Just over a quarter of residents had reduced their car ownership on moving there, mainly from two cars to one, and a third of residents reported lower car use. These changes were partly explained by proximity to the town centre, bus and rail stations but the parking limitations also contributed. The site had been developed at higher than usual densities for that area (108 dwellings/ hectare) which meant that, even with the lower than usual parking ratios, the area between the housing was largely filled with parked cars. An area designated as a home zone (Fig. 5) was rarely used, as intended, for children's play. The most frequently cited problem, by over half of the respondents, was lack of parking and conflict between neighbours over limited parking spaces was mentioned by several interviewees. When residents were asked why they moved to Poole Quarter, most mentioned the accessibility of the site but none mentioned anything relating to the low-car concept or the travel plan – this was a notable difference from the European carfree developments.

Melia et al. (2013) researched the potential UK demand for housing in European-style carfree developments. They found the strongest demand amongst 'carfree choosers' or people who live without cars by choice. Ninety-one per cent of these people were already living in urban areas, particularly in larger cities. They differ from the low-income groups who are constrained to live without a car. They tend to cycle and use rail more but use buses less. Most of the 'carfree choosers' displayed pro-urban attitudes, favouring higher density living in flats and terraced houses. Their views on

Fig. 5. Poole Quarter.

access to public transport and services suggest the potential demand for carfree living can be most easily satisfied in the inner areas of larger cities.

BENEFITS AND PROBLEMS OF CARFREE DEVELOPMENT

Although the literature on European carfree developments is limited, there is evidence that these developments reduce car use and increase walking and cycling. The literature also suggests some other potential benefits, which this section reviews.

Scheurer's (2001) surveys found levels of car ownership varying between 8% of households in Vienna Florisdorf to 54% of households in Vauban, which was then at an early stage in its development. Scheurer's method of measuring modal share was rather unusual, asking respondents to fill in the frequency of trips per month under seven specific categories with no 'other' category, so comparisons with all-purpose modal share statistics may not be precise. Nevertheless, a clear pattern of very low-car use (5–16% of journeys) and high levels of walking and cycling (38–73%) emerges from these surveys.

Nobis (2003), surveying Vauban two years later, found a similar proportion of carfree households ('over 40 %') and using different questions from Scheurer confirmed the low level of car use: cycling was the most frequent mode for commuting, shopping and leisure. Both of these studies were conducted before the extension of the tram system to Vauban in 2006, which may have further influenced both car ownership levels and travel patterns.

The studies of European carfree development have mainly concentrated on mobility aspects although containing some evidence of other benefits. Ornetzeder et al. (2008) explored questions of social cohesion and social contacts in Vienna's Florisdorf carfree development. 85–87% of respondents agreed that there were 'good neighbourly relationships', 'solidarity within the settlement' and that people helped each other. They found that residents of the carfree project had more friends within the settlement than those of the slightly larger reference settlement. They also knew more people by sight. The authors ascribe these differences to the carfree nature of Florisdorf, although there were also differences in the extent of resident involvement in the planning of the two developments which could explain differences.

Scheurer also comments on the favourable environment for children in Vauban where household sizes were particularly high. Nützel (1993) found that children were allowed to play out on the carfree streets of Nuremberg-Langwasser at a younger age (average 3.8) than on conventional streets nearby (average 5.6). The observations made during the study visits by the author support these findings. There was considerable evidence of young children playing and cycling without direct supervision in several of the developments visited.

No specific research has been found on the health or economic impacts of carfree development, although some benefits could be deduced from the observations about travel patterns and traffic generation. The health benefits of walking and cycling have generated a substantial literature. Both are associated with improved fitness, bone and muscle strength and flexibility of joints (BUPA, 2007) and improvements in mental health (Glenister, 1996). Although the issues are not fully understood, air pollution caused by motor traffic is associated with a range of respiratory illnesses (RCEP, 2007) and so a reduction is likely to provide health benefits.

The European studies provide fairly strong evidence for the three intermediate consequences illustrated in Fig. 1 (relating to land, car use and active travel). Ornetzeder et al. (2008) found evidence to support two of the ultimate benefits: sociability, as discussed above, and reductions in CO_2 emissions: residents of the carfree area had a lower carbon footprint than a more conventional reference development nearby, and considerably lower than the national average.

The benefits for residents from carfree developments in general may be inferred with a reasonable degree of confidence, although the extent depends upon the individual circumstances of each development. The benefits to the wider local area and the global environment are more problematic to assess and whether they are achieved in practice depends upon a number of other factors, including supportive policy and design issues.

The land-related benefits depend on how the land saved from parking and roads is re-allocated. In Vauban, the developers were obliged to reserve an area of land as a form of insurance, in case car ownership exceeded the capacity of the car parks. This did not occur and the land has been used as informal public open space since then. In Slateford Green, Edinburgh, land set aside for parking has been used to provide more semi-private space including a children's play area (Eastwood, 2008). In other developments it is difficult to identify how the 'land saved' from parking was used, since developments were planned with the low or zero parking in the first place. The benefits may nonetheless be inferred from a notional counterfactual where additional land for parking would either reduce public space, gardens or reduce the number of dwellings built on the site, which in turn might increase building on undeveloped land elsewhere.

Reduced congestion depends upon wider policy and practice in the city and the immediate area surrounding the carfree development. Some of the benefits would also depend upon behavioural change by residents for which there is some evidence from the European studies. Carfree developments reduce driving and increase active travel because they attract residents predisposed towards non-car travel and they change the behaviour of residents (compared to conventional developments). If lower car use in carfree developments were solely due to the former, then national and global benefits would not be achieved and the benefits to the wider local area would be achieved at the expense of other areas. However, this is not the experience identified in Europe.

The evidence from European studies suggests that carfree developments do indeed change the behaviour of their residents. Nobis found that 81% of the carfree households in Vauban had previously owned a car; 57% gave up their cars after moving there. Scheurer found proportions varying from 10% (in GWL Terrein) to 62% (in Florisdorf) of households had reduced their car ownership since moving to the carfree developments. In

Florisdorf, Ornetzeder et al. (2008) found only one car owner (who was violating the rules of occupation) amongst the 50% of male and 30% of female residents who had previously owned a car. Forty-one per cent of respondents said they were 'using the bicycle much more than before'.

The existing examples in continental Europe and the study of demand in the United Kingdom both suggest considerable potential for carfree development, particularly in the inner areas of larger cities, where population densities are high and many households do not own a vehicle. These areas are also likely to benefit most from the reduced traffic generation. Many cities and countries have adopted policies of urban intensification, sometimes for transport reasons but mainly where development land is scarce or where there is a desire to protect undeveloped land. As Melia, Barton, and Parkhurst (2011) argue, urban intensification tends to reduce car driving but the effect is less than proportional, so doubling the population density in an area will generally reduce but rarely halve the traffic generation and car ownership of each household. This produces the *paradox of intensification*: global benefits at the price of worsening local conditions. Carfree development is one means of attenuating the localised externalities of intensification. Where implemented over an area wider than an individual housing development, this benefit would depend upon effective control of parking.

The main problems of carfree developments relate to parking and the control of vehicular access. Scheurer found dissatisfaction amongst 39% of residents with the arrangements in Vauban. Carfree households were unhappy that some car owners were flouting the rules by parking on the *stellplatzfrei* streets. Some car owners were unhappy about the inconvenience of parking separated from the housing. Nevertheless, Nobis found carfree households were more satisfied overall with the arrangements than car owners. This finding is consistent with Borgers, Snellen, Poelman, and Timmermans (2008) who found that car owners in the Netherlands preferred parking to be adjacent rather than separated from their housing (there was no mention of any carfree housing in the sample).

Overspill parking can also be a problem. The Vauban system of annual declarations and expensive parking spaces has given some residents an incentive to cheat, by registering cars in other names and parking them nearby. Freiburg City Council had taken legal action against two persistent offenders. The suburban location of Vauban made parking enforcement more difficult. There were no parking controls in the adjoining district of Merzhausen and statutory enforcement of parking rules within Vauban itself was rare. Vehicles were often parked on the *stellplatzfrei* streets in contravention of the rules, although this did not significantly detract from the traffic-free nature of these streets as there were very few vehicle movements.

The Limited Access model avoids the latter problem, although overspill parking in the surrounding area was sometimes an issue. Most of the examples were in more urban locations than Vauban. In GWL Terrein, parking in the surrounding areas was already controlled, so the development did not significantly change the parking situation there. In Stellwerk 60, some complaints had been made about overspill parking which was then addressed by the extension of controls in the surrounding area.

The criteria for exceptional vehicular access to Stellwerk 60 had caused differences of opinion amongst the residents. One contested issue was whether older or disabled residents should be allowed to drive into the interior of the site. The rules adopted by the residents' association allowed minibuses for older and disabled residents inside the site but not private cars.

The annual declarations of car ownership used in German carfree developments, are not believed to be enforceable under English or Scottish law (A. Chandler, Bristol Law School, personal communication, 11 March 2009). There does not appear to be any legal means of preventing home owners from owning vehicles, although a tenancy agreement may allow a landlord to take action where a tenant infringes a clause preventing them from parking in a defined area. This method is sometimes used for car-free student accommodation. Scepticism over the likely effectiveness of such enforcement often contributes to opposition towards such developments (e.g. Kingston Federation of Residents, 2013; Scotsman.com, 2007).

CONCLUSIONS

The parking challenges around carfree and low-car development epitomise several of the challenges of urban parking policy in general. Where road space is limited, parking controls can be used to ration that space, to reduce traffic within a particular area and to improve the urban environment. Carfree or low-car development can be used to pursue the same objectives. Parking controls in defined geographical areas will often create pressure on the surrounding areas. Carfree and low-car development will likewise create pressures for surrounding parking controls, where these do not yet exist.

Where comprehensive parking controls already exist, in places like Inner London, it is relatively easy for planning authorities to impose no-permit conditions on residents of newly built housing. Although a few individuals may find private or uncontrolled spaces elsewhere, a no-permit rule prevents car ownership for the vast majority of residents. In car-free housing of this kind, the no-permit condition is the only factor reducing car ownership. In all other respects, these dwellings may be no different to any others in the area. By contrast, the European carfree developments create a degree of self-selection through design and conception or marketing. Many of the people who move to them are attracted by the concept but this self-selection can never be absolute. Where parking within the development is limited and particularly where its cost is significant, some residents will always be tempted to park in surrounding areas unless and until controls are extended there (which in practice occurs).

The low levels of trip generation by residents of European carfree developments (where a minority continue to own cars) are consistent with the aggregate data for the United Kingdom. Households without cars generate very few car movements. Although some households without cars occasionally borrow or hire cars, they generate on average less than 2% of the car trips per person of households with cars (DfT, 2013, Table NTS 0702). Thus any policy which reduces car ownership in a particular area will also reduce traffic generation as well as demand for parking spaces.

From a policy perspective, the advantages of carfree (or to a lesser extent low-car) development are greatest in densely populated urban areas with limited road space. In some of the densest areas, unconstrained car ownership may be physically impossible. Melia et al. (2013) suggest that the potential demand for carfree housing is greatest in the inner areas of larger cities, so there is a considerable overlap between areas of greatest benefit and areas of greatest potential. For cities undergoing urban intensification, carfree development offers a response to the paradox of intensification, enabling development at higher densities without the usual problems caused by traffic generation. This may be particularly useful for development sites where road capacity is a planning constraint.

One of the most common objections to car-free housing in the United Kingdom is the fear of overspill parking from residents of surrounding areas. However, the extension of controlled parking zones in several British cities over recent years offers an opportunity to plan for new development with lower parking standards.

Unlike low-car development and the UK-style low-car housing, the European carfree developments offer more tangible benefits to their residents. These benefits flow from the removal of traffic and the re-use of parking land to improve the immediate environment. The two different approaches of the UK and European cities illustrate a different policy emphasis: the European approach reflects a greater concern for the immediate environment of residents.

The European examples described in this chapter all involved the public sector − particularly local authorities − in the initial development of what was an unfamiliar concept to private developers. However, unlike most other sustainable transport interventions, carfree development requires no more public funding than a 'business as usual' scenario. In a context where pressure for housing growth is coupled with constraints on public expenditure, carfree development is a concept which merits greater attention from planners, transport planners and policymakers.

NOTE

1. Although the spelling of the terms is often inconsistent, UK documents tend to separate (car free) or hyphenate (car-free) the adjective. The word carfree is more frequently used to describe the broader concept promoted by the international carfree movement, and the developments described as *autofrei* in German speaking countries. This convention is used in this chapter.

REFERENCES

BBC News Online. (2007). *Waiting over for would-be buyers.* Retrieved from http://news.bbc.co.uk/1/hi/england/devon/6706825.stm. Accessed on June 24, 2013.

Borgers, A., Snellen, D., Poelman, J., & Timmermans, H. (2008). Preferences for car-restrained residential areas. *Journal of Urban Design, 13*(2), 257−267.

Bouvier, D. (2005). *GWL terrein à amsterdam, les potentialités d'un quartier sans voitures.* Lille, France: Agence de développement et d'urbanisme de Lille Métropole.

Brighton, & Hove City Council. (2005). *Brighton and Hove local plan policy HO7: Car free housing.* Brighton, UK.

BUPA. (2007). *Cycling and health.* Retrieved from http://www.bupa.co.uk/health_information/html/healthy_living/lifestyle/exercise/cycling/cycling_health.html. Accessed on March 26, 2007.

Camden L. B. (2012). *Annual monitoring report 2011/12.* Retrieved from www.camden.gov.uk. London Borough of Camden, UK.

CLG. (2006). *Planning policy statement 3 (PPS3): Housing.* London: Department of Communities and Local Government.

Crawford, J. H. (2000). *Carfree cities*. Utrecht, UK: International Books.

DETR. (2000). *Planning policy guidance note 3: Housing*. London: The Stationery Office.

DETR. (2001). *Planning policy guidance note 13: Transport*. London: The Stationery Office.

DfT. (2005). *Making residential travel plans work: Good practice guidelines for new development*. Retrieved from www.dft.gov.uk. Department for Transport, Transport 2000 Trust, London.

DfT (2013). *National travel survey: 2012*. London, UK: Department for Transport.

Eastwood, M. (2008). *Slateford green transport study*. Edinburgh, UK: Dunedin Canmore Housing Association.

Gemeente Groningen. (2008). *Statistisch jaarboek*. Groningen, the Netherlands.

Glasgow City Council. (2009). *City plan RES 7 - car free housing*. Retrieved from http://www.glasgow.gov.uk/index.aspx?articleid=7861. Accessed on June 24, 2013.

Glenister, D. (1996). Exercise and mental health: A review. *Journal of the Royal Society of Health, 116*(1), 7–13.

Hass-Klau, C. (1993). Impact of pedestrianization and traffic calming on retailing: A review of the evidence from Germany and the UK. *Transport Policy, 1*(1), 21–31. doi:10.1016/0967-070X(93)90004-7

Kingston Federation of Residents. (2013). *Plan for huge student block unites opposition*. Retrieved from http://www.kingstonfed.org/wordpress/plan-for-huge-student-block-unites-opposition/. Accessed on June 2013

Melia, S. (2009). *Potential for carfree development in the UK*. Unpublished PhD. University of the West of England, Bristol, UK. Retrieved from www.stevemelia.co.uk

Melia, S., Barton, H., & Parkhurst, G. (2011). The paradox of intensification. *Transport Policy, 18*(1), 46–52.

Melia, S., Barton, H., & Parkhurst, G. (2013). Potential for carfree development in the UK. *Urban Design and Planning, 166*(2), 136–145.

Melia, S., Parkhurst, G., & Barton, H. (2010). Carfree, low car: What's the difference? *World Transport Policy & Practice, 16*(2), 24–32.

Nobis, C. (2003). The impact of car-free housing districts on mobility behaviour: Case study. *International conference on sustainable planning and development*, Skiathos Island, Greece (pp. 701–720).

Nützel, M. (1993). *Nutzung und Bewertung des Wohnumfeldes in Großwohngebieten am Beispiel der Nachbarschaften U und P in Nürnberg-Langwasser No. 119*. Bayreuth, Germany: Universitat Bayreuth.

ONS. (2013). *2011 census*. Retrieved from www.nomisweb.gov.uk. Accessed on June 2013.

Ornetzeder, M., Hertwich, E. G., Hubacek, K., Korytarova, K., & Haas, W. (2008). The environmental effect of car-free housing: A case in Vienna. *Ecological Economics, 65*(3), 516–530.

Parkhurst, G. (2003). Regulating cars and buses in cities: The case of pedestrianisation in Oxford. *Economic Affairs, 23*(2), 16–21.

Pucher, J., & Buelher, R. (2007). At the frontiers of cycling: Policy innovations in the Netherlands, Denmark and Germany. *World Transport Policy & Practice, 13*, 13.

RCEP. (2007). *The urban environment No. 26*. Norwich, UK: Royal Commission on Environmental Pollution, The Stationery Office.

Scheurer, J. (2001). *Urban ecology, innovations in housing policy and the future of cities: Towards sustainability in neighbourhood communities*. Unpublished Thesis (PhD), Murdoch University Institute of Sustainable Transport, Perth, Australia.

Scotsman.com. (2007). *I'm sorry but you can't park here, there, or anywhere.* Retrieved from http://www.scotsman.com/news/i-m-sorry-but-you-can-t-park-here-there-or-anywhere-1-1348372. Accessed on June 2013.

Tsubohara, S. (2007). *The effect and modification of the traffic circulation plan (VCP)-traffic planning in Groningen in the 1980s No. 317.* Groningen, the Netherlands: Urban and Regional Studies Institute.

World Carfree Network. (2013). *Homepage.* Retrieved from www.worldcarfree.net. Accessed on June 2013.

Wright, L. (2005). *Sustainable transport: A source book for developing cities, carfree development No. 3c.* Eschborn, Germany: GTZ.

CHAPTER 11

THREE FACES OF PARKING: EMERGING TRENDS IN THE U.S.

Rachel R. Weinberger

ABSTRACT

Purpose – *Parking policy in the United States is dominated by zoning codes with minimum parking requirements stipulated for a variety of uses. Some cities have realized that this approach has not yielded the desired policy outcomes; instead, it may be causing unintended consequences including added auto-travel, dispersed development, congestion, and air pollution that cities now wish to mitigate.*

This paper identifies historic and contemporary trends in United States' parking policy as cities gain additional insight and embrace new priorities.

Methodology/approach – *Three emerging trends in the U.S. context are identified: Rethinking zoning codes that require parking with development; introducing pricing to better manage curb resources thereby cutting down curb-space competition; and looking for urban design solutions to parking access, location and on-site placement which can lead to more efficient mode use decisions.*

The chapter provides an analysis of cases showing how cities are now seeking alternative approaches.

Parking: Issues and Policies
Transport and Sustainability, Volume 5, 235–258
Copyright © 2014 by Emerald Group Publishing Limited
All rights of reproduction in any form reserved
ISSN: 2044-9941/doi:10.1108/S2044-994120140000005021

Findings — *After many years of policy intervention focused on the alleviation of parking shortages by requiring additional off-street parking, cities are now seeking alternative approaches.*

Practical implications — *Cities can learn from each other's experiences. New paradigms in parking policy will lead to different social outcomes: they could increase the cost of auto use (disadvantaging the poor) but decrease auto dependence (favoring the poor).*

Originality/value of paper — *The originality of this chapter is in the juxtaposition and analysis of trends that have, heretofore, had little exposure.*

Keywords: Parking minimums; curbside management; off-street parking; performance pricing; adaptive reuse; shared parking

INTRODUCTION

It was once believed that providing abundant parking was the key to making desirable, successful urban places: the primary objective of parking regulation was to ensure enough parking to accommodate everyone while avoiding negative spillovers on adjacent land uses. A negative spillover occurs when patrons to your neighbor's establishment park in such a way as to impede your ability to park in the most convenient location for your own needs. The solution to this concern is embodied in minimum off-street parking requirements, which have been applied nearly universally, though far from uniformly, across the United States (Goodman, 2013; see Institute of Transportation Engineers, 2010).

These requirements, applied through zoning codes, oblige developers to provide a certain number of parking spaces per square meter of development to ensure enough parking. The explicit question of "enough parking for what?" has almost never been posed, but the implicit answer is "enough to satisfy demand for free parking generated by demand for access to the land use." Initially it seemed like a reasonable way to have developers mitigate potentially negative impacts of their developments on existing uses. Further, it was believed that this requirement would alleviate excess demand on existing street parking. Instead, the result of parking minimums has been the creation of three to four parking spaces per automobile in the United States (Davis, Pijanowsi, Robinson, & Engel, 2010), an artificial "market" in which 99% of parking is free to the user (Shoup, 2005), and a culture of entitlement with respect to parking that makes it difficult to implement policy and operational changes. Further, the original problems of spillover and excess demand at the curb have been left largely unsolved. Perceived parking shortages, manifest in over-crowding at the curb, persist in many locations.

With greater recognition of how parking supply figures in a cycle of car-dependence, parking minimums are now understood to contribute to dispersed land uses, depressed development, and degradation of the pedestrian and cycling environment (see Weinberger, Kaehny, & Rufo, 2010). Dysfunction caused by poorly conceived parking policies is seen as an impediment to creating an effective and balanced urban transportation system. Because parking supply induces auto use, it is also tied to increased traffic and air pollution. Several cities, as they tally the unintended consequences of their minimum parking requirements, have begun to question the planning assumptions that drove their policies in the first place. Little by little cities are leaping into the unknown and rethinking their zoning with respect to parking requirements. That leap is one of three trends that this chapter explores.

This changing perspective, combined with new technology, has spurred changes in curbside parking practices in the downtown areas of several American cities. Increasingly cities understand that curb parking shortages in a given area may well be coupled with excess capacity off-street and even excess capacity at nearby curbs. This understanding has led to an increased focus on better managing curb parking demand, rather than attempting to ease perceived on-street constraints by increasing off-street supply. Cities are recognizing that without managing the entire parking system, generation of additional off-street space only leads to off-street surpluses. Curb management constitutes the second trend explored in this chapter.

Design and placement of parking spaces relative to the land uses they serve make a difference in terms of how a neighborhood is perceived and the decisions that residents make with respect to how they will access a particular use – that is, by car or some other means. Street design can facilitate or present barriers that also affect parking utilization. These urban design issues constitute the third theme of this chapter.

After establishing the context by briefly reviewing the history of parking regulation in the United States, these themes are explored in depth. All three trends – rethinking parking minimums; applying performance standards as a management tool for curb parking; and employing better urban design principles to parking locations – mitigate negative environmental impacts frequently associated with auto dependence. These trends represent a departure from early thinking that had assumed only benign impacts of increased automobile accommodation. Eliminating minimums (introducing maximums), applying performance standards, and revisiting design decisions promise to result in higher quality of life, less pollution and congestion, and more vibrant and safer urban centers.

HISTORY

Parking supply and management has been a matter of public policy in the United States since the early twentieth century when cars began to compete for urban space. City leaders suspected that parking operations and parking shortages added to congestion (Weinstein, 2004) and studies dating to at least 1927 show that drivers cruising for parking can comprise a large proportion of traffic on downtown streets (Shoup, 2005). Vehicles maneuvering in and out of spaces can impede traffic flow, and double-parked vehicles have a detrimental effect on street capacity, not on on-street capacity. In fact, such remedies as on-street parking bans, charging for curb parking, building off-street lots, using remote lots, and implementing transit-based park-and-ride lots had been suggested as early as the mid-1920s and in some cases earlier (Weinstein, 2004).

In 1956, the year the interstate highway construction was initiated, the Bureau of Public Roads (BPR) published a book defining the parking problem and solution (BPR, 1956). The authors explicitly promoted parking solutions to ease auto use, not necessarily to improve accessibility and, unfortunately, without a sense of how that might affect the rest of a city's functions. The underlying philosophy was that motorists should not have to pay much, if anything, for parking. They should not be inconvenienced with time-wasting searches or walks that exceed more than a few minutes. Any competition for parking among new motoring visitors and existing users was meant to be eliminated. Planners steeped in the BPR philosophy defined parking demand to be the level experienced at the development's thirtieth busiest hour (for U.S. shopping centers, e.g., this would be during the weekends leading up to Christmas when shopping is heaviest). Thus, the definition of demand ensures that parking would be over-supplied 99% of the time.

American city leaders responded to this guidance and to the political pressure for parking by increasing the supply of both curbside and off-street parking. Cities removed curbside parking bans, built government-funded parking garages, allowed the construction of privately funded garages, metered curbside parking on shopping streets, and, ultimately, required that both new residential and commercial development include off-street parking. Such is the thirst for new parking that a Brooklyn City Council member, in 2011, proposed increasing curb parking by marking New York City's 450 broken fire hydrants as legal parking spots (Goldenberg, 2011).

This new thinking and implementation of these policies had an immediate and lasting effect on urban and suburban densities and land use patterns. The low marginal cost of land in suburban locations meant the cost of developing parking there was also very low but urban development, where land was more costly, suffered. It was considered a foregone conclusion that "[p]arking is the prime convenience advantage of the [suburban] shopping center over the central business district" (American Society of Planning Officials, 1954, p. 4). So in an effort to maintain a competitive edge over suburban destinations, cities built garages in their downtowns, sometimes sacrificing existing buildings to do so. New zoning codes required developers to incorporate, at a minimum, sufficient off-street parking to meet the highest projected demand under the assumption that all visitors would come by private automobile.

Because we better understand the endogenous relationship between supply and demand, we can say with confidence that the increase in parking induced additional demand for driving and, in turn, greater demands for parking (Guo, 2013; McCahill, Haerter-Ratchfrod, Garrick, & Atkinson-Palombo, 2014; Weinberger, 2012). By creating accommodations for potential auto trips, cities inadvertently induced them. It was not auto traffic per se that changed U.S. cities but the cities' accommodations to cars that invited and induced more auto traffic. Center City Philadelphia provides a classic, and nearly contemporary, example. Data collected in Philadelphia from 1980 to 2000 show a 40% increase in off-street parking in the region's core, an area well served by transit. The increase in parking was attended by an equivalent increase in drive-alone commute trips and complementary drop in transit trips – albeit with no drop in transit services (Philadelphia City Planning Commission, 2005, Chap. 2, p. 5). The additional parking added no net gain in accessibility nor economic growth; it simply accommodated, and very likely induced, an increase in auto trips with related increases in congestion and pollution.

Even with ample transit capacity and a population loss of 500,000 people since its 1950 peak, Philadelphia felt compelled to build more parking spaces. In 2004, the city destroyed three landmarked buildings to add 600 more parking spaces as part of a larger project; the project foundered and all that remains is a surface parking lot where the buildings were razed (Harris, 2003; Kostelini, 2013).

Planners and transportation system managers are coming to appreciate that requiring parking to meet unconstrained demand may not be efficient nor is it a desirable objective. Instead, as will be explored in the next section, strategies to better manage supply and demand or, in some cases, to reduce demand, are being tested. Parking policy is increasingly nuanced. It is used to generate revenue, as in the Chicago case where the parking meter system was sold to close a budget gap. With straightforward price signals, it is used to decrease the "cruising" for free spaces that contributes to unwanted congestion and unnecessary emissions; such pricing also mitigates parking in bus stops, the travel lane, at fire hydrants, and other illegal locations. New York has instituted "peak-period" parking charges and San Francisco, Los Angeles, Seattle, and Washington, DC have been using performance pricing to accomplish these goals. Parking policy is being reinvented to mitigate disruptions to the urban fabric and to recalibrate the allocation of land, both rights-of-way and parking lots, among users of all modes as in Portland, Oregon, where parking development rights may be transferred among properties.

EMERGING TRENDS

After the introduction of parking minimums in the 1960s, there was very little innovation in parking policy until the new century. Recently a number of initiatives have been undertaken to correct the unintended consequences of past parking policy. These initiatives seek to use parking policy to restore urban centers, mitigating some of the congestion, air pollution, and infrastructure and public health costs associated with over-reliance on automobiles. We now turn to the three emerging trends identified in the introduction. The first is the increasing call to reduce or eliminate minimum parking requirements; this is sometimes coupled with implementation of maximum parking allowances. The second is a trend to manage curb inefficiencies, where spot shortages or underutilization are norms, with performance targets – this is typically manifest in pricing strategies. The third, a natural outgrowth of the first two, looks at urban design elements that create barriers to reaching physically proximate but psychologically distant parking spaces. Failure to address these barriers promotes the perception of shortage even where none may exist.

Parking Requirements in the Zoning Code: Minimums and Maximums

There are two tools in the zoning kit that are used to regulate the amount of parking in a city. These are parking minimums, which are fairly ubiquitously applied across the United States – indeed, even Houston, Texas, which boasts of having no zoning code, has parking minimum requirements embedded in its building code – and parking maximums, which have been implemented in a small number of jurisdictions.

Minimum requirements prescribe a lower bound on the number of parking places that must accompany development. Developers are free to supply more than the minimum. However, because minimums tend to err on the side of over-requiring, they rarely do (Guo & Ren, 2013; McDonnell, Madar, & Been, 2011). Because minimums represent only a lower bound on parking, they can have no mitigating impact on traffic generated by new land uses. Therefore, these regulations will either have no effect or they will increase traffic by creating a market distortion that artificially inflates parking supply. In addition to induced auto traffic, this often results in underutilized parking. Minimum parking requirements can also increase housing costs and commercial-lease rates, as developers recoup the cost of providing excess parking by inflating prices for dwelling units or building space.

In addition to the market distortion, there are two problematic issues with how minimums are set. Minimum parking requirements are nearly universally set as a function of the building size and use and seldom as a function of automobile capacity. As discussed in the next section, buildings are durable so their size is fairly fixed; meanwhile, land uses are dynamic and may change throughout the building's functional life. Furthermore, as consistent as is the practice of setting use-based requirements, the number of spaces required for equivalent uses is extremely varied, to the point of seeming arbitrary. Fig. 1, for example, shows the distribution of parking requirements per 400 congregants for houses of worship in a sample of 38 U.S. cities with similar densities and transit systems.

Durable Infrastructure

A fantastic example of the durability of buildings, and what planners call adaptive reuse, is the Musée d'Orsay in Paris. Once a train station, it is now a museum. The conversion prompts the question: are the parking requirements for a museum the same as they are for a train station?

A more typical example of adaptive reuse is illustrated in Fig. 2. This building, in Berkeley, CA, was built and opened in the 1940s as The Berkeley Bowl, a recreational bowling alley with 16 lanes. In the early 1970s

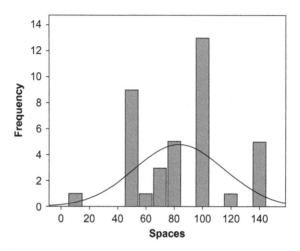

Fig. 1. Number of Parking Spaces Required for a 400-Person House of Worship.
Source: Goodman; Analysis: author

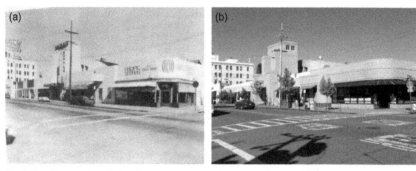

Berkeley Recreational Bowl circa 1970   Any Mountain circa 2013

Fig. 2. Berkeley Bowl Then and Now. (a) Berkeley Recreational Bowl, circa 1970.
(b) Any Mountain, circa 2013. *Source*: (a) Photo courtesy of the Berkeley
Architectural Heritage Association. (b) Photo by Gordon Hansen.

the bowling alley shut its doors and the building stood empty for several
years. In 1977 the building was reinvented as a grocery store, and playing
off the double meaning of "bowl," the owners kept the original name for
the business. The new Berkeley Bowl operated for 22 years before decamp-
ing to a larger location. A new use was soon found for the building and it

opened as a sporting goods store – its current incarnation. Do a 1940s bowling alley, a 1970s grocery store, and a 21st century sporting goods store have the same parking requirements? According to the Institute of Transportation Engineers' *Parking Generation* report, the bowling alley should have had 5.6 spaces per lane, or, 90 parking spaces; the grocery store should have had 120 spaces (140 if it were a discount grocery store); and the sporting goods store also about 120 spaces[1] (ITE, 2010). When a use pre-dates the zoning requirement it is customary that the requirement be waived but subsequent uses are usually required to comply with the zoning code (see the Minnesota example on page 246). Fortunately, in spite of the local code's requirement for 70 spaces (lower than the 120 suggested by ITE), the planning board allowed each use change without the additional parking. All three uses have functioned exceptionally well with the site's 12 parking spaces.

Not quite as well-known as the Musée D'Orsay, but perhaps as dramatic a conversion, is the 1844 Church of the Holy Communion depicted in Fig. 3. The congregation held services for over 125 years in Manhattan but joined with another church and sold its building in the early 1970s. After several years as a drug rehabilitation center, the property was again re-purposed when it was converted to the Limelight nightclub.

Fig. 3. Limelight Shops Nee Limelight Nee Church of the Holy Communion. *Source*: Photo by Rachel Weinberger.

The Limelight opened in 1983 and was a primary Manhattan night life destination until 2007. Today it stands as a shopping center with 19,000 square
feet of retail space (New York City Department of City Planning, PLUTO
database, 2013). According to ITE's Parking Generation report, a church of
that size should have at least 210 parking spaces. An adult cabaret – the
closest land use category to "nightclub" found in the ITE's guidance on
parking – would require fewer (only 115 spaces) and a shopping center,
fewer still at about 90. Had the church been built with its original suggested
complement of parking spaces, then the converted use would have had 95
surplus spaces. What should the nightclub have done with 95 excess parking
spaces? And the shopping center with 120 excess? Fortunately, there are no
spaces at all on the site and it is situated in a zone of parking maximums,
so neither "new" owner had to contend with all that excess. But had this scenario played out in a typical U.S. city or town, rather than in the heart of
Manhattan where parking maximums are in effect, the story would have
been quite different. And what if the conversion had gone the other way?
Could a shopping center be turned into an adult cabaret? Subsequently,
could it be converted into a house of worship? In most places, for want
of additional parking spaces, the conversion could not have gone the
other way.

The Berkeley Bowl and the Limelight are stories of successful reuse but a
far more typical story is of the restaurateur in Minnesota who, despite having contracted with nearby property owners to allow his wine bar customers
to park in their excess spaces, was denied permission to open his establishment because he didn't comply sufficiently with the zoning code's parking
requirements. The site which had previously housed a toy store had three
parking spaces, the number required for the original use. The zoning code
requires 10 for the new use. The proprietor of the restaurant arranged to
sub-lease additional spaces from a nearby dry cleaning business. This is an
ideal arrangement as the dry cleaner's hours of operation have very little
overlap with the wine bar's hours. But the dry cleaner wished to retain the
right to reclaim two of the spaces in the event they, themselves, needed
the spaces in the future. For want of two spaces, the city council denied permits to open the wine bar, preferring to leave an empty storefront, forego
jobs, tax revenue, and a more lively streetscape (Russo, 2012). This is a common story in the U.S. though one that is rarely documented. A proposed
use may fit in a built space but, without the requisite number of parking
spaces, the new use is not allowed. The storefront remains vacant causing
the city to lose tax income and damaging the vibrancy of the district where
the property is located.

Even when the use does not change, for example with residences, the parking "needs" can change. Minimums are typically set to accommodate the maximum number of cars that the household might choose to own, given an unconstrained supply of parking. For example, a three-bedroom home might have four parking spaces associated with it under the assumption of a nuclear family with two driving parents and the possibility of two children of driving age living there. But assuming the same family occupies the house for forty years, there may be only five, or at most, ten years during which both the children live at home after they have reached driving age. Simple arithmetic shows that for 75–87% of this family's life-cycle, the minimum parking requirement exceeds the number of drivers in the home.

Rethinking Accessory Use Minimums and Turning Away From Single-Use Requirements
In spite of the problems detailed above, parking minimums are alive and well in most U.S. cities, but there is a marked trend to revisit them. Emerging evidence shows that minimums are expensive in terms of added construction costs as well as opportunity cost. Parking is space intensive – typical space requirements in a lot or garage are 325–400 square feet per automobile (ITE, 2010), compared with:

- An office cubicle about 75 sq. ft. in 2010[2] (4 people could work in the space it takes to park one car);
- A table at a restaurant with 12–15 sq. ft. allotted per person (22 people could dine in the space it takes to park one car);
- A house of worship in the U.S. requires about 4.8 times more space for parking than it does for the physical building (Goodman, 2013).

An abundance of underutilized parking across the country and some recent high profile parking fiascos have caused more and more municipalities to consider reducing parking minimums. Many people would advocate abandoning them entirely. The three examples highlighted here represent almost $250 million spent by municipalities and private developers creating parking spaces for which there is, simply, no demand.

East River Plaza, a mall development in New York City consists of a 485,000 sq. ft. retail area accompanied by a 688,000 sq. ft. garage. Recent research shows that at the time of expected peak parking demand – a Saturday in the height of the Christmas shopping season – the garage was about 38% full (Gebhart, 2013). While the developers and neighborhood critics feared and expected much more auto access (based on suburban experiences) more than 50% of shoppers come to this mall on foot. The garage was estimated to have cost the developer $62.5 million yet it seems a $25 million dollar garage would have been sufficient. Early on in the project, the parking garage financing threatened to stop the development. This phenomenon is consistent with other findings that show parking requirements have a retarding effect on development.

Another mall development, the DC USA shopping center in Washington, DC, hosts 546,000 sq. ft. of retail space. As part of their package to woo the developer, the DC government agreed to finance the project's garage. The city's zoning requirements called for a 2,000 space garage. Ultimately, planners in the District Department of Transportation and the Office of Planning persuaded others in the city that the 2,000 spaces would be excessive. After internal negotiations, the city was able to persuade the developer and the prospective tenants that the city's own parking requirements were too high (personal communication with Karina Ricks, Principal, Nelson\Nygaard Consulting Associates [former Transit-Oriented Development Coordinator Washington, D.C. Department of City Planning.]). The city built a 1,000 space garage with a construction cost of $47 million. The total subsidy, which included a substantial reduction in land cost, was closer to $64 million. To date, the 1,000 spaces remain underutilized; about half are ever used (Hudson, 2013). The city is still liable to operate the garage and is now attempting to mitigate losses by permitting long-term leases on the parking spaces. These lease agreements guarantee commuter driving by ensuring cheap commuter parking to a very transit-oriented hub. While parking is still overbuilt, the city can take some comfort in knowing that there are only 500 spaces too many and not 1,500 spaces too many.

A final example of a garage fiasco is another project that was financed by a city as a contribution to a public-private partnership. The New York Yankees sought to build a new baseball stadium. As a condition of remaining in New York City, the team's owners negotiated an agreement by which the city substantially underwrote the stadium parking garage (O'Grady, 2012). The city provided $100 million in subsidies for the 9,000 space garage[3] and underwrote an additional $237 million in bonds. On game days the garage is partially filled but seldom more than 40%, the corporation that runs it has defaulted on their bond payments (O'Grady, 2012) and has yet to make a single payment to the city in rent or taxes (Gonzalez, 2013). The 2013 third quarter debt is $42 million (Gonzalez, 2013). Local politicians have called for the garage to be demolished and the 21 acres of donated parkland returned to the city.

Limiting Rather than Requiring Accessory Parking

A city might look to limiting, rather than requiring accessory parking to reduce traffic, to remove barriers to redevelopment, and/or to balance competing needs for space. In the 1970s, recognizing that more parking can lead to more driving and wishing to reduce driving, Portland, OR, New York, NY, and Boston, MA implemented parking maximums. They did so as part of their strategies to comply with the requirements of the Clean Air Act. By implementing parking maximums they sought to reduce auto use, thus they took a proactive step to reduce traffic-related air pollution and growth in emissions. Just as a reduction in parking would limit car use, an increase in parking would, in many cases, increase car use.

Trying to avoid the Minnesota outcome described earlier, Sacramento, California changed its parking code effective January 1, 2013. Recognizing that "[P]arking requirements for new land uses are outdated and designed primarily for suburban development, as opposed to existing urban and traditional neighborhoods," (Sacramento Community Development Department, 2012, p. 3) they eliminated minimums in some parts of the city and for some uses. They also allowed businesses to use off-site spaces and on-street parking to demonstrate how they will accommodate people coming by car. The new law empowers the Zoning Administrator to further reduce requirements by up to 75% if doing so promotes the city's goal of spurring in-fill development. It is too soon for rigorous analysis but early indications are that the code has worked as desired (personal communication with Greg Sandlund, Associate Planner, Community Development Department, City of Sacramento).

Another California city, Santa Monica, provides a model for Sacramento's expectations. Santa Monica has a small flexible parking district on one side of one of its main boulevards and "traditional" parking requirements on the other side. With a pedestrian friendly character, the "flexible" side generates eight times more sales tax revenue per square meter than the "traditional" side and does so with a more limited dedicated parking supply (Rubin, 2013).

Cities are waking up to the fact that over the years they have adopted suburban style parking requirements that frequently run counter to urban goals. Several have taken steps to reverse this course.

Performance Parking: Managing On-Street (Aka Curb) Parking

Some cities have recently adopted strategies of performance parking wherein they set a performance target for availability and use price and time limits to affect those targets. The major U.S. cities to adopt performance standards are Los Angeles, CA; San Francisco, CA; Seattle, WA; and Washington, DC. These cities have adopted dynamic pricing strategies to achieve the performance targets. New York City has adopted a related scheme in which the parking cost is higher during the afternoon "parking peak." Performance parking derives from behavioral economics and uses the idea that price can be, and should be, raised or lowered to attain a desired behavior outcome – in this case a certain level of parking demand.

Curbside parking meters were introduced in 1935, in downtown Oklahoma City, Oklahoma, at the behest of a department store owner who wanted to make parking more available for potential shoppers. His own employees had been parking at the curb and making it harder for customers to access the front door. Metering, recognized as an efficient way of encouraging "turnover" on the curb, spread quickly. By 1955, all major U.S. cities had metered their central business districts and retail shopping streets. Ensuring curb space for short-term shoppers and deliveries remains a primary goal of curbside parking management in the United States (Zalewski, Buckley, & Weinberger, 2011).

Although metering has been commonplace for more than fifty years, in recent history the political will to increase meter rates has been lacking (Zalewski et al., 2011). As a result, meters have become ineffective for promoting turnover. Oklahoma City's parking meter rates have more or less kept pace with inflation since 1935. But there has been no adjustment for the greater demand that came with the explosion of car ownership since their introduction in 1935. As a result, the typical price of metered parking today is just high enough to be an annoyance and far too low to effectively redistribute demand or maintain availability.

Using occupancy targets as their performance standards, cities are working to make their curb use more efficient. San Francisco has developed a branded system called SF*park* which adjusts rates at the block level and by time of day, when and where average occupancy rises above, or falls below, targeted thresholds. SF*park* employs a complex system of parking sensors and smart meters. The technology dependent system tracks occupancy to a very detailed level and has permitted the city to make rate adjustments relatively frequently. The city increases the price by $0.25 if the occupancy on a block exceeds 80%, and reduces the price if the occupancy is less than 60%. By increasing and decreasing the price in small increments they expect to distribute parking demand from very crowded blocks to less crowded ones. Analysis of the first two years of data show modest progress in attaining the project's goals (Millard-Ball, Weinberger & Hampshire, 2014).

Seattle has established similar goals for *SeaPark*, their curb management program. They have set a performance goal of one to two vacancies per block and then calculated the percentage occupancy target that corresponds to the vacancy they seek. The use of space available as a performance measure has a slight advantage over a uniform average occupancy because what is important to motorists is whether or not they find a space. For the same average occupancy, the probability of finding a space declines with block size. The Seattle approach does not include the technology employed in SF*park;* instead they rely on manual surveys and less frequent rate adjustments. Seattle also uses parking duration as a policy lever to achieve their targets.

The underlying principle of both systems is the same: set a performance goal for your system and then manage the system to meet that goal. Part of the success in each case is that the rate setting was taken out of the political process and pegged to a measurable outcome. Table 1 summarizes the key features of these projects.

Urban Design, Parking, and Alternatives to Driving

Design decisions include parking lot layout, street design, location relative to the destination and on-site placement. The evidence suggests that the location and placement of parking resources can profoundly affect street life and mode choice. Furthermore, poor street design can impede efficient use of parking supply. These phenomena are illustrated in the final three cases.

The Jefferson National Expansion Monument (Gateway Arch)
The Jefferson National Expansion Monument in St. Louis is maintained and operated by the United States Department of the Interior National Park Service. To accommodate visitors, the Park Service maintains a 1,200-space parking garage at the northern end of the monument grounds. A typical visit to the park involves driving across the bridge depicted in the southern part of Fig. 4, traveling north on the Interstate highway and then turning into the Monument grounds. Once on the Monument grounds, a visitor would park in the garage and walk for five to seven minutes to reach the Monument and the museum. At the end of the visit, the visitor walks back to the garage, drives out of the park back onto the Interstate highway, and continues their journey. Of course some people come from the north and leave toward the south but their journey is essentially the same − in either case, the downtown of St. Louis is completely by-passed. Visitors miss the opportunity to see the city and the city does not benefit from

Table 1. Two Approaches to Performance Parking

	San Francisco SF*park*	Seattle SeaPark
Program goals/expected benefits	Easier parking, faster transit (reduced congestion)	Increase parking availability; reduce congestion
Performance standard	60–80% occupancy	1–2 spaces free/block depends on average block size in area
Policy levers	Vary price	Vary price and time limits
Vary prices	By block and time of day	By area and subarea and by time of day
External funds	~$20 m (Partner with Federal Highway Administration)	~$0
Data collection	Continuous	"at least once/year"
Technology	High	Low
Politics	Politics are taken out of the day-to-day operations: The respective agencies in charge are authorized to vary prices according to the performance goal.	
Public Information	Highly dynamic (web based)	Relatively static (extensive use of signage)

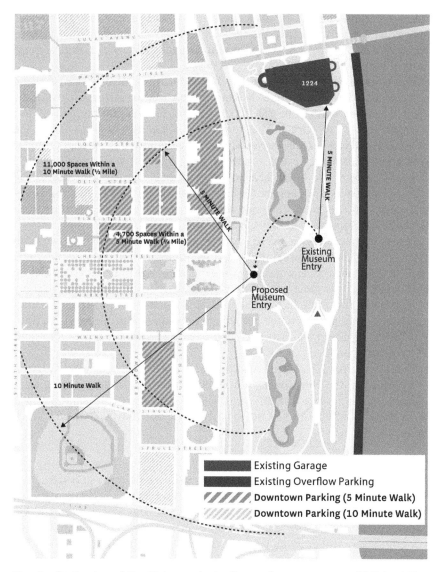

Fig. 4. St. Louis and the Gateway Arch. *Source*: Image courtesy of Michael Van Valkenburgh Associates, modified by Alyssa Pichardo, Nelson\Nygaard Consulting Associates.

tourist trade that should be associated with hosting a national Monument and major tourist attraction. As the diagram shows, the monument lies to the east of St. Louis, a city replete with partially empty parking lots and garages.

The contour lines in Fig. 4 show how much available parking can be found in the city at the same distance as tourists would have to walk to reach the Monument from the Park's garage. Eliminating the garage and directing visitors to park in the downtown is a potential win/win for the visitor and the city. The visitor experience is enhanced by enjoying both the Monument and the city and for those who still prefer to avoid the city, they may park at one of the nearest alternate sites and walk directly to the Monument. There are benefits to the city by adding foot traffic and probable sales and this plan does not require visitors to walk any further to reach the Monument than they currently do.

Although the garage is already built and considered a sunk cost, at some point it will need to be rebuilt. In the meantime, it has to be maintained and the use of the garage site for alternate park activities could be considered. At the time of rebuilding, or when considering the parking arrangements for other such attractions, it is worth noting that garage construction is estimated to range between $26k and $45k per space (ITE, 2010 – inflation adjusted) and hence a 1,200 space garage costs between $31 and $54 million to build.

Eliminating the Park's garage and directing visitors to the already available parking in the downtown will not inconvenience visitors (as there is no increased walking requirement), and will save millions of dollars and put an average of 8,000 tourists on the streets of downtown St. Louis every day.

Medford, Massachusetts
The city of Medford experiences an acute parking shortage in a particular part of its downtown. When Medford Square's derelict downtown garage collapsed, the city proposed to replace it with a new $7.5 million garage. Their expectation was to relieve pressure on parking. A planning analysis was conducted to better understand the city's parking inventory and the pressures on the specific area where the shortage was felt. The study revealed that the parking shortage was highly localized and that within a relatively short distance there was ample available parking.

For advocates of performance parking the obvious solution would be to increase the price of parking in the high pressure area and to drop the price for parking in the area of greater availability. This would, in theory, shift the demand and solve the problem of the parking shortage. But the theory misses the complexity introduced by physical and psychological obstacles such as those encountered in the Medford case.

As Fig. 5 reveals, the parking surplus was separated from the area of shortage by a complex intersection which created such a serious impediment that performance pricing would not have been a straightforward exercise. The price differential would have to have been sufficiently exaggerated to overcome the obstacle presented by the arterial. In his research on

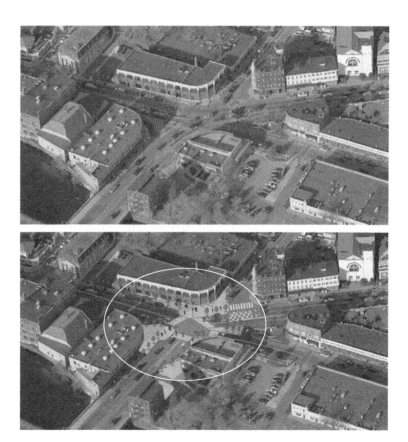

Fig. 5. Medford Square showing how a combination of traffic calming, signal improvements and streetscaping could make crossing Medford Square's intersection safer, faster, and more pleasant ("before" (above) and "after" (below)). *Source*: Nelson\Nygaard Consulting Associates.

"T" communities, Grannis (2005) shows that arterial crossings are an out-sized barrier to pedestrian access. Pedestrians have to have an extraordinary incentive to cross an arterial; most prefer to stay within the sub-street system circumscribed by the arterial boundaries. In the Medford case, long crossing distances and unfavorable signal timings exacerbated the arterial effect by making the available parking even further in time than the distance alone would have indicated. A redesign of the crossings could mediate the distance by improving the signal timing and recasting the arterial as a local business street. At $1.5 million, the intersection redesign would cost a fraction of the garage and could be considered a must do experiment before investing in the garage. Furthermore, it could have an effect similar to that in St. Louis in knitting together the two sides of the arterial — and in this case the two sides of the city — in a way that would improve opportunities for all. This improved design has not been implemented but it was sufficiently convincing that the city council decided to abandon its plan to build the garage while the intersection is under consideration.

Driving to Shop

The final case in this series examines the placement of parking. By looking at on-site parking placement, Maley and Weinberger (2011) took a fresh perspective on parking supply and its influence on mode choice. Most studies have looked simply at quantity of parking supplied and at what price but this study looked at parking placement and found that placement matters, perhaps profoundly. The case looked at six grocery stores in the City of Philadelphia. Three of the stores had a "suburban" design in which a grocery store was placed at the center of a large lot surrounded by the requisite parking spaces as stipulated in the zoning codes. The other three grocery stores were built up to the lot lines and had entrances at the side-walk thus contributing to a continuous street wall typical of what is referred to as pedestrian-oriented design. These "urban" stores had their requisite parking allotments arrayed in garages, typically built above the store. In some cases the parking was shared by other uses within the devel-opment; thus reducing the total parking built in the area but still ensuring a sufficient amount for parkers at these groceries. The difference in design is captured in Fig. 6. In all cases the stores were situated within relatively dense neighborhoods, all of them well within the city boundaries with simi-lar access characteristics.

Looking only at people who lived within a one-half-mile walk shed of the grocery stores, Maley and Weinberger (2011) found that more people drove to shop to the grocery stores that were surrounded by parking while

Fig. 6. Suburban and Urban Parking Layout. *Source*: Photos by Rebecca Wetzler.

more walked to the stores that fronted on the street. The result was made more surprising by controlling for income and car ownership; people who drove to the grocery store drove from neighborhoods where income and car ownership were lower – usually a predictor of less, not more, driving. The placement of the parking in the suburban style layout created an environment that was not conducive to walking while the urban style layout could accommodate the cars but did not favor them. One might say that the suburban style stores "invited" drivers while the urban style stores "invited" walkers. The parking placement affected mode choice and should, in turn, affect the amount of parking space that planners and developers might deem a reasonable complement to the primary use.

CONCLUSION

After several years of urban population loss, U.S. cities are growing again. As they do, they realize that competing with the suburbs on suburban terms is a losing proposition. One of the many powerful tools that cities have with which to reinvent themselves is parking policy. Parking is an asset and should be managed as such, particularly where competition for land and curb space is high. Providing too much drives the price lower, undermining development, and inadvertently subsidizing auto use. There are many promising trends such as the three outlined here that suggest a seismic shift in how parking has been viewed and how it is beginning to be used.

Cities are coming to realize that there is little or no direct demand for parking. Demand for parking is simply a manifestation of demand for access and the provision of parking may be understood as an amenity in an environment rich with alternatives to driving. Parking capacity should be sized consistently with the street system. If more spaces are provided than the street system has capacity to feed, those spaces, and the real estate they consume, will be wasted. Conversely, permitting fewer spaces can provide a check on congestion and provide more opportunities for "complete street" retrofits that play into cities' multimodal mobility strengths.

Long-term practice in over-requiring accessory parking, failing to tie parking infrastructure to the transportation system and under-managing curb parking resources have induced unsustainable levels of demand, contributing to congestion, air pollution and auto dependence along the way. Cities that have tried to reverse declining fortunes by replicating the conspicuous, low-cost parking abundance of suburban commercial centers have failed from an economic development perspective as well. Parking's voracious consumption of real estate has meant that these ill-fated efforts have come directly at the expense of the walkability, transit-viability, and urban design virtues that cities require to thrive on their own terms.

NOTES

1. It seems surprising that a grocery store which relies on a much greater volume of sales, and presumably customers, would have the same recommended level of parking as the lower volume sporting goods store.
2. http://theweek.com/article/index/211935/americas-workspaces-are-shrinking-unless-youre-the-boss
3. Although the Yankee's old stadium had more seats, the new garage has more parking spaces.

ACKNOWLEDGMENTS

Many thanks to the anonymous reviewers, the editors of this volume, and my Nelson\Nygaard colleagues — particularly Thomas Brown and Jennifer Gennari — for thoughtful insights on earlier drafts. Thanks to Rebecca Wetzler and Gordon Hansen for their journeys to the field in pursuit of legal photographs and to James Bennett for the St. Louis image.

REFERENCES

American Society of Planning Officials. (1954). *Site design, parking and zoning for shopping centers.* Information Report No. 59. Retrieved from http://www.planning.org/pas/at60/report59.htm

Bureau of Public Roads. (1956). *Parking guide for cities.* Washington, DC: Bureau of Public Roads.

Davis, A., Pijanowsi, B., Robinson, K., & Engel, B. (2010). The environmental and economic costs of sprawling parking lots in the United States. *Land Use Policy, 27*(2), 255–261.

Gebhart, K. (2013). *Parking oversupply in East Harlem: An analysis of parking occupancy and mode usage at East River Plaza in New York City.* Transportation Research Board Annual Meeting, Washington, DC.

Goldenberg, S. (2011, March 21). Pol plugs parking at broken fire hydrants. *New York Post.* Retrieved from http://nypost.com/2011/03/21/pol-plugs-parking-at-broken-fire-hydrants/

Gonzalez, J. (2013, April 2). Yankee stadium garage deep in the hole, missing April 1 payment on $237M in bonds. *New York Daily News.* Retrieved from http://www.nydailynews.com/new-york/yankee-stadium-garage-company-strikes-opening-day-article-1.1305278

Goodman, S. (2013). *Graphing parking accessible parking wonkery.* Retrieved from Graphingparking.com

Guo, Z. (2013). Does residential parking supply affect household car ownership? The case of New York City. *Journal of Transport Geography, 26,* 18–28.

Grannis, R. (2005). T-communities: Pedestrian street networks and residential segregation in Chicago, Los Angeles, and New York. *City and Community, 4*(3), 295–321.

Guo, Z., & Ren, S. (2013). From minimum to maximum: Impact of the London parking reform on residential parking supply from 2004 to 2010? *Urban Studies 50*(6), 1183–1200.

Harris, L. (2003, September 24). Panel OKs 3 demolitions on Sansom. The Historical Commission also approved a multiuse development in the same area near Rittenhouse Square. *Philadelphia Inquirer.* Retrieved from http://articles.philly.com/2003-09-24/news/25458007_1_historic-buildings-demolition-request-development-plan

Hudson, K. (2013, July 9). Cities cut parking mandates: To Promote Transit, District of Columbia considers easing rules on developers. *The Wall Street Journal.* Available at http://online.wsj.com/news/articles/SB10001424127887324251504578579982643189770

Institute of Transportation Engineers. (2010). *Parking generation* (4th ed.). Washington, DC.

Kostelini, N. (2013, January 25). Prominent property is back up for sale: 1911 Walnut Street. *Philadelphia Biz Journal.* Available at http://www.bizjournals.com/philadelphia/print-edition/2013/01/25/prominent-property-is-back-up-for.html?page=all

Maley, D. & Weinberger, R. (2011). *Food shopping in the urban environment: Parking supply, destination choice and mode choice.* Transportation Research Board Annual Meeting. Washington, DC.

McCahill, C., Haerter-Ratchfrod, J., Garrick, N., & Atkinson-Palombo, C. (2014). *Parking in urban centers: Policies, supplies, and implications in six cities.* Transportation Research Board Annual Meeting. Washington, DC.

McDonnell, S., Madar, J., & Been., V. (2011). Minimum parking requirements and housing affordability in New York City. *Housing Policy Debate, 21*(1), 45–68.

Millard-Ball, A., Weinberger, R., & Hampshire, R. (2014). Is the curb 80% full or 20% empty? Assessing the impacts of San Francisco's parking pricing experiment. *Transportation Research Part A, 63,* 76–92

New York City Department of City Planning. (2013). *Primary land use tax output (PLUTO)* [Data file].

O'Grady J. (2012, October 11). Yankee Stadium Parking Company defaults on its bonds. Transportation Nation (WNYC radio). Retrieved from http://www.wnyc.org/story/285430-yankees-stadium-parking-company-defaults-on-its-bonds/

Philadelphia City Planning Commission. (2005). Center City Parking Evaluation Final Report. Philadelphia, PA.

Rubin, C. (2013). *Curbing downtown parking requirements: Its effects on Santa Monica land uses, urban form and municipal finances.* Unpublished Master's Thesis, University of California, Los Angeles and report to the Los Angeles Department of City Planning Design Studio, Los Angeles, CA.

Russo, L. (2012, February 21). Striking out on cupcakes, pizza, parking and business development. *Star Tribune.* Retrieved from http://www.startribune.com/local/yourvoices/139584884.html

Sacramento Community Development Department. (2012). *Zoning code parking update.* Report to the City Council Report ID 2012-00697. Retrieved from http://www.cityofsacramento.org/dsd/planning/long-range/parking/documents/Council_Report_103112.pdf

Shoup, D. (2005). *High cost of free parking.* Chicago, IL: American Planning Association.

Weinberger, R. (2012). Death by a thousand curb-cuts: Evidence on the effect of minimum parking requirements on the choice to drive. *Transport Policy, 20*(March), 93–102.

Weinberger, R., Kaehny J., & Rufo, M. (2010). *U.S. parking policies: An overview of management strategies.* New York, NY: Institute for Transportation and Development Policy.

Weinstein, A. (2004). Curing congestion: Competing plans for a "loop highway" and parking regulations in Boston in the 1920s. *Journal of Planning History, 3*(4), 292–311.

Zalewski, A., Buckley, S., & Weinberger, R. (2011). *Regulating curb space: Developing a framework to understand and improve curbside management.* Transportation Research Board Annual Meeting. Washington DC.

CHAPTER 12

PARKING SUPPLY AND DEMAND IN LONDON

David Leibling

ABSTRACT

Purpose — *The purpose of this study is to measure the supply and demand for parking in London to determine whether there is sufficient provision for night-time residential needs and to determine whether policies designed at controlling car ownership by restricting residential parking are effective.*

Methodology/approach — *The history of parking controls and early studies of parking in Central London are reviewed to put into context recent surveys of parking supply undertaken by MVA. Data from the National Travel Survey, the English Housing Survey and various travel demand surveys by Transport for London have been analysed to determine the overnight demand for parking and the supply both off-street and on-street.*

Findings — *The study shows that there appears to be saturation in inner London for controlled on-street parking (which is the majority of available parking) and high utilisation for off-street parking. In outer London, there is more spare capacity. The evidence suggests that restricting residential parking space does not limit the growth in car*

Parking: Issues and Policies
Transport and Sustainability, Volume 5, 259–289
ISSN: 2044-9941/doi:10.1108/S2044-994120140000005013

ownership especially in outer London where the car is an essential part of modern living.

Practical implications — *Restrictive policies on parking supply in new developments leads to unsightly and dangerous parking on streets not designed for parking or illegal parking on footways. Policy makers must appreciate that car ownership will continue to rise and that parking spaces must be provided, if necessary, underground.*

Originality/value of study — *The study uses several different sources of data to investigate the under-researched area of parking availability which is of considerable importance to transport planners and policy makers.*

Keywords: Parking; supply and demand; London

INTRODUCTION

This chapter provides an introduction to parking policies in London, the history of controls and how they are presently managed. Data from the National Travel Survey (NTS), annual London Travel Demand Surveys undertaken by Transport for London (TfL) and the national census are used to investigate where motorists park at night in inner and outer London. Alongside these studies, two surveys of available parking spaces in London by MVA in 1999 and 2004 are reviewed together with the residential parking data provided by the English Housing Survey (EHS) to give information on supply. The demand and supply data are combined to see whether there is adequate residential parking on- and off-street, leading to the conclusion that there is saturation for residents' spaces on-street and a very high utilisation for residents' off-street parking. The recent trend to reduce off-street car parking (whether by planning restrictions or builders trying to increase the density of housing) will accentuate the pressure on parking space. The evidence for the link between car parking supply and car ownership in London is also reviewed and the conclusion is that there is only a weak negative correlation.

PARKING CONTROLS IN LONDON

The metropolis of London, as defined by the Greater London Authority Act of 1999, covers 159,000 hectares and is over 50 km wide from east to west and 40 km from north to south with a population in 2011 of 8.2 million, 3.3 million homes and 2.7 million cars. To this must be added a daily immigration of over a million people who work in London.

There are 33 boroughs (including the City of London which has slightly different constitutional powers) which are responsible for most transportation and planning issues, including the provision of parking and its pricing. The main roads, comprising about 5% of the total road length but accounting for some 30% of traffic, are controlled by TfL which also provides virtually all of the public transport in London. TfL is responsible to the elected Mayor of London who is monitored by elected local representatives sitting on the Greater London Assembly.

A large proportion of inner London (the lighter coloured areas in Fig. 1) was built in the nineteenth century before the age of the car, so the streets are narrow and not designed for large vehicles. Most of the homes in inner London are two or three storey buildings, originally single family homes but now often split into several individual dwellings, each potentially with

Fig. 1. Inner and Outer London Boroughs.

a car. They usually do not have off-street parking (Fig. 2) and, unlike city centres in other countries with purpose-built multiple occupancy homes, they rarely have underground car parks. Even in the leafy outer suburbs, with family houses built in the middle of the twentieth century, the facilities for parking cars did not anticipate the number of multi-car households and the garages provided are often too small for today's cars (Fig. 3). There is therefore a conflict between the need to keep roads free for moving traffic while also providing scarce road space for parking cars.

Until 1997, the provision of parking in residential development was subject to minimum standards, set by each borough, with builders required to provide a minimum number of off-street parking spaces usually based on the number of bedrooms, and hence inhabitants, in the property. When the Labour government was elected in 1997, one of its policies was to encourage public transport usage and restrict car use (although not explicitly car ownership). They reversed the parking standards to a maximum and restricted the number of off-street parking spaces (but encouraged the

Fig. 2. Nineteenth Century Terraced House with No Off-Street Parking and Controlled On-Street Parking. *Source:* Picture by the author.

Fig. 3. Wide Residential Street with (Unnecessary) Parking Control. Car Too Big to Fit into 1920s Garage. *Source:* Picture by the author.

provision of cycle spaces). Building developers welcomed this change as it meant that they could build more homes in the same space. However, car ownership has continued to rise and the extra cars are now parked on narrow residential roads. The Conservative government, elected in 2010, has removed this restriction and is encouraging local authorities to take account of increased car ownership in approving new building plans. However in some areas with good public transport, town planners are insisting on car-free developments with no off-street parking and no access to controlled on-street parking. It is clear that in the past 20 years the amount of additional parking provision has decreased (and is discussed further below) but it is too early to see whether this reversal of policy is now increasing the supply of parking spaces.

The first on-street parking restrictions in London were introduced in the 1920s, with the first meters (in Manchester Square) in 1958. Various studies were done between 1954 and 1965 looking at the impact of introducing parking meters and subsequently to study the impact of raising charges

(Inwood, 1965). The studies involved driving to a specific location in central London and then measuring the time it took to find a parking space within approximately 0.5 km. Measurements were made in February 1965 and then July 1965 after charges had been doubled or quadrupled (from 2½ p to 10 p). The report shows pictures of double parking which was not uncommon. The effect of the price increase was to reduce parking search times from 3.46 minutes to 1.40 minutes when the price was doubled and from 6.10 minutes to 1.04 minutes when it was quadrupled.

As car ownership and use has grown, the pressure on parking has increased and local authorities have introduced increasingly strict controls on the use of limited kerb space. A plan to introduce underground car parks in London squares was abandoned because of criticism of the disruption during building and the desire to try to reduce car commuting.

Parking in all of central London (within a 3 km radius of the centre), virtually all of inner London and a large part of outer London is now controlled by a system of single and double yellow lines, kerb markings and street signs which define when parking and loading are not allowed. On the most important through routes, managed by TfL, the markings are in red and the signage not only shows where parking and loading are *not* allowed, it also specifically shows where they *are* allowed. Infringements of parking controls are treated as civil offences and offenders are given or sent by post a Penalty Charge Notice (PCN) which outlines the details of the offence and the amount to be paid to the local authority.

Much of the control is done by Controlled Parking Zones (CPZs) where the hours of control are shown at the entry to a zone and do not have to be repeated in each street. Many London boroughs now have dozens of CPZs, ranging from a few streets to a wide area and covering the total borough, with hours varying from zone to zone. In areas where there is inadequate residential parking the controls act as a form of rationing. In other areas the parking restriction is for an hour or two each day and is designed to discourage all day parking by commuters − the hours vary so that enforcement officers can visit different streets at different times. Many restrictions are for the whole of the working day (8.00 am to 6.30 pm), often with additional loading restrictions in rush hours on main roads, and some extend into the evening to protect parking spaces for late coming residents. Very busy roads and dangerous junctions have 24 hour restrictions, marked by double yellow lines. The wide variation in times can lead to confusion amongst motorists.

Residents apply for permits to enable them to park in specially designated areas within the CPZs; prices range from around £120 per year in inner London to around £60 in outer London, often in a range based on engine emissions, with a higher charge for a second car. Visitors' permits are also available for residents to purchase and to give to visitors. The number of permits issued usually exceeds the number of on-street spaces available and a parking space is not guaranteed for a resident. Paying bays are now being reserved for car club vehicles and electric charging points as well as for disabled drivers, doctors, diplomats and loading. With London land values at around £6 million per hectare, a car parking space (5 m by 2.4 m = 12 m^2) is worth £7,200, equivalent to an annual cost of £360 using a 5% yield. A resident's parking permit is therefore good value. Nevertheless, motorists object to the level of parking charges, whether for annual residential permits or hourly charges, mainly because they feel that they have already paid for the road space with their other taxes. However, parking is a small proportion of the total cost of motoring, where fuel alone costs the average motorist around £1,600 per year.

The number of parking penalties in 1993/1994 was 2.8 million; this rose to 5.9 million in 2003/2004 and has now fallen to 4.0 million in 2012/2013 as a result of more rigorous enforcement, greater compliance by motorists and a reduction of traffic in London.

In July 2007, parking offences were categorised into higher and lower level penalties, determined originally by London Councils for the London boroughs and then used in the rest of the country. Higher penalty offences (which account for three quarters of the total) include parking on yellow lines or in resident parking zones without a permit, while the lesser offences include overstaying the time on a meter or parking in an off-street car park without paying. Penalties range from £60 to £130 in London (£40–70 outside London) which are halved if the payment is made within 14 days. These penalties can be compared with the cost of parking which is typically £2–4 an hour in inner London and £1–2 an hour in outer areas.

Local authorities in London generated £557 million in income, half of which comes from permits and hourly charges and the rest from penalties (RAC Foundation, 2013). After expenses, they made a surplus of £254 million which by law must be reinvested in transport-related activities. In 2013, Barnet Council tried to raise its permit charges to increase its general income at a time of reduced government subsidies but this was overruled by the courts and the charges had to be reduced.

With the introduction of the Congestion Charge in central London, traffic fell by about 15% and space at parking meters became available. Many meters, previously limited to 2 hour stays, were converted to 4 hour stays to encourage their use. Nevertheless, TfL in its annual monitoring reports calculated the loss of parking income to local authorities was only worth around £15,000 per annum, although they did not measure the equivalent loss of commercial off-street car parks (TfL, 2007).

EARLY SUPPLY STUDIES

In 1966, Michael Thompson of the London School of Economics carried out a survey of parking in central London together with the GLC (Thompson, 1966). The GLC had identified that there were 125,000 parking spaces (paying and free, on- and off-street) and it was decided to survey 5% of them over one day using 44 observers. At the same time a short questionnaire was given out to drivers asking how far they had come, the reason for their journey, the frequency of their travelling by car to London and what they would do if parking was not available.

Occupancy, defined as whether the space was in use or not, peaked at around 2 pm when commuters and shoppers combined. On-street occupancy was nearly 90%, off-street around 70%. Occupancy at 6 am is likely to be mainly residents, so Thompson concluded that more than a quarter of spaces were taken up by overnight (resident) parkers; this rose to nearly a half if the parking was free (Table 1).

The survey also found a high level of illegal parking – meter feeding (putting in extra money after the original time has expired), moving the car between bays in the same zone and overstaying on meters (over a third of motorists exceeded the permitted time). The Thompson survey measured the turnover of spaces over the working day – once per day for off-street parking, nearly six times for meters, and just over twice for free spaces.

Table 1.   Parking Spaces in Central London in 1966.

	No. of Spaces	% of Spaces	Occupancy at 6 am (%)	Peak Occupancy (%)
Off-street public	25,500	20	24	68
Off-street private	55,000	44	18	73
On-street – metered	14,500	12	28	84
On-street free	30,000	24	47	87
Total	125,000	100	28	76

Source: Thompson (1966).

In 1977 the study was repeated in the same area by the GLC Department of Planning and Transportation (Carr, Potter, & Baker, 1979). They surveyed the whole of central London (roughly the area inside the inner ring road, an area approximately 7 km by 4 km). This study also looked at non-compliance. Eleven per cent of cars in residents' bays did not have a valid permit; a third of meters showed a level of infringement (16% feeding, 9% excess charge,[1] 7% penalty). It was difficult to measure non-compliance on single yellow lines as some parking could be legitimate (e.g. vehicles displaying a disabled driver badge) and offences were generally of a short duration.

Carr did a separate survey (1976) of 35 private non-residential car parks around Tottenham Court Road in central London and found that 50% of the spaces were used by commuters who could use public transport as an alternative and 70% could be removed without affecting priority users such as disabled people, those on shift work or deliveries.

WHERE MOTORISTS PARK AT HOME

While the previous section considered parking behaviour during the day, i.e. at the destination, this section looks at where cars are actually parked at home, i.e. the demand for residential parking. Two sources have been used. The first is the NTS, an annual survey of 8,200 households, covering over 19,000 individuals who complete a weekly diary of their travel. The second source is the London Travel Demand Survey (LTDS) a continuous household survey undertaken by TfL, covering 8,000 households in the London area, including the London boroughs as well as the area outside Greater London but within the M25 motorway. The survey is a successor to the household survey component of the London Area Transport Survey (LATS) which was last carried out in 2001 when 30,000 households were sampled. Each of these sources gives a different aspect to the residential parking picture and their information is combined in Table 2.

Table 2 combines the different sources and estimates the total number of cars parked at home in different places. The proportion of vehicles parked off road, at just under 60%, increased from 1995/1997 to 2012 according to the NTS but has hardly changed between 2001 and 2007/2008−2009/2010 according to LATS/LTDS. There has been a notable shift from garage

Table 2. Comparison of Different Data on Where Cars are Parked at Home.

% of Vehicles	NTS[a] 1995/1997	NTS[a] 2012	LATS[b] 2001	LTDS[c] 2007/ 2008–2009/ 2010	Estimated no. of Vehicles 000 2011		
					Inner	Outer	London
Garage	17	9			30	190	240
Off-street	36	47			160	1,110	1,250
Garage/off-street total	53	56	58	57	190	1,300	1,490
On-street – with permit			12	17	290	190	480
On-street – without permit			29	25	160	500	660
On-street total	42	41	41	42	550	690	1,140
Other	4	2	1	1	20	10	30
Total					660	2,000	2,660

[a]National Travel Survey.
[b]London Area Transport Survey.
[c]London Travel Demand Survey.

(17% falling to 9%) to off-street (36% rising to 47%). This reduction in the use of garages can be due to a number of factors

- garages are increasingly used for storage of other items besides cars, particularly in modern houses which tend to be less well equipped with storage
- garages have been converted into living accommodation
- modern cars tend to be larger and do not fit into the garages of older houses
- modern cars are more reliable with better corrosion protection and can be parked in the open with the confidence that they will start; they also have better theft protection
- the growth in multi-car households – the extra cars cannot be parked in the garage
- inconvenient access to garages in blocks of flats as they may be poorly lit and subject to vandalism and unsocial behaviour

The effect of the increased number of streets with parking restrictions can be seen in the switch from on-street without permit to on-street with permit and off-street parking. In some boroughs, such as Camden, Islington, Kensington and Chelsea and Westminster in central London, the proportion of on-street parking which is subject to permits is well over 90%. As more permit zones are created, motorists try to avoid charges by parking off road on their own premises, converting their front gardens into parking spaces (Fig. 4). However, this does not lead to much additional parking space as the additional crossover from the highway to the garden takes up two thirds of a car length. Councils have been banning additional crossovers to discourage garden conversion which also leads to problems with water run-off.

These surveys and the census provide an opportunity to estimate the total demand for residential parking which is shown in Table 3. Table 3 is derived from the LTDS analysis by number of vehicles in the household combined with the total number of cars by borough in the 2011 census (ONS, 2011). Borough by borough figures are given in the Appendix.

There are nearly 2.7 million cars in London, three quarters of which are in outer London where the car ownership per household is twice that in

Fig. 4. Nineteenth Century Houses with Gardens Converted to Off-Street Parking with Controlled on-Street Parking. *Source:* Picture by the author.

Table 3. Total Demand for Residential Parking in London (2011).

	Garaged/ Off-street	On-Street Permit	On-Street No Permit	Other	Total	Vehicles Per Household
Inner	190	296	178	17	681	0.54
Outer	1332	156	482	13	1983	0.99
London	1522	452	660	29	2664	0.82

Source: London Travel Demand Survey (LTDS) and 2011 Census.

inner London. A quarter of cars in inner London are housed overnight in a garage or off street, compared with two thirds in outer London.

AVAILABILITY OF RESIDENTIAL AND DESTINATION PARKING IN LONDON

In 1999 the Government Office for London, prior to the formation of TfL, commissioned MVA Consultancy to measure the availability of parking in London as input into policy making about workplace parking levies and congestion charging. The study (MVA, 2000) involved inspection on-street of a sample of 300 areas each 500 metres square (25 hectares) in London. This study was updated in 2004 (MVA, 2005) when 50 of the original squares were resurveyed to take into account changes that may have occurred as a result of changes in land-use and parking regulations (including the extension of CPZs) and changes associated with traffic management initiatives, such as bus priority schemes and congestion charging.

The types of parking considered were:

- On-Street Controlled parking (OSC) – this mainly comprises parking at meters or Pay-and-Display bays; and parking in residential (permit) bays.
- On-Street Non-controlled parking (OSN) – this covers free parking on-street, and comprises unrestricted parking where there are no yellow or red lines; and parking at single yellow or single red lines, which is normally allowed overnight.
- Public Off-Street car parks (POS) – these are car parks open to the public and often charged.
- Private Non-Residential car parks (PNR) – these are car parks related specifically to the organisation that owns it. Examples are car parks for employees of offices, factories and shops; or car parks for customers of shops, leisure centres or sports grounds. Admittance is normally

restricted to employees, suppliers or customers respectively. Sometimes there will be charges for customer parking. In practice there is overlap with POS as a car park for a supermarket may also be used by motorists who are not necessarily shopping at that retail outlet.

• Private Residential parking which comprises parking in private residential drives or garages (driveway), or in communal car parks at blocks of flats and houses (communal).

The study was particularly interested in PNR and POS car parks, where charges or planning restrictions could control usage and OSC parking, which by definition was already restricted in supply to fulfil the objectives of planners in the boroughs. OSN parking supply could be reduced by extending the areas covered by CPZs. Private residential parking supply could generally be affected only when new developments were planned, and there was no intention to regulate parking on private driveways.

The 1999 study surveyed just under 5% of the surface-area of London with a concentration of sampling points in strategic town-centres, where a large proportion of public car parks and CPZs exist, and in the central area where similar conditions apply. For PNR car parks the surveyors counted the number of maximum possible parking spaces rather than just the marked spaces − in practice in small car parks, the effective capacity may be greater as cars are often parked in the access areas and moved when other cars need to exit.

The main findings were that there were some 6.8 million parking spaces within London, with a range of ±0.6 million. Of these about 40% were in private driveways, garages, shared residential car parks (i.e. overnight residential parking), 35% available on the road, without restrictions, 12% on-street with restrictions (although these could be used for residential parking at night when the restrictions did not apply) and 15% in public and private off-street car parks which would be used as destination parking (Table 4).

The number of spaces in Central London from the MVA study in 1999 can be compared with the estimates of Carr undertaken in 1977 although the categories are not quite the same and this is shown in Table 5.

In 2004 MVA carried out an update of the 1999 study (MVA, 2005) and revisited 50 out of the original 300 squares. OSC spaces were again obtained from Borough sources, where available, and more categories were used: Meter Spaces, Pay & Display Spaces, Pre-paid voucher Spaces, Free Parking Spaces, Resident Spaces, Business Spaces and Shared Use Spaces. PR parking was excluded as it was felt there would be little change. Evidence from the EHS (discussed in more detail below) suggests that this

Table 4.   Estimated Number of Parking Spaces in London (1999).

		Spaces	Lower Range	Upper Range
Private residential	Driveway	1,835,700	1,700,300	1,971,100
Private residential	Shared	855,700	768,600	942,800
On-street non-controlled	Unrestricted	2,355,300	2,185,400	2,525,100
On-street non-controlled	Single yellow line	631,000	574,500	687,500
On-street controlled	Meter	86,900	78,900	95,000
On-street controlled	Resident	79,200	72,500	86,000
Public off-street	Public	229,900	171,000	288,800
Private non-residential	Employee	558,400	502,400	614,300
Private non-residential	Other	216,600	161,900	271,200
Total		6,848,700	6,215,500	7,481,800

Source: MVA London Parking Supply 2000.

Table 5.   Parking Spaces in Central London.

'000s of Spaces	Carr 1977	MVA 1999
Public on-street	32	25
Private non-residential	57	34
On-street	31	67
Residential	21	25
Total	141	151

study might have failed to take account of the reduction in garage spaces. Nevertheless, the conclusions of the update study were that there had been:

- a reduction in Private Non-Residential employee parking spaces in central and inner London. It seems likely that some of this change had been associated with the introduction of congestion charging in 2003;
- an increase in spaces available to the public, whether in public or private car parks, in inner and outer London;
- a reduction in on-street non-controlled parking, especially in central London.

Table 6 shows changes between 1999 and 2004 but these must be treated with caution because of the small scale of the original study and the even smaller scale of the update. Some of the large change in the 'Other' category may be due to the use of different classifications.

Table 6. Change in Number of Non-Residential Off-Street and On-Street Parking Bays (1999–2004).

% Change	Off-Street Non-Residential				On-Street Non-Controlled			On-Street Controlled
	POS[a] public	PNR[b] employee	PNR[b] other	All non-residential car parks	OSN[c] uncontrolled	OSN[c] single yellow/red line	OSN[c] total	OSC[d] total[e]
'000s of bays (2004) London	222	671	378	1,272	2,132	604	2,736	459
Change in no. of bays (1999–2004)								
Central area, inside inner ring road	−21	−46	235	−26	0	−28	−43	n/a
Between inner ring road and north/south circular roads	18	3	84	24	−9	−14	−11	n/a
Between north/south circular roads and London boundary	−3	29	71	31	−9	3	−7	n/a
All London	−4	20	74	27	−9	−4	−8	177

Source: MVA (2005).
[a]Public off-street car parks.
[b]Private non-residential car parks.
[c]On-street non-controlled parking.
[d]On-street controlled parking.
[e]These OSC figures are not available for the central and other areas as defined, being based on Borough estimates. They also exclude (at least) Lewisham, where no estimates are available.

Table 7. No. of On-Street Parking Bays in Controlled Areas (OSC) (London Local Authority Returns).

'000s of spaces	Meter spaces (1)	Pay & display spaces (2)	Voucher spaces (3)	Free parking spaces (4)	Resident spaces (5)	Business spaces (6)	Shared use spaces (7)	Shared Spaces Included under Both Headings		
								Spaces available for general public (sum of columns 1–4 and 7)	Spaces available for residents and business (sum of columns 5–7)	Total spaces (sum of columns 1–7)
Inner	8	25	0	6	117	9	105	144	230	269
Outer	2	15	1	11	98	7	55	84	162	190
London	10	40	1	17	215	16	161	228	392	459

Source: MVA (2005) (note that many of the figures are from earlier years or are imputed).

In the 1999 study MVA attempted to measure on-street residents' bays but as many of these schemes were only just coming into use at that time the data were very patchy because of their limited sampling method. MVA also tried to survey local authorities in London with limited success. In 2004 MVA again surveyed local authorities via the Association of London Government (now called London Councils) but found the data were very inconsistent and out of date. Part of the problem is that local authorities often measure the length of street subject to parking restrictions rather than converting it to the number of bays (5 m per bay is a typical conversion factor). One or two councils do publish, in their annual parking reports, the number of bays and even the number of permits in use (which generally exceeds the number of bays). Westminster's 2010 report stated that there were currently just over 35,000 permits in use and approximately 32,000 resident bays. This is the same number as recorded by MVA in 2004.

Table 7 shows on-street parking bays by type and then sums by characteristics. The number of spaces available for the general public includes meter, pay-and-display, voucher, free and shared spaces. The number of spaces for residents and business also includes shared spaces. The total spaces column only counts the shared spaces once. This table, based on local authority returns, shows a total of 459,000 on-street controlled spaces (i.e. areas with yellow lines and/or CPZs) whereas the study by the MVA's on-street survey shows 603,000 (±50,000). MVA did not survey areas where on-street parking was not allowed (e.g. double yellow lines, crossings or bus cages).

This can be compared with the figures for private off-street residential bays from the MVA earlier study which were not updated in the 2005 study, in Table 8. These figures suggest there is off-street space for every car (total according to 2011 census 2.66 million cars), whereas Table 2 shows that there are 1.49 million cars parked off-street and 1.17 million

Table 8. Private Off-Street Residential Bays (1999).

'000s of Bays (1999)	Garage or Driveway	Communal, e.g. Flats	Total Private Off-Street
Central area, inside inner ring road	7	18	25
Between inner ring road and north/south circular roads	111	192	303
Between north/south circular roads and London boundary	1,717	646	2,363
All London	1,836	856	2,692

Source: MVA (2005) (as noted, these were not updated from the 1999 study).

parked on-street or elsewhere. This supply/demand balance is further discussed below in a dedicated section.

AVAILABILITY OF RESIDENTIAL
PARKING – ALTERNATIVE DATA

This section looks at the available capacity to meet the demand for residential parking through an analysis of the EHS. The EHS is a continuous national survey of 17,000 households commissioned by the Department for Communities and Local Government (DCLG). The following data are based on a physical inspection of an 8,000 sub-sample of the properties by a trained surveyor and give information on availability of parking spaces. The data are the average of the two survey years 2009/2010 and 2010/2011 (referred to henceforth as EHS 2009−2011).

Table 9 shows the total availability of on- and off-street parking places in London based on the EHS survey for 2009−2011. There were 3.1 million homes with 3.5 million spaces for 2.6 million cars. In London 61% of households have a car compared with Great Britain as a whole where 74% of households have a car. This reflects the excellent public transport in inner London making a car much less necessary than in the outer suburbs. Even so, a third of households are judged by the surveyors as having inadequate or no parking.

Table 9. No. of Dwellings with Different Parking Availability in London.

	2009−2010			
	'000	%	Avg. spaces per household	No. of spaces
Garage	591	19	1.17	690
Other off-street parking	675	22	1.80	1,220
Adequate street parking	838	27	0.97	813
Inadequate street or no parking	994	32	0.74	735
All	3,098			3,458
Households with a car	*1,889*	*61*		
No of cars[a]	*2,567*			
Cars/dwelling with adequate space	*1.22*			

Source: English Housing Survey 2009−2011 special analysis.
[a]Total number of households in London in 2011 census was 3,266,000 and number of cars was 2,664,000.

Table 10 shows how houses in London are older than England as a whole. The houses most likely to have garages were built between the two World Wars, when motorisation was just beginning, and in the post-war period. More recently a higher proportion of properties have been built with parking spaces rather than garages, as builders reflect the same factors as noted above for the use of garages. Builders of new estates generally try to maximise their profits by achieving the highest density per hectare within local planning constraints, thus restricting off-street availability. In addition, local authorities have tried to limit off-street parking to preserve the amenity of the developments (see below).

As well as the age of dwelling, it is also of interest to investigate parking availability by type of dwelling as shown in Table 11. This shows the high proportion of flats, which do not have adequate parking. There has been a tendency for local authorities not to approve the provision of any off-street parking at all for new blocks of flats in areas with good public transport: at the same time owners of such properties may be prevented from applying for residents' parking permits. While this will discourage car ownership, property owners may still own cars and park them some distance away in other residential streets.

Further analysis by car ownership, shown in Table 12, shows that households with more than one car are more likely to have a garage, reflecting the higher income and the greater probability of living in a less densely populated area. Almost a half of the 37% of households without a car

Table 10. Per cent of Dwellings with Differing Parking Availability by Age of Housing in London.

% of Locations	Dwelling Age			Total
	Pre-1919	1919–1980	Post-1980	
Garage	5	28	12	19
Other off-street parking	14	20	41	22
Adequate street parking	36	24	21	27
Inadequate street parking	37	24	22	27
No parking provision	8	3	4	5
All	100	100	100	100
% of dwellings in London	*29*	*55*	*16*	*100*
% of dwellings in England	*21*	*58*	*21*	100

Source: English Housing Survey 2009–2011 special analysis.

Table 11. Per cent of Dwellings with Differing Parking Availability by
Type of House in London (2009).

% of Locations	Houses	Terraces	Flats	Total
Garage	51	16	7	19
Other off-street parking	28	27	16	22
Adequate street parking	12	32	31	27
Inadequate street parking	8	23	39	27
No parking provision	1	2	8	5
All	100	100	100	100
% of dwellings in London	*22*	*29*	*50*	*100*
% of dwellings in England	*52*	*29*	*20*	*20*

Source: English Housing Survey 2009–2011 special analysis.

Table 12. Per cent of Dwellings with Differing Parking Availability by
Number of Vehicles in household in London.

| % of Locations | Number of Vehicles Owned or Available for Use | | | | |
	3 +	2	1	0	Total
Garage	46	39	22	5	19
Other off-street parking	33	28	26	14	22
Adequate street parking	9	18	26	34	27
Inadequate street parking	12	13	23	39	27
No parking provision	1	2	3	8	4
Total	100	100	100	100	100
% of dwellings in London	*3*	*15*	*45*	*37*	*100*
% of dwellings in England	*7*	*26*	*44*	*23*	*100*

Source: English Housing Survey 2009–2011 special analysis.

would not be able to park their car, if they had one, on their own premises
or the street. Fourteen per cent of those with two or more cars (equivalent
to 4% of households in London) do not have adequate parking – some
will be parked illegally or in off-street non-residential car parks.

In 2011 TfL, working with AECOM, undertook a large-scale postal survey in November with residents of developments having 10 or more units
and built between 2004 and 2009. The purpose was to determine the influence that parking provision has on travel choices (TfL, 2012). In total,

around 3,000 responses were received from more than 800 developments across London. Two thirds of respondents were residents of Outer London, many living in areas with poor access to public transport with the remainder residents of Inner London typically living in areas with better public transport provision. This enables a comparison to be made between the type of housing and the parking provision being made for new developments and existing homes in London as a whole shown in Table 13.

Table 13 shows a higher proportion of purpose-built flats in new developments as they are cheaper to build and provide more accommodation in a limited area. How this affects parking is shown in Table 14.

Table 14 shows that, even in new developments, there is insufficient off-street parking with only 66% of cars being parked off the road. A review borough by borough (see Appendix) shows that in 18 out of the 33 boroughs (including the City of London) the residential planning standards, defining the permitted maximum number of car parking spaces, are

Table 13. Type of Housing in New Developments Compared with London as a Whole.

% of Locations	New Developments (TfL)	London (EHS)
Flats – conversion	17	11
Flats – purpose built	44	38
Terraced houses	16	29
Semi-detached houses	11	17
Detached houses	9	4
Other	3	

Source: TfL (2012) and EHS 2009–2011 special analysis.

Table 14. Where Parked by Type of Parking in New Developments Compared with London as a Whole.

% of Locations	New Developments	LTDS/NTS (All London)
Garage	15	9
Driveway	29	47
Private car park	22	
On-street permit	15	17
On-street no permit	11	25
Other	7	3

Source: TfL (2012), London Travel Demand Survey (LTDS) and National Travel Survey (NTS).

more restrictive (i.e. provide fewer spaces) than the Mayor of London's London Plan. A number of boroughs do not restrict parking spaces in private detached houses but may restrict them in affordable housing or where there is a high level of public transport provision. Ten of these 18 boroughs are in outer London where space is less likely to be at a premium suggesting that these boroughs have policies designed in part at least to try to restrict car ownership. In some boroughs the restrictions are quite severe. In Tower Hamlets and Islington, for example, the maximum, even where public transport is poor, is 0.5 spaces per household compared with a recommended 1 space for 1–2 bedroom homes and 2 for larger homes.

SUPPLY/DEMAND BALANCE

This section combines the data on the amount of residential parking that is available in London from the MVA and EHS surveys with the demand for parking from NTS and LATS survey to determine the degree of pressure on the available space both on- and off-street.

There is a considerable gap between MVA's estimate (for 1999) of available off-street parking of 2.69 million spaces (Table 8) and the EHS estimate of 1.81 million. The EHS figure is likely to be more reliable as it is based on a larger sample and is more recent.

The NTS and LTDS data for parking demand in London (Table 2) show 0.24 million cars parked in a garage overnight and 1.25 million in other off-street spaces. The EHS figure of 0.69 million for the supply of garage spaces includes 11% in homes where there are no cars, so only 0.61 million are needed for parking. Comparing this with the 0.24 million cars parked in garages gives a garage utilisation of 39% which is somewhat lower than the average for the whole of England of 44% (and the reasons for non-use of the garage have been highlighted above). It also implies that 0.37 million cars which could be parked in garages are parked elsewhere on site or in the street.

Table 15 compares the maximum available residential parking with cars in use and must be treated with extreme caution as it is based on small samples and several different years of data which are largely out of date. On-street includes controlled (with permit) and uncontrolled areas; off-street includes garages and drives.

The MVA availability figures suggest a virtual 100% saturation of on-street permit spaces in all areas of London. This is certainly true in inner London but there are large areas of outer London where residential

Table 15. Approximate Residential Supply Demand Balance for London.

'000s	Max Available Residential Spaces	Max Available Residential Spaces	Max Available Residential Spaces	Max Available Residential Spaces
	On-street permit	On-street no permit	Off-street	Total
Cars parked				
Inner	286	166	193	645
Outer	165	506	1,314	1,985
All London	451	672	1,507	2,630
Available space (MVA 1999–2004)				
Inner	292	611	328	1,231
Outer	167	2,125	2,363	4,655
All London	459	2,736	2,692	5,886
Available space (EHS 2009–2010)				
All London	1,548		1,810	3,358
Utilisation (MVA)				
Inner	98%	27%	59%	52%
Outer	99%	24%	56%	43%
All London	98%	25%	56%	45%
Utilisation (EHS)				
All London	73%		83%	78%

Source: MVA, London Travel Demand Survey, Census, English Housing Survey 'other' parking places excluded.

permit bays are provided to prevent commuter parking during the day than being motivated by rationing overnight residential parking. This suggests that MVA (or rather the local authorities which provided the data) have underestimated the number or that the local authorities have increased them substantially since the data were supplied between 2000 and 2004, (the more probable explanation). MVA seem to have over-estimated the amount of off-street parking with utilisation of only 59% in inner and 56% in outer London. The EHS figure of 83% for the whole of London is more credible but may be a little on the high side.

These figures can be compared with the 85% maximum occupancy of parking bays which is considered good practice for satisfactory turnover of vehicles.

CHANGES IN CAR OWNERSHIP IN LONDON AND THE LINK WITH PARKING SUPPLY

This section looks at the changes in car ownership in London in the past 20 years and examines whether the increase in parking restrictions and a decrease in parking supply has led to a reduction in car ownership.

Data from the national census carried out every 10 years shows that in the decade between 1991 and 2001 there was a growth in car ownership per household but there was a decline in the decade to 2011. The decline is larger in inner London which accounts for a third of the population but only a quarter of the number of cars as shown in Tables 16 and 17.

Table 16. Changes in Population, Households and Car Ownership in London.

'000		Inner	Outer	London	% change decade on decade		
					Inner	Outer	London
Population	1991	2,245	4,334	6,579			
	2001	2,520	4,652	7,172	12	7	9
	2011	2,923	5,250	8,173	16	13	14
Households	1991	1,016	1,748	2,764			
	2001	1,129	1,887	3,016	11	8	9
	2011	1,261	2,005	3,266	12	6	8
Cars	1991	594	1,631	2,225			
	2001	703	1,913	2,616	18	17	18
	2011	681	1,983	2,664	−3	4	2

Source: ONS Censuses.

Table 17. Changes in Car Ownership Per Household.

	Cars/Household			% of Households with Car		
	Inner	Outer	London	Inner	Outer	London
1991	0.58	0.93	0.80	44	68	58
2001	0.62	1.01	0.87	50	70	63
2011	0.54	0.99	0.82	47	67	59

Source: ONS Censuses.

Table 18. Comparison of Inner and Outer London.

	Inner London (%)	Outer London (%)
Area	19	81
Population	36	64
Households	39	61
Cars	26	74

Source: ONS 2011 Census.

Of the two boroughs with the biggest percentage decline in car owner-ship, Kensington and Chelsea (12% decline) has a tight parking policy while Hammersmith and Fulham (11%) does not, so no conclusion can be reached on the impact of restricted parking availability. There are many economic factors other than parking controls which affect car ownership such as income effects of the recession, improved public transport services, particularly in inner London and possibly the influx of immigrants who may not be able to afford cars or are more used to using public transport as well as young people who are less likely to own cars (RAC Foundation, 2012).

In outer London, which consists of boroughs with more individual homes and wider roads, there has been a smaller increase in population but, as in inner London, a smaller increase in households implying more people per household. The number of cars has continued to grow but at a slower rate. While parking restraints may have affected this growth, eco-nomic effects and to a lesser extent better public transport may have played a part (Table 18).

The subjective scoring of the restrictiveness of parking standards by bor-ough in the appendix (based on data in the 2011 TfL study into new devel-opments (TfL, 2012)), has been compared with various parameters from the census which indicate car ownership to see whether restriction on parking has affected car ownership:

The results in Table 19 suggest only a weak negative relationship between restrictions on car parking and the level of car ownership. A more statistically rigorous approach was undertaken by MVA in conjunction with TfL (Whelan, Crocker, MVA Consultancy, & Vitouladiti, 2011). Their modelling included:

- Price of cars — initial costs and operating costs
- Quality of cars and highway network — vehicle quality, level of service on network(s), and parking supply
- Price and quality of substitutes — price, availability and quality of alternative means of travel
- Income — well-defined relationship between household/individual income and car ownership with richer households typically owning more vehicles
- Need — strongly influenced by household size, structure, employment, location(s), and subsequent trip productions/attractions
- Tastes and preferences — aspects of decision-making processes as well as broader, societal trends (e.g. attitudes, lifestyles, interests and values)

Statistically significant explanatory variables included household structure, income, tenure and nationality, but parking (defined by whether there was a CPZ in the area) had an imperceptible influence. However they did not include an explicit variable on the *availability* of residential parking which is much more likely to have an impact.

Looking at the reasons for *not* owning a car, the LATS in 2001 gave a number of options but parking was not specifically mentioned. Economy

Table 19.   Correlation of Changes in Car Ownership and Parking Restrictions.

	Correlation Coefficient
Change in number of vehicles 2011 compared with 2001	−0.18
% Change in number of vehicles 2011 compared with 2001	−0.28
Change in vehicle per household 2011 compared with 2001	−0.30
Change in number of vehicles 2011 compared with 1991	−0.38*
% Change in number of vehicles 2011 compared with 1991	0.00
Change in vehicle per household 2011 compared with 1991	−0.48*

Sources: ONS Censuses and author (as shown in the appendix).
*Significant at 95% level.

(40% respondents), ability to drive (39% respondents) and use of other modes (36% respondents) were the main reasons for not owning a car.

Financial reasons are much more likely in the inner boroughs such as Tower Hamlets, Newham and Hackney (52%) than in the outer suburbs, where it only accounted for 25% of the mentions, and where not being able to drive was more prevalent.

In an update to this study, TfL asked SDG to carry out a follow up survey to the 2011 LTDS study (SDG, 2012) which gave the following reasons in declining order of importance for not owning a car:

- Cost: can't afford to own and run a car
- Car unnecessary: don't want the hassle of owning a car and choose to live somewhere where a car is unnecessary
- Do not own a car due to a disability
- Do not own a car due to difficulties with car parking
- Do without a car for environmental reasons

As with the earlier MVA/TfL study, the level of car ownership is much more likely to be economic or related to the access to alternative transport than the availability of car parking. This is contrast to New York where studies by Guo (2013) suggest that parking availability is more important than economic factors. The conclusion is therefore that the relationship between parking availability and car ownership in London is still to be proven.

CONCLUSIONS

This chapter shows that, based on London data, it is possible to construct a supply/demand balance for parking to determine the pressure on parking both on-street and off-street. The data are extremely patchy and inconsistent but it appears that there is saturation in inner London for controlled on-street parking and high utilisation for off-street parking. Detailed roadside surveys of available space on and off-street are required before accurate assessment can be made of the supply/demand balance. Many local authorities do small scale local surveys before introducing CPZs and it is possible that some councils have done larger scale city wide projects (e.g. Nottingham before introducing the workplace parking levy) but these have not been published.

While public transport availability and usage has improved enormously in the past 10 years, car ownership has continued to grow in outer London where geography makes the car an essential for much of everyday life, for its convenience and perceived cheapness to run. However restrictive policies on parking supply in new developments, partly as a perceived method of reducing car ownership and partly because developers can increase the number of housing units on scarce and expensive land, will cause further pressure on limited on-street parking. This leads to unsightly and dangerous parking on streets not designed for parking or illegal parking on footways. The evidence does not appear to show that controls on parking supply to restrict car ownership have had a great effect in London and policy makers must appreciate that car ownership will continue to rise and that parking spaces must be provided, if necessary, underground. Much more information is needed in order to make a wider assessment, and to understand the implications of increasing car ownership.

NOTE

1. In the early years of parking meters, there was a half hour period of grace (excess period) for which a higher hourly rate was payable.

ACKNOWLEDGEMENTS

The author wishes to thank Qinyi Chen at Imperial College London who undertook the special analysis of the English Housing Survey and the EHS team at the Department of Communities and Local Government for their technical help.

REFERENCES

Carr, R. (1976). *Some characteristics of private non-residential parking in greater London.* London: GLC.
Carr, R., Potter, H. S., & Baker, L. L. H. (1979). *The central London parking and car usage survey.* London: GLC.
Guo, Z. (2013). Does residential parking supply affect household car ownership? A case of New York City. *Journal of Transport Geography, 26,* 18–28.

Inwood, J. (1965). *Some effects of increased parking meter charges in London.* Crowthorne: Road Research Laboratory Report LR7.

MVA. (2005). Update of London parking supply. MVA on behalf of Transport for London. TfL, London.

MVA in association with Data Collection Ltd. (2000). London parking supply study: Main report. Prepared for Government Office for London. TfL, London.

ONS Census: KS404EW Car or van availability, local authorities in England and Wales. (2011). Retrieved from http://www.ons.gov.uk/ons/rel/census/2011-census/key-statistics-for-local-authorities-in-england-and-wales/rft-table-ks404ew.xls

RAC Foundation for Motoring. (2012). On the move. RAC Foundation for Motoring, London.

RAC Foundation for Motoring. (2013). Local authority parking finances in England 2012–2013. RAC Foundation for Motoring, London.

SDG. (2012). London travel demand survey – Follow-up survey. SDG on behalf of TfL. TfL, London.

TfL. (2007). Central London Congestion Charging Scheme: Ex-post evaluation of the quantified impacts of the original scheme. Transport for London, London.

TfL. (2012). *Residential parking provision in new developments.* Travel in London Research Report 2012, TfL, London.

Thompson, M. (1966). *Some characteristics of motorists in central London.* Greater London Papers No. 13. Greater London Council, London.

Whelan, G., Crocker, J., MVA Consultancy, & Vitouladiti, S. (2011). *A new model of car ownership in London: Geo-spatial analysis of policy interventions.* London: Transport for London.

APPENDIX: WHERE CARS ARE PARKED BY BOROUGH

'000 Vehicles	Garaged	On-Street Permit	On-Street No Permit	Other	Total	Vehicles Per Household	Parking Standards[a]
Inner							
Camden	13	28	2	3	47	0.48	4
City of London	1	0	0	0	2	0.39	5
Hackney	6	15	20	1	42	0.41	3
Hammersmith and Fulham	8	32	2	1	44	0.54	4
Haringey	15	17	28	1	62	0.60	0
Islington	9	28	1	0	39	0.41	5
Kensington and Chelsea	7	36	1	1	45	0.57	4
Lambeth	22	19	25	1	67	0.51	0
Lewisham	33	7	36	1	77	0.66	0
Southwark	24	12	23	1	60	0.50	5
Tower Hamlets	15	21	4	2	44	0.43	6
Wandsworth	26	44	18	1	90	0.69	0
Westminster	13	27	3	5	49	0.46	3
Outer							
Barking and Dagenham	33	3	21	0	57	0.82	0
Barnet	92	15	37	0	145	1.06	0
Bexley	88	2	18	0	109	1.17	0
Brent	49	23	15	1	88	0.80	0
Bromley	120	4	30	1	154	1.18	2
Croydon	103	6	30	1	140	0.97	2
Ealing	62	20	30	1	113	0.91	3
Enfield	80	3	35	1	120	1.00	0
Greenwich	44	7	26	0	78	0.77	2
Harrow	73	5	22	1	100	1.19	3
Havering	94	2	21	1	118	1.21	2
Hillingdon	97	2	22	2	122	1.22	1
Hounslow	60	6	27	0	94	0.99	1
Kingston upon Thames	48	10	13	0	70	1.11	0
Newham	13	15	32	1	61	0.60	0
Merton	38	11	22	1	73	0.92	0
Redbridge	78	3	24	1	106	1.07	0
Richmond upon Thames	40	15	29	1	85	1.06	0
Sutton	74	2	14	1	91	1.17	1

(*Continued*)

'000 Vehicles	Garaged	On-Street Permit	On-Street No Permit	Other	Total	Vehicles Per Household	Parking Standards[a]
Waltham Forest	29	9	36	2	76	0.79	3
Inner London	193	286	166	19	664	0.54	
Outer London	1314	165	506	15	2000	0.99	
London	**1507**	**451**	**672**	**34**	**2664**	**0.82**	

Source: London Area Travel Survey 2007–2010 and 2011 Census.
[a]Parking standards is a subjective assessment of the severity of residential standards for parking compared with the London Plan. Derived from TfL 2012, where the range is 0 = borough standards conform to London Plan to 6 = much tighter standards than London plan. (Tower Hamlets only allows 0.5 of car space for a 4 bed house even in the areas with the lowest public transport availability, compared with the London Plan standard of 2 spaces.)

CHAPTER 13

EXPLORING THE IMPACT OF THE MELBOURNE CBD PARKING LEVY ON WHO PAYS THE LEVY, PARKING SUPPLY AND MODE USE

William Young, Graham Currie and Paul Hamer

ABSTRACT

Purpose − *The pricing of parking is a common tool used by governments to facilitate the efficient movement of traffic, raise revenue and, more recently, influence travel behaviour. An important and under-researched by-product of parking pricing schemes is the impact of these schemes on parking supply.*

Methodology/approach − *This chapter offers a review of prior research and literature, and explores: who pays the parking levy, the impact of the Congestion Levy on the provision of parking and an overview of the transport impacts of the levy.*

Findings − *The direction of the levy at parking operators and owners rather than the vehicle drivers does not provide a direct link between users and the levy and results in many parking providers not passing the levy onto commuters. The study of parking supply impact shows that,*

Parking: Issues and Policies
Transport and Sustainability, Volume 5, 291−316
Copyright © 2014 by Emerald Group Publishing Limited
All rights of reproduction in any form reserved
ISSN: 2044-9941/doi:10.1108/S2044-994120140000005022

since the introduction of the levy, the supply of commercial off-street parking spaces has declined while the growth in private, non-residential, parking spaces has slowed. Over the same period, there has been a decrease in the number of parking spaces provided for long-stay parking (which attract the parking levy), and an increase in the number of spaces provided for other uses. Understanding these parking supply impacts are important, not only because a reduction in the number of long-stay car parking spaces is an objective of the levy, but also because any such reduction could magnify the travel behaviour impacts that may have occurred solely as a result of an increase in parking price. Investigation of the overall transport impacts of the levy indicate that the parking levy did have an impact on mode choice. However the extent of this impact was not clear due to a large number of associated changes in policy and economic conditions that took place at the same time as the levy.

Practical implications *– The chapter shows that the parking levy was positive in its impact on transport use, however there were a number of improvements that could be made to the way the levy was implemented that could improve these. Interestingly, there have been a number of recent changes in the implementation of the levy that address some of these issues. Most importantly, following its own investigation into the impact of the levy, from January 2014 the cost of the levy was increased by 40% to $1,300 per annum, and its coverage extended (Victorian State Revenue Office, 2013). The impact of this change has not been considered in this research.*

Originality/value of paper *– The uniqueness of the chapter lies in its exploration of how increased prices of parking has influenced supply and how the levy, as a new form of congestion pricing, has influenced the supply of parking in the context of the case study of the Melbourne parking levy in Australia.*

Keywords: Parking; parking tax; parking supply; transport pricing

INTRODUCTION

Price mechanisms, including taxes, fees, penalties and subsidies, are a common tool used by governments' to improve market and social outcomes. Recently, governments have been giving consideration to pricing road use, as a means of easing traffic congestion. There are many different ways to charge for the use of a road network. One indirect approach which is frequently used is parking charges.

Given the potential of parking charges to deliver preferred transport and economic outcomes while generating a consistent revenue stream, the Victorian Government introduced a 'congestion levy' on long-stay, off-street parking spaces within the Melbourne central business district (CBD) and surrounding inner city areas in January 2006:

> The levy was designed to reduce traffic congestion in Melbourne's inner city by acting as a financial deterrent to drivers who arrive and leave during commuter peak hours and park all day in the city car parks. The levy aims to encourage suburban commuters to use public transport to travel into the city and car park owners/operators to convert long-stay car parking spaces, which will attract the levy, into short stay parking spaces, thereby creating more parking options for shoppers and visitors. (Parliament of Victoria, 2005, *Congestion Levy Bill*)

The levy was initially set at $A400 per annum, rising to $A800 per annum in January 2007, and with inflation each year thereafter (Parliament of Victoria, 2005). Although revenue was not an express aim of the levy, its introduction raised almost $A38 million in 2007 (Victoria: State Revenue Office, 2007). It should be noted that the Victorian Government (Victoria: State Revenue Office, 2013) has made significant changes to the levy as a consequence of the investigation on its impact of transport users.

This chapter provides an overview of three aspects of the Melbourne parking levy. The first is who pays the levy. The second, the major focus of the chapter explores how the supply of off-street car parking spaces in Central Melbourne, Australia has changed since the introduction of a parking levy. Understanding these parking supply impacts are important, not only because an increase in short-stay car parking spaces was a stated parking levy objective, but also because any reduction in the supply of long-stay car parking spaces could act to magnify the travel behaviour impacts that may have occurred as a result of an increase in parking price. The chapter initially reviews previous research on parking supply and its relationship to parking price. Parking supply in this case concerns the quantity of spaces where parking can be made. The chapter describes the context for the supply of municipal, commercial, private, non-residential parking in Melbourne. The overall impact of the levy on parking supply of long-stay (leviable) and short-stay (non-leviable) parking spaces is then investigated. The third section of the chapter provides an overview of the overall transport impacts of the parking levy. The chapter closes with a summary of key points and implications for future research.

The chapter follows previous studies on aspects of the implementation of the parking levy (Hamer, Young, & Currie, 2012). It summarises the findings of these previous studies and adds a discussion on the impacts of the levy on the supply of parking. This uniqueness of the chapter lies in its exploration of how increased prices of parking has influenced supply and how the levy, as a new form of congestion pricing, has influenced the supply of parking in the context of the case study of the Melbourne parking levy.

WHO PAYS THE PARKING LEVY?

The impact of the levy depends on the linkage between the payment and the person paying the levy, i.e. who pays the levy. This aspect of the levy was covered in detail in Hamer et al. (2012). This section of the chapter summarises the main findings of this study before moving to an exploration of the impact of the levy on parking supply in the next section.

The following paragraphs briefly explain the operation of the levy, as described in the *Congestion Levy Act 2005* (Vic) (Parliament of Victoria, 2005). This applies a levy on all long-stay parking spaces in the Melbourne CBD and adjacent inner city areas. The congestion levy covers an area of approximately 14.6 km^2. Under the Act, a long-stay parking space is defined as:

(a) a parking space in a private car park,
(b) a parking space in a public car park that is:

    (i) set aside or used for ongoing parking by the owner of the space (or another person under lease or licence), or
    (ii) used for the parking of a motor vehicle for a period of at least 4 hours on a working day, commencing at or before 9.30 a.m. and ending at or after 9.30 a.m.

Under the definition provided in the legislation, a private car park refers to any car park that is not a public car park. Subject to the levy exemptions and concessions set out the in legislation, all parking spaces in a private car park attract the congestion levy. The legislation defines a public car park as a car park in which 'the predominant number of parking spaces are set aside for, or used by, the general public, whether on a casual basis or under any kind of longer-term arrangement'.

The *Congestion Levy Act 2005* (Vic) identifies that the owner of premises is liable to pay the levy on leviable parking spaces. In the case of a publicly accessible car park (regardless of ownership), the car park operator is liable with the owner of the premises to pay the levy. As a result, both the owner and operator of a public car park must register their details (and the details of the car park) with the State Revenue Office (VSRO, 2007). It is clear from the previous discussion that the responsibility for the payment of the levy rests solely with car park owners and operators, a fact confirmed by the Victorian State Revenue Office (VSRO, 2007). Since there is no direct link between payment for the parking levy and parker, the remainder of this section highlights who pays the parking levy, and hence the potential directness of the influence on commuter travel decisions.

Hamer et al. (2012) found that both the real and nominal costs of public long-stay parking within the levy area have increased since December 2005. In the period December 2005–June 2008, the real cost of parking reached a maximum of $14.28, prior to declining to $13.39 by June 2008. This June 2008 price represented a real cost increase from December 2005 of just one-third of the average daily cost of the levy ($3.28). Over the same period, the real cost of casual parking within the levy increased by a similar amount to long-stay parking costs. The payment mechanism is complicated since commercial car park facilities offer customers a range of parking choices including casual (e.g. hourly/daily) and periodic (e.g. weekly/monthly)·parking. The pricing regime in 2009 in Melbourne is shown in Table 1. It can be seen clearly that commuter parking, or early bird parking, is extremely cheap when compared to short-term weekday parking but is comparable to long-term parking rates on the weekend and in evenings (McGuigan, 2009). Casual parking is parking that is available for use by the public on an ad hoc basis. Casual parking charges can be set at a fixed rate per entry, or may be varied according to the length of stay or time of entry or exit. Many parking facilities located in inner Melbourne also offer 'early-bird' parking with a discounted, flat fee charged for long-stay users who arrive before a specified time, and stay for a minimum period (McGuigan, 2009). 'Early-bird' rates are offered at approximately two-thirds of the car parks located within the Melbourne CBD, with most charging between $A10 and 20 per day, and a weighted average cost of $13 per day (McGuigan, 2009). This rate provides a discount of up to 70% on the full (i.e. undiscounted) cost of all-day parking (McGuigan, 2009). Additional data collected from car parks outside the CBD showed that the cost of discounted 'early-bird' parking at these locations was similar to that offered in the CBD. However, these discounted rates were available at fewer car parks (22 of 50) and, except for car parks located on the edge of the CBD, represented a smaller discount to the full cost of all-day parking. Many commercial parking facilities also

Table 1. The Rates that Parkers Pay.

Item	0–0.5 Hours	0.5–1.0 Hours	1.0–1.5 Hours	1.5–2 Hours	2–3 Hours	Over 3 Hours	Early Bird	Over-Night
Weekday work day rates per bay	$4.76 ($2.82)	$11.40 ($3.40)	$23.30 ($8.99)	$23.96 ($8.50)	$33.07 ($11.52)	$37.49 ($9.82)	$13.45 ($2.57)	
Weekday evening rates per bay	$8.14 ($2.32)	$8.14 ($2.32)	$8.64 ($2.36)	$8.64 ($2.36)	$9.89 ($3.42)	$10.62 ($4.18)		$10.16 ($3.77)
Weekend rates per bay	$7.13 ($2.82)	$7.34 ($2.82)	$9.13 (3.16)	$9.13 (3.16)	$11.00 ($4.76)	$12.63 ($6.77)		

Source: McGuigan (2009, Table 2, p. 13).

offer customers the option of entering into a license or contract for the use of a parking space on a periodic basis. Customers of these spaces may include organisations who lease or license these spaces for use by their employees, and individuals who prefer to drive into the city, or require the availability of a car at all times.

In summary the parking levy is only a small proportion of the total cost of parking and the price of parking is set by the prevailing market and local consumer preference. Hamer et al. (2012) concluded that although the parking levy provides considerable income to the state government the parking levy did not drive the price of parking.

Accordingly, across public and private car parking facilities, Hamer et al. (2012) suggested that less than one-quarter of trips that terminate in an off-street car park within the levy area are being paid for directly by the driver. If these results are correct, it suggests that the way in which the levy is being implemented by parking providers is undermining the stated purpose of the levy to influence long-term commuter parking and may be limiting its impact to generate a change in travel demand.

Finally, a close analysis of who was paying for parking, by Hamer et al. (2012), suggests that in public car parking facilities, just 34% of total revenue is sourced directly from long-stay users. Employers contribute the single largest proportion of revenue (38%), although short-stay (i.e. casual) users appear to be subsidising long-stay users as the former group contribute 26% of the total revenue, but account for only 17% of total parking stays. These findings tend to reinforce the fact that, as commercial car parks are profit-driven businesses, operators may be recouping the cost of the levy by passing the levy charge on to other users (e.g. casual users), in order to retain market share. Operators may also be partially absorbing the charge (and thus reducing their profit margin). The evidence to support this hypothesis is further strengthened by the reduction in the real costs of long-stay parking (both inside and outside the levy area) after September 2007, a time that coincided with the first signs of the Global Financial Crisis. In an effort to retain market share in a time of falling demand, parking operators appeared to have reduced parking rates and hence absorbed more of the levy themselves.

In private car parking facilities, Hamer et al. (2012) found the imposition of the congestion levy does not appear to have encouraged organisations to pass on the charge to the actual users unless the user was already being charged for a parking space at market rates suggesting that the link between the parking levy and the user is far from clear and that the stated aims of the levy may not be met because of the approach used for implementation.

THE IMPACT OF THE LEVY ON PARKING SUPPLY

The second and major aspect of this chapter is the impact of the parking levy on parking supply. In general, research literature focussing on parking supply has tended to focus on the impact that parking supply has on travel demand (e.g. Bly & Dasgupta, 1995; Hidas & Cuthbert, 1998; Morrall & Bolger, 1996; Shoup, 2005; Transport Co-operative Research Program, 2003). Parking supply can be used as a travel demand management measure on its own, without any pricing signals. However, reducing parking supply without introducing price signals can lead to a non-optimal distribution of traffic flows (Verhoef, Nijkamp, & Rietveld, 1995). One cause of these inefficiencies is the lack of driver information as to whether a parking space will be available at their destination (Verhoef et al., 1995).

Restricting parking supply, but leaving it unpriced, also rations parking spaces on a first-come-first-served basis rather than on a willingness-to-pay principle (Verhoef et al., 1995). When those drivers who arrive first are not confronted with the implicit search costs they pose on successive drivers, the first-come-first-served rationing principle leads to inefficient patterns of parking space occupation over the course of the day. For example, it is unlikely that a car park facility that can be used free of charge will provide sufficient capacity for shoppers who may wish to park later in the day, unless an oversupply of parking is provided or the existing spaces are restricted to certain users. Either way, this provides for an inefficient use of the available parking facilities. Although drivers may respond to a first-come-first-served rationing principle by rescheduling their trips (which implies a loss of utility and therefore serves as a proxy for a driver's willingness-to-pay), such rescheduling generates important welfare losses (Verhoef et al., 1995).

In practice, many cities implement parking pricing and supply measures in tandem (see case studies cited in European Co-operation in Science and Technology, 2001), and their effects are interrelated. If parking is restricted for regulatory reasons, its scarcity supports pricing. If supply is restricted for commercial reasons (e.g. if there are higher value uses for the land), the capital cost is also greater and it is likely to be priced accordingly. While many inner city areas maintain some form of regulatory parking restrictions (even on private, off-street facilities), most commercial car parks are priced to maximise revenue to the owner (TCRP, 2003). However, the relative scarcity of supply and the higher cost of land and construction in these areas support higher prices than could be charged in suburban locations. Conversely, where planning regulations require a *minimum* number of parking spaces, parking supply often exceeds the demand, necessarily reducing the marginal cost of parking particularly in locations outside the central business district (Shoup, 1999; Transport Co-operative Research Program, 2005).

The cause and effect of parking pricing and supply is also said to work in reverse. As parking prices increase, optimal parking supply (i.e. the number of parking spaces required to meet demand) tends to decline (Litman, 2006). Where parking is free or under-priced, consumers have little incentive to use parking facilities efficiently and car park operators have little incentive to efficiently manage such facilities. Free or under-priced parking therefore increases parking demand and total parking costs (Litman, 2006; Shoup, 2005). By increasing the cost of parking, consumers are encouraged to shift to alternative modes, forcing parking operators to manage their facilities more efficiently.

Due to the interdependence of parking supply and parking pricing policies, it is difficult to identify the extent to which supply and pricing individually influence travel behaviour. In particular, little research has been undertaken to explore supply aspects of this link. However, statistical analyses typically show a stronger direct relationship between travel behaviour and price than between travel behaviour and supply (TCRP, 2003). As Verhoef et al. (1995, p. 149) conclude, 'In a setting in which regulatory parking fees are equivalent to the first-best policy of road pricing, mere physical restrictions on parking space supply certainly are not'. However, the contributing role of parking supply in this chain of relationships cannot be overlooked.

The following section aims to explore how increased prices of parking have influenced supply using a case study of the Melbourne parking levy.

The General Parking Supply Context in Central Melbourne

General parking supply policy in Melbourne is the most firmly planned parking policy in the Melbourne metropolitan area (MMA), the state capital city of the State of Victoria, Australia. The City of Melbourne is the local government area including Melbourne CBD but is just one of 31 local government areas which comprise the wider MMA. The Victorian Planning Scheme (Department of Planning and Community Development, 2012) was developed in order to provide a consistent planning basis across all of the state. Within the Planning Scheme, Clause 52.06 governs the parking standards in terms of rates, dimensions and related considerations. Specifically,

Clause 52.06's purpose is to ensure that car parking facilities are provided in accordance with the State Planning Policy Framework and the Local Planning Policy Framework, including the Municipal Strategic Statement and local policies such as a Local Parking Precinct Plan (State of Victoria, 2008). Clause 52.06 aims to ensure that the design and location of car parking areas does not adversely affect the amenity of the locality; achieves a high standard of urban design; enables easy and efficient use; and protects the role and function of nearby roads.

Generally speaking, new developments must provide parking based on Clause 52.06−5. Table 2 provides some of the standardised land uses that have a predetermined parking standard or rate (which specifies the number of supplied spaces required per development) as set out in the Victorian Planning Scheme (Department of Planning and Community Development, 2012). The parking rate specified in the Scheme is that required for development. Rarely do developers in the inner suburb provide more parking than that required by the Scheme due to the cost of providing a parking space. In outer suburbs, where the cost of land is lower, some developers may exceed that required by the Scheme.

The centre of Melbourne does not follow the Victorian Planning Scheme categories of parking supply outlined in Table 2. Rather it has a flat rate of 5 spaces per 1,000 square meters of net useable floor area or 12 spaces per 1,000 square meters of floor area, whichever is the larger (Department of Planning and Community Development, 2012). For both approaches the parking provision would be smaller than the general rate shown in Table 2.

Table 2. Victorian Car Parking Requirements, Clause 52.06 Victorian Planning Scheme (2012).

Land Use	Car Space Measure	Parking Rate
Shop, other than specified in this table	Car spaces to each 100 m^2 of leasable floor area	4
Office other than specified in this table	Car spaces to each 100 m^2 of net floor area	3.5
Restaurant	Car spaces to each seat available to the public	0.4
Hotel	Car spaces to each 100 m^2 of leasable floor area	3.5
Post Office	Car spaces to each 100 m^2 of net floor area	4.0

Source: Department of Planning and Community Development (2012).

Further, parking pricing in Central Melbourne is much more vigorously implemented then in other parts of Greater Melbourne.

The relationship between parking provision and demand across Greater Melbourne is investigated next. The number of parking events and jobs in each local government area is presented in Fig. 1. It shows that there is an increase in parking demand as the number of jobs increases. However, for Central Melbourne, which is the far right hand point in Fig. 1, the parking events per job is considerably lower than in other parts of the city. This is due to the lower parking supply, higher parking price and higher provision of alternate means of getting to the central city, primarily public transport.

In summary the parking supply in Central Melbourne is relatively lower than that in the rest of the MMA and the demand for parking per usage category is also lower.

The actual parking supply in the central city is further complicated by the fact that parking is provided by a number of different parking providers. The impact of the parking levy on the provision of parking will differ for each of these providers. The following sections look at the amount of parking provided by the municipal authority, by commercial parking operators and for private non-residential use to set the scene for investigating the impact of the parking levy on parking supply in Central Melbourne.

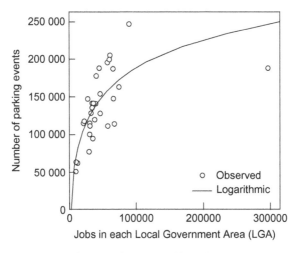

Fig. 1. Number of Jobs and Parking Events (Demand).

Municipal Parking

The City of Melbourne owns two off-street car parking facilities within the levy area (Hamer et al., 2012). These car parks provide a total of 499 car parking spaces (Hamer et al., 2012), a level of supply which has remained unchanged since at least 2004 (MCC, 2004). As discounted long-stay parking is not offered at either car park, the introduction of the levy has had minimal, if any, impact on the supply of municipal car parking spaces.

In addition to off-street parking, the City of Melbourne manages more than 4,000 on-street parking spaces within the Melbourne CBD and the area immediately north of the CBD (MCC, 2008a). On average, 41,000 drivers use these 4,000 car parking spaces each day (MCC, 2008a). None of these on-street parking spaces attract the congestion levy.

Commercial Parking

Parking is also supplied commercially to the general public as a turn up and pay arrangement or can be provided to companies for individuals on a periodic basis. All day public parking is termed 'early bird' parking and offers a discount for those arriving before a given time (usually around 10 a.m. on weekdays) and is normally used by commuters or those on all day business trips.

The supply of commercial off-street parking has been recorded in two statistical local areas of the City of Melbourne (Inner Melbourne and Southbank/Docklands) since 1997 and in the remaining areas of the City of Melbourne since 2002. Fig. 2 shows that, between 1997 and 2006, the number of commercial off-street car parking spaces in the Inner Melbourne and Southbank/Docklands statistical local areas increased by more than 10,000. This increase represents a 32% growth in the supply of parking within the levy area, or an annualised growth rate of 3.2% per annum. This increase accounts for the majority of parking supply growth recorded in the levy area, with parking supply in other parts of the levy area remaining relatively steady since its inclusion in the data set in 2002.

Between 2006 and 2008, after the levy was introduced, the total number of commercial off-street parking spaces within the levy area declined by almost 2,000 (or 3.3%); the majority (88%) of this decline resulted from a reduction in the number of commercial car parking spaces within the Southbank and Docklands area of Melbourne CBD. While this period coincided with the introduction of the congestion levy, it was also a period of major development in the Docklands precinct, with large parcels of land (that were previously being used for off-street car parking) being redeveloped for residential and commercial purposes.

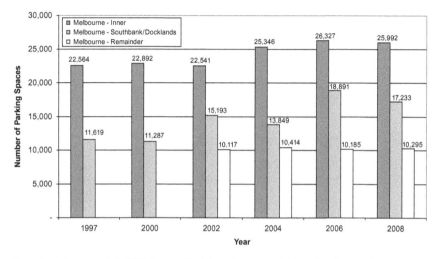

Fig. 2. Commercial Off-Street Parking Spaces within the Levy Area. *Note*: Excludes parking spaces outside the City of Melbourne. *Source*: CLUE (MCC, 1997, 2000, 2002, 2004, 2006, 2008a, 2008b).

The number of commercial parking spaces, within the City of Melbourne boundaries, but outside the levy area, increased by 17% over the period 2006 and 2008. This growth is larger than that in the levy area, but is based on a lower sample size since, in 2006, the number of commercial car parking spaces outside the levy area comprised less than 10% of the total commercial off-street parking supply within the municipality.

Private, Non-Residential Parking
The supply of private, non-residential parking within the City of Melbourne has also been recorded over the same time-frame (i.e. Inner Melbourne and Southbank/Docklands since 1997, and in the remaining areas of the City of Melbourne since 2002). Fig. 3 shows that steady growth in private, non-residential parking was recorded in all three statistical local areas up until 2006, with an additional 10,400 private car parking spaces (equivalent to a 35% increase) being provided across the levy area between 2002 and 2006. From 2006 to 2008, the total number of private, non-residential car parking spaces within the levy area increased by a further 2,300, or 6%. The number of private, non-residential car parking spaces within the Inner Melbourne and Southbank/Docklands statistical local

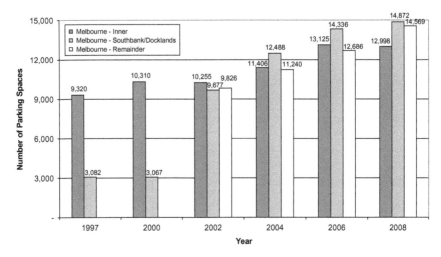

Fig. 3. Private, Non-Residential Off-Street Parking Spaces within the Levy Area. *Note*: Excludes parking spaces outside the City of Melbourne. *Source*: CLUE (MCC, 1997, 2000, 2002, 2004, 2006, 2008a, 2008b).

areas remained relatively steady between 2006 and 2008, with 82% of the increase in supply being provided outside of these areas.

Fig. 4 shows the number of private, non-residential car parking spaces within the entire City of Melbourne. From 2002 to 2006, the number of car parking spaces provided within the levy area increased at a rate of 2,600 per year, compared to an increase of 570 per year outside the levy area. In the two years following the levy's initial introduction, this change partially reversed, with car parking numbers increasing by 1,470 per year outside the levy area compared to only 1,150 per year inside the levy area.

Overview of Supply Changes

Table 3 summarises how parking supply within the levy area varied between 2004 and 2008. This shows that, prior to the introduction of the levy, there was strong growth in both private, commercial and total parking. Following the introduction of the levy, in the period between 2006 and 2008, total parking has continued to increase but at a substantially lower rate. The supply of public off-street car parking decreased slightly, reversing the trends from earlier survey periods. By contrast, the supply of private, non-residential off-street car parking has increased slightly over

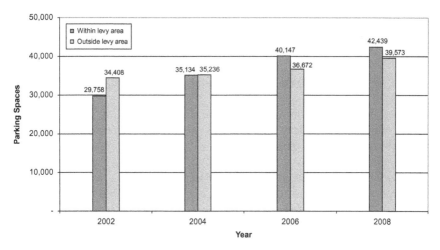

Fig. 4. Private, Non-Residential Parking Spaces Inside and Outside Levy Area. *Note*: Excludes parking spaces outside the City of Melbourne. *Source*: CLUE (MCC, 2002, 2004, 2006, 2008a, 2008b).

Table 3. Summary of Off-Street Parking Supply in the Levy Area (MCC Area Only).

No. of Spaces				Change (2004–2006)		Change (2006–2008)	
	CLUE 2004	CLUE 2006	CLUE 2008	No.	%	No.	%
Commercial	49,609	55,403	53,520	5,794	11.7%	−1,883	−3.4%
Private	35,134	40,147	42,439	5,013	14.3%	2,292	5.7%
Total	84,743	95,550	95,959	10,807	12.8%	409	0.4%

Source: CLUE (MCC, 2004, 2006, 2008a, 2008b).

the same period, although the growth in the number of car parking spaces is far slower than it was between 2004 and 2006.

From these results alone, it is difficult to gauge the extent to which the levy may be causing observed changes in parking supply. It might be hypothesised that the higher parking prices resulting from the levy might have reduced parking demand and therefore encouraged parking providers to reduce their parking supply. However, over the same period (2006–2008), the global financial crisis took place which may have also acted to influence demand and supply.

Quantifying the Supply Impacts of the Levy

This section quantifies the changes in the supply of parking consequent on the introduction of the levy and explores the impact of the price of parking on short- and long-stay parkers.

Aggregate Changes in Long/Short-Stay Parking Supply

The Explanatory Memorandum of the Congestion Levy Bill (Parliament of Victoria, 2005) anticipated that imposing a levy only on long-stay parking spaces in commercial car parks would encourage car park owners and operators to convert these spaces into short-stay car parking spaces.

While the overall reduction in the supply of commercial parking that has occurred since 2006 (Fig. 2) appears to support sustainable transport objectives, the data cannot reveal whether this reduction has been accompanied by a similar (or greater) reduction in the number of commercial long-stay parking spaces. Some evidence of how the mix of parking types has changed since the introduction of the levy comes from the *Inner Melbourne Car Park Price Study* (2008b), which revealed that, over the two and a half year survey period, 5 (of 50) car park sites ceased offering discounted daily (early bird) parking rates.

Annual returns provided by car park operators to the State Revenue Office (DTF, 2010) provide a further indication of the shift in the parking mix. Fig. 5 compares the number of leviable parking spaces to non-leviable parking spaces within the levy area. Leviable parking spaces include all non-exempt parking spaces in private, non-residential car parks; all non-exempt parking spaces in commercial car parks provided for periodic parking; and all non-exempt parking spaces in a municipal or commercial car park that satisfy the levy's entry time and duration criteria (Parliament of Victoria, 2005). Non-leviable parking spaces include all other non-exempt parking spaces and primarily service the needs of weekday casual users and daily users arriving after 9.30 a.m.

Between 2005 and 2007, the number of leviable parking spaces within the levy area fell slightly (by 2.1% or about 1,000 spaces), but remained relatively steady thereafter. The number of non-leviable parking spaces dropped sharply in the year immediately following the introduction of the levy (2006), but more than recovered in 2007 to the point where there was a 25%

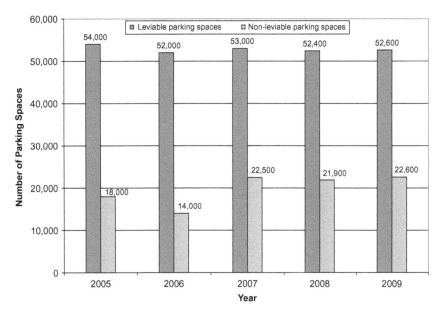

Fig. 5. Supply of Leviable and Non-Leviable Spaces in the Levy Area. *Note*: Excludes parking spaces within Docklands. *Source*: DTF (2010).

increase in non-leviable parking spaces between 2005 and 2007. The number of non-leviable parking spaces has remained relatively steady since 2007.

Overall this data suggests long-term parking supply has fallen but not by much. Short-term parking has increased considerably, which is also consistent with expectations. However the growth in short-term parking supply is much greater than the small decline in long-stay parking. Rather than the levy causing a shift from long-stay to short-stay parking it seems to be having the effect of restricting growth in long-stay parking and encouraging growth in short-stay parking. This is not quite the result expected of the levy.

These conclusions are however speculative and reliant on the quality of the data from the annual returns. This data is known to have quality issues.[1]

Disaggregate Changes in Parking Supply and Price
The link between the introduction of the levy and changes in parking price and supply can be considered in more detail by exploring the relationship between early-bird (long stay) and weekday casual (short stay) parking

prices (as outlined in Hamer, 2012) and the supply of leviable and non-leviable parking spaces.

Because supply data is only available on an annual basis it is assumed that the supply of parking remains unchanged within any given year. For ease of presentation, the analysis only uses data from those months in which the highest and lowest price (in any given year) were recorded.

Fig. 6 demonstrates the relationship between early-bird parking price and the supply of non-leviable parking spaces.

Based on the literature, it may be expected that increases in early-bird parking prices (precipitated by the levy) would generate an increase in the supply of non-leviable parking spaces, as the operator converts (long-stay) leviable parking spaces into non-leviable spaces. Fig. 6 suggests that a moderately strong positive correlation ($r_{xy} = 0.58$) which confirms this expectation.

Fig. 7 compares the relative price of early-bird parking to the supply of leviable parking spaces. If all data points are used, a moderately weak negative correlation ($r_{xy} = 0.35$) is shown. The substantial change after the introduction of the levy was possibly a short-term reaction to the levy.

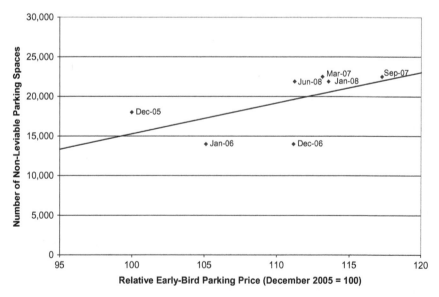

Fig. 6. Correlation between Early-Bird Price and Non-Leviable Supply. *Source*: DTF (2010), MCC (2008a, 2008b).

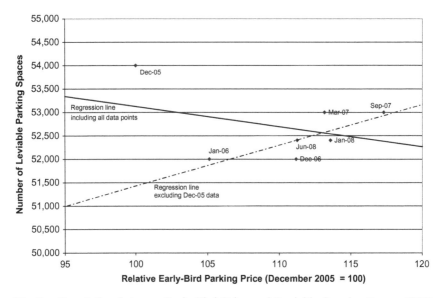

Fig. 7. Correlation between Early-Bird Price and Leviable Supply. *Source*: DTF (2010), MCC (2008a, 2008b).

This can be illustrated by removing the December 2005 data point. The remaining data (January 2006–June 2008) shows a strong, positive correlation between long-stay parking price and supply ($r_{xy} = 0.77$). The overall trend shown by all data points is likely to be the consequence of movement towards a pseudo equilibrium point.

Fig. 8 compares the relative price of weekday casual parking to the supply of non-leviable parking spaces. Despite the levy not applying to casual parking, the price of casual parking has increased above inflation since the levy was introduced (Hamer et al., 2012). This might be expected to have reduced casual parking supply. However, the analysis shows a moderately strong ($r_{xy} = 0.69$) positive correlation between casual parking price and supply. This overall trend is likely to result from the progressive movement towards a pseudo equilibrium of supply and demand, complicated by a changing pricing mechanism.

In general, the findings suggest that parking price and supply are positively correlated, with the possible exception of long-stay parking price and supply (Fig. 7). The results shown in Figs. 6 and 7 (including all data points) might be expected, given the hypothesis that increases in parking prices lead to an optimisation of parking supply. However, the results

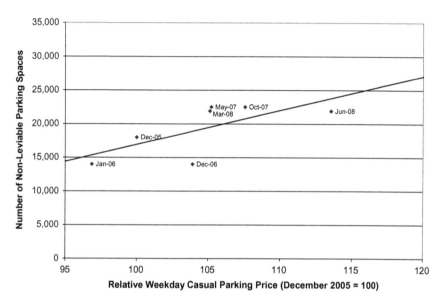

Fig. 8. Correlation between Weekday Casual Price and Non-Leviable Supply.
Source: DTF (2010), MCC (2008a, 2008b).

shown in Fig. 8 (and those shown in Fig. 7, if the 2005 data is excluded)
tend to contradict both this hypothesis and the aims of the levy itself.

One possible explanation for the confounding results is that early-bird
parking is only one element of long-stay parking supply. Perhaps other
long-stay commercial parking or private non-residential long-stay supply
has reacted differently? Data on this is not available.

An alternative explanation may be that there is some other (external)
factor that is influencing the supply of leviable parking spaces. Despite the
Global Economic Crisis, Melbourne CBD is one of the few areas where
employment has been growing consistently. This suggests that employment
growth may also be influencing the extent to which leviable parking spaces
are provided.

Fig. 9 shows a correlation analysis of full-time and total employment
against the supply of (all non-residential) off-street parking spaces.
Although, again, the data set is quite small, the results nevertheless demonstrate strong positive correlations for both full-time employment ($r_{xy} = 0.97$)
and total employment ($r_{xy} = 0.93$) and supply. Both of these correlations are
stronger than the correlations shown between parking price and parking
supply, suggesting that employment may be a stronger influencing factor.

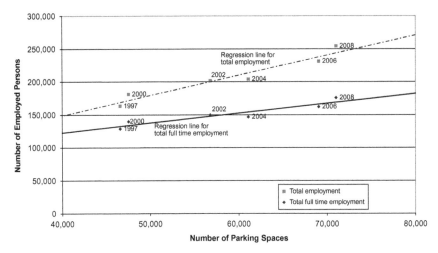

Fig. 9. Relationship between Off-Street Parking Supply and Employment. *Source*: CLUE (MCC, 2002, 2004, 2006, 2008a, 2008b).

Thus, while the levy may be having some impact on the supply of long-stay parking spaces, measuring the extent of its contribution is complicated by changes to inner city employment numbers and the resultant parking demand that this may be generating.

TRANSPORT IMPACTS OF THE LEVY

The overall transport impacts of the congestion levy are outlined in Hamer (2012). Hamer (2012) showed that the introduction of the congestion levy has resulted in significant reductions in total car travel demand to the levy area and a significant reduction in car (as driver) mode share for journey to work trips. This has corresponded with a significant increase in the public transport mode share for journey to work trips. However, the data cannot demonstrate the extent to which the introduction of the levy may have caused these changes. Analysis of longer-term trends and public transport user surveys suggest that the congestion levy is just one of many factors that users have taken into consideration when making their travel decision. In particular, while the relationship between parking pricing and travel demand is inelastic, the pricing of parking — and the extent to which it is passed on to the driver — is clearly a factor in the effectiveness of the levy.

Hamer's (2012) analysis of the travel and parking demand impacts of the levy suggests that, because the levy is largely not being borne by the drivers themselves, its effectiveness has been greatly reduced. It is estimated that following the introduction of the levy only 11% of the theoretical reduction in car travel demand has actually been achieved. Thus, the extent to which the levy is not being passed on by parking providers is undermining the stated purpose of the levy, and is limiting its effectiveness as a travel demand management tool. These findings suggest that the actual price increase, as experienced by users, is a critical determinant of the extent to which the supply of long-stay may be reduced and travel behaviour may be modified. Although some of the final results have relied on relatively small sample sizes (and must therefore be treated with a degree of caution), the results nevertheless highlight the importance of passing on the full cost of the congestion levy to the motorist, if the levy's supply and travel demand impacts are to be maximised.

Hamer (2012) indicates that while the travel demand impact of parking charges have formed the basis of much previous research (see, for example studies cited in TCRP, 2005), to date there has been little consideration – the review of the San Francisco commercial parking tax (Kulash, 1974) excepted – of the actual impact of area-wide parking pricing schemes despite their relatively widespread use. The research presented here has provided a better understanding of the impact of such schemes and their ability to effect a change in travel behaviour. In particular, the research has highlighted that if parking charges are to make a substantial contribution towards a change in travel behaviour, then it is critical that parking owners, operators and tenant organisations pass on the charge as an additional personal cost to users. This finding has important implications for other researchers and policy makers, who are promoting similar area-wide parking initiatives as an alternative to other more contentious policies such as cordon pricing or road-user charging. These findings may be applicable to more direct forms of road-user charging. If a large proportion of drivers have all of their vehicle operating costs paid for by their employer, the objective of the pricing mechanism may be undermined.

CONCLUSION

This chapter has explored three aspects of the Melbourne Congestion Levy.

The first is the question of who pays the levy. Hamer et al. (2012) showed that the parking price was set by market conditions and that the parking levy contributed only a small proportion (less than a third) to the overall cost payed by the users.

The second and major aspect of the chapter is the exploration of how the supply of off-street car parking spaces in Central Melbourne has changed since the introduction of a parking levy. Prior to the levy parking supply in both commercial and private, non-residential parking was growing. When the levy was introduced the following changes occurred:

- Within the levy area:

    - Total supply continued to increase but at a much lower rate. The total number of commercial spaces declined slightly while the number of private, non-residential spaces increased by a similar number. These trends may have been influenced by the global financial crisis as well as the levy itself.
    - The number of leviable parking spaces declined slightly immediately after the levy was introduced but remained stable thereafter. Growth occurred in the number of non-leviable spaces (however this finding warrants caution as source data is suspect).
    - As the price of early bird parking grew, the number of non-leviable spaces increased as expected. However, there is also evidence that the number of leviable parking supply increased. This is an unexpected result. It is hypothesised that growth in employment has increased demand for parking and may have counteracted the price signals that have been introduced.
    - After the introduction of the levy, the supply of short-term and casual parking increased as intended. However, unexpectedly, the introduction of the levy also coincided with increases in the price of short-term and casual parking. Consequently, short-term parking supply has been positively linked to price after the levy was introduced − a very unusual result.

- In the area immediately outside of the levy area:
    - The number of parking spaces supplied increased more than trend after the levy was introduced.

The message in these findings for the parking levy is unclear. The levy hoped to reduce long-term parking and encourage short-term parking. From a supply perspective there is no evidence of a meaningful decline in long-term parking while growth appears to have occurred in short-term parking. Some small increases in parking supply outside the levy area are noted. Parking prices meanwhile appear to have increased for all parking (including casual parking) which is contrary to the aims of the levy.

What these findings demonstrate is a very complex picture of the influences of supply, demand and price. The levy was introduced during a period of economic change and employment growth, both factors which also appear to have had a significant influence on supply.

Overall it is difficult to see positive outcomes for the aims of the levy from these findings. If reducing peak congestion was a central aim of the levy then there is little evidence of a decline in long-stay commuter parking supply.

From the perspective of future research this analysis has demonstrated that understanding the influences of parking supply, demand and price are a considerable challenge. Access to supply and price data from commercial sources is problematic due to confidentiality constraints. The quality of published data obtained in the application of the levy is also of limited value. This could have been addressed if a more comprehensive survey of parking supply had been undertaken prior to introducing the levy. This might also have acted to increase valid returns on leviable parking. It would also have been helpful if statements from parking suppliers in paying for the levy had included collection of some data relating to the use of parking.

There is clearly more scope for understanding the wider influences on parking supply into the future. For instance, parking supply outside the central city is rarely associated with pricing. The impact of this on the supply of parking over the entire urban region needs investigation. Further the relationship between parking supply and the provision of various levels of public transport is in need of investigation. More importantly there appears to be two parking policies in Australian cities, the central city and suburban areas. The impact of this on transport and land-use activity requires investigation.

The final area covered was the transport impacts of the levy. Hamer (2012) showed that the parking levy did have an impact on mode choice but the level of the impact was unclear due to the large number of other policy, infrastructure and economic changes that occurred during the study period.

Overall this chapter has reinforced the positive aspects of the parking levy, however refinement and improvement of the approach is required. Recent changes by the Victorian Government have addressed some of these aspects and the impact of these changes requires investigation. Most importantly, following its own investigation into the impact of the levy, from January 2014 the cost of the levy was increased by 40% to

$1,300 per annum, and its coverage extended to include short-stay parking spaces (VSRO, 2013). The impact of this change has not been considered in this research.

NOTE

1. If the results from Fig. 5 are compared to those in Figs. 2 and 3, it can be seen that the number of leviable parking spaces as determined from the annual returns differs from the number of parking spaces within the City of Melbourne that would be considered to attract the levy. Even accounting for the slight difference in the survey frame (CLUE excludes car parks outside the City of Melbourne's municipal boundaries; the data excludes parking spaces within the Docklands precinct) and the 13,500 non-residential levy exemptions that have been granted (VSRO, 2007), the results suggest a discrepancy of at least 10,000 car parking spaces on which the levy is not charged, equating to more than A$8 million in foregone revenue. The reason for this undercounting is unclear, given that the State Revenue Office used the City of Melbourne's database to identify relevant car park owners within the municipality (C. Phang [State Revenue Office] 2008, personal communication, 24 June). One possible explanation is that, in the interests of keeping administrative costs to a minimum, the State Revenue Office has relied, without sufficient verification, on parking owners and operators to provide a truthful account of the number of car parking spaces under their control.

REFERENCES

Bly, P. H., & Dasgupta, M. (1995). Urban travel demand: A growing business, but can it last? In L. J. Sucharov (Ed.), *Urban transport and the environment* (pp. 89–97). Southampton: Computational Mechanics Publications.

Department of Transport, Planning and Local Infrastructure. (2014). Planning Schemes Online. Retrieved from http://planningschemes.dpcd.vic.gov.au/. Accessed on May 6, 2014.

DTF. (2010). *Review of the effective of the congestion levy.* Melbourne, Victoria: Department of Treasury and Finance. Available at www.dtf.vic.gov.au/CA25713E0002EF43/WebObj/CongestionLevy2010/$File/CongestionLevy2010.pdf. Accessed on May 6, 2014.

European Co-operation in Science and Technology (COST). (2001). *COST 342: Parking policy measures and their effects on mobility and the economy.* Luxembourg: Community Research and Development Information Service (CORDIS).

Hamer, P. (2012). *Impact of parking price policies: A case study of the Melbourne Congestion levy.* Master of Engineering Science thesis, Department of Civil Engineering, Monash University.

Hamer, P., Young, W., & Currie, G. (2012). Do long stay parkers pay the Melbourne congestion Levy? *Transport Policy, 21*(2012), 71–84.

Hidas, P., & Cuthbert, M. (1998). Parking policy as a TDM measure in CBD areas. *Proceedings of the 22nd Australasian Transport Research Forum*, Australian Transport Research Board, Sydney.

Kulash, D. (1974). *Parking taxes as roadway prices: A case study of the San Francisco experience.* Washington, DC: The Urban Institute.

Litman, T. (2006). *Parking management best practice.* Chicago, IL: APA Planners Press.

McGuigan, D. (2009). *Car parking price policy of Melbourne CBD.* Clayton: Monash University Student Research Report.

Melbourne City Council (MCC). (1997). *Census of land use and employment.* Melbourne: Melbourne City Council.

Melbourne City Council (MCC). (2000). *Census of land use and employment.* Melbourne: Melbourne City Council.

Melbourne City Council (MCC). (2002). *Census of land use and employment.* Melbourne: Melbourne City Council.

Melbourne City Council (MCC). (2004). *Census of land use and employment.* Melbourne: Melbourne City Council.

Melbourne City Council (MCC). (2006). *Census of land use and employment.* Melbourne: Melbourne City Council.

Melbourne City Council (MCC). (2008a). *Census of land use and employment.* Melbourne: Melbourne City Council.

Melbourne City Council (MCC). (2008b). *Inner Melbourne car park study: Car park levy price impact assessment.* Melbourne: Collie Pty Ltd.

Morrall, J., & Bolger, D. (1996). The relationship between downtown parking supply and transit use. *Institute of Transportation Engineers (ITE) Journal, 66*(February), 32–36.

Parliament of Victoria. (2005). Congestion Levy Act 2005. Available at http://www.legislation. vic.gov.au/Domino/Web_Notes/LDMS/PubStatbook.nsf/f932b66241ecf1b7ca256e92000 e23be/bb8881c465167b52ca2570ad001f05eb/$FILE/05-074a.pdf. Accessed on May 6, 2014.

Shoup, D. C. (1999). The trouble with minimum parking requirements. *Transportation Research Part A, 33*, 549–574.

Shoup, D. C. (2005). *The high cost of free parking.* Chicago, IL: APA Planners Press.

State of Victoria. (2008). *Melbourne 2030: A planning update – Melbourne @ 5 million.* Melbourne, Victoria: Department of Planning and Community Development.

Transport Co-operative Research Program (TCRP). (2003). *Chapter 18 – Parking management and supply.* Traveler response to transportation system changes. TCRP Report 95, National Academy Press, Washington, DC.

Transport Co-operative Research Program (TCRP). (2005). *Chapter 13 – Parking pricing and fees.* Traveler response to transportation system changes. TCRP Report 95. T. R. Board. National Academy Press, Washington, DC.

Verhoef, E., Nijkamp, P., & Rietveld, P. (1995). The economics of regulatory parking policies: The (im)possibilities of parking policies in traffic regulation. *Transportation Research A, 29*(2), 141–156.

Victoria: State Revenue Office (VSRO). (2007). *Review of the administration of the congestion levy – Final report.* Melbourne: State Revenue Office.

Victoria: State Revenue Office (VSRO). (2013). *Recent changes to congestion levy.* Melbourne: State Revenue Office.

CHAPTER 14

A PARKING SPACE LEVY: A CASE STUDY OF SYDNEY, AUSTRALIA

Stephen Ison, Corinne Mulley,
Anthony Mifsud and Chinh Ho

ABSTRACT

Purpose – *This chapter provides a case study of the implementation of the Parking Space Levy (PSL) in Sydney, Australia. Introduced by the Parking Space Levy Act 1992, the scheme places a levy on business use of off-street car parking spaces with the revenues from the levy being hypothecated to public transport improvements. The chapter outlines the implementation of what is now a relatively mature scheme and examines how the revenues raised by the scheme have been spent.*

Methodology/approach – *This chapter offers a review of the introduction of the levy in Sydney and explores its impact in implementation with respect to changes to the number of parking spaces and an analysis of the way in which the hypothecated revenue has been spent. The implementation of the PSL is evaluated against the literature on hypothecation of funds and includes a discussion of policy issues for Sydney in the light of the evidence presented.*

Findings – *Whilst off-street parking availability is a major contributor to peak period traffic, the implementation of the PSL as a single rate of*

Parking: Issues and Policies
Transport and Sustainability, Volume 5, 317–333
Copyright © 2014 by Emerald Group Publishing Limited
ISSN: 2044-9941/doi:10.1108/S2044-994120140000005023

application has not led to a decrease in total number of available parking places in the City of Sydney. The number of concessions for unused spaces, whereby the levy was not imposed, increased when the levy rate was doubled in 2009 although this was accompanied by a fall in the number of exemptions from the levy. The revenue from the PSL has been dedicated to improvements in public transport infrastructure, primarily interchanges and commuter car parks although the more recent provisions to spend on 'soft' measures to improve sustainable travel have not been taken up.

Practical implications − *Whilst a stated objective of the PSL was to reduce congestion, the chapter concludes that the PSL had more than this single objective which makes it more difficult to assess whether its implementation has been a success.*

Originality/value of chapter − *This chapter provides an overview of the introduction, implementation and outcomes of the PSL in Sydney, relating it to the PSL in Melbourne (Chapter 13) and the WPL in Nottingham (Chapter 15). No other study to date evaluated the PSL in Sydney against the literature relating to hypothecation nor tracked the impacts of implementation of the PSL to evaluate its success.*

Keywords: Parking space levy; Sydney; revenue; implementation; exemptions

INTRODUCTION

Sydney has a unique importance in Australia. It is a Global city, the capital of the New South Wales state and the economic and cultural centre for the Greater Metropolitan Area (GMA) and the rest of Australia. The city centre, or CBD, is the location of significant employment and also congestion. Of all Australian and New Zealand cities, Sydney was ranked number 1 for traffic congestion with an estimated 40 minutes delay for each hour driven in the peak period and 92 hours delay per annum for a 30 minute commute and getting worse with an extra 2 minutes delay for each hour driven in the peak period and additional 2 hours delay per annum being identified between 2012 and 2013 (Tom Tom, 2013a). Worldwide, in a similar analysis, Sydney ranked 7th out of 161 cities across five continents for 2012 (Tom Tom, 2013b).

In 2013, 630,000 trips were made daily to the CBD and this is expected to grow to 775,000 by 2031 as a result of population growth and major developments in the CBD which is expected to generate jobs in excess of 20,000 (TfNSW, 2013). Access to the CBD by car creates a significant demand for parking which exists both on-street and off-street.

Introduced by the Parking Space Levy Act 1992, the Parking Space Levy (PSL) is well established in Sydney. The Act 1992 provided the legal background and the PSL was introduced on business use of (marked and unmarked) car parking spaces from 1 July 1992. The introduction of the PSL together with subsequent amendments to vary the level of the tax (the most recent of which is the Parking Space Levy Act 2009 which replaces the NSW Parking Space Levy Act, 1992, now repealed) identifies two objectives:

> The object of this Act is to discourage car use in leviable districts by imposing a levy on parking spaces (including parking spaces in parking stations), and by using the revenue to encourage the use of public transport (in particular, public transport to and from, or within, those districts).

Sydney's PSL, in common with the PSL in Melbourne (Australia) (see Chapter 13), is levied on off-street parking but is distinguished from the Parking Levy in Nottingham (UK) (see Chapter 15) by being levied on all off-street parking and not only those parking spaces attached to businesses. Similarly to Melbourne, the PSL was intended to encourage the use of public transport although there is not the stated intention, as in Melbourne, to create a shift from long-stay to short-stay spaces.

This chapter first outlines the implementation of the PSL in Sydney. This is followed by an examination of how the revenues raised by the PSL have been disbursed. As the revenues are hypothecated to specific expenditure items, this is undertaken against the background of elaborating the literature on hypothecation or 'earmarking'. The penultimate section discusses policy issues for Sydney in the light of the evidence presented before presenting conclusions in the final section.

THE PARKING SPACE LEVY, SYDNEY, AUSTRALIA

Collecting taxes or implementing a charge which is subsequently 'earmarked' or 'hypothecated' for a particular purpose is not a new idea. In Sydney, the PSL was introduced in 1992 by a Coalition government and retained by the following Labor government with clear state-wide 'earmarking' to public transport related activities embedded in the legislation.

The Levy and Its Implementation

The Sydney PSL is aimed at business parking and includes a significant number of exemptions. The levy is imposed on off-street commercial and office parking spaces, parking spaces in parking stations and vacant land used for parking cars. The exemptions include residential parking (on the same or adjoining premises), casual parking to provide 'services' such as tradespeople and visitors where there is no parking charge to local government offices, charities, religious organisations and where a vehicle is garaged overnight for emergency services. Since its introduction in 1992, the levy has been increased a number of times, and extended in area as shown in Table 1.

Table 1 shows that the levy was doubled in 1997, 2000 and 2009 with increases in between being tied to the Consumer Price Index (CPI) since 2003. In comparison to Melbourne where a parking space levy was introduced at roughly the same time, the initial levy was lower at introduction

Table 1. The PSL and the Levy Imposed by Year.

	Category 1 Areas: Sydney CBD, North Sydney and Milsons Point	Category 2 Areas: Bondi Junction, Chatswood, Parramatta and St Leonards
1-July-1992	$200	
1-July-1996	$200	
1-July-1997	$400	
1-July-2000	$800	$400
1-July-2003	$840	$420
1-July-2004	$860	$430
1-July-2005	$880	$440
1-July-2006	$900	$450
1-July-2007	$930	$460
1-July-2008	$950	$470
1-July-2009	$2,000	$710
1-July-2010	$2,040	$720
1-July-2011	$2,100	$740
1-July-2012	$2,160	$770
1-July-2013	$2,210	$780

Source: NSW Office of State Revenue.

in Sydney but is now higher than that of Melbourne. Moreover, a second category parking space levy with a lower levy was introduced in 2000 to cover areas outside Sydney CBD and North Sydney (referred to as the Category 2 PSL). Whilst these might be thought of as lower order business districts, both Chatswood and St Leonards are included in the 'global arc' area of high income (business and residential) areas which has been developed and reinforced by high technology industries and Sydney's universities.

Fig. 1 shows the geographical distribution of the areas subject to the PSL. This identifies that the Sydney CBD is only one of a number of areas covered by the legislation and reflects the way in which the Sydney Metropolitan area consists of a hierarchy of centres (referred to as a 'City of Cities' (NSW Government, 2012).

Fig. 2 shows the spatial distributions of car parks within the City of Sydney for both tenanted spaces and public car parking spaces. The levy is effectively only applied when the parking space is in use so for tenanted spaces only when leased and on public car parking spaces, defined as parking places set aside for members of the public to park, only when in use.

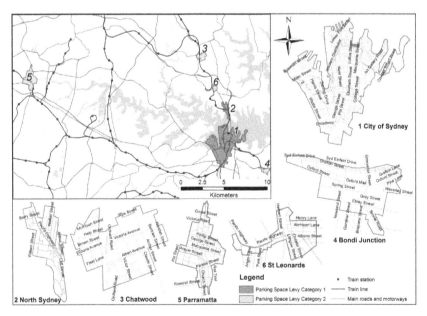

Fig. 1. Geographical Distribution of the PSL and Liveable Districts in Sydney, NSW. *Source*: Developed from GIS Layers and Parking Space Levy Maps (2009).

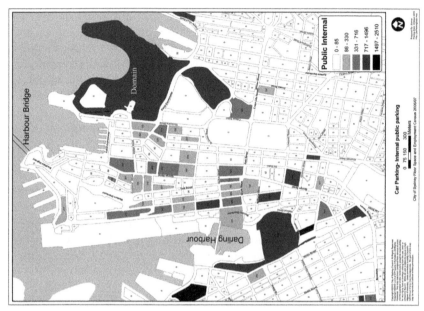

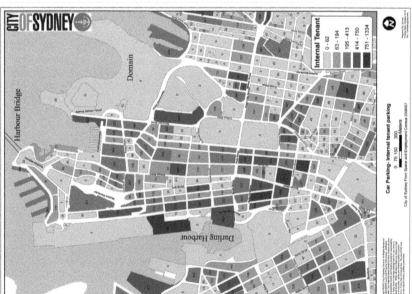

Fig. 2. Spatial Distribution of Car Parking Spaces in the City of Sydney. *Source:* City of Sydney.

For public parking spaces, a concession is granted for the time period when the car parking space is unused, calculated on a daily basis.

In Fig. 2, the map on the left shows internal tenant parking. This is parking for which a lease is granted for a dedicated space and for which the levy is chargeable on each leased space with exemptions only for unleased spaces. This map shows that there are large car parks in the core of the CBD along each of the arterial routes which creates congestion through drivers accessing these spaces in the peak hours. On the right, the map shows the distribution of car parking for public spaces in the City of Sydney. A comparison with the map of the distribution of tenanted spaces shows a lower density of large car parks in the core but two very large car parks at the Domain and a number of car parks adjacent to Darling Harbour which are particularly used for special harbour-side events. One of the issues for parking management for the City of Sydney is that access to the Darling Harbour car parks, being alongside a main arterial route to the Sydney Harbour Bridge, is particularly detrimental to traffic flow in the peak whereas the Domain car park does not have this impact. The parking levy does not appear to be reflected in the pricing of these car parks with 'Early Bird' parking rates being offered for entry during the peak that are significantly lower than the hourly rate (e.g. an 'Early Bird' rate of $14 (entry between 6.00 and 9.00am with departure between 3.00 and 7.00pm as compared to $11 for the first hour, $25 for between two and three hours and $32 for three or more hours (Wilson's Harbourside car park, 2013 rates[1]).

Within the boundaries of the City of Sydney, which includes the CBD, an examination of the data shows that the total number of parking places has not changed dramatically since 2007/2008 apart from a temporary increase in 2009/2010 for Sydney CBD with the total parking spaces returning to the previous levels in the following financial year. Fig. 3 combines tenanted and public car parking spaces but the constancy of total spaces masks the different trends in exempt and concessions for casual parking spaces which are unfilled.

Exemptions and concessions are an important part of the implementation of the PSL Act with Fig. 3 showing how exemptions and concessions for unused casual parking have changed over the period from 2007 to 2008. The unused casual car parking space is defined as a space set aside for public parking but remains unused for this purpose and a concession is given on a daily basis by parking operators for each unused space. The parking operator is required to keep records of the number of liable spaces, the number of spaces within this which are set aside as casual parking spaces

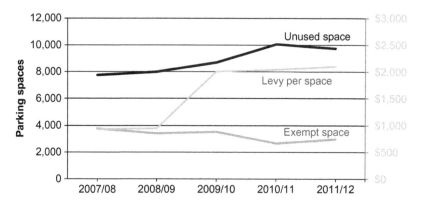

Fig. 3. Exemptions and Unused Casual Spaces in the City of Sydney 2007/
2008–2011/2012 *Source*: Data provided by City of Sydney.

and the number which remain unused on each day, with the determination
of 'unused' being related to the time of day of maximum daily usage, designated as 1.00 pm unless another determination is established.

In Fig. 3, the number of unused casual spaces is calculated by dividing
the total monetary value of the unlet lease and unused casual space concessions (disclosed by parking operators) by the levy applied to a parking
space, converting the concession value into relevant spaces. This
figure shows that whilst the exemptions have declined over the period by
21% there was a 25% increase in the number of unused car parking spaces.
For the exempt spaces, these have fallen from being 8% of the total number of parking spaces in the City of Sydney to 6% between 2007/2008 and
2011/2012. The proportion of unused spaces increased from 16% of the
total spaces at the beginning of the period to 19.5% at the end with a 2.5%
jump in the 2009/2010 financial year when the levy was increased to $2,000
per space from $950. More disaggregate figures show that the highest
increase occurred in the CBD and areas closeby (Millers Point and the
Rocks) where the increases in unused space exceeded 50%. The response to
the increase in levy rate suggests either that the new levy rate had an impact
on reducing the demand for parking or that parking operators found the
new rate provided a higher incentive to better monitor and declare spaces
as unused. Exemptions, on the other hand, may have declined because of
reductions in residential parking as a result of City of Sydney planning policy on restricting parking on redevelopments leading to a reduction in the
stock of exempt parking, since the other categories of exemption (outlined

above) are unlikely to have reduced in demand. This highlights the importance of using multiple tools, including planning restrictions, in an overall
strategy to manage parking.

The Disbursement of Parking Space Levy Revenues

The PSL is collected by the NSW Office of State Revenue (OSR) and is
hypothecated to spending on public transport related activities.
'Hypothecation' or 'earmarking' is the designation or allocation of particular tax revenues to particular forms of government spending (Teja &
Bracewell-Milne, 1991, p. 43). As such, it refers to an alternative to funding
of provision from a pool of undifferentiated tax revenue (*ibid.*, p. 45).
Before discussing whether or not the disbursement of the PSL in Sydney has
helped to meet the aims of its implementation, this section first reviews the
literature on hypothecation so as to provide a framework for evaluation.

The Literature Context for Understanding the Pros and Cons of the Hypothecation of Revenues

As far back as 1984 the Brookings Institution identified that 'Earmarking
is prompted by a desire to protect particular programs, agencies, or regions
from competition and to provide them larger or more stable shares of
resources than they would otherwise obtain ... ' (Brookings Institution,
1984, p. 12). It is against this backdrop that this chapter considers the
hypothecation of the PSL in Sydney.

Deran (1965), in referring to hypothecation, highlighted a number of criticisms as well as a justification. The criticisms include the way in which
hypothecation is argued to hamper effective budgetary control by removing
degrees of freedom in spending taxation revenue (which explains why
Treasuries do not favour earmarking); to lead to a misallocation of
resources with 'excess' revenue being devoted to some functions and other
activities, not included in the earmarking, being unsupported; to inflexibil-
ity in revenue structure, making it difficult for authorities to enact
suitable adjustments when there is a change in conditions. Moreover, the
hypothecating of revenue can remain in place long after the need for which
it was established has disappeared, leading to a situation where a portion
of fiscal policy is removed from periodic review and control which in turn
impinges on the power of policy-makers.

Against this, Deran presented a number of economic and non-economic
factors which justify the use of hypothecation. In particular, hypothecation

applies the benefit theory of taxation; it assures a minimum level of expenditure to 'desirable' and identified authority functions; it assures continuity of funding for specific projects and hence is beneficial for long-term planning. Importantly, in the transport context, hypothecation can help in overcoming resistance to new taxes or increased rates, especially those designed to elicit behaviour change giving rise to more of a win−win situation. Whilst some of Deran's arguments depend on value judgements, these arguments have resonance for transport funding in an environment where limited funding is advanced as the reason for lack of implementation of transport projects.

Ring fencing revenue raised from a particular measure as a way of overcoming the resistance to a new tax is borne out by various studies in the international literature. For example, Ison (2000) sought the views of UK local authority officials and councillors to road pricing and found that support for such a measure increased dramatically if the road pricing scheme revenue was spent on specific policy options. In this regard 11.3% perceived road pricing as being totally/fairly acceptable before specific revenue allocation, whereas the figure was 54.6% if the revenue was allocated to specific policies such as improved local public transport. This line of argument was supported by Thorpe, Hills, and Jaensirisak (2000) who found that acceptance of road pricing increased with guaranteed revenue allocation. Not surprisingly, the first implementations of road pricing, such as London, Singapore and Stockholm all had some element of hypothecation to increase acceptability.

As highlighted by Deran (1965), the issue of policy acceptance is important but in many jurisdictions the potential to assure continuity for specific projects has also played a significant role in terms of hypothecation. For example, the Norwegian toll-ring schemes, namely Bergen in 1986, Oslo in 1990 and Trondheim in 1991, generated revenue specifically for a package of transport improvements ranging from new infrastructure (safety and environmental improvements (see Larsen, 1995)) which would have taken much longer to introduce if the tolls had not been implemented.

This literature suggests a number of issues are important in discussing the disbursement of the PSL revenues. Are businesses accepting of it? Has the objective of the PSL been met? Are the revenues spent in a transparent and supportive way to promote the success of the PSL? Next, the use of PSL revenues in Sydney are examined before returning to these questions in the following section.

Collection and Spending of the PSL Revenues
The levy is collected by the NSW Office of State Revenues and deposited into a special account called the Public Transport Fund. In 2011, receipts to the fund were in the order of $100m per annum (OSR Annual Reports).

From the date of implementation, the Public Transport Fund has been spent on bus priority and bus facilities (such as new layover spaces), commuter car parks, new ferry wharves, interchanges, new infrastructure for light rail and bus and maintenance. Fig. 4 shows the fund distribution between these different elements and reveals the greatest contribution has been to the provision of interchanges, although one interchange in particular, Parramatta, dominates this expenditure at $142m. Without the spend on Parramatta, the greatest part of the Fund has been used to fund 36 different commuter car parks, both new and to provide upgraded facilities.

The PSL Act 1992, Section 18(3) defined the way in which the Fund could be deployed as 'money for the construction and maintenance of car and bicycle parking facilities, and other infrastructure, which facilitate access to public transport services to and from the City of Sydney and any other areas covered by the PSL or in accordance with a direction of the Minister' (NSW Parking Space Levy Act, 1992, Section 18, 3–4). In the

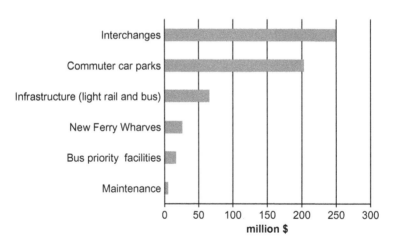

Fig. 4. Expenditure of the Public Transport Fund (Completed Projects) 1992–2011. *Source*: Public Transport Fund, Transport for NSW (http://www. transport.nsw.gov.au/content/parking-space-levy).

Table 2. Expenditure from the Public Transport Fund 2009–2011.

Parking Space Levy Act 2009	Expenditure from the Public Transport Fund	2009–2010 ('000$)	2010–2011 ('000$)
s11.3(a)	*Public transport services*	*0*	*0*
s11.3(b)	*Public transport infrastructure*	*97,108*	*73,346*
	Infrastructure maintenance	5,310	4,825
	Project development	420	573
	Car parks and interchanges	86,651	62,593
	Other transport infrastructure	4,727	5,355
s11.3(c)	*Communication to commuters*	*0*	*0*

Source: Public Transport Fund, Transport for NSW (http://www.transport.nsw.gov.au/content/parking-space-levy).

2009 Act which replaces this, the use of the Fund has been extended to finance:

(a) 'public transport services, and
(b) projects that facilitate access by public transport to and from, or within, leviable districts, including projects for the construction, maintenance and ongoing management of parking facilities, and other such infrastructure, and
(c) initiatives for the communication of information to commuters, including initiatives that make use of new technologies'. (NSW Parking Space Levy Act, 2009, Section 11 (3))

The extension in 2009 allows the Public Transport Fund to be used for current or revenue subsidy of public transport and to invest in 'soft' policy options of delivering information and improvements using new technology whereas previously it was reserved for capital expenditure. This change in potential use of the PSL has not so far been used as shown by the Fund statements for 2009/2010 and 2010/2011 in Table 2.

DISCUSSION

The discussion in this section is based on a review of levy documentation in Sydney covering the issues raised in the literature concerning the success and challenges faced by the PSL. In doing so, this section highlights issues which are being raised as part of current transport policy.

Are businesses accepting of it? Has the objective of the PSL been met? Are the revenues spent in a transparent and supportive way to promote the success of the PSL? How well has the PSL met its objectives?

How Accepting Are Businesses of the PSL?

Although the PSL is being charged on business and casual parking spaces in Sydney, it is businesses that have the most direct link between a lease or ownership of a specific parking space and the payment of the levy. An alienated business community coupled with a reluctance of businesses to move to the area because of the levy could be a serious concern, given the economic status of Sydney in the generation of economic activity for NSW and Australia more generally. However, a PSL which delivers a reduction in congestion and the improvement in use of public transport could easily outweigh the impact of businesses moving from precincts where the levy is imposed.

In Sydney, the attitude of businesses has not been a key feature of the PSL implementation. This is perhaps unsurprising since the PSL is low relative to incomes (approximately 2% of median incomes (ABS, 2011 Census)), and the journeys to work in the CBD by public transport already attracts a mode share of over 70%. However, the PSL has attracted media coverage for the way Sydney has been identified as the city with the 4th highest parking costs in 2011 (comparison of median prices for 20 capital cities (Colliers International, 2011)) as well as the earlier cited Tom Tom studies on congestion (2013a, 2013b). Periodic reviews of the PSL legislation have prompted advocates to argue against the PSL. The Property Council (2004), for example, which advocates for the property industry, argued not so much against the tax per se but for its failure to control congestion particularly in the Sydney CBD. Related to this is the bigger issue as to whether the PSL has the intended 'bite' to encourage behaviour change with little and mostly anecdotal evidence that users are not aware of the PSL being passed directly to car users, whether in dedicated employer spaces or in casual parking. Clearly behaviour change could be stronger if there was greater awareness of the levy and its motivation rather than relying solely on a price signal.

Are the Revenues Spent in a Transparent and Supportive Way to Promote the Success of the PSL?

In Sydney, whilst there is a clear link between the hypothecation of the PSL to the Public Transport Fund, there is no such transparency on how spending *from* the Public Transport Fund is planned to be linked to the objectives of the PSL in encouraging public transport use to the areas where the PSL is applied. As with all fixed period, all day taxes, the PSL does not distinguish between those travelling at congested times of the day, and those travelling at other times. On the positive side, and in common with all property based taxes, taxes on parking spaces are difficult to evade. Moreover, property-based taxes, because of their tax base, provide a stable and predictable source of revenue that is typically unaffected by business cycles.

The introduction of a hypothecated stream of revenue is often associated with a specific policy (London congestion charge and public transport, the workplace parking levy in Nottingham and the funding of tram extension (see Chapter 15)). In contrast, the Sydney PSL seems to have been introduced more as producing a 'pot of money' from which improvements to public transport access can be funded rather than a planned process of improving access to the specific centres where the PSL is applied.

How Well Has the PSL Met Its Objectives?

A single rate of application of PSL (whether Category 1 or Category 2) undoubtedly makes the scheme relatively simple to administer. However, this single rate of application does not allow a differentiation between areas within the spatially differentiated centres nor does it allow for differentiation between car park access which contribute more or less to congestion. It is therefore somewhat of a crude instrument and only an indirect instrument for government since its objectives (to reduce congestion) do not necessarily align with car park operators' objectives (to maximise or protect their revenue).

Off-street parking is the major contributor to peak period traffic into the CBD and initiatives by car park operators through 'earlybird' rates and 'book a space' (pre-booking of a space with a big discount) encourage car drivers to access the CBD and other centres (where the PSL is in operation) during the morning peak when the impact of such access is most severe with traffic congestion being at its highest. This could be addressed by complementing the PSL with the approach of Melbourne, Australia where the PSL places the tax on long-stay parking places only (see Chapter 13). Perhaps more importantly, the single rate of PSL within the CBD which covers a significant spatial area, means that there appears to be significant variability in car park occupancy rates with car parks towards the fringe of the PSL area being relatively underused. This maybe a reflection of the success of the PSL in discouraging car parking and car use (especially since the significant price increase in 2009) or alternatively, it could be a reflection of the more recent ability of car park owners to claim reductions for unused 'casual' parking spaces on a daily basis. This exemption of course militates against the stability of the tax revenue and is the basis of an action in the Sydney City Centre Access Strategy ' ... [to] work with car park owners and operators to review the current management and pricing of parking facilities at different times of the day' (TfNSW, 2013, p. 26).

For Sydney, in all the centres where PSL is applied, the tax on parking spaces has more than one objective. In addition to the revenue raising properties of the tax there are additional objectives that the PSL seeks to address. A reduction in congestion is a stated objective with the implicit objective of encouraging transfer to public transport modes through improving the quality with the spending of hypothecated funds. However, congestion in Sydney remains an issue and over 50% of respondents to the Sydney Household Travel Survey identified the use of public transport was to 'avoid parking problems' (Hey & Shaz, 2012). There is however no direct evidence as to whether parking difficulties are related to expense or lack of supply and, of course, there is no counterfactual evidence to know what would have happened if the PSL had not been implemented.

CONCLUSIONS

Earmarking revenue for particular purposes is not a recent phenomenon, with the introduction of the PSL dating back 20 years. Hypothecation can assure a minimum level of expenditure for a particular project, can assure continuity, as well as being beneficial for long-term planning and aiding in overcoming resistance to the introduction of a new levy.

Since it is the business community who in theory pay the levy then how they react is clearly important. It is possible that they may choose to relocate and/or that businesses considering relocating to the area may think again although the current rate of the PSL is probably only a very small proportion of location costs in Sydney. Against this small cost, Sydney centre locations offer benefits associated with being such a prime location. For a PSL to work effectively as a 'stick' to reduce congestion by achieving the behaviour change in employee travel to work patterns, businesses need to pass on the levy to their employees. It is of serious concern that the anecdotal information in Sydney suggests employees are not generally aware of paying for the PSL in their salary package if their employment is associated with a reserved car parking space.

Commuters in particular may not benefit from the spending of earmarked revenue if it is spent, for example, on a car park or interchange to which they do not have easy access. This is particularly true in Sydney where the Public Transport Fund is used more as a 'pot of money' for eligible projects.

Whilst not explicit at the time of introduction, the success of a parking levy might be seen as a reduction in the number of car spaces used for parking in the designated area. In Sydney, parking spaces at the fringes of the taxed area are more likely to be unused and therefore not generate levy revenue. As part of a policy of taxing off-street car parking spaces, policymakers should give thought to design developments and land use solutions which include car parking spaces to ensure that if not required in the future, car parking spaces can be converted into alternative uses, such as commercial or rental spaces. The City of Sydney, as one of the local government areas where the PSL is levied, has embraced the principle of addressing car parking as part of its planning process but the other local government areas are not as proactive.

On the positive side the PSL, as a land-based tax, is capable of providing a more stable source of revenue that is relatively simple to administer, as compared to an income-based tax which can be seriously affected in its revenue generation by economic cycles. But the revenue raising potential is critically affected by the type of exemptions that are granted. More than the revenue stream guarantee, the exemptions also dictate how easily a parking levy can meet its other objectives. Although the PSL was introduced to reduce congestion, the policy's failure to include on-street parking and the agreement to exempt key categories such as unused casual parking in Sydney, will compromise the message to car-based commuters.

Having more than one objective, the PSL aims to raise revenue, aid in reducing congestion, encourage alternative modes of transport and stimulate the uptake of 'softer' measures to increase sustainable travel. However, policies which have more than one objective are more difficult to evaluate for their success and, in particular, give opportunities for opposition on the grounds that one element of the policy is not working.

NOTE

1. http://www.wilsonparking.com.au/go/wilson-car-parks/nsw/harbourside

REFERENCES

ABS (Australian Bureau of Statistics). (2011). *Census quick stats.* Retrieved from http://www. censusdata.abs.gov.au/census_services/getproduct/census/2011/quickstat/1GSYD. Accessed on 1 August 2013.

Brookings Institution. (1984). *Government finance in developing countries.* Washington, DC: Brookings Institution.

Colliers International. (2011). Media release, August 8. Available at Colliers International Global CBD parking rate survey. Available at http://newcastle.colliers.com.au/sitecore/ content/Colliers_Corporate/News/News-details.aspx?NewsId={90377C21-B011-4F2A-B2CF-517B724A4617}. Accessed on 12 March 2013.

Deran, E. (1965). Earmarking and expenditures: A survey and a new test. *National Tax Journal, 18*, 354–361.

Hey, A., & Shaz, K. (2012). *Parking and mode choice in Sydney: Evidence from the Sydney Household Travel Survey.* 35th Australasian Transport Research Forum 2012, Perth, Australia. Retrieved from patrec.org

Ison, S. G. (2000). Local authority and academic attitudes to urban road pricing: A UK perspective. *Transport Policy, 7*(4), 269–277.

Larsen, O. I. (1995). The toll cordons in Norway: An overview. *Journal of Transport Geography, 3*, 187–197.

NSW Government. (2012). *Metropolitan Plan for Sydney 2036.* Retrieved from http:// metroplansydney.nsw.gov.au/Home/MetropolitanPlanForSydney2036.aspx. Accessed on 21 February 2013.

NSW Parking Space Levy Act. (1992). *Act 32 of 1992.* Retrieved from http://www.austlii.edu. au/au/legis/nsw/repealed_act/psla1992189/. Accessed on 1 July 2013.

NSW Parking Space Levy Act. (2009). *Act 5 of 2009.* Retrieved from http://www.austlii.edu. au/au/legis/nsw/consol_act/psla2009189/. Accessed on 1 July 2013.

OSR (Office of State Revenue). (various dates). *Annual reports.* Retrieved from http://www. osr.nsw.gov.au/about/publications/annual/archive/. Accessed on 21 February 2013.

Property Council of Australia. (2004). *Parking space levy review.* Retrieved from www. propertyoz.com.au. Accessed on 12 March 2013.

Teja, R. S., & Bracewell-Milnes, B. (1991). *The case for earmarked taxes: Government spending and public choice.* Research Monograph 46. Institute of Economic Affairs, London.

TfNSW. (2013). *Sydney city centre access strategy for further consultation.* Retrieved from transport.nsw.gov.au/content/sydney-city-centre-access-strategy. Accessed on 5 October 2013.

Thorpe, N., Hills, P., & Jaensirisak, S. (2000). Public attitudes to TDM measures: A comparative study. *Transport Policy, 7*, 243–257.

Tom Tom. (2013a). *Australia and New Zealand congestion index.* Q2 report 2013. Retrieved from www.tomtom.com/en_au/congestionindex. Accessed on 2 February 2014.

Tom Tom. (2013b). *Congestion index.* Retrieved from tomtom.com/en_gb/congestionindex/. Accessed on 10 October 2013.

CHAPTER 15

A CASE STUDY OF THE INTRODUCTION OF A WORKPLACE PARKING LEVY IN NOTTINGHAM

Simon Dale, Matthew Frost, Jason Gooding, Stephen Ison and Peter Warren

ABSTRACT

Purpose − *A Workplace Parking Levy (WPL) scheme represents a major transport demand management intervention which raises a levy on private non-domestic off street parking provided by employers to employees, regular business visitors and students. It therefore increases the average cost of commuting by car and stimulates a contraction in the supply of workplace parking places. Under UK legislation the revenue from such a scheme is hypothecated funding for further transport improvements. As such it is potentially an important mixed policy instrument available to transport authorities to tackle traffic congestion and create extra transport capacity by using the additional funding such a scheme provides. At present, in the United Kingdom, only Nottingham City Council has implemented such a scheme and thus an understanding of*

Parking: Issues and Policies
Transport and Sustainability, Volume 5, 335−360
ISSN: 2044-9941/doi:10.1108/S2044-994120140000005024

how that scheme was implemented, how it operates and the outcomes after a full year of operation are of importance to transport academics and other local authorities considering utilising a similar approach.

Methodology — *This chapter presents an overview of the WPL scheme in Nottingham. The legislation, implementation experience, monitoring framework and outcomes for this scheme after the first year of full operation are discussed by drawing on current literature, documentary evidence and monitoring data.*

Findings — *The Nottingham WPL scheme was fully implemented in April 2012. The gap between the provisions of the underpinning legislation and the functioning scheme has necessitated the formulation of policy in line with the spirit of the legislation. Acceptance by the business community and the public were further barriers to implementation which were mitigated by a consultation process and a Public Examination. However acceptance remains a concern until the scheme has been shown to meet its key objective of reducing congestion. To date there is no evidence that the scheme has had a negative impact on business investment and, while there is as yet no evidence traffic congestion has reduced, it is still early for such impacts to be identified especially as the majority of the associated public transport improvements are yet to be implemented. However the WPL has already raised £7 million in net revenue in its first year of operation which is hypothecated for public transport improvements which may help encourage inward investment and reduce car travel.*

Practical implications — *At present the Nottingham WPL scheme has only been operational for a short time and a limitation to the research presented here is that the major public transport improvements part funded by revenue hypothecated from the WPL are not yet in place. It will be necessary to wait at least a further 3 years before more definite conclusions as to the success of the WPL package can be drawn.*

Originality/value of the chapter — *As the first of its kind in the United Kingdom or indeed in Europe, the WPL scheme in Nottingham provides a unique contribution to the literature, comparing and contrasting implementation and outcomes with those in Australia and Canada. Geographical and cultural differences between the United Kingdom and these countries mean that conclusions drawn concerning existing schemes in other continents are not necessarily transferable to the United*

Kingdom. This chapter provides evidence in a UK framework to assess if the approach could be suitably applied more widely.

Keywords: Workplace; parking; levy; Nottingham; hypothecation; implementation

INTRODUCTION

This chapter aims to present an overview of the Workplace Parking Levy (WPL) scheme in Nottingham, a medium-sized city in the United Kingdom. This scheme represents a major transport demand management intervention by increasing the average cost of commuting by car by the introduction of a new cost element to parking at the workplace. The revenue raised is hypothecated under UK legislation for transport improvements. In the case of Nottingham the majority is to be spent on public transport improvements, although there is support, for workplace travel planning and cycle infrastructure.

The legislation, implementation experience, monitoring framework and outcomes to date for this scheme are discussed with a view to informing the viability of such an approach for other cities in the United Kingdom or indeed world-wide.

The Workplace Parking Levy Scheme and Nottingham

The Nottingham WPL scheme operates by charging a levy or tax on each parking place occupied by an employer, student or regular business visitor attending their place of work. This is intended, therefore, to impact specifically on commuting by car. Thus the WPL can be a more targeted alternative to other forms of congestion charging such as road user charging (RUC). A WPL will therefore have a dual purpose:

1. To act as a transport demand management tool by either:
   - increasing the cost of commuting by car when the charge is passed on by the employer to the employee or;
   - by the reduction in the supply of workplace parking places due to employers reducing their provision.

2. To fund transport improvements: While the statutory hypothecation for any WPL revenue in the United Kingdom is for all transport

improvement purposes, the City of Nottingham Workplace Parking Levy Order, 2008 (Annexes 1 and 2) restricts this further during the first 10 years of operation mainly to supporting named large scale public transport improvements. However it does also include measures to encourage the adoption of workplace travel plans and cycling. While it is anticipated that it is the WPL and large scale public transport schemes that will provide the major stimulus for any mode switch, these softer measures will complement the package and contribute progressively over time.

Nottingham is one of eight English core cities, situated 180 km north of London it is the largest conurbation in the East Midlands with a population of 670,000. Fig. 1 shows its location and principal transport links. With a smaller population of 304,000, the Nottingham City Council administrative area covers the central area of the city only. The urban suburbs of Beeston, West Bridgford, Hucknall, Gedling and Arnold lie in the surrounding boroughs for which Nottinghamshire County Council is the administrative authority.

Nottingham has long experienced peak period traffic congestion which is estimated to cost the economy £160 million per year (NCC, 2013). A population growth of around 9% over a 15-year period from 2011 is also expected (NCC, 2013) which, without intervention, would be expected to lead to a 15% increase in car journeys to City Centre destinations (NCC, 2008). Tackling congestion by promoting sustainable transport choices is at the heart of the City Council's transport policy and a central pillar of this approach has been the introduction of a WPL with the dual purpose of acting as a transport demand management tool in its own right as well as funding large scale public transport improvements.

The WPL is a public policy instrument option which has been made available to local authorities. Howlett and Ramesh (1995) identified three classifications of public policy instruments and this classification framework is of relevance to WPL. Their classification is as follows:

1. Voluntary Instruments – These leave the market to determine the policy based on a basic framework of rules set by government. Outcomes include free services provided by a community, voluntary work; the government may prompt this by cutting back on state provision while actively employing initiatives to encourage voluntary behaviour.
2. Mixed Instruments – This is a 'middle road' approach whereby government does not direct particular behaviour but rather encourages it by introducing financial incentives. An example of this is increasing taxation

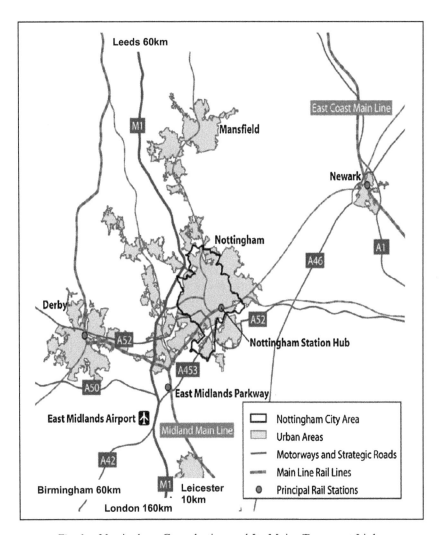

Fig. 1. Nottingham Conurbation and Its Major Transport Links.
Source: Nottingham City Council (2013).

on aviation fuel to curb the growth in cheap flights to address environmental concerns.

3. Compulsory Instruments – These are coercive actions which direct
   behaviour. Environmental speed restrictions in a National Park or

introducing Urban Clear Zones controlled by Traffic Regulation Orders are good transport examples of such policies.

The WPL is a classic example of a Mixed Instrument as it does not prohibit commuting by car but seeks to discourage it by increasing the cost of doing so while helping to provide viable alternative travel options.

THE LEGISLATIVE BACKGROUND TO WPL IN THE UNITED KINGDOM

The legislative background to the WPL can be traced back to the 1998 transport White Paper 'New Deal for Transport: Better for Everyone' which set out, amongst other measures, to allow local authorities to introduce either RUC or WPL schemes provided the revenue raised was hypothecated for transport improvements (DETR, 1998a, 1998b). Details of how a WPL scheme could be formulated are included in the UK government's Department for Transport's (DfT) consultation paper 'Breaking the Logjam' (DETR, 1998b). This included a number of issues for consultation, including exemptions and how the revenue should be spent. Effectively this sets out how the DfT thought a WPL should be constituted and asked the public and practitioners to comment. These documents and subsequent consultation informed the legislative background to WPL enshrined in the Transport Act (2000). This legislation defines a workplace parking place along with other key definitions and also grants the powers to local authorities to introduce WPL schemes and to enforce them.

The final piece of national legislation was put in place in 2009 in the form of the Workplace Parking Levy (England) Regulations (2009) (SI 2009/2085). This strengthened existing legislation for the issuing of penalty charges for non-compliance and for managing this process.

POLICY AND LEGISLATIVE BACKGROUND TO THE NOTTINGHAM WPL

In the United Kingdom it is mandatory for each local authority to produce a Local Transport Plan (LTP) and submit it to the DfT in order to receive a share of the funding available from central government. An LTP presents the overall transport strategy and the plan for implementing that strategy.

Nottingham City Council's LTP 2011–2026 (NCC, 2013) provides a summarising statement for the Council's vision for Transport in the City:

> A vision for improving Nottingham's transport Nottingham 2026: contributing to a safe, clean, ambitious, proud city.
>
> Transport provision, in all its various forms, is an issue for everyone affecting everyday lives. We want transport in Nottingham to provide the network for a dynamic international city of significance where people want to live, work, study and visit with a premiere economy built on success and fairness. We want to see a culture change amongst Nottingham's citizens and visitors, where walking, cycling and public transport becomes the logical first choice. We aim to tackle congestion, assist in city economic regeneration and promote greater accessibility and equality of opportunity which will contribute to a safer and healthier environment, whilst also reducing emissions and reducing carbon consumption. At the heart of this Plan is a commitment to make smaller scale improvements in local neighbourhoods which can have a huge impact on citizen's lives. In this way the overall quality of life for Nottingham and its citizens and visitors will be assured.

The issues which are drivers for investment in public transport in Nottingham can be summarised as follows:

1. Congestion: The City Council estimates that peak period congestion costs the city economy £160 million a year and is particularly acute on key radial routes.
2. Connectivity: The City Council believes that strong connectivity to other urban centres and national and international gateways is essential if Nottingham is to remain competitive as a location to do business.
3. Significant Growth: Using data from the Office for National Statistics, the City Council forecasts indicate that population is set to rise by 9% over a 15-year period from 2011 from increased job opportunities driven by a growth in science and technology, knowledge intensive and creative industries (NCC, 2013).

The City Council has justified its transport policy on these key issues and the statistics which define them. Although this policy framework has been derived within a political environment, the costs of congestion have been well documented both in the academic literature (Grant-Muller & Laird, 2006) as well as by Central Government (DETR, 1998b) with the available data demonstrating significant peak period congestion (NCC, 2008).

The WPL Business Case (NCC, 2008) used modelling which predicted a relatively modest reduction in congestion directly attributable to the WPL on its own. This was due to the relatively low charge per place, uncertainty over the extent to which employers would pass on the charge and the relatively small percentage of turnover that WPL liability would represent to the majority of employees (less than 1% (NCC, 2005)). Hence it is the combined effect of the WPL package which was anticipated to have a much larger constraining effect on congestion.

A cost benefit analysis was carried out, based on the UK government's appraisal framework. This placed the package in the 'High value for money' category. However the Business Case stresses the importance of the non-monetised wider social, environmental and economic benefits resulting from constraining congestion and providing connectivity via high quality public transport.

The drivers for intervention are also the raison d'être for the programme of major transport interventions due to be introduced by 2015, included in the current and previous LTPs. Table 1 summarises how each intervention interacts with the policy frame work set out above.

Although relevant to transport policy in Nottingham, the improvement to the A453 (see Fig. 1) is a Highways Agency Trunk road funded scheme (supported by Nottingham City Council).

The WPL has a dual role to play in the City Council's strategy both as a transport demand management tool and a major source of funding. In its first year of full operation the WPL has raised £7 million of hypothecated revenue for large scale public transport improvements (Dale, Frost, Ison, & Warren, 2013). Table 2 shows the cost of each scheme and the contribution proposed by WPL revenues.

This data shows how funds raised by WPL are leveraged by investment from Central Government, notably for NET Phase 2 where the WPL is funding the £150 million local contribution, with the remaining £371 million coming from non-local sources. It is noted in the Nottingham LTP (NCC, 2013) that one benefit of investing in large scale public transport schemes is the significant temporary boost to the local economy while they are being built prior to implementation.

Public Consultation Process

The Nottingham WPL scheme was developed and approved after a period of scheme development and subsequent extensive public consultation by Nottingham City Council. The Council began investigating the feasibility of implementing a WPL scheme in Nottingham in 2000 with the Council's

Table 1. Issues Tackled by Programmed Transport Schemes in Nottingham.

Intervention	Description	Constrain Congestion	Fund Public Transport Improvements	Provide for Growth	Improve Connectivity
Workplace Parking Levy	Levy payable by employers on parking places provided to employees, regular business visitors and students	✓	✓		
Nottingham Express Transit Phase 2	Provision of two additional tram lines to Chilwell and Clifton linked to the central public transport hub at Nottingham Station	✓		✓	✓
Regeneration of Nottingham Station	Refurbish Nottingham Station to provide high quality public transport hub	✓		✓	✓
Ring Road Major Scheme	Improvements to junctions to ease congestion and improved public transport interchanges along the Nottingham Ring Road	✓			✓
Provision of Link Buses	Provide high quality link bus services between the tram corridors	✓		✓	✓
A453 Dualling	Convert the link road from junction 24 of the M1 motorway to dual carriageway	✓		✓	✓

Table 2. Funding of Programmed Major Transport Schemes in Nottingham.

Scheme	Total Cost (£millions)	NCC 'Local' Contribution Not Including WPL Contribution (£millions)	WPL Contribution (£millions)	Non-Local Sources (£millions)	Completion Date
Nottingham Express Transit Phase 2	570	29	170 (30%)	301	2014
Ring Road Major	16.175	3.2	0	12.975	2015
Provision of Link Buses (Capital only)	8.8	0.3	3.78 (42%)	4.72	On going
Local Transport Plan	6 pa	0	0	6 pa	On going
Refurbishment of Station	60	0	11.7 (19.5%)	48.3	2014

first and second LTPs (2001–2006 and 2006–2011) (NCC, 2000, 2006) containing commitments to develop proposals for a WPL scheme.

The Council liaised with the business community and other stakeholders regarding initial proposals and options for the WPL or other charging methods. By July 2007 the WPL proposals had been sufficiently developed to a stage where by widespread public consultation could be undertaken. In accordance with the powers contained within the Transport Act, the Council resolved in July 2007 to consult with the public, the business community and other relevant stakeholders with the purpose of seeking views on both the principle of introducing a WPL and on the detail of the proposed scheme.

In order to encourage public participation in the consultation process and to allow for independent scrutiny of the proposals, the Council held a one week non-statutory 'Public Examination' of the proposals as part of the consultation exercise. Prior to this 685 representations had been received (Dodd, 2007). The Public Examination took place towards the end of the consultation period between 1st and 5th October 2007. One hundred and nine employers, residents and other stakeholders were invited to take part and of these 28 took up that offer (Dodd, 2007). It was led by an independent chairman, the 'Examiner' (nominated by the Planning Inspectorate) who issued a report 'The Proposed Nottingham Workplace Parking Levy, Report of the Public Examination' (Dodd, 2007) on the Public Examination in which various recommendations were made in respect of the proposed scheme. These recommendations are presented under five topic headings based on the representations made prior to and during the Examination. Nottingham City Council responded to the recommendations and these recommendations and responses were as follows (NCC, 2007):

Topic 1 – Transport Impacts of the WPL Scheme.
The Examiner stressed the need to promote workplace travel planning, develop a strategy to offset likely problems of displaced parking and to promote a clear ticketing strategy on the City's public transport. This was largely accepted by the City Council and provision was made to implement using projected WPL revenues.

Topic 2 – Economic Impacts of the WPL Scheme.
The Examiner report stressed the need to take steps to mitigate any economic impacts by promoting workplace travel plans and by encouraging salary sacrifice schemes for employees who were to have the WPL charge passed on by their employer. The report stressed the need to clearly link the WPL charge to the public transport improvements which it funds. Again, these recommendations were largely accepted by the City Council.

Topic 3 – Alternatives to the WPL Scheme.
While the Public Examiner accepted the Council's case that the WPL was the only feasible means to implement a revenue raising scheme within the timescale dictated for funding the tram extensions (NET phase 2), he disputed the City Council's position that it was a better means of congestion charging for Nottingham than a targeted RUC scheme or a local lottery. The Council did not accept this point arguing that a RUC was costly to implement with a high technological risk for a city the size of Nottingham.

An investigation into the viability of a local lottery revealed that it would be costly to implement due to anticipated high marketing costs required to achieve sufficient public awareness to attract a viable take up. Even with this investment in marketing, the amount of revenue raised would still most likely be insufficient given the relatively small population of Nottingham.

Topic 4 – Scope of the WPL Scheme.
The Examiner made recommendations regarding how the proposed discounts and exemptions would operate, i.e. what was in scope or out of scope when it comes to paying the actual charge. These recommendations were largely impractical or un-economic and were ultimately not taken up by the City. However, the discounts and exemptions that *were* taken forward are discussed in the next section, 'Operation of the Nottingham WPL'.

Topic 5 – Operational Issues of the WPL Scheme.
The Examiner made only one recommendation under this heading to suggest the WPL should only levy a charge on places occupied by 'regular' business visitors who regularly commute to the premises. The City Council accepted this.

Subsequent to the issues identified in the consultation being addressed to the satisfaction of the Public Examiner and Secretary of State for Transport, the key piece of local legislation, The City of Nottingham Workplace Parking Levy Order (2008), was approved by the Secretary of State for Transport. It is worth noting that this predated and indeed informed the 2009 national regulations which followed. This Order is a legal order setting out the scheme as specific to Nottingham and making it legally binding and enforceable. To do this it draws on the provisions of the Transport Act (2000) for its key definitions such as that for workplace parking places (WPP).

During the implementation stage there was extensive engagement with employers to explain the scheme, how it operated and how to manage their liability. This included written material as well as employer workshops. Nottingham City Council has an ongoing policy to use WPL revenue to provide business support in the form of workplace travel planning and parking management advice as well as supporting the provision of infrastructure to encourage cycling. This approach was in accordance with the Public Examiner's recommendations pertaining to topic 2 at the Public Examination.

OPERATION OF THE NOTTINGHAM WPL

Basic Characteristics

The WPL scheme levies a charge on occupied private non-domestic off-street parking places, i.e. those occupied by vehicles used by employees, regular business visitors or pupils/students. These are referred to as workplace parking places (WPP). In order to be liable for the WPL, the location must be occupied by a vehicle but need not be a marked parking space, hence the term 'place' is used rather than space. The scheme covers the entire area administered by Nottingham City Council but not the outlying areas of the conurbation which lie in the surrounding Nottinghamshire County Council area. In the 2013/2014 financial year the charge per WPP is £334 per year although this is set to rise above the rate of inflation up to 2016. This escalator aims to coincide with the completion of the public transport improvements which the levy part funds. While the exact amount is linked to inflation the escalator raises the relative charge for a parking place by about a third after inflation is taken into account from its original level in 2012 to its 2016 level. It is worth noting that the cost of licensing a workplace parking place per day is far lower than the prevailing charge for daily parking, either within public car parks or on street pay and display bays.

Employers apply for a licence for each of their premises (where such places are provided) which states the number of WPP they wish to use and then pay the appropriate levy, subject to not qualifying for a discount. The following receive a 100% discount from the WPL:

- Premises from which frontline health services are provided by or on behalf of the NHS.
- Premises occupied by the emergency services.
- Places occupied by disabled blue badge holders.
- Employers with 10 or fewer WPP.

Places occupied by vehicles loading or unloading or by those occupied by customers are exempt and do not qualify as WPP.

Licensing was introduced in October 2011 and charging commenced six months later on 1 April 2012. There was thus a six-month period to allow the licensing procedures to 'bed in' prior to the commencement of charging.

Policy Interpretation

Because the Nottingham WPL is the first scheme of its type in the United Kingdom, the implementing legislation does not benefit from experience gained elsewhere. As a result it is not surprising that the legislation does not fully address all definitions, all the desired discounts and some aspects of compliance and enforcement. This has resulted in the necessity for 'policy' to plug this gap. While it is beyond the scope of this chapter to fully explore all such policy issues, Table 3 summarises a selection of issues that have required a policy statement to expand on the legislation, prevent legal challenge and ensure a consistent approach. This illustrates the gap between the design of a functioning WPL scheme and the provisions for this in the legislation.

One option to narrow this 'gap' between the legislation and the working scheme would be for Nottingham City Council, as the implementing body, to apply to the Secretary of State for Transport to amend the City of

Table 3. Policy Issues.

Issue	What the Legislation Says	Policy Approach
Definition of a workplace parking place (WPP)	The Transport Act, 2000 (*Transport Act, 2000, c.38 Part III Chapter II*) and the City of Nottingham Workplace Parking Levy Order, 2008 (paragraph 3) definition includes any location used to park for the purpose of attending a place of employment; this therefore includes on-street parking and paid for public parking.	The policy approach is to exclude on-street parking and individually arranged parking in public car parks, so it is purely WPP provided by the employer. This is because enforcement of individually arranged parking would be very difficult.
Definition of a Regular/ Occasional Business Visitor	The term 'Business Visitor' is defined in the Transport Act (2000, *c.38 Part III Chapter II*): "Business Visitor, in relation to the relevant person (e.g. an employer), means an individual who (i) In the course of his employment, or (ii) In the course of carrying on a business or for the purposes of a business carried on by him, is visiting the relevant person or any premises occupied by the relevant person." Acting on the recommendations of the Public Examiner, the Council has chosen to distinguish between occasional and regular business visitors so as not impede the day to day running of employers and to target commuter parking places. Thus the Nottingham WPL Order 2008 provides that only workplace parking places occupied by business visitors attending their regular place of work will be chargeable. Places occupied by Occasional business visitors are exempt from the scheme and do not need to be licensed.	The criteria to differentiate between regular and occasional business visitors is not included in any legislation and is thus a matter of policy. A regular business visitor is defined as a consultant, supplier, agent or other business visitor who attends their regular place of work on three or more days over a 14-day period.
Discount versus Exemption	The Transport Act (2000, *c.38 Part III Chapter II*) legislation allows for certain exemptions; places used for customers or for loading as examples. The City of Nottingham Workplace Parking Levy Order (2008)	As the scheme was implemented it became apparent that it was desirable not to charge other categories not specified in the legislation, e.g. unpaid charity workers. It was not possible to exempt these as they are be covered by the

(paragraph 4) also allows for some categories to enjoy a 100% discount, e.g. places occupied by disabled blue badge holders.

National Health Service (NHS) discount

The City of Nottingham Workplace Parking Levy Order (2008) (paragraph 4 (4)) provides for 100% discount for Qualifying NHS premises and defines these as follows:

(a) a health service hospital within the meaning of the National Health Service Act 2006(a);

(b) premises that are used by a National Health Service trust for the purpose of providing ambulance services; or

(c) premises that are primarily used for the provision of primary medical services under arrangements made by a Primary Care Trust under section 83 of the National Health Service Act 2006.

definition of WPP contained within the legislation so they are given a 100% discount. However in order to be aligned with other such discounts contained within the legislation these places would still need to be licensed. This was considered to be an unreasonable administrative burden and, as a matter of policy, such places are simply not required to be licensed or pay the charge.

The definition for (c) became obsolete as the NHS commissioning regulations evolved, thus requiring further policy clarification. The Council's policy now makes provision for the 100% discount to be available to premises occupied by private employers that are commissioned by the NHS to provide primary medical services, regardless of the commissioning route, subject to meeting the following test:

A premises occupied by a private employer commissioned by the NHS under one or more contract will be eligible for the 100% discount from the **WPL**, provided that:

The primary purpose of the premises must be the delivery of primary medical services.

(i) The monetary value of the services delivered to the NHS under the contract(s) from that premises must be more than 80% of the total financial turnover for that premises.

(ii) More than 80% of patients treated at that premises must be under the NHS contract(s).

(iii) The provider must provide evidence to support the above mentioned requirements to the satisfaction of the Council – this must include evidence from the current accounting period which covers the licensing period in respect of which the discount is being sought.

Nottingham Workplace Parking Levy Order (2008) to include some of these key policies. While this would strengthen the scheme legally, it reduces the flexibility to amend policy as circumstances dictate or the scheme evolves. It is therefore necessary to allow the scheme to bed in to check that the policies operate as intended before any amendments to the existing Order are requested from the Secretary of State for Transport.

Operations and Enforcement

Clearly, as with any tax or levy, the WPL must be enforceable. The Transport Act empowers the licensing authority to authorise individuals to exercise the power of entry to premises where there is reason to believe that workplace parking is being provided. Any person who intentionally obstructs such enforcement commits a criminal offence. To this end and to facilitate administration of the scheme Nottingham City Council maintains a team of officers who are 'duly authorised' to undertake compliance and enforcement work in addition to the general administration and operation of the scheme.

The City Council states (NCC, 2008) that it conducts its compliance and enforcement activities based on the following principles intended to complement the scheme objectives:

- Focus on compliance rather than enforcement
- Build and maintain relationships with employers
- Negotiation being the preferred route to resolution
- Fair opportunities for the employer to alter their licence or behaviour to comply with the scheme
- Efficient and rigorous delivery of the process

Nottingham City Council's policy is therefore to make every effort to engage, advise and assist employers to correctly license any workplace parking places that they provide. To this end WPL staff make a site visit on an employer's premises with a view to engaging and building a relationship with the employer and to establish if any workplace parking is provided and that this is licensed correctly. Only if the outcome of such a site visit indicates that workplace parking is being provided without a licence, or appears to exceed the licensed number, will a compliance survey be conducted.

The intention of a compliance survey is to gather data as to the number of vehicles parked in order to establish the number of workplace parking places being provided.

Employers are then notified if they are correctly or incorrectly licensed. If an employer persistently refuses to licence their WPP correctly and pay the appropriate charge they will ultimately receive a Penalty Charge Notice (PCN).

The Workplace Parking Levy (England) Regulations (2009) (SI 2009/2085) contain the detailed provisions for the issuing of PCNs. However the Regulations leave the Local Order, The City of Nottingham Workplace Parking Levy Order (2008) (paragraph 1(2)(b)) to specify how the amount of the penalty charge is calculated and within what period it must be paid, together with any reductions for early payment. The Local Order (paragraph 9) specifies the level of penalty charges. In Nottingham, the penalty charge for providing unlicensed workplace parking places is half the annual charge payable at that time for each unlicensed workplace parking place. The penalty charge for contravention of a licence condition is the annual charge payable at that time for one workplace parking place.

A PCN may be issued by the Council if, following the completion of a compliance investigation, an employer is found to be:

(a) providing workplace parking places without a licence; or
(b) providing more workplace parking places than the maximum amount stated on their licence; or
(c) in breach of a licence condition.

As a matter of policy, the Council seeks to communicate with the employer to understand the reasons for non-compliance rather than moving straight to issuing a PCN. Up to three compliance surveys may be completed before a PCN is issued. This process allows a non-compliant employer up to two opportunities to obtain a licence, or increase their WPL licence accordingly, or reduce the number of workplace parking places provided, before the PCN is formally issued.

The above enforcement strategy would seem to be successful in that the WPL scheme has operated smoothly in its first year with no legal challenges and 100% compliance from known WPL liable employers.

BARRIERS TO IMPLEMENTATION

The major barrier to the implementation of any congestion charging scheme is that of public acceptance (Frost & Ison, 2008) and this is closely linked to the issue of political risk for the decision makers. Evidence from Nottingham City Council's consultation prior to and during the 'Public Examination' and subsequent press coverage, suggests that typically the WPL is criticised on three grounds (Dodd, 2007; *Nottingham Post*, 2012; Westcott, 2012), namely being:

1. an additional burden on business and thus damaging to a city's economy;
2. ineffective as a tool to combat congestion;
3. unfair on the motorist who already carries a high tax burden.

There is little academic literature as to how acceptable the UK general public would find a WPL scheme partly because until Nottingham's WPL, there was no reference point for understanding what it is. However, some research has been carried out to assess business attitudes to a WPL scheme and not surprisingly the business community are less than positive (Burchell & Ison, 2012; NCC, 2005; Nottingham and Derby Chamber of Commerce, 2012).

A survey of key stakeholders, mainly transport policy decision makers, conducted in 1999 (Ison & Wall, 2002) showed that they considered peak period congestion and its associated problems to be fairly serious. They also viewed a WPL as one of the least acceptable measures but most effective measures to combat this problem. A study carried out by Price Waterhouse Cooper (PwC) on behalf of Nottingham City Council (2005) showed that, although WPL charge was likely to be less than 1% of a business turnover, businesses were highly critical of having to bear this cost. Sixty per cent of businesses interviewed in this 2005 study said they would relocate some activities away from Nottingham and more than 50% said they would reduce planned investment. Sixty-six per cent felt the levy would not be offset by improvements in public transport. This identifies a contradiction in both the general non-specific perception that a high quality transport system is important to business location and the relatively low percentage of turnover being asked to fund this and the strong reaction of businesses to this cost.

This then leaves a question of what will businesses actually do? The barrier of acceptability to the business community has been strengthened as a result of the present government's 'Red Tape Review' which included a consideration of WPL schemes as shown below. This stressed the requirement that any future scheme must be acceptable to the business community (Cabinet Office, 2013).

"Within the Road Transport Red Tape Challenge theme, DfT placed over 400 regulations online for your views. After removing those that have already lapsed, 376 remain – of which 142 will be scrapped or improved following a vigorous process of challenge. Plans include:

– local authorities will now have to ensure business interests are properly considered as part of any future proposed Workplace Parking Levy scheme. They must show they have properly and effectively consulted local businesses, have addressed any proper concerns raised and secured support from the local business community."

Given the evidence of business views presented above and the change in the government's perspective, this could prove a challenge. Clearly, no local authority wishes to damage the economy of their area and if there is evidence that the presence of the WPL is damaging to the economy in the medium term, then such a scheme may need re-thinking. However there is inevitably a lag between the introduction of a WPL and the completion of any concurrent public transport improvements and some short-term 'pain' may be acceptable to decision makers.

The relative political stability of Nottingham allows decision makers to take a medium- to long-term view as they know it is extremely unlikely they will be voted out of office over a single issue such as the WPL, provided the economy of the city performs adequately over the medium term. This is not the case in other similar UK Cities where a WPL could be implemented. For example, the city of Bristol is more finely balanced politically (Bristol Liberal Democrats, 2011) and politically motivated reaction to an initially unpopular idea can make a big difference electorally. Bristol in the last decade has considered and rejected the idea of a tram scheme, major bus improvements and a WPL (BBC News, 2012). It could be speculated that this is probably more due to political factors than an objective Examination of the pros and cons of such schemes in what is accepted as a congested City.

The decision makers within Nottingham City Council took the view that in the medium term, a world class public transport system providing both high levels of mobility and accessibility, combined with the image of a modern progressive city will enhance Nottingham's offer to inward investors and more than offset the cost of the WPL. Moreover, the introduction of the WPL is predicated on high quality public transport once in place, decreasing the need for car parking at employment sites and/or promoting parking management schemes which pass on the cost of WPL to employees thus making the cost of WPL to employers a void issue.

EVALUATING PERFORMANCE; EVALUATION FRAMEWORK, METHODOLOGIES AND AVAILABLE DATA TO DATE

The Evaluation Framework

The 2008 Business Case for the WPL scheme (NCC, 2008) contained a commitment to carry out an evaluation of the scheme. To this end Nottingham City Council has identified six key objectives for the WPL scheme and a framework of indicators to measure performance of the scheme against these objectives has been developed. These are shown in Table 4.

Clearly these indicators are subject to non-local factors such as the price of fuel or the national and global economy. In order to gain a fuller evaluation of the scheme's outcomes and impacts it will be necessary to undertake two further steps:

1. Benchmarking against comparator cities where comparable data is available to identify how Nottingham has performed in terms of the six WPL objectives.
2. Further qualitative research aimed at attribution of the causes of these impacts to the WPL and the other public transport improvements. It will also be important to consider the contribution of other WPL supported initiatives such as workplace travel planning or support for measures to encourage cycling.

It may be necessary to monitor the indicators for several years post implementation before any robust conclusions can be drawn concerning the medium-term outcomes and longer term impacts of the Nottingham WPL scheme and its associated transport improvements.

Monitoring Results after Year 1 of WPL Operation

Dale et al. (2013) present some initial data for the indicators in Table 4 following year 1 of operation of the scheme. This concludes that there is little or no evidence of the WPL effecting congestion or business investment at this early stage. However they also report that bicycle usage has increased by 15% between the 2010 baseline year and 2012 and that increasing numbers of the larger employers are taking up Workplace Travel Plans and Parking Management schemes which seek to pass on the

Table 4. WPL Evaluation Framework.

WPL Objective	Performance Indicators	Metrics
Objective 1: Constrain congestion in the AM and PM peak periods	Congestion (Car Journey Times)	AM peak period journey time per vehicle mile (dec mins)
	Area-wide traffic mileage	Millions of vehicle miles p.a.
	Single occupancy car journeys	% of single occupancy
	Bus services running on time	Excess waiting time (dec mins) for frequent services
		% of non-frequent buses on time at timing points in City
		% of buses starting on time in City
Objective 2: Increase uptake of workplace travel plans and responsible parking management strategies	% of employees covered by a travel plan	% of employees covered by a travel plan
	Number of WPP and employers covered by workplace parking management schemes	Number of WPP and employers covered by parking management schemes
	Take-up of support packages number by type	Number of employers taking up travel planning or parking management support packages
Objective 3: Contribute to the implementation of major transport schemes and the Local Transport Plan	Net WPL Revenue	Total Revenue (£) minus operating costs, business support and traffic management expenditure
	City Council WPL expenditure on Business Support	Expenditure on business support and traffic management
	City Council WPL operating costs	Expenditure on WPL admin and enforcement
	Analysis of WPL revenues	Breakdown of WPL revenue by employer size/type
	Number of WPP places, covered by the 100% discount	Total number of WPPs enjoying the 100% discount excluding those occupied by disabled Blue Badge holders
Objective 4: Encourage sustainable travel and mode choice	Mode share of public transport at Inner Area Traffic Cordon in AM peak period	% of travel by public transport on main radial routes + rail
	Local bus and light rail passenger journeys	Millions of passengers on trams and buses

Table 4.   (*Continued*)

WPL Objective	Performance Indicators	Metrics
	Cycling trips	Cycle counts at strategic points in City
	Mode of journeys to school	Proposed 'Hands up survey' at schools
	Single occupancy car journeys	% of single occupancy cars
Objective 5: Enhance the attractiveness of Nottingham as a location for business investment	Employee numbers Business location decisions	Number of jobs in the City Research Project
Objective 6: No significant displaced parking problems	Displaced parking analysis	Number of WPL related complaints per year and type of scheme delivered

cost of the WPL to their employees. Around 36% of liable workplace parking places (WPP) are now covered by such parking management schemes,
mainly implemented by larger employers who have the organisational
resource to run such schemes. It should be noted that, although it is desirable from a transport demand management perspective for the employer to
pass on the cost of the WPL to employees, this is not always viable from a
business perspective. For example, in the case of lower paid manual
workers, especially shift workers where the public transport options may
be more limited, the additional cost of WPL may make it unattractive
to work in Nottingham causing recruitment issues for the employer.
Some employers have recognised this and have absorbed the cost of the
WPL. This is less of an issue for employers with a more highly paid
workforce.

Additionally the number of WPP licensed by employers is approximately
17% lower than the number identified in the 2010 pre scheme Off Street
Parking Audit Surveys (OSPA). While it should be noted that the OSPA
surveys represented a 'best estimate' rather than actual numbers licensed
and that since those surveys additional discounts have been provided, it is
still safe to conclude that this represents a contraction in the supply of
workplace parking places in real terms. So although the WPL would
appear to be effecting employer behaviour in a way that is likely to contribute to a reduction in commuting by car, this would not appear to be

reflected in the reduction of peak period journey times or other indicators measuring congestion. This could be for the following reasons:

1. Parking is being displaced from employer's premises to on-street parking and there is much anecdotal comment on this in the media (e.g. a recent *Daily Telegraph* article (Milward, 2013) but little supporting evidence). This is likely to be a temporary effect since, as issues come to light, parking controls are introduced to combat them, particularly in residential areas. However, there is a tendency for the public and the media to blame all displaced parking on the WPL when this may not be the case, e.g. there is considerable displaced parking surrounding the hospitals which charge staff for parking but enjoy the NHS 100% discount from the WPL.
2. Infilling by suppressed demand for peak period travel.
3. The numbers of journeys being affected at liable employers is relatively small compared to the number of peak period trips. The total number of trips recorded crossing the City's inner area traffic cordon in the AM peak period inbound is 66,000 (which is only a sample of the total trips on the network) while the reduction in WPP is only around 7,000 places (Dale et al., 2013).

The absence of evidence for the WPL to be causing a reduction in inward investment in the City is a positive outcome for the WPL scheme at this point in time as employers will have been aware that the scheme was going to be introduced since 2009. Indeed, Dale et al. (2013) report that Nottingham City Council's inward investment team have enjoyed a significant increase in enquiries and subsequent investment successes in 2012/2013 over previous years. While this data is far from a complete reflection of levels of investment, it is more current than the other macroeconomic indicators, numbers of jobs and the balance of VAT registrations (and it will be interesting to see if these figures mirror the macroeconomic data when they become available later in 2013). It may be that the planned public transport improvements, funded by a WPL, are seen as attractive by potential inward investors.

CONCLUSION AND LESSONS FOR OTHERS LOOKING AT WPL

The Nottingham WPL scheme is the first of its kind in the United Kingdom. The outcomes from this scheme, and the public transport improvements which it makes possible by part funding, may determine if the WPL option is adopted by other UK local authorities to fulfil the dual role of acting as a transport demand management measure, while providing hypothecated funding for transport improvements.

At present there is a 'gap' between the provisions and definitions contained in the underlying legislation in the Transport Act (2000) and the Workplace Parking Levy (England) Regulations (2009) and the requirements of a functional WPL scheme that needs to be filled by a consistent policy approach. Going forward it could be an option to migrate some of these policy elements into the legislation at a local level. For the Nottingham scheme this would require varying the local enabling legislation, The City of Nottingham Workplace Parking Levy Order (2008), which at present only contains minor additional detail to the national legislation. However, for any future UK schemes, this could be considered in drafting the local legislation by using the experience gained in Nottingham.

Literature and experience shows that acceptance by the public and business community is a key barrier to implementing a WPL. This has been reinforced by the present government's 'Red Tape Review' which stressed the need to gain the acceptance of the business community before a WPL can be implemented. This makes it increasingly important that the Nottingham WPL is evaluated. It will need to result in a successful outcome with respect to its stated objectives if other UK local authorities are to implement a similar WPL scheme. At present the Nottingham scheme is operating smoothly with little or no non-compliance and has not been legally challenged by employers (Dale et al., 2013). This outcome is partly due to the public consultation undertaken, the Public Examination and subsequent practical advice and support provided to employers. Obviously the need and method for undertaking this process prior to any future scheme will vary according to cultural and legislative context. However not withstanding this, it should be considered as good practice.

In its first year of full operation the WPL has raised £7 million of hypothecated revenue for public transport improvement (Dale et al., 2013). While the data from Nottingham to date suggests that, as yet, the scheme has had minimal impact on levels of congestion in Nottingham, the evidence from macroeconomic indicators is demonstrating that Nottingham has fared no worse economically than other similar sized UK cities since the chosen base year for WPL monitoring, 2010. It should be noted that, although the WPL has only been fully operational for a year, the business community has been aware of its implementation since 2009 and thus it is possible that any negative economic impact has had 4 years to take effect.

It is important to note that, of the overall package of transport interventions that will take place in Nottingham between 2010 and 2015, only the WPL and some of the Linkbus services are currently in place. While it is proposed that the WPL will have a positive impact on some of the scheme objectives even as a standalone measure, the main benefits may not be realised until all the interventions which the WPL part funds are in place.

There is evidence of positive changes in employer behaviour. Take up of travel planning has increased since 2010 as has the implementation of parking management schemes which seek to pass on the cost of the WPL to employees. There is also some evidence that the number of workplace parking places has fallen following the introduction of WPL.

REFERENCES

BBC News Website. (2012). *Bristol workplace parking levy scrapped by Bristol City Council.* Retrieved from http://www.bbc.co.uk/news/uk-england-bristol-19743418. Accessed on 24 December 2013.

Bristol Liberal Democrats. (2011). *News: Hung council re-elects Barbara Janke as leader.* Retrieved from http://www.bristol-libdems.org.uk/2011/05/hung-council-re-elects-barbara-janke-as-leader/. Accessed on 24 December 2013.

Burchell, J., & Ison, S. G. (2012). Employers attitudes to the workplace parking levy: A case study of Nottingham, UK. *92nd annual meeting of the Transportation Research Board*, TRB, 09-0249, Washington, DC.

Cabinet Office. (2013). *Red Tape Review website.* Retrieved from http://www.redtapechallenge. cabinetoffice.gov.uk/2011/12/road-transport-announcement/. Accessed on 13 June 2013.

Dale, S., Frost, M. W., Ison S. G., & Warren, P. (2013). Workplace parking levies: The answer to funding large scale local transport improvements in the UK? Thredbo 13 Conference. *The 13th international conference on competition and ownership in land passenger transport*, Oxford.

Department of the Environment, Transport and the Regions (DETR). (1998a). *A new deal for transport: Better for everyone, the government's white paper on the future of transport.* London: The Stationery Office. Retrieved from http://www.nottinghamcity.gov.uk/ CHttpHandler.ashx?id=2510&p=0. Accessed on 3 May 2013.

Department of the Environment, Transport and the Regions (DETR). (1998b). *Breaking the Logjam: The government's consultation paper on fighting traffic congestion and pollution through road user and workplace parking charges.* London: The Stationery Office. Retrieved from http://www.nottinghamcity.gov.uk/CHttpHandler.ashx?id=2511&p=0. Accessed on 3 May 2013.

Dodd, B. (2007). *The proposed Nottingham workplace parking levy. Report of the Public Examination.* The UK Planning Inspectorate. Retrieved from http://www.nottingham-city.gov.uk/CHttpHandler.ashx?id=2681&p=0. Accessed on 5 May, 2013.

Frost, M. W., & Ison, S. G. (2008). Implementation of a workplace parking levy: Lessons from the UK. *88th annual meeting of the Transportation Research Board*, TRB, 09-0249, Washington, DC, 15 January.

Grant-Muller, S., & Laird J. (2006). *Costs of congestion: Literature based review of methodological and analytical approaches.* Scottish Executive. ISBN 07559 6306 7.

Howlett, M., & Ramesh, M. (1995). *Studying public policy: Policy cycles and policy subsystems.* Oxford: Oxford University Press. ISBN 0195409760, 9780195409765.

Ison, S. G., & Wall, S. (2002). Attitudes to traffic related issues in urban areas of the UK and the role of workplace parking charges. *Journal of Transport Geography, 10*(1), 21–28.

Milward, D. (2013). *Flagship workplace parking levy 'creating chaos'.* Journalistic article. Retrieved from http://www.telegraph.co.uk/motoring/news/10243004/Flagship-workplace-parking-levy-creating-chaos.html. Accessed on 27 August 2013.

Nottingham and Derby Chamber of Commerce. (2012). Unpublished e-survey summarised and retrieved from http://www.thisisnottingham.co.uk/Firms-look-leaving-city-parking-levy/story-17018942-detail/story.html. Accessed on 4 June 2013.

Nottingham City Council (NCC). (2005). *Workplace parking levy economic impact.* PwC for Nottingham City Council. Nottingham: Nottingham City Council. Retrieved from http://nottinghamcity.gov.uk/CHttpHandler.ashx?id=2492&p=0. Accessed on 20 May 2013.

Nottingham City Council (NCC). (2007). *Appendix E – NCC's responses to the examiner's recommendations.* Nottingham: Nottingham City Council. Retrieved from http://www.nottinghamcity.gov.uk/CHttpHandler.ashx?id=2391&p=0. Accessed on 20 May 2013.

Nottingham City Council (NCC). (2008, April). *Workplace parking levy business case.* Nottingham: Nottingham City Council. Retrieved from http://www.nottinghamcity.gov.uk/CHttpHandler.ashx?id=2672&p=0. Accessed on 5 June 2013.

Nottingham City Council (NCC). (2013). *Nottingham Local Transport Plan 2011 to 2026.* Nottingham: Nottingham City Council. Retrieved from http://nottinghamcity.gov.uk/index.aspx?articleid=24051. Accessed on 14 June 2013.

Nottingham City Council (NCC) and Nottinghamshire County Council. (2000). *Local Transport Plan for greater Nottingham (LTP 1) 2000/2001 to 2005/6.* Nottingham: Nottingham City and County Council.

Nottingham City Council (NCC) and Nottinghamshire County Council. (2006). *Local Transport Plan for greater Nottingham (LTP 2) 2006/7 to 2010/11.* Nottingham: Nottingham City and County Council.

Nottingham Post. (2012). Levy may see us move on after 27 years, claims depot manager. Journalistic article. *Nottingham Post.* Retrieved from http://www.thisisnottingham.co.uk/Levy-27-years-claims-depot-manager/story-15678012-detail/story.html. Accessed on 3 December 2012.

The City of Nottingham Workplace Parking Levy Order. (2008). London: Bircham Dyson Bell LLP. Retrieved from http://www.nottinghamcity.gov.uk/CHttpHandler.ashx?id=1830&p=0. Accessed on 5 February 2014.

Transport Act. (2000). *c.38 Part III Chapter II.* London: HMSO. Retrieved from http://www.legislation.gov.uk/ukpga/2000/38/part/III/chapter/II. Accessed on 4 February 2014.

Westcott, S. (2012). *Anger at stealth tax on parking at work.* Journalistic article. Retrieved from http://www.express.co.uk/posts/view/312004/Anger-at-stealth-tax-on-parking-at-work. Accessed on 3 June 2013.

Workplace Parking Levy (England) Regulations (2009). *SI 2009/2085.* London: HMSO. Retrieved from http://www.legislation.gov.uk/uksi/2009/2085/contents/made. Accessed on 4 February 2014.

CHAPTER 16

ON-STREET PARKING

Wesley E. Marshall

ABSTRACT

Purpose – *To overview the gamut of issues that on-street parking impacts in mixed-use centers including: parking demand, land use, vehicle speed, road safety, the pedestrian environment, and travel behaviors.*

Methodology/approach – *In addition to reviewing existing literature, the following two case studies are presented. The first study explores the impact in centers built before the advent of parking regulations as compared to more contemporary, conventional developments. The second study investigates how street design factors affected vehicle speeds and safety, based on a study of over 250 roads.*

Findings – *On-street parking typically: serves the highest demand; is efficient in terms of land use and cost; induces lower vehicle speeds; increases safety on low-speed streets; enhances walkability; and fosters less driving, more pedestrian activity, and increased vitality.*

Practical implications – *On-street parking is one piece of a larger puzzle of complementary factors that influence issues such as travel behavior and safety, and therefore, it is difficult to isolate. On-street parking plays a crucial role in helping create places that are walkable, require less parking, and have more vitality. On-street parking is not purely*

Parking: Issues and Policies
Transport and Sustainability, Volume 5, 361–380
Copyright © 2014 by Emerald Group Publishing Limited
All rights of reproduction in any form reserved
ISSN: 2044-9941/doi:10.1108/S2044-994120140000005014

a device to be used in the right environment; rather, it is a tool to help create that right environment.

Originality/value of chapter – *Prevailing thought on the subject of on-street parking has shifted back-and-forth for generations, in part because most studies focus on one or two impacts. This chapter takes a more comprehensive approach in order to increase our understanding of on-street parking in mixed-use, commercial centers.*

Keywords: Parking; on-street; land use; walkability; speed; safety

INTRODUCTION

Cities and towns around the world have struggled to revitalize their downtown – many of which have been dormant for generations. As early as the 1920s, in trying to improve automobile flow, the solution many downtowns sought revolved around the elimination of on-street parking (Norton, 2008; Shoup, 2005). Cities such as Los Angeles first tried banning on-street parking in these early days of the automobile after car traffic started to restrict the flow of streetcars. While this ordinance was reversed just 19 days later, in part due to claims that parking restrictions were discriminatory against motorists, the debate about on-street parking was just beginning. Los Angeles went back-and-forth on the issue for decades, an indecisiveness representative of policy-makers everywhere. Even San Francisco, a city where you will find pictures of its on-street parking on postcards (Fig. 1), banned the practice in 1970 from 7 am until 6 pm on most streets (Highway Research Board, 1971).

While many planners and engineers now consider on-street parking a fundamental element of any successful downtown, the debate still rages because conventional engineering practice continues to regard on-street parking as a safety issue and a nuisance to through traffic. One difficulty is that both supporters and critics of on-street parking seem to have little problem finding examples to support their side of the argument. Another issue is that there has been little academic research on the subject, especially with respect to studies that cover the wide-ranging gamut of issues that on-street parking has the potential to impact. At a minimum, these issues include: user demand, land use, congestion, traffic calming, road safety, walkability, pricing and the economic success of a downtown. Since most studies focus on one or two aspects, finding a definitive overall answer has proven to be

Fig. 1. Emblematic Street Parking in San Francisco. *Source*: W. E. Marshall.

exceedingly difficult. Thus, it is not all that surprising that prevailing thought on the subject has shifted back-and-forth over the years.

How did we get to this point? Why is on-street parking ubiquitous in some downtowns but conspicuously absent from others? Furthermore, why have some places been so successful when it comes to incorporating on-street parking into their downtowns while others have failed? Though the inconsistent history of restricting on-street parking traces back to the early part of the twentieth century, such as in Los Angeles, many point to the 1950s as the defining era for such decisions, particularly in the United States. A 1955 policy statement from the U.S. Chamber of Commerce exemplifies the predominant line of thinking at the time. This document called for giving the first priority of any street to the:

> movement of people and goods with such restrictions on curb usage as this principle may dictate. (Highway Research Board, 1971, p. 161)

The U.S. National Parking Association further highlighted this issue with a 1959 report recommending the elimination of on-street parking in downtown areas under the premise that through traffic should be the priority in the street realm (Highway Research Board, 1971). In 1971, the Highway Research Board, which later became known as the Transportation Research Board, joined the debate with their take on issues of traffic capacity and safety. Their published comprehensive guide to parking describes the issues surrounding the provision of on-street parking in the following manner:

> Curb parking can seriously impede traffic movement along major routes. It typically contributes to or is directly involved with some 20 percent of urban street accidents.

One of the best and most economical methods of increasing capacity and safety is the removal of curb parking. (Highway Research Board, 1971, p. 5)

According to this guide, on-street parking would only be acceptable in situations: where the street is not required to function as part of the street network; where the through movement of traffic can be prohibited; and where the need for parking is so great that it trumps vehicular movements (Highway Research Board, 1971).

Despite appearances to the contrary, research to support these claims were limited. For example, a 1965 Wilbur Smith study found that on-street parking reduces road capacity and that off-street parking in downtowns enhances retail activity (Wilbur Smith & Associates, 1965); they concluded that on-street parking should be minimized wherever possible and that off-street parking would be the key determinant of economic success. As a result of such studies, the high costs of structured parking garages seemed trivial in comparison to the potential losses due to traffic congestion, crashes, retail activity, and maintaining parking meters. Not surprisingly, cities in the United States and abroad undertook a systematic effort to shift street space away from parking in favor of increased vehicle movement. For example, over the course of 40 years, Hartford, Connecticut in the United States strategically removed on-street parking while more than tripling the 15,000 off-street parking spaces that were available in 1960 (McCahill & Garrick, 2010). Unfortunately in this case, the effort to improve Hartford nearly destroyed any semblance of vitality; only now is the city beginning to climb back from a 25% drop in population and a more than twenty point increase in driving mode share.

This reallocation, and the underlying premise that streets are primarily intended for the through movement of traffic, is still prevalent in many places. However in the last couple of decades, a growing number of urban planners have pointed out that the centers that have retained on-street parking — along with other compatible features of pre-1950s centers — are some of our most successful downtowns. In order to address this dichotomy between conventional practice and emerging urban theory, this chapter evaluates the current state of research attempting to evaluate or assess the impact of on-street parking in mixed-use, commercial districts. It also presents the results of a set of research projects designed to study the range of issues relating to the provision of on-street parking and its impact on downtowns. One set of research questions was based upon case studies for six New England town centers in the United States with a focus on the impact of parking at mixed-use, walkable commercial centers built before the advent of parking regulations as compared to more contemporary, conventional development patterns. The second study investigated how street design affected vehicle speeds and safety, based on a study of over 250 Connecticut roads. The sites were selected to represent a wide array of street types with different speed limits, adjacent land uses, and levels of on-street parking.

By relying on multiple lines of research, the intention was to forge a more complete understanding of on-street parking and its effects. This includes an assessment of the benefits and shortcomings of on-street parking vis-à-vis the other common methods of supplying parking (off-street surface parking and structured garage parking) in addition to looking at the context in which on-street parking can be successfully employed. This chapter covers the fundamental impacts of on-street parking on a downtown, including: parking demand, land use, vehicle speed, road safety, the pedestrian environment, and travel behaviors.

PARKING DEMAND

On-street parking – as compared to off-street surface lots and structured parking garages – is thought to have the highest demand in commercial and mixed-use districts. This is because on-street spaces are typically public, highly visible, and often convenient to multiple destinations (Litman, 2006). The existing research supports this claim, primarily through studies focused on setting the appropriate price for various types of spaces, which typically suggest the highest fees for on-street spaces (Shoup, 2005). The first of the research projects investigated this question in six New England town centers where on-street parking spaces not only charged higher fees than the off-street parking but also had the shortest maximum time allotments. The study itself was organized around the selection of three case study sites, which can be characterized by having traditional mixed land uses supported by a fee-based, organized system of parking; and three more contemporary sites supported by free, privately owned surface parking lots with similar land areas and land uses. The selected sites included:

Traditional Sites   Contemporary Sites

1. Brattleboro, Vermont   1. Avon, Connecticut
2. Northampton, Massachusetts   2. Glastonbury, Connecticut
3. West Hartford, Connecticut   3. Somerset Square; Glastonbury, Connecticut

Table 1.   Parking Occupancy.

	Peak Occupancy (%)	Average Non-Peak Occupancy (%)
On-street parking	94.5	81.6
Off-street surface parking	59.2	48.8
Structured garage parking	75.5	49.4

Source: Derived from Marshall, Garrick, and Hansen (2008).

Following site selection, a boundary around each downtown was established; the boundary lines incorporated each commercial district and any parking lots intended to serve the center. Data were gathered detailing the provision of parking by first mapping and categorizing each space as on-street parking spaces, off-street surface lots, or off-street structured garages. On-site work included parking occupancy counts carried out a minimum of five times at each site in an effort to collect what could be considered a typical peak usage (i.e., during the busy holiday shopping season) as well as an average non-peak occupancy (i.e., on a summer day with good weather).

Table 1 shows the parking occupancy results. The results suggest that users of the downtowns consistently selected on-street parking spaces over and above less expensive off-street surface lots and garage parking. In other words, visitors to downtowns place a premium on on-street parking, often because of their convenience to a wide variety of uses. The combination of higher fees and the shortest maximum time allotment in these particular on-street spaces also helped maintain high turnover in these most convenient spaces, seemingly without negatively impacting overall usage. The goal of the parking fees in general should be focused more on parking management and less on maximizing revenue.

LAND USE

One often overlooked fact in assessing on-street parking is its efficiency in terms of land use.

The impact can be felt at multiple levels in terms of the land consumed by the parking space itself and in terms of the opportunity cost that comes with devoting excessive land to parking. On the first point, one on-street space is typically between 7 and 8 feet wide and between 20 and 22 feet long. Off-street surface lots, however, consume additional land for driveways and access lanes. Practitioners typically use a rule of thumb of 300–400 square feet per space (Litman, 2006). Our results suggest that this is an optimistic estimate. For the six sites studied, off-street surface lots averaged 513 square feet of land consumed per parking space. Driveways and access lanes were indeed the main culprits, but landscaping – as required by many municipalities to mitigate heat island effects – also played a significant role. Fig. 2 depicts these differences.

As for the land use opportunity cost of providing parking in the form of off-street surface lots, this difference in land consumed per space can add up quickly. The centers in this study averaged slightly more than 2,000 total parking spaces; if only 15% of those 2,000 spaces were provided via on-street parking, this would equate to more than 2.3 acres of additional land not needing to be designated as parking. With land being a limited resource – particularly in downtowns where density and high activity are important – the benefit of being able to conserve such vast amounts of land by providing parking on the street rather than with an off-street surface lot is immeasurable. This calculation does not even consider the fact that if parking is not provided on the street, street space would still not likely be usable for uses other than transportation and that this area would increase significantly in larger cities with much more parking.

On-street parking supports greater efficiency in land use, which can facilitate higher density commercial development than would be possible

Fig. 2.   Land Use of On-Street Parking versus Off-Street Surface Lot.
Source: W. E. Marshall.

368   WESLEY E. MARSHALL

for a center reliant solely upon off-street surface lots. To assess this, land use data was collected in terms of retail space, office space, and residential units. The traditional sites, where on-street parking was prevalent, also exhibited:

- 58% greater building density;
- 176% greater floor to area ratio; and
- 90% more leasable building space in each of those town centers.

This suggests that on-street parking results in a more efficient use of land, in part because using the curbside for parking saves considerable amounts of land from life as an off-street surface parking lot. However, parking can also be provided in structures or underground, which has additional land use efficiency advantages. Given that each of the traditional town centers had one parking garage, this played a role in the increased development numbers. The trade-off, however, is in the cost. This cost is not limited strictly to construction costs, but also should include land acquisition, operations, maintenance, and interest. Taking all of this into account, Litman's work estimates the following annual costs per space for urban (but not CBD) parking: $578 per space for on-street parking; $780 for off-street surface lots; and $1,598 for structures; and $2,298 for underground parking (Litman, 2006). When assessing the advantages of structured parking, one should also discount the number of off-street surface lot spaces the same parcel of land could accommodate (Shoup, 2005) as well as take into account the development that can be built around or above a parking structure or underground lot.

VEHICLE IMPACTS

Two of the drawbacks most often cited when it comes to on-street parking are congestion and safety. Congestion is thought to come primarily from not being able to allocate enough street space to the through movement of automobiles, and secondarily from the traffic created by vehicles attempting to parallel park. However, research by simulation modelers and empirical results from road diet[1] conversions have shown that in urban settings, actual road capacity is largely controlled by the capacity of the signalized intersections as opposed to the number of travel lanes on the street (Huang, Stewart, & Zegeer, 2002; Litman, 2007; Welch, 2000). While such delays might seem substantial, particularly for those being delayed, left-turn lanes and cross street traffic volumes are far more significant factors in vehicle throughput than the number of travel lanes. The one congestion issue surrounding on-street parking that has been shown to be significant in several studies has to do with cruising for parking (Arnott, de Palma, & Lindsey, 1991; Arnott & Inci, 2005; Glazer & Niskanen, 1992; Shoup, 2006). The underlying issue these authors found, however, is not the on-street parking itself but the price of on-street parking often being less than nearby off-street spaces.

The issue of road safety leads into the second strand of research, which investigated the impact of on-street parking on traffic safety and vehicle speed via over 250 roadway segments. Crash records were obtained for a six-year period and aggregated in order to obtain a reasonable count for statistical analysis. The severest injury from each crash was assigned as the overall severity level for that crash. Previous research looking into on-street parking and safety did not separate crashes by severity (Hansen, Garrick, Ivan, & Jonsson, 2007). Thus, on-street parking has previously been associated with increased crash risk (Greibe, 2003; Pande & Abdel-Aty, 2009; Roberts, Norton, Jackson, Dunn, & Hassall, 1995). Earlier studies show that 16% of crashes in American cities directly involved cars parking along the road (Highway Research Board, 1971). In a before-and-after study of curbside parking prohibition on arterial streets, another study found that non-intersection crash rates reduced by an average 37% with the banning of on-street parking (Desjardins, 1977).

Table 2 presents the safety results in terms of crash rate per mile per site for low speed streets with on-street parking; high speed streets with on-street parking; low speed streets with no on-street parking; and high speed streets with no on-street parking. The results suggest that on-street parking

Table 2. Crash Rates.

	Street Speed Category	No. of Sites	Total Miles	Crash Rate per Mile per Site (1998–2003 Aggregated)				
				Fatal	Severe Injury	Minor Injury	PDO[a]	Total Crashes
On-street parking	Low (<35 mph)	13	3.06	0	11.1	47.7	231.1	289.9
	High (≥35 mph)	5	1.45	0.7	29	89.7	222.8	342.1
No on-street parking	Low (<35 mph)	13	2.36	0.0	28.0	48.3	192.0	268.2
	High (≥35 mph)	24	5.12	0.2	17.2	44.7	114.8	177.0

Source: Marshall et al. (2008).
[a]PDO, property damage only.

can help to create a safer environment. While this statement seems to contradict most people's perception, the reality is that lower speed streets (less than 35 mph) with on-street parking have far fewer crashes resulting in a severe injury or fatality. More specifically, the fatal and severe crash rate on low speed streets with on-street parking is 11.1 per mile compared to 28.0 for low speed streets with no parking. Also, only 3.8% of the crashes that occurred on low speed streets with parking resulted in a severe injury; on the other hand, 10.4% of the crashes resulted in severe injuries on low speed streets without parking. This severe injury crash rate is more than two times higher than the streets with on-street parking. Streets with speed limits above 35 mph, however, found contrary results. On these streets, on-street parking was significantly associated with higher crash rates at all severity levels (although only five street segments in our study fell into this category). Thirty-five miles per hour was selected as the delineation point because we found a very different outcome for facilities with speeds less than 35 mph versus those with speeds greater than 35 mph (e.g., there were no recorded fatalities occurring on facilities with speeds greater than 35 mph).

This divergence in safety between low speed and high speed streets with on-street parking might help explain why these results differ from studies where such streets were not considered separately. Moreover, these results highlight the need to consider context in assessing the potential use of on-street parking. In Europe, urban street speeds are often less than 20 mph (Mitchell, 2007), and such conditions seem necessary in ensuring the safe use of on-street parking. This type of thinking is also making strides in the United States; in a street design manual recently published by the Institute of Transportation Engineers (ITE) in conjunction with the Congress for the New Urbanism (CNU), the recommended practice is to maintain speeds of less than 35 mph on streets with on-street parking (ITE & CNU, 2010). Our results concur with this recommendation and suggest that under these low speed conditions, on-street parking helps improve safety, and in particular, these roads with on-street parking show a significantly reduced crash rate for the most severe types of crashes. The obvious question is: why?

One reason for this difference in crash severity outcomes has to do with vehicle speed. Part of this same research strand included an investigation to identify the street elements in the driving environment that significantly influenced drivers' choice of speed. In addition to the presence and occupancy of on-street parking, this study controlled for: roadway type, land use type, posted speed limit, lane width, roadway width and shoulder width where present, presence of sidewalks, planting strips, road edge delineation, side curbs, and medians. The segment lengths of the streets were determined by the consistency of the variables of interest. Thus, segments began and ended with the presence and/or termination of any or all of the variables mentioned. On-street parking was measured at three levels of occupancy: 50–100%, 30–49.9%, and less than 30%. The results revealed that the 50–100% and the 30–49.9% occupancy levels did not show any statistical difference in mean free flow speeds; thus, these categories were merged.

Speeds for a minimum of 100 free flowing vehicles were then measured for each site. The assumption for this study is that the driver's chosen speed is influenced only by the street itself and adjacent driving environment. Accordingly, free flow speed was used to ensure that other vehicles did not influence the drivers' choice of speed. With mean free flow speed as the dependent variable, the analysis of variance model constructed in this study explained almost 80% of the variability in the mean free speeds chosen by drivers (Hansen et al., 2007). A previous paper shows these results in additional detail (Marshall et al., 2008). Significant factors included land use type, posted speed limit, building setback, the presence of a vegetated strip, and the presence of on-street parking. With respect to the presence of on-street parking, the reduction in vehicle speeds was in the order of 2.3 mph as compared to streets without parking and all other variables held constant. In other words, this study suggests that drivers tended to travel statistically significantly slower speeds in the presence of occupied on-street parking. Overall, the speed study showed that the largest speed reductions occurred on those roadways with a combination of street variables that many urban designers would consider complementary to on-street parking. For example with building setbacks, small setbacks were correlated with a 1.5 mph reduction in vehicle speed as compared to segments with large setbacks and all other variables held constant. Fig. 3 depicts an example of these mean speed results for two 25 mph segments.

The empirical results found in these speed and safety studies differ from conventional engineering theory. This mindset is emphasized in a recent driver simulation study of speed and hazard for streets with and without on-street parking (Edquist, Rudin-Brown, & Lenne, 2012). While they found slower vehicle speeds with the presence of on-street parking, they concluded that the reduction in speed was not enough to compensate for the longer perception-reaction times found in more complex environments. This type of thinking does not seem to hold up empirically, in part because it only accounts for the fact that people are driving slower in these environments. In reality, drivers also tend to have different expectations of hazard in more complex environments, and in turn, they compensate for these risks

Fig. 3. Speed Study Example Outcomes. *Source*: G. Hansen and W. E Marshall.

accordingly (Adams, 1995). It is similar in concept to the empirical examples that have found better road safety outcomes for shared spaces and multiway boulevards, both with more conflict points and complexity than any engineering traffic textbook would deem acceptable (Bechtler, Haenel, Laube, Pohl, & Schmidt, 2010; Jacobs, Macdonald, & Rofé, 2002). In the context of the type of streets seen in the three traditional downtowns from the first study, on-street parking and the other factors that coalesce with such environments – such as increased cyclist and pedestrian activity – can change the way people drive, and in turn, the road safety outcomes (Marshall & Garrick, 2011). Studies such as the simulation study also do not account for the potential difference in crash severity. While they acknowledge that slower vehicle speeds provide pedestrians, cyclists, and drivers with more time to react, they fail to recognize that when a crash does occur, the chance of it being life-threatening is greatly reduced. It also does not account for the implications of the additional off-street parking needed to compensate for not providing on-street parking, as off-street parking normally requires curb cuts and driveways, which have also been shown to reduce safety. It is important not to underestimate such differences when assessing the complete pedestrian environment.

PEDESTRIAN ENVIRONMENT AND TRAVEL BEHAVIOR

In terms of the pedestrian environment, the strip of parked cars along the street serves as a buffer to pedestrian activities immediately beyond the curb. In planning circles, this type of advantage does not find much debate. For instance, all of the main pedestrian level of service methodologies score streets with more on-street parking as better for pedestrians (Byrd & Sisiopiku, 2006). This is thought to be due to the buffer between pedestrians and through traffic imparted by on-street parking, but these numbers do not begin to take into account the potential for increased walkability due to less parking and denser development. It is also important to remember, however, that on-street parking can easily be misused in situations without complementary street design features (i.e., generous sidewalks) and the associated development patterns with appropriate densities, land uses, building setbacks, and pedestrian connections. In other words, on-street parking — for example, with its traffic calming abilities — is part of a complete street package that offers pedestrians a safer and more comfortable built environment. But how does on-street parking impact behavior?

This is a difficult question to answer because ideally in a study of this nature, one would want to find locations with various combinations of some features and not others, in order to isolate the contribution of each individual feature. However, this is very difficult to achieve in a real-world setting, and few studies have been able to accomplish this because on-street parking generally comes as part of a package with these other features such as compact development and mixed land use. For example, a recent paper examined the impact of on-street parking on car ownership in residential neighborhoods (Guo, 2013). While the study attempted to overcome methodological challenges such as the weak endogeneity between the provision of parking and car ownership and the low correlation between on-street and off-street supply, it did not account for any other street design factors nor differences in price (as the study only considered free parking). So while it would be nice if our case study could isolate on-street parking as a factor, the reality is that these results need to be contextualized and understood as attributable to a larger number of complementary factors, of which on-street parking is just one.

The study results showed that centers with on-street parking and other compatible characteristics such as generous sidewalks, mixed land uses, and higher densities recorded more than six times the number of pedestrians walking in these areas compared to the control sites, which lack these traits. At similar times, on similar days, the traditional sites averaged well over 300 pedestrians compared to less than 50 at the contemporary sites. Combined with an estimate of the on-site employees, the traditional sites averaged 1,300 more people on site, a level of activity successfully sustained with only 400 more parked cars. This means that the traditional sites averaged 1.80 people per car on site compared to 1.06 people per car at the contemporary sites on a typical day.

Fig. 4 depicts two sidewalks cafes during the lunch hour on the same day; the one at the traditional site is heavy with pedestrian activity while the one at the contemporary site is empty. While factors such as the quality of the food or service at these restaurants were not controlled for, the images do speak more to a qualitative assessment of the relative appeal of dining beside a street buffered by on-street parking as compared to one buffered by an off-street surface lot. In a recent book by Eran Ben-Joseph, he derisively places off-street surface lots at the bottom of the parking totem pole (Ben-Joseph, 2012). In other words, on-street parking is often an urban design tool used by planners to do far more than provide parking while structured garage parking can be extremely land use efficient and can also be delivered in a manner supportive of a downtown. Off-street parking detracts from such environments and does not provide much value beyond the parking itself.

Some of the difference in the level of pedestrian activity at these sites can clearly be attributed to differences in mode share. While only 9% of those surveyed traveled to the contemporary sites via a mode other than the automobile, this number reached 25% for the traditional sites. Other than driving, walking was the most important mode in each of these town centers. The user survey showed that at the traditional sites, almost 15% of trips to the town center were walking trips while at the contemporary sites, only 7% walked to the site. Bicycle use reached 2.5% in the user survey at the traditional sites compared to negligible bicycle use at the contemporary sites. In terms of public transportation, nearly 7% of those at the traditional

Fig. 4.   Sidewalk Cafe Comparison. *Source*: W. E Marshall.

sites used transit compared to only 1.4% at the contemporary sites. The difference was noteworthy because both the contemporary and traditional sites had similar levels of transit available (Marshall & Garrick, 2006).

Another potential reason for this difference has to do with multi-task trip making. In other words, people at the traditional sites were far more likely to park once and walk to do multiple errands instead of driving and parking again. In the user survey, drivers were asked if they always, sometimes, or never park once and walked to multiple errands (Marshall & Garrick, 2006). Over 70% of traditional site drivers said "always" compared to only 25% at the more contemporary sites; furthermore, while only 7% of those at the traditional sites never parked once and walked, this number exceeded 32% at the more contemporary sites. With regard to parking, this distinction is significant. Parking once and running multiple errands within a downtown as opposed to driving from store to store results in less parking being required to accommodate the same activity; this is a more efficient use of resources. Litman suggested reducing parking requirements by 5−15% in more walkable communities where parking once and running multiple errands is favored (Litman, 2006). Our results suggest that this potential for increased efficiency in parking could be greater than 15%.

THE FUTURE OF ON-STREET PARKING

The vitality afforded to these more walkable downtowns is in part due to the presence of on-street parking as a design feature in itself, but the corresponding reduction in off-street parking spaces needed can also play a role. Fewer off-street parking can potentially be replaced with more residences, restaurants, stores, and offices − the very uses that get people to want to come there in the first place. This begs the question as to the differences in economic output. For instance during one of Los Angeles' on-street parking bans, the city found a noticeable decline in retail business (Jakle & Sculle, 2004). Without on-street parking, convenience seemed to diminish and people decided to shop elsewhere. These sorts of questions have yet to be studied extensively.

Movements such as tactical urbanism are also beginning to ask the question as to whether vehicle parking is the highest and best use of street space in the first place. The current incarnation of what is generally known as tactical urbanism sprouted from the first Park(ing) Day in San Francisco in 1995, when activists turned a parking space into a park for a day (Lydon, Bartman, Garcia, Preston, & Woudstra, 2012; Patton, 2012). The first image in Fig. 5 shows a Park(ing) Day temporary installation in Denver, Colorado. The other two images depict more permanent tactical urbanism installations. The middle image is from Portland, Oregon where

Fig. 5. Tactical Urbanism Examples. *Source*: W. E. Marshall for Denver and Portland; M. Lydon for Long Beach.

two parking spaces were converted into a bicycle corral. The bottom image is from Long Beach, California of what is known as a parklet. It represents a growing trend of what appears to be outdoor seating for a restaurant in the form of an extended sidewalk; in reality, the parklet is open to the public and not just for patrons of the adjacent uses. When changes such as the bike corrals and parklets were first being introduced, many business owners objected to losing parking spaces and potential customers; however, anecdotal evidence suggests that such installations can increase revenue (Gandy, 2012). Innovative street space solutions – where on-street parking might normally be found – are now succeeding across the United States and around the world.

In addition to methodological improvements to on-street parking studies, future research trends also suggest a shift in the availability of technology in, for example, being able to track parking space occupancy in real-time. For example, San Francisco is currently undertaking a study called SFpark where they have outfitted over 440,000 public parking spaces with occupancy sensors (Pierce & Shoup, 2013; Simons, 2012). As part of the dynamic pricing pilot study, the cost of parking in 7,000 parking spaces spread across seven San Francisco neighborhoods changes over the course of a day and is being adjusted every six weeks. The target price is to ensure 85% occupancy, so that there is always one or two spaces available on every block face (prices can vary by block face). The overall intent is to reduce the amount of cruising for parking and perhaps even increase user satisfaction. Parking meters have come a long way since first being installed in Oklahoma City in 1935; new technologies and studies such as SFpark will hopefully bring a greater understanding to the complex world of on-street parking.

In terms of the provision of on-street parking and the state of the research, it will also be interesting to see the influence of the current proliferation of car sharing as well as with the changes that may come with autonomous cars, which the head of Nissan recently stated they would be selling by 2020 (Wasserman, 2013).

CONCLUSIONS

Beyond being convenient to multiple destinations, on-street parking is a great way to provide for parking shared among a number of land uses. Combining high occupancy rates, high demand, and high turnover help make on-street parking more efficient than other common forms of parking.

Efficiency also comes in the form of land use, as on-street spaces do not require access lanes, driveways, or landscaping (Litman, 2006). Such off-street parking requirements help off-street surface spaces consume more than double the land needed for on-street parking (Marshall et al., 2008). Providing parking solutions on the street tends to also be less expensive than both off-street surface lots, primarily in terms of land use efficiency, and structured garage parking, due to actual dollars spent (Shoup, 2005). Our investigation also points to on-street parking helping create safer roads. Although prior studies claim otherwise, this study considered crash severity and found that lower speed streets without parking had a severe and fatal crash rate more than two times higher than the streets with parking. This result was in part due to the fact that drivers tended to travel slower in the presence of features such as on-street parking. On-street parking — combined with lower vehicle speeds — also impacts the pedestrian environment. The case study presented here suggests that on-street parking plays a crucial role in pedestrian comfort, and in turn, the sites with on-street parking were more walkable, required less parking, and had much more vitality.

On-street parking should be used in situations where the street is a vital part of the destination and where the intent is to get drivers to slow down and recognize that they have arrived. There are many cities and towns that fail to provide on-street parking in these potentially beneficial situations. In many cases, the land needed for on-street parking is already available in the form of excess street capacity or existing paved shoulders that are entirely unwarranted for a town center setting. Other researchers have shown that street capacity is actually limited by intersection throughput; thus, a reduction in the number of through traffic lanes along street segments rarely impacts travel times. Many cities and towns have street space available that can be reallocated toward a more productive use such as on-street parking, which in the right context can help make these places safer and more walkable, while encouraging increased vibrancy and vitality. Unfortunately, these same places are still being influenced by the long standing idea that the focus in street allocation should be on automobile movement.

Getting parking right requires a more comprehensive approach than simply considering issues such as demand with respect to land use, as is common in most parking regulations. Overall, our results suggest that on-street parking is not purely a device to be used in the right environment; rather, it is a tool to help create that right environment in the United States and internationally.

NOTE

1. The typical "road diet" reconfiguration converts an undivided four-lane roadway into a two-lane roadway with turning lanes at intersections and other features such as bike lanes and on-street parking.

REFERENCES

Adams, J. (1995). *Risk*. London: UCL Press.

Arnott, R., de Palma, A., & Lindsey, R. (1991). A temporal and spatial equilibrium-analysis of commuter parking. *Journal of Public Economics*, *45*(3), 301–335. doi:10.1016/0047-2727(91)90030-6

Arnott, R., & Inci, E. (2005). *An integrated model of downtown parking and traffic congestion*. Cambridge, MA: National Bureau of Economic Research.

Bechtler, C., Haenel, A., Laube, M., Pohl, W., & Schmidt, F. (2010). *Shared space: Examples and arguments for vibrant public spaces*. Vienna, Austria: Road Safety Board.

Ben-Joseph, E. (2012). *Rethinking a lot: The design and culture of parking*. Cambridge, MA: MIT Press.

Byrd, J.,& Sisiopiku, V. (2006). Comparison of level of service methodologies for pedestrian sidewalks. *Transportation Research Board annual meeting CD-ROM*.

Desjardins, R. J. (1977). Effective low cost traffic engineering. Paper presented at the Compendium of Technical Papers of the 47th annual meeting of the Institute of Transportation Engineers at the Fourth World Transportation Engineers.

Edquist, J., Rudin-Brown, C. M., & Lenne, M. G. (2012). The effects of on-street parking and road environment visual complexity on travel speed and reaction time. *Accident Analysis and Prevention*, *45*, 759–765. doi:10.1016/j.aap.2011.10.001

Gandy, C. (2012). *Gazelles and the art of placemaking*. Retrieved from http://www.pps.org/blog/gazelles-the-art-of-placemaking/ Accessed on June 25, 2012.

Glazer, A., & Niskanen, E. (1992). Parking fees and congestion. *Regional Science and Urban Economics*, *22*(1), 123–132. doi:10.1016/0166-0462(92)90028-Y

Greibe, P. (2003). Accident prediction models for urban roads. *Accident Analysis and Prevention*, *35*(2), 273–285. doi:PiiS0001-4575(02)00005-2, doi:10.1016/S0001-4575(02)00005-2

Guo, Z. (2013). Residential street parking and car ownership: A study of households with off-street parking in the New York city region. *Journal of the American Planning Association*, *79*(1), 32–48. doi:10.1080/01944363.2013.790100

Hansen, G., Garrick, N. W., Ivan, J. N.,& Jonsson, T. (2007). Variation in free-flow speed due to roadway type and roadside environment. *Transportation Research Board Annual Meeting CD-ROM*.

Highway Research Board. (1971) *Special report 125: Parking principles*. Washington, DC: National Academy of Sciences.

Huang, H. F., Stewart, J. R., & Zegeer, C. V. (2002). Evaluation of lane reduction "Road Diet" measures on crashes and injuries. *Transportation Research Record*, *1784*, 80–90.

ITE, & CNU. (2010). *Designing walkable urban thoroughfares: A context sensitive approach, an ITE recommended practice*. Washington, DC: Institute of Transportation Engineers, Congress for the New Urbanism.

Jacobs, A. B., Macdonald, E., & Rofé, Y. (2002). *The boulevard book: History, evolution, design of multiway boulevards*. Cambridge, MA: MIT Press.

Jakle, J., & Sculle, K. (2004). *Lots of parking*. Charlottesville, VA: University of Virginia Press.

Litman, T. (2006). *Parking management best practices*: Victoria, BC: Planners Press.

Litman, T. (2007). *Congestion reduction strategies: Identifying and evaluating strategies to reduce traffic congestion*. Retrieved from www.vtpi.org/tdm/tdm96.htm

Lydon, M., Bartman, D., Garcia, T., Preston, R., & Woudstra, R. (2012). *Tactical urbanism 2*. New York, NY: The Street Plans Collaborative.

Marshall, W. E., & Garrick, N. (2006). Parking at mixed-use centers in small cities. *Transportation Research Record, 1977*, 164–171.

Marshall, W. E., & Garrick, N. (2011). Evidence on why bike-friendly cities are safer for all road users. *Journal of Environmental Practice, 13*(1), 16–27.

Marshall, W. E., Garrick, N. W., & Hansen, G. (2008). Reassessing on-street parking. *Transportation Research Record, 2046*, 45–52. doi:10.3141/2046-06

McCahill, C. T., & Garrick, N. W. (2010). Influence of parking policy on built environment and travel behavior in two New England cities, 1960 to 2007. *Transportation Research Record, 2187*, 123–130. doi:10.3141/2187-16

Mitchell, C. G. B. (2007). Old world ways: Roadway designs in Britain and other European countries emphasize maintaining the safety and mobility of older pedestrians. *Public Roads, 70*(March/April), 2–9.

Norton, P. D. (2008). *Fighting traffic: The dawn of the motor age in the American city*. Cambridge, MA: MIT Press.

Pande, A., & Abdel-Aty, M. (2009). A novel approach for analyzing severe crash patterns on multilane highways. *Accident Analysis and Prevention, 41*(5), 985–994. doi:10.1016/j.aap.2009.06.003

Patton, Z. (2012). Parklets: The next big tiny idea in urban planning. *Governing Magazine*, June.

Pierce, G., & Shoup, D. (2013). Getting the prices right: An evaluation of pricing parking by demand in San Francisco. *Journal of the American Planning Association, 79*(1), 67–81. doi:10.1080/01944363.2013.787307

Roberts, I., Norton, R., Jackson, R., Dunn, R., & Hassall, I. (1995). Effect of environmental-factors on risk of injury of child pedestrians by motor-vehicles – A case-control Study. *British Medical Journal, 310*(6972), 91–94.

Shoup, D. (2005). *The high cost of free parking*. Chicago, IL: American Planning Association.

Shoup, D. (2006). Cruising for parking. *Transport Policy, 13*, 479–486.

Simons, D. (2012). SFpark: San Francisco knows how to park it. *Sustainable Transport, 23*(Winter), 26–27.

Smith, W., & Associates (1965). *Parking in the city center*. New Haven, CT: the Automobile Manufacturers Association.

Wasserman, T. (2013). Nissan: We'll have a self-driving car on roads in 2020. *CNN*. Retrieved from http://www.cnn.com/2013/08/27/tech/innovation/nissan-driverless-car. Accessed on August 27, 2013.

Welch, T. (2000). The conversion of four-lane undivided urban roadways to three-lane facilities. Paper presented at the Urban Street Symposium. Transportation Research Circular No. 501, Transportation Research Board, Washington, DC.

CHAPTER 17

PARKING IN GUANGZHOU: PRINCIPLES FOR CONGESTION REDUCTION AND IMPROVING QUALITY OF LIFE IN A GROWING CITY

Rachel R. Weinberger and Lisa Jacobson

ABSTRACT

Purpose — *In Guangzhou, the largest city in southern China, car ownership is increasing beyond the capacity of the road system. This leaves streets gridlocked and parking facilities inaccessible, thus under-utilized. At the same time, Guangzhou's zoning code calls for additional off-site parking which is likely to encumber development. This chapter documents and discusses policies in Guangzhou that affect and are affected by parking and how they relate to City goals.*

Methodology/approach — *The chapter explores the relationship between three interrelated topics: (1) today's parking policies in Guangzhou, regulated by a variety of municipal agencies, (2) case studies of two large developments and their respective parking supplies and demands, and (3) city goals and objectives.*

Parking: Issues and Policies

Transport and Sustainability, Volume 5, 381–407

Copyright © 2014 by Emerald Group Publishing Limited
ISSN: 2044-9941/doi:10.1108/S2044-994120140000005025

Findings — *There is opportunity for Guangzhou to implement strategies to manage its parking supply relative to its roadway capacity, plus integrate its parking policies to the overall transportation system.*

Practical implications — *Emerging cities can learn from other's experiences. Parking supply affects the decisions people make about how they will travel and this in turn affects congestion, air quality and quality of life. Using smart parking regulations means an end to inadvertently fostering dependency on the car and the start of creating sustainable communities.*

Originality/value of chapter — *The value of the chapter comes from the way it builds from existing evidence to further understand the challenges of an emerging, fast-growing city.*

Keywords: Parking supply; congestion management; parking governance; parking utilization; parking maximums; parking building setbacks

INTRODUCTION

A critical yet poorly understood element of urban development policy is parking supply and management. Misapplied parking policies undermine a host of economic development, mobility, and sustainability goals. They lock cities into development trajectories, and all but guarantee unacceptable levels of congestion. In Guangzhou, the largest city in southern China, car ownership is increasing beyond the capacity of the road system. To address congestion, Guangzhou has focused on traffic engineering solutions and recently, by auctioning only a limited number of new license plates, set upper bounds on the number of cars allowed on the road. The latter policy is prevalent in other Chinese cities, including Shanghai and Beijing. However, the City may be missing opportunities to reduce congestion by better managing its parking resources.

Even with relatively low auto mode shares and evidence that off-street parking supply is underused, the planning department has mandated increased parking supply with new development. Increasing parking supply attracts more vehicles onto the streets and highways, exacerbating congestion, delay, and contributing to more pollution. Cities that have developed according to principles that ease auto use tend to engender high levels of auto dependence. They also tend to share the common characteristic of excess parking, which implies wasted resources. On the other hand, cities that emphasize multimodal access rather than auto access tend to be more prosperous. These latter cities still tend to have high levels of vehicle congestion but, because they also have high transit ridership and nonmotorized mode use, there are fewer people directly affected by or subject to traffic congestion (Shrank, Eisele, & Lomax, 2011).

Guangzhou could manage its parking resources to alleviate its congestion problem but to do so several hurdles must be overcome. First, there is a lack of coordination between the multiple players responsible for parking management and policy. The Communications Commission, the Price Bureau, the Planning Bureau, and other bodies have authority over different aspects of parking, yet they appear to work quite independently. Moreover, these bodies lack coordination with land use planning and development agencies. Examples include the determination of parking price where there is no coordination between the on- and off-street prices, and the pronounced conflict between traffic management, economic development, and convenient parking. One agency will mandate a parking garage in an area that another agency designated as a low parking/historic preservation district. This fragmentation among agencies, and the policies within these agencies, is common in many cities beyond Guangzhou and represents a serious obstacle to moving forward with a comprehensive parking policy.

Another inherent conflict in Guangzhou is that, regardless of how much parking is provided, parts of the street system are so congested that they cannot deliver additional vehicles to some parking locations. This leaves parking facilities under-utilized, and they will remain unused due to the congestion and the effect of high-density development (see case studies of two recent, high-end developments on page 396). The case studies also reveal that the amount of parking required in the zoning code far exceeds the amount required to ensure a "successful" real estate development. Indeed, confident that the transportation system is adequate for their needs, developers frequently negotiate to lower their parking burden. An abundant parking supply encourages auto use although the current preference is for walking and transit (with a mode split of more than 80% taking transit).

Recognizing that increased parking leads to increased driving, many cities – including Antwerp, Seoul, New York City, and Zurich – have implemented parking maximums. The purpose of the maximums is to ensure smooth traffic movements and to reduce private vehicle use. There is no reason for cities today to repeat the errors of their counterparts. Guangzhou and other growing cities can revisit their parking policies by unpacking zoning regulations, better managing use of building setbacks, and by coordinating management of on- and off-street parking.

The primary purpose of this chapter is to document policies in Guangzhou that affect and are affected by off-street parking. The identification of issues is accompanied by an analysis of these policies to show how they support or undermine City goals. This chapter concludes with findings and considerations of adopting alternative policies in Guangzhou.

BACKGROUND INFORMATION

Population and Auto Ownership

The population of Guangzhou grew 33% from 2005 to 2010 (Statistics Bureau of Guangzhou, 2006), reaching 12.7 million (Guangzhou Transport Planning Research Institute [GTPRI], 2010); meanwhile, growth in private vehicle ownership is greatly outpacing population growth. In 2005, of the 1.8 million registered vehicles, 31% were private cars. As of 2010, there were 2.15 million motorized vehicles of which 1.34 million (GTPRI, 2010) (or 62%) were private cars. Some have estimated the private vehicle fleet to be as high as 1.7–2 million (Guangzhou Daily, 2011).

Car ownership is predicted to nearly double from 2010, increasing to 3.65 million by 2020 (Statistics Bureau of Guangzhou, 2011), while the population will reach 15 million (China Academy of Urban Planning and Design, 2010). This results in auto ownership of 243 vehicles per 1,000 residents, compared to today's 170 vehicles per 1,000. The city is unlikely to be able to absorb the traffic that will accompany this kind of growth in auto ownership (Fig. 1).

Parking Policy

It has proven extremely difficult to pin down the policies and requirements that govern parking in Guangzhou. Information is inconsistent and often contradictory. The complexity is not unique to Guangzhou but illustrates an obstacle to assessing the effectiveness of policies as well as highlighting the difficulty that developers may face in deciding whether to build in Guangzhou.

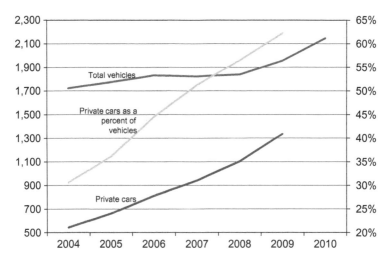

Fig. 1. Guangzhou Vehicle Growth. *Source*: (GTPRI, 2010).

Guangzhou employs the following explicit tools to implement and manage their parking policies:

1. *Minimum parking requirements*, which require developers to build at least the number of parking spaces set by the City.
2. *Parking price limits*, which are price maximums established by the City (in Guangzhou, there are three tiers of pricing).
3. *Increasing supply of public parking garages*, where the City has proposed an increase of 130,000 underground parking spaces.

A fourth but implicit policy is the permissive position toward using building setbacks as impromptu, or ad hoc, parking lots. A "setback" is frequently required in zoning codes to regulate bulk and to ensure that adequate light can reach lower floors of buildings. A typical requirement stipulates the number of meters required between the property line and the building line, thus regulating how far the building is setback from the property line. This area, though not intended for parking automobiles, has become a de facto parking lot for many modern buildings in Guangzhou. This phenomenon is illustrated in Fig. 2. Research indicates that surrounding buildings with parked cars represents a significant

Fig. 2. Setback Buildings with Front-Yard Parking (Adam Millard-Ball).

deterrent to pedestrian and bicyclist access (Maley & Weinberger, 2010; Marshall, Garrick, & Hansen, 2008). This policy has implications for other transportation policy areas and for performance of the transportation system.

Several municipal agencies implement conflicting policies in different areas of the city. Most simply, agencies divide the city into zones or areas, and each zone has different parking rules and requirements. One scheme describes areas where parking should be "restricted," "moderate," or "encouraged" as illustrated in Fig. 3. As expected, restricted parking is in the historic core of the city; moderate mostly surrounds the core; encouraged is the lower density outer zone. A second scheme divides the city into areas labeled "A" and "B" and delineates specific levels of required parking minimums. Generally, parking minimums in Area A are between 20% and 50% lower than in Area B. Fig. 4 shows the A and B spatial designations, and a comparison of parking requirements is presented in Table 1 (GTPRI, 2011).

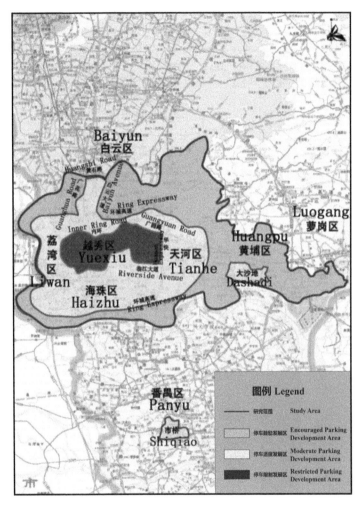

Fig. 3. Parking Intensity Designations. *Source*: GTPRI (2010).

A third system delineates three different off-street parking "charging" areas. The first level includes the three major business districts. The second level includes districts south of Beihuan highway, Xinjiaon North Road, Gongye Avenue, the north of Chongxi West Road, east of the Pearl River main channel, and west of Huanan high-speed artery. The third level designates residual areas. These three levels are illustrated in Fig. 5.

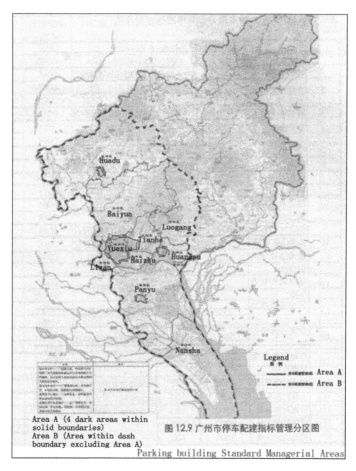

Area A (4 dark areas within
solid boundaries)
Area B (Area within dash
boundary excluding Area A)

图 12.9 广州市停车配建指标管理分区图

Parking building Standard Managerial Areas

Fig. 4.   Area A, Area B, and Nondesignated areas of GZ. *Source*: GTPRI (2010).

There is no obvious relationship among these competing geographic designations.

As of spring 2013, the Guangzhou Municipal Transport Commission was considering an additional policy to limit vehicles in the city by banning nonlocal cars from entering downtown areas and using main roads between 7 a.m. and 9 a.m. and 5 p.m. and 7 p.m., Monday through Friday (Huifeng, 2013). The same expected outcome could conceivably be achieved by better managing the city's parking supply.

Table 1. Off-Street Parking Requirements.

Building Types	Subtypes	Unit	Spaces Required		Bicycle Spaces Required
			Area A	Area B	
Residential	Development	/100 m² floor area	0.5–0.8	0.7–1.0	1
	Economic housing	/100 m² floor area	0.3	0.4	1
	Low-rent housing	/100 m² floor area	0.2	0.3	1.5
	Dormitory	/100 m² floor area	0.2–0.3	0.3	2
Hotel	Hotels	/100 m² floor area	0.3–0.4	0.5	0.25
	Hostels	/100 m² floor area	0.1–0.12	0.15	0.25
Office	Administration	/100 m² floor area	0.6–0.8	1.2	0.7
	Business (>15,000 m²)	/100 m² floor area	0.5–0.6	0.9	0.7
	Business (≤15,000 m²)	/100 m² floor area	0.6–0.7	1.0	0.7
Commercial	Retail and mall	/100 m² floor area	0.5–0.6	0.8	1
	Wholesale market	/100 m² floor area	0.8–1.2	1.5	1
	Warehouse supermarket	/100 m² floor area	1.0–1.5	2.5	1
	Single-used restaurant and entertainment	/100 m² floor area	1.0–1.5	2.5	1
Culture	Theater	/100 seats	3–5	5	3
	Conference center	/100 seats	3–5	10	3
	Museum/library	/100 m² floor area	0.3–0.4	0.8	3
	Exhibition center	/100 m² floor area	0.4–0.6	0.8	2
Stadium	Large-scale	/100 seats	–	6	10
	Small-scale	/100 seats	4–5	6	15
Hospital	Hospitals	/100 m² floor area	0.5–0.7	0.8	3
	Clinic	/100 m² floor area	0.6–0.8	1.0	3
	Sanatorium	/100 m² floor area	0.3–0.5	0.5	3
School	Primary schools	/100 m² floor area	0.1–0.15	0.15	3
	Middle schools	/100 m² floor area	0.1–0.15	0.15	8
	Colleges	/100 m² floor area	0.5–0.8	0.8	5
Tourism	Historic sites/theme parks	/100 m² land area	4–8	12–15	30
	City parks/resorts	/100 m² land area	1–2	4–6	20
Industry/Warehouse	Industrial factories	/100 m² floor area	0.1–0.2	0.2	1
	Warehouse facilities	/100 m² floor area	0.1–0.2	0.2	1

Source: GTPRI (2010).

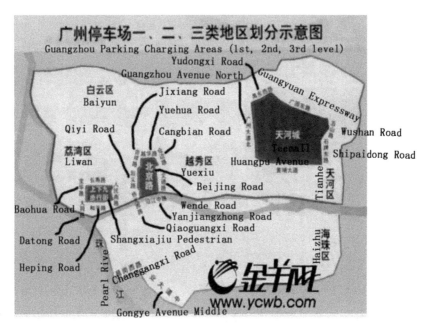

Fig. 5. Parking Charging Districts. *Source*: http://www.ycwb.com/news/2008-06/
26/content_1920883.htm.

Parking Policy Management

As in most cities, Guangzhou's parking policy divides into two distinct sub-sets. The stakeholder tree in Fig. 6 shows the agencies and organizations that play a role in parking decisions. The Planning Bureau, with approval of the municipal government, sets *off-street* parking policies and therefore supply. The Communications Commission, an operating agency responsible for street management, including road and bus/tram transport, governs *on-street* parking. From a user perspective and from the view of a functioning city, on- and off-street parking management are mutually dependent and should be managed in tandem. However, in Guangzhou, off-street parking management does not take into account the goals and operations of the agency responsible for on-street parking. The reverse is also true, when setting policy for on-street spaces the Communications Commission does not consider the needs, goals, or actions of the Planning Bureau, nor does it consider existing off-street supply. An additional element is parking price,

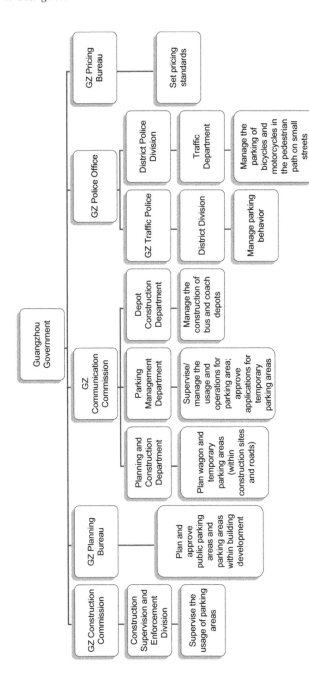

Fig. 6. Stakeholder Tree of Parking Interests in Guangzhou. *Source:* GTPRI (2011).

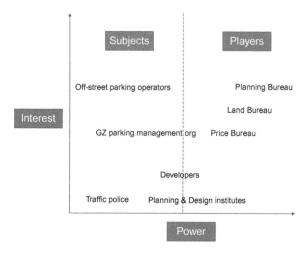

Fig. 7. Power Interest Grid Off-Street Parking. *Source*: Institute for
Transportation & Development Policy (ITDP) (2011).

managed by yet another agency, the Price Bureau. The Price Bureau is
responsible for setting maximum parking rates; one of the Bureau's objectives
is to resolve the tension between "affordable parking" and prices that are
high enough to make parking development attractive to the private sector.

Fig. 7 shows power and interest of agencies involved in managing off-street
parking. The Planning Bureau, Land Bureau, and Price Bureau all have the
most influence and power on the off-street parking system. It is noteworthy
that the Communications Commission is not identified as an interested party
nor an empowered agency on off-street parking policy, which has a well-
documented impact on transportation and travel behavior (Weinberger, 2012).

Frequently, ineffective management of on-street parking leads to the
perception of insufficient space overall. A 2009 analysis of setback parking,
undertaken as part of the Guangzhou Bus Rapid Transit (BRT) corridor
study, documents a concern regarding parking shortages, but data analysis
shows no shortages. The case studies, detailed in the next section, show a
maximum occupancy of 58% on the weekend and 38% on a weekday for
the major development of Taikoo Hui with average occupancies of 33%
and 18% for weekend days and weekdays during the prime opening hours
of 10 a.m. to 8 p.m. At the International Finance Center (IFC), another
successful development, the maximum weekday and weekend occupancy
rates are 35% and 30%, respectively. Both developments are in the Tianhe

district, which, in spite of this excess capacity, has been identified by the Planning Bureau as needing additional off-street space (see Table 2). These data suggest that poor management and coordination are the problems that need to be addressed, even though the problem presents itself as insufficient supply.

Nevertheless, the Guangzhou Transport Planning Research Institute (GTPRI) has developed a plan to provide 130,000 new public off-street parking spaces throughout the city (GTPRI, 2011). Table 2 outlines the proposed new distribution of spaces. Assuming four different car drivers use each space each day, the 130,000 spaces will result in over 1,000,000 additional daily, one-way trips.

A 2009 interview with representatives of GTPRI revealed a belief among Guangzhou's planners that developers sought opportunities to build parking because it is profitable (Interview by Adam Millard-Ball with representatives of GTPRI, August 2009). In more recent interviews with the Transportation Planning Research Institute, it was revealed that, in the face of compelling evidence, the city's planners have come to believe the opposite. The new belief was seeded by the way no private developer could be persuaded to build the additional spaces that the Planning Bureau has programmed (Interview by Rachel Weinberger with representatives of GTPRI, December 2011). The IFC and Taikoo Hui developments are further evidence that developers prefer fewer parking spaces. These developers negotiated parking reductions resulting in one case in a parking supply that is two-thirds of the as-of-right requirement. The evidence further suggests that providing less parking has been beneficial as parking utilization is well below supply with most visitors arriving by public transportation. Furthermore, regardless of parking supply provided, Guangzhou's street system may lack the capacity

Table 2. Distribution of Proposed Parking Spaces.

District	Parking Spaces Planned	Parking Spaces Planned/District Land Area (m²)
Baiyun, Tianhe, Haizhu, Liwan, Yuexiu, Huangpu, Luogang	76,716	0.016
Panyu	32,950	0.038
Huadu	13,050	0.035
Nansha	7,200	0.030
Total	129,916	0.021

Source: GTPRI (2011).

to bring more vehicles to the sites. The next section takes a closer look at the parking at the IFC and Taikoo Hui developments.

CASE STUDY: TWO DEVELOPMENTS IN TIANHE

To get a deeper and more nuanced understanding of how travel and transportation work in Guangzhou, two developments with similar characteristics were surveyed on a weekend day and a Friday. Table 3 describes the sites and shows that they are both relatively new, large, mixed-use developments that have on-site, paid parking facilities, and are located near public transit.

At every entrance to each site, surveyors counted people entering on foot or by automobile. Efforts to ascertain the access mode and origin were hampered by security guards who forbade the survey team from engaging with site visitors; however, valuable information was inferred from these entrance counts. The IFC had more visitors on the weekday, likely due to more office tenants, while Taikoo Hui had about a third more visitors on the weekend.

In two days, over 18,000 people visited the IFC. The vast majority walked or came by public transit. Few visitors arrived by car: 12% of weekday visitors and 16% of weekend visitors came by car. This corresponds to over 1,500 auto trips. Though the IFC is zoned for 0.5 parking spaces per 100 m^2, the developers supplied 0.37 spaces per 100 m^2. The other site, Taikoo Hui, had nearly 55,000 visitors in two days. Similar to the IFC, the majority of people arrive by transit or walked from nearby locations, with arrivals by car in the single digits: 7% on the weekday and 9% on the

Table 3.   Development Site Comparison.

	Taikoo Hui	Guangzhou IFC
Site size (m^2)	50,000	31,000
Floor area (m^2)	358,000 (Swire Properties Ltd, 2014)	450,000
Uses	Retail, office, hotel, serviced apartments	Retail, office, hotel, conference center, serviced apartments
Parking spaces	859	1,700
Parking/100 m^2	0.19	0.37
Parking price	8 a.m.–10 p.m.: 10RMB/hour	8RMB/hour
Year opened	2011	2010
District	Tianhe	Tianhe
Transport context	Shipai Qiao BRT and Metro Station	Zhujiang Xincheng Metro Station

Source: ITDP (2011).

weekend, generating 3,000 auto trips. Taikoo Hui attracted double the number of auto trips than IFC, yet Taikoo Hui had three times as many visitors. Taikoo Hui also has half the number of parking spaces than the IFC. Both sites are located along the new metro and Taikoo Hui is also accessible by BRT. The price difference in parking cost between the two developments is almost negligible, with a marginal difference of 2RMB/hour.

The prevalence of parking appears to have a larger impact on the way in which people choose to access the sites rather than affecting the total number of trips to these sites (Table 4). IFC, with more auto infrastructure, has disproportionately more auto trips. Taikoo Hui, with far more overall trips suffers no ill consequence of having provided fewer parking spaces. Site access by weekday and weekend is shown in Fig. 8 and Fig. 9.

An analysis of parking utilization (Table 5) shows that there is an excess of available parking at both sites. At Taikoo Hui, the development with fewer parking spaces, average weekday and weekend occupancy was 20% and 36%, respectively. Peak occupancy did not exceed 60%. At IFC, average occupancy is 27% on weekdays and 23% on weekends. Peak occupancy was 35%.

PARKING-RELATED GOALS

Parking policy directly affects several of Guangzhou's overall goals for the city. City policy documents, official presentations, and discussions with public officials together helped to identify several of the City's goals and objectives. The relationship between Guangzhou's goals and current parking policies is, overall, disconnected. This section describes the expected impact of current parking policies and the mismatch of the policy outcomes and goals.

Table 4. Site Access.

	Pedestrian or Metro Access	Auto Access	Auto Mode Share
International Financial Center	**15,728**	**2,420**	**13%**
Weekend	5,770	1,076	16%
Weekday	9,958	1,344	12%
Taikoo Hui	**49,768**	**4,557**	**8%**
Weekend	28,483	2,861	9%
Weekday	21,285	1,696	7%

Source: ITDP (2011).

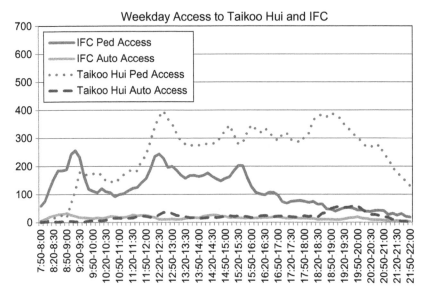

Fig. 8.   Weekday Access by Time of Day. *Source*: ITDP (2011).

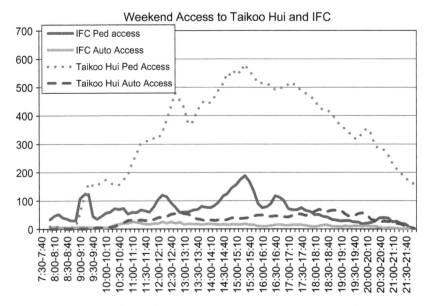

Fig. 9.   Weekend Access by Time of Day. *Source*: ITDP (2011).

Table 5. 10 a.m.–10 p.m. Parking Occupancy (Taikoo Hui and IFC).

	Taikoo Hui		IFC	
	Weekday	Weekend	Weekday	Weekend
Average occupancy (10 a.m.–10 p.m.)	19.5%	35.8%	27.2%	23.1%
Peak occupancy	38.4%	57.6%	34.6%	29.6%
Average parking duration	1:22	1:48	2:19	2:21

Source: ITDP (2011).

Guangzhou's specific parking objectives (GTPRI, 2011):

1. Developing an integrated transport system; ensuring the balance of parking supply and demand.
2. Parking in private developments is the major method of achieving the right supply, supplemented by public off- and on-street parking. The scale and location of parking to be coordinated with road and transit capacities.
3. Increasing citywide supply of underground parking by 130,000 spaces.

Guangzhou's transportation objectives (Guangzhou Municipal Communications Commission, 2011):

4. Maintain travel speeds of 25 kph or higher.

Supplemented by [pertinent] economic development goals:

5. Encourage additional land development.
6. Encourage purchase of automobiles by residents in order to support three automobile manufacturing plants in the city (Transport Planning Research Institute [Planning Bureau] meeting, December 12, 2011).

Goal Analysis

The first goal of developing an integrated transport system is laudable but, given the structure of parking minimums, it is unobtainable. To address this goal, the amount of parking that is allowed to be constructed must be set in accordance with the capacity of the road system. The current policy (illustrated in Table 1) of requiring minimum amounts of parking space consistent with levels of development, and regardless of road capacity, undermines this important integration. In general, parking minimums should be reduced or eliminated since:

1. When parking demand is lower than the mandated standard, minimum requirements will oversupply parking. This leads to three additional problems:
   a. Because supply and demand are codetermined, such an oversupply may actually be *inducing* rather than simply accommodating car ownership and use (Weinberger, 2012).
   b. Some developers will be forced to incur direct and indirect costs related to providing parking that they might not otherwise incur. With added costs, some will choose to forego development altogether (McDonnell, Madar, & Been, 2009). Research shows that each parking space adds significantly to the cost of residential buildings (Jia & Wachs, 1999; U.S. Environmental Protection Agency, 2006) and commercial development (Shoup, 2005). The additional costs may reduce developer profit margins — sometimes to the point of foregoing development as indicated above. In other cases the additional costs may be passed through to the tenants and customers of the development whether they are car and parking users or not (Shoup, 2005).
   c. Parking takes up valuable land thereby forcing dispersion of primary uses. An opportunity cost of parking is the preclusion of other land uses. The implied density decrease associated with that dispersion degrades pedestrian, bike, and transit environments contributing to a cycle of auto-dependence (Weinberger, Kaehny, & Rufo, 2010).
2. Minimum requirements provide only a lower bound on parking supply. These regulations exert no control over the parking supply when developers want to provide more than the mandated standard.
3. Minimum requirements are set as a function of developed area (space/m^2), that is, they are considered a function of land planning. But parking is part of the transportation system and must be considered both as part of the transportation system as well as part of the development function.

The imposition of minimum standards is undergirded by the fallacy that anticipating and meeting parking demand is of paramount importance to successful development. This is based on the idea that there is an exogenously determined parking demand. What planners, traffic engineers, and other urban policy makers frequently fail to grasp is that there is no demand for parking per se. There is demand for access to locations and to the extent that access is available via walking, biking or riding transit — in all of its manifestations – the demand is met and no parking need be provided. A particularly well-known modern development, which rose on the principle of demand for access, is the Swiss Re building at 30 St. Mary Axe in London. The Swiss Re building comprises 40 stories and 76,400 m^2 of commercial space (Foster and Partners, 2011). The building, completed in 2004 and able to accommodate 4,000 employees in the office area, includes only five car parking spaces with those five spaces being reserved for use by people with physical disabilities.

If the London requirements matched the Guangzhou parking requirements, at 0.5 spaces per 100 m^2 (GTPRI, 2011), the developers of the Swiss Re building would have had to provide 373 additional spaces. The developers understood that, in a transit rich context, access needs were satisfied without adding parking. They saved \$7.8 to \$13.7 million in construction costs (based on estimates by Shoup, 2005 op cit and Litman, 2010; USD \$20–\$35,000 per structured space), reduced the size of their building by 11%, and eliminated thousands of weekly auto trips to, and within, downtown London (auto use is highly dependent on the cost and supply of parking; See: Vaca & Kuzmyak, 2005; Pratt, Kuzmyak, Weinberger, & Levinson, 2003).

The reduction in auto trips translates directly to cyclical reinforcement of reductions in congestion, air pollution, and greenhouse gas emissions. By not accommodating auto trips, users will avail themselves more of transit and nonmotorized modes. By increasing demand on transit, the transit operators can justify higher frequencies and better service, which, in turn, makes transit more attractive and further draws more people to transit services (Mogridge, 1997). By supplying the additional parking spaces, the converse would have occurred; weaker transit would have required additional transit subsidies.

The second part of this goal, ensuring the balance of parking supply and demand, fails to recognize that supply and demand are codetermined and mediated by a price. Little is understood about parking demand in the context of price because most parking – throughout the world – is subsidized. The subsidy is an outcome of the oversupply that usually accompanies parking minimums. Unless parking price is unbundled from the primary development and priced to cover its cost, "demand" is simply an expression of desire for an underpriced good.

Guangzhou's second goal of providing parking in private developments to achieve the right supply (supplemented by public off- and on-street parking) reinforces the objective in Goal 1 of achieving the right supply. The arguments against this approach are found in the preceding paragraph.

Depending on the context, on-street parking should be a primary, not sup-plementary, piece of the parking supply. There are three critical advantages of on-street parking:

1. On-street parking offers the most flexibility across uses and time of day. Whereas development-based parking is typically limited to users of the specific development, on-street parking may be used by anyone seeking to park whether they are going to one development or another. This provides particular efficiencies when developments have different time of day use profiles. Shared parking, in which multiple developments with different time of day demands rely on the same spaces, is a more efficient use of space (Urban Land Institute, 2005). The classic example is a hardware store and a movie theater. The hardware store needs to accommodate customers during the day and the theater accommodates customers at night. Rather than require each development to supply a full complement of parking with one set idle while another nearby is oversaturated, a shared parking arrangement can lead to more efficient use of both. On-street parking provides the ultimate efficiency by providing maximum sharing.
2. On-street parking is safer than parking in building setbacks or off-street parking because drivers are not required to travel across the pedestrian path to access the parking spaces (Marshall et al., 2008).
3. When appropriate, a row of cars parked between moving traffic and the pedestrian space can serve as a traffic calming device. It buffers pedestrians from moving traffic (Marshall et al., 2008), particularly when situated between the carriageway and bicycle and pedestrian lanes.

Public off-street parking can also provide an important opportunity for shared parking, thus limiting the amount of time that spaces are idle. New York City has recently adopted a change in their zoning code that makes all parking in new developments in part of the city public (New York City Department of City Planning, 2013). Rather than being the primary source for parking spaces, private development parking should be limited to the maximum extent possible.

Finally, as Goal 2 states, it is critically important that the scale and location of parking facilities coordinate with road and transit capacity. At present, there is no mechanism by which this can occur.

The City's third goal is a proposed increase in citywide supply of under-ground parking by 130,000 spaces. This stands in stark contrast to the other objectives and to other city policy on the distribution of parking supply. In particular, the additional spaces are proposed for the areas identified by

Observed parking utilization at these developments does not necessarily imply that parking shortages are not felt in other parts of the city. However, caution must be expressed in the view that a perceived parking shortage can be addressed by appropriate pricing concomitant with provision of other access modes and that requiring excess parking in new developments will not alleviate spot shortages experienced in historic districts.

Furthermore, and of paramount importance, the existing parking rules seem to be set to ensure the convenience of drivers and car owners, irrespective of any urban planning or urban design principles that correspond to livable, sustainable, and economically successful cities. Rapidly growing cities have distinct advantages over shrinking and slow growth cities, and there are many opportunities to set a city on a good trajectory for the future. Sometimes, in their haste to accommodate rapid growth, growing cities also miss opportunities and put in place policies that bode ill for the future. In Guangzhou, the GTPRI has indicated that, in the short term, increasing parking supply is the main method for addressing the perceived parking shortage. They indicate parking demand management as a supplementary strategy, which includes limiting vehicle license plate registrations. In the long term, they expect to reverse these approaches (GTPRI, 2011). Yet the short-term strategy locks the City into excess parking and may preclude the long-term strategy from being implemented.

Given the particular advantages of Guangzhou, the following strategies are likely to have a substantial impact on parking demand:

Eliminate parking minimums. Guangzhou has an opportunity to turn its attention from trying to determine how much parking to require and instead think about how much parking to allow. While it is not always prudent to take cues from developers, it is certainly telling that high-end and luxury developers, such as the developers of Taikoo Hui and the IFC, have negotiated with the City to reduce their parking supply well below the amount required. These developments cater to clients who are among the most likely to be auto reliant and yet the developers are confident that other modes of access will be sufficient to attract their customers. Indeed, even with the significantly lowered parking supply, both Taikoo Hui and IFC have excess parking spaces. Eliminating parking minimums allows a city to build parking supply to real demand.

Establish parking maximums according to the street capacity. The street system can accommodate a fixed and limited number of vehicles in any given time period. When parking standards are set according to development and not transportation capacity, there are guaranteed imbalances that result in congestion when people choose cars beyond the level that is socially optimal. Guangzhou has an opportunity to set proactive parking limits, guided by the existing transportation capacity. When determining street capacity, the City may also look forward to the point when it may wish to reserve additional lanes for future BRT corridors. The conversion of auto lanes to BRT lanes greatly enhances the person capacity of a corridor while frequently reducing the auto capacity. Reductions in auto capacity can easily result in redundant or excess parking capacity but preventing excess parking by maintaining automobile capacity would be a very peculiar outcome.

Set parking regulations in tandem with transit and other elements of the transportation system. Development sites do not experience parking demand per se, rather, they experience demand for access. In transit rich areas, most access needs can be met by transit. These areas will thrive with much lower levels of parking than areas that do not have good transit. Guangzhou should use transit district zoning overlays or other tools that tie parking reductions to good transit and nonmotorized access.

Eliminate Setback Parking. Setback parking has a corrosive effect on the pedestrian environment. Most intrusions to pedestrian environments lead to additional private auto reliance (preference for the automobile), which further erodes the pedestrian environment and ultimately leads to auto dependence (lack of alternatives) and inescapable congestion. Vehicles crossing and driving on the sidewalk present a serious danger to non-auto users and even to auto users who must walk the last few meters from their parking place to their destination. Research on this issue shows that parking at the front of buildings discourages people from using nonmotorized modes when nonmotorized modes would otherwise be preferred (Maley & Weinberger, 2010). To foster a built environment conducive to pedestrian and bicycle mobility, placing provided parking in the rear of buildings can be critical (U.S. Environmental Protection Agency, 2006).

CONCLUSIONS

Unlike European and U.S. cities, many of which have developed their mass transit and auto systems during different historical periods, mass transit and mass auto ownership in China are a relatively recent phenomenon. As a result, Chinese cities face a tremendous opportunity to develop these systems in a complementary, rather than competitive fashion. Cities can use appropriate land use context, urban design guidelines, and reduced parking requirements to steer development to highly accessible transit corridors. Using metros and BRT systems as accessibility tools and mechanisms by which to shape regions, zoning regulations can encourage growth along transit corridors to create better, people-oriented places.

To avoid worsening traffic conditions and placing a drag on the growing economy, Guangzhou would be wise to rethink off-street parking as a solution to its on-street parking problems and consider access planning instead. Parking supply affects the decisions people make about how they will travel and this in turn affects congestion, air quality, and quality of life. Using smart parking regulations means an end to inadvertently fostering dependency on the car and the start of creating sustainable communities.

Guangzhou city leaders have put considerable but disjointed thought into developing a parking program. Their plan, which builds on common practice more than best practice, addresses some of their goals and threatens others. Rather than adapting outdated and incomplete zoning regulations, including off-street parking minimums from U.S. suburbs and other car-dominated societies, Guangzhou has the opportunity to forge a new path by creating best practices and serving as an exemplar for cities across China and around the world.

ACKNOWLEDGMENTS

Work in this chapter was substantially supported by the Institute for Transport and Policy Development (ITDP). The text draws from the unpublished white paper, *Parking Policy in Guangzhou*. Special thanks to Bram van Ooijen, Li Shuling, Liu Shaokun, Michael Kodransky, Zoltan Gymarti, and Jessica Morris for help, support and intellectual contributions as well. Thanks also to the reviewers and editors of this volume and our Nelson\Nygaard colleagues —particularly Jennifer Gennari and Liu Qingnan for their help.

REFERENCES

China Academy of Urban Planning and Design (CAUPD). (2010). Guangzhou Urban Planning and Research Centre, Guangzhou Urban Planning and Design Survey Research Institute & GZTPRI (Guangzhou Transport Planning Research Institute).

Foster and Partners. (2011). Projects: Swiss Re Headquarters, 30 St Mary Axe. Retrieved from http://www.fosterandpartners.com/projects/swiss-re-headquarters-30-st-mary-axe/

Guangzhou Daily. (2011). *Car Ownership of Guangzhou Will Exceed 2 Million Next Year*. Retrieved from http://gzdaily.dayoo.com/html/2011-07/17/content_1419228.htm. Accessed on January 18, 2012.

Guangzhou Municipal Communications Commission. (2011). *Scheme on Mitigating Traffic Jam in Central Areas of Guangzhou City after Asian Games*. Guangzhou: Guangzhou Municipal Communications Commission.

Guangzhou Transport Planning Research Institute (GTPRI). (2010). Guangzhou Transport Development Annual Report.

Guangzhou Transport Planning Research Institute (GTPRI). (2011). *Guangzhou Urban Comprehensive Transport Planning*, pp. 189–199.

Guangzhou Transport Planning Research Institute (GTPRI). (2011, October). Existing conditions, problems and future visions for parking in Guangzhou. Presentation to Communications Commission.

Holtzclaw, J., Clear, R., Dittmar, H., Goldstein, D., & Haas, P. (2002). Location efficiency: Neighborhood and socio-economic characteristics determine auto ownership and use-studies in Chicago, Los Angeles and San Francisco. *Transportation Planning and Technology*, 25, 1–27.

Huifeng, H. (2013). Guangzhou closer to ban on non-local cars in rush hours. *South China Morning Post*. Retrieved from http://www.scmp.com/news/china/article/1218689/guangzhou-closer-ban-non-local-cars-rush-hours

Institute for Transportation & Development Policy (ITDP). (2011) *Parking Guidebook for Chinese Cities*. Retrieved from http://www.itdp.org/documents/Parking_Guidebook_for_Chinese_Cities.pdf

Jia, W., & Wachs, M. (1999). Parking requirements and housing affordability: Case study of San Francisco. *Transportation Research Record, 1685*, 156–160.

Kain, J. (1967). Postwar metropolitan development: Housing preferences and auto ownership. *The American Economic Review, 57*(2), 223–234.

Litman, T. (2010). Parking requirement impacts on housing affordability. *Victoria Transport Policy Institute*, 2–34.

Maley, D., & Weinberger, R. (2010). *Food shopping in the urban environment: Parking supply, destination choice and mode choice. Paper presented at the transportation research board annual meeting*, Washington, DC.

Marshall, W., Garrick, N., & Hansen, G. (2008). Reassessing on-street parking. *Transportation Research Record: Journal of the Transportation Research Board, 2046*, 45–52.

McDonnell, S., Madar, J., & Been, V. (2009). *Minimum parking requirements, transit proximity and development in New York City*. Furman Center for Real Estate and Urban Policy, New York, NY. Manuscript in preparation.

Mogridge, M. J. H. (1997). The self-defeating nature of urban road capacity policy: A review of theories, disputes and available evidence. *Transport Policy, 4*(1), 5–23.

MoHURD. (2010). Ministry of Public Security and National Development and Reform Commission.

New York City Department of City Planning. (2013). Manhattan Core Text Amendment Approved. Retrieved from www.nyc.gov/html/dcp/html/mn_core/index.shtml. Accessed on July 16.

Pratt, R., Kuzmyak, R., Weinberger, R., & Levinson, H. (2003). Parking management and supply. *TCRP report 95, traveler response to system changes handbook*. Washington, DC: Transportation Research Board.

Schimek, P. (1996). Household motor vehicle ownership and use: How much does residential density matter? *Transportation Research Record: Journal of the Transportation Research Board, 1552*, 120–125.

Shoup, D. (2005). *The high cost of free parking*. Chicago, IL: American Planning Association.

Shrank, D., Eisele, B., & Lomax, T. (2011). Texas Transportation Institute Annual Urban Mobility Report. Retreived from http://mobility.tamu.edu/ums/

Siegman, P. (n.d.). *Reforming parking requirements: Less traffic, better places*. Local Government Commission. Retrieved from http://www.lgc.org/freepub/community_ design/presentations/siegman_sgzc_oak04/index.htm. Accessed on December 16, 2011.

Statistics Bureau of Guangzhou. (2006). 1% Sample Survey of Population (2005). Retrieved from http://www.gzstats.gov.cn/pchb/pc/. Accessed on January 18, 2012.

Statistics Bureau of Guangzhou. (2011). Ownership per 100 Urban Households of Consumer Durables (2010). Retrieved from data.gzstats.gov.cn/gzStat1/chaxun/ndsj.jsp. Accessed on January 18, 2012.

Swire Properties Ltd. (2014). Our Portfolios: Taikoo Hui, Guangzhou. Retrieved from www. swireproperties.com/en/our-portfolios/mainland-china/Pages/taikoo-hui-guangzhou.aspx. Accessed on February 15, 2012.

Urban Land Institute. (2005). *Shared parking*. Washington, DC: Urban Land Institute.

U.S. Environmental Protection Agency.(2006). *Parking spaces/community places: Finding the balance through smart growth solutions*. Washington, DC: Development, Community and Environmental Division (1807T), U.S. Environmental Protection Agency.

Vaca, E., & Kuzmyak, R. (2005). Parking pricing and fees. *TCRP report 95, traveler response to system changes handbook*. Transportation Research Board, Washington, DC.

Weinberger, R. (2012). Death by a thousand curb-cuts: Evidence on the effect of minimum parking requirements on the choice to drive. *Transport Policy, 20*, 93–102.

Weinberger, R., Kaehny, J., & Rufo, M. (2010). *U.S. parking policies: An overview of management strategies*. New York, NY: Institute of Transportation and Development Policy.

CHAPTER 18

CONCLUSIONS

Corinne Mulley and Stephen Ison

ABSTRACT

Purpose — *The purpose of this chapter is to synthesise the issues and debates raised in the book as a whole.*

Methodology/approach — *This chapter reviews the content of the book, drawing together the threads to provide conclusions on parking issues and policies around the world.*

Findings — *The chapter reveals the way in which parking is fundamentally a land-use issue and the importance of parking to different travel demands. As cars spend most of their time parked at home, the issue of residential parking is important and determines the shape and nature of our cities. Planning for parking has a key role to play in determining the outcome of how walkable the built environment becomes. The synthesis of the chapters of the book reveals how the type of parking is intrinsically linked to the activity undertaken and the type of destination, whether the trip is for commuting or for retail or leisure.*

The chapter identifies strategies such as car-free developments, park and ride and workplace parking levies used to provide solutions and the way in which the number of stakeholders involved influences the ease with which the complex interplay of issues in parking can be resolved.

Parking: Issues and Policies
Transport and Sustainability, Volume 5, 409–416
Copyright © 2014 by Emerald Group Publishing Limited
All rights of reproduction in any form reserved
ISSN: 2044-9941/doi:10.1108/S2044-994120140000005026

Practical implications — *Understanding that parking is primarily a land-use policy, dependent on the home location and destination of the trip, has implications for the development of parking policy within the package of measures making up travel demand management strategies. The chapter shows how parking for a stationary vehicle can influence the flow of moving vehicles and the built environment.*

Originality/value of chapter — *This chapter draws on the chapters of this book which offer a multidimensional investigation into parking issues and parking policy, providing a wealth of case study material providing evidence to underpin the design of effective parking management approaches.*

Keywords: Parking; land-use demand; supply; management; policy; planning

Everyone has a view on transport issues because of the way in which transport touches everyday lives and impacts on personal wellbeing. Parking, as a topic, unsurprisingly evokes strong reactions from car owners and non-car owners alike as well as being an area of key debate in land-use and transport policy.

Parking as a land-use issue is raised in all chapters to different degrees. For example, the parking space allocation required for the 29.1 million cars currently in the UK is an area equivalent to about one quarter of Greater London with the average car being in use for 3—4% of the time and parked at home or elsewhere for the remaining 96% (Marsden, Chapter 2). This makes parking a significant land-use issue. Why such extensive use of land should be allocated to parking on land which has a high opportunity cost, particularly in city centres, is echoed by McCahill and Garrick (Chapter 3), Manville (Chapter 7) and Weinberger and Jacobson (Chapter 17). Moreover, the amount of space set aside for parking has varied significantly over time and is clearly impacted by policies beyond those relating simply to parking (McCahill & Garrick, Chapter 3).

Land-use issues go beyond simply the amount of space set aside for parking. Land-use considerations need to distinguish between cities built for cars and cities where parking is being retrofitted. For residential parking, cities built before mass car ownership primarily rely on on-street parking, setting the stage for extensive policy discussion. In contrast, for new or recent build, the determination of the space set aside is impacted by planning considerations and discussion as to the impact of, in particular, minimum parking standards. Whether on-street or off-street, parking for residential use clearly has implications for the built environment. Marshall (Chapter 16) shows how on-street parking plays a key role in making the built environment walkable, albeit in the context of destinations and not residential neighbourhoods but a parallel for residential parking can be easily drawn. A walkable built environment has many knock on effects, not only for parking but for wider travel behaviour. In this context, residential parking policy for on-street parking can be used to reduce car ownership, on the basis of reducing car trips with mixed outcomes as detailed by Leibling in Chapter 12.

For residential parking, there is a greater debate in the literature between the common use of minimum parking requirements in the planning domain and the outcome for residents, for the urban areas under consideration and for the economy. The evidence is now clear that minimum parking requirements by planners have led to oversupply of parking (Shoup, Chapter 5), raised house prices through the provision of unnecessary parking (Weinberger, Chapter 11) and have an impact on the economy (in the context of China, Weinberger & Jacobson, Chapter 17). The counter debate is that maximum parking requirements lead to spillover effects and parking difficulties in adjacent areas. In various chapters, the impacts of maximum parking requirements are identified as less serious than the distortions created by minimum parking specifications as well as being to some extent ameliorated by implementing policy to control spillover effects. For example, the City of Sydney, Australia, uses maximum parking spaces in its planning control but adds to this a prohibition of entitlement for on-street parking for dwellers of these brownfield site developments with the aim of limiting spillover effects, influencing car ownership and car use behaviour, as explained by Ison, Mulley, Mifsud, and Ho, Chapter 14.

Planning considerations aside, on-street residential parking is primarily influenced by housing type and residential density and becomes a problem when the housing type required to support the population density results in competition for on-street parking, turning it into a more general urban issue (Bates, Chapter 4). Cars spend the majority of their time parked at home and so this makes residential on-street parking an issue, particularly as this parking space is rarely paid for or paid for at a rate that affects behaviour.

Travel behaviour for residential parking is perhaps most starkly shown in the development of car-free parking (Melia, Chapter 10) where residents of these developments are making a lifestyle choice in living without proximity to cars. However, the study of the balance of supply and demand in London (Leibling, Chapter 12) also shows the way in which parking controls can have an impact on travel behaviour by residents.

For non-residential parking, it is convenient to separate workplace parking from other parking issues. Retail parking is the dominant parking activity outside residential and workplace parking and the activity is associated with the lowest duration of parking. Here the debate divides into the impact of parking policy on congestion, on the built environment and on travel behaviour. Linked to this is the determinants of parking choice and the way in which the combination of factors interplay in shaping the eventual decision of where to park and how this can be used in forming parking policy (Brooke, Ison, & Quddus, Chapter 6). The planning controls and their impacts are persuasively explained by Weinberger (Chapter 11) with the behavioural aspects being highlighted by Marsden (Chapter 2) who identifies how more information is needed to truly gauge the extent to which parking restraints, in particular, provide positive benefits for the economy.

The mantra that parking is never free is relevant here as retail parking, particularly retail activity on the edge of cities, provides parking which may be free to car users but of course is recouped through the rent of the retailers. Perhaps more importantly, the case study of Guangzhou (Chapter 17) shows how parking for retail and business activity can differ because the demand for parking is confused with a demand for access. In Guangzhou, the development with good public transport access was able to meet a significant proportion of the demand for access through use of public transport with demand for parking consequentially being lower. Moreover, access by public transport brings other benefits through a reduction in car-based trips (congestion, emissions) as well as providing opportunities to grow public transport (higher ridership leading to increased frequencies, for example) that leads to greater urban sustainability.

Parking for commuting is important for a number of reasons. Bates (Chapter 4) identifies that demand for commuter parking dominates by being the single largest demand for parking away from home. Moreover, the effects of commuter parking are compounded because the onset of work times are more concentrated in time than for other journey purposes and exacerbated by the way in which there are often no charges for destination parking. The British evidence is that commuter parking is not well handled by pricing although the recent move by Nottingham City Council to implement a workplace parking levy (WPL) is an exception.

Parking for commuting is the result of cars moving on roads at busy times. Using parking as a way of reducing congestion is the aim behind the workplace parking levy in Nottingham (Dale, Frost, Gooding, Ison, & Warren, Chapter 15) and the parking space levies (PSL) of Sydney and Melbourne (Chapters 13 and 14, respectively). In Melbourne the evidence shows there is not a strong link between who pays for parking and the existence of the levy since the levy is imposed on the owners of the parking spaces, making it more difficult for the PSL to influence behaviour. Importantly too, the Melbourne PSL originally targeted long stay parking so as to influence the travel behaviour of commuters and one outcome has been that supply has changed to give both an overall reduction in supply but also a shift towards the provision of short stay parking as parking owners respond to the 'incentives' of the levy. The WPL of Nottingham and the PSL of Sydney both have explicit aims to reduce congestion using hypothecation of the revenue to public transport improvements to make the levy more palatable. As a mechanism, and as a way of raising revenue for hypothecation, levying commuters has possibilities but to work well commuters have to be payers of the levy and with the commuters knowing specifically the use of the hypothecation, as in Nottingham, rather than being treated as a 'pot of money' as in Sydney. In this context, the Nottingham WPL is more likely to meet its objectives since all aspects of the scheme are under the control of a single agency and the impact of the WPL is designed to impinge directly on car users.

Whilst the price mechanism is used in parking policy, Manville (Chapter 7) argues that it provides perverse signals. On-street parking is often free or priced below off-street parking with conservative estimates (see Chapter 4, Table1) suggesting US cities only charge for a small percentage of their on-street parking. But on-street parking is using more valuable space because of its proximity to destinations than the off-street garage spaces. This means that car drivers prefer on-street parking and are prepared to cruise to find it when it appears unavailable thereby adding to traffic flow and, in some cases congestion. Cruising creates driver frustrations which are unnecessary because off-street parking is vacant but not demanded because the price is higher. However, if on-street parking is correctly priced to minimise the negative externalities it has the potential to contribute to urban vitality as shown by Marshall (Chapter 16). Marshall argues that on-street parking should be used to provide the right environment in mixed use destinations, creating a built environment which is walkable and creating positive travel behaviour traits, slowing down traffic and increasing safety, particularly of pedestrians.

Setting the price to send the right signals to car drivers wanting to park is only part of the story in terms of parking management. Parking management is ubiquitous in urban centres and central to many of the chapters in this book thus emphasising the point that there is no single solution that fits all places. Rye and Koglin (Chapter 8) provide a comprehensive overview of how parking management policy arises through both conflicts and complex relationships between parking, revenue raising and the desire for economic vitality. They also show how solutions rely on the interaction of a number of actors. However, as Weinberger and Jacobson demonstrate (Chapter 17), it is often the number of stakeholders involved which frustrates the development of parking policy to push in the same direction.

Whilst parking management has grown to be associated with increasing controls, particularly with on-street parking, the issues are different for areas identified as destinations as compared to residential areas where supply is insufficient to meet demand. In the former case, a lack of supply is often associated with pressure to build off-street parking but this is likely to exacerbate the situation unless pricing correctly values the difference between off-street and on-street parking places. Increasingly, parking management has driven the demand for parking down to the extent that parking off-street is being converted to alternative uses (Rye & Koglin, Chapter 8).

Park and Ride is perhaps the most explicit parking management tool used to control congestion, protect urban centres (often heritage centres) by displacing parking from the urban core to land which is cheaper together with public transport links with the urban centre. Parkhurst and Meek (Chapter 9) examine this management strategy in depth, concluding that it is most successful when used to promote economic activity rather than simply to enhance mobility. Perhaps more disappointingly, park and ride schemes are not universally associated with lower car use and often with a net traffic increase. This raises the question as to whether making it easy for car users to park – as with Park and Ride – actually promotes a car culture thus lessening the opportunities to develop sustainable transport policies promoting walking and cycling or creating walkable built environments which encourage more sustainable mobility.

Parking cannot be seen as an activity in itself but is part of a bundle, associated with car use. It is clear that planning policies can make an empirically detectable difference (McCahill & Garrick, Chapter 3) and that the outcome is often exacerbated by context and constrained by the number of actors involved in the policy and regulatory process (Rye & Koglin, Chapter 8; Weinberger & Jacobson, Chapter 17). The evidence to date supports the implementation of maximum parking places as part of the planning process, replacing the minimum parking place policy still in operation in many places.

The aims of parking policy are often multi-faceted and subject to a complex interplay of objectives but overall, if policy is to be successful, it must not promote mixed messages. It is clearly important to take account of the area under consideration (Brooke, Ison, & Quddus, Chapter 6) but also the nature of the parking, whether for residential, retail or commuters. The chapters of this book highlight that there is no single solution but the range of case studies demonstrate an evidence base to influence policy makers' choice. Important here too is the conclusion of Marsden (Chapter 2) that parking policy must stop looking only at the detail and recognise that parking is part of a larger urban issue, ensuring consistent policies are developed at that spatial level.

In the future, cities should aim for rapid turnover in the higher rent street spaces and longer durations in the off-street parking. Increasing parking charges or at least making the relative price between on-street and off-street parking more of an incentive to push appropriate travel behaviour responses is an implication of many of the chapters in this book. This may raise acceptability problems (Rye & Koglin, Chapter 8) but the argument that parking charges are regressive requires further investigation. The evidence suggests that parking charges (or increased parking charges) might be regressive for the population of drivers but not necessarily for the population as a whole. Indeed, as Manville (Chapter 7) points out, concerns over the regressiveness of parking charges can be, and maybe better ameliorated by increasing the subsidy for public transport. This would also support the objectives of many cities to move towards a more sustainable mobility for their citizens. Indeed, combined with a pricing policy that reflects the true worth of the resource being consumed in parking, it would provide a better signal to car drivers who currently think that car parking should be provided almost as of right in satisfying their automobility demands. In this context it is crucially important to understand the policy message and context as to what pricing for parking is designed to achieve. Is it a charge for the use of scarce resources or is it a way of managing congestion? If used to manage congestion it is a second best solution, bringing with it some of the welfare costs associated with ignoring the first best solution of road pricing.

It is clear that parking is central to urban mobility and that it is primarily a land-use issue. Parking policy, pricing and management can be employed, alongside effective planning controls, to provide a more sustainable environment. However, it is also clear that the future brings many uncertainties, especially in relation to the growth of car use and whether parking policies can effectively be deployed to avoid the negative effects of the automobile era on our urban areas. The longer term solution may well be travel behaviour solutions, aimed at changing the travel behaviour associated with single car ownership to something more co-operative – such as car sharing schemes – which can lead to a reduction in pressure for car parking and a better balance between demand and supply for parking. Alternatively, built environment approaches such as transport orientated developments which reduce the demand for car use can bring a reduction in the demand for car use and lower the demand for parking.

ABOUT THE AUTHORS

John Bates is a mathematical economist, with over 40 years' experience in transportation modelling, with particular reference to travel demand. He has a detailed understanding of the principles which bind the various modelling components and has contributed substantially to the modelling guidance sections of the Department for Transport's WebTAG. He has been a leading figure in the development of stated preference techniques within the transport field and has international expertise in evaluation methodology, in particular the valuation of time savings and reliability. He works as an independent consultant, based in Abingdon near Oxford. He has considerable experience as a Peer Reviewer/Auditor and has a proven ability to get through the details of complex (and often poorly documented) models with a view to assessing their strengths and weaknesses. Based on his experience of working with many other consultants, his collaborative but demanding approach has earned considerable respect.

Sarah Brooke is undertaking a PhD in the area of Parking Search within the Transport Studies Group, School of Civil and Building Engineering, Loughborough University. Sarah is researching the factors that influence on-street parking search, using quantitative driver questionnaires conducted across four cities within the East Midlands region of the United Kingdom, and qualitative semi-structured interviews of East Midlands Local Authority Transport and Parking Officers. Prior to commencing her PhD, Sarah completed a BSc. in Social Psychology at Loughborough University, before commencing a career which encompassed various marketing, teaching, and transportation positions in the private, public, and voluntary sectors. In 2012, she obtained a MSc. in Sustainable Transport and Travel Planning, graduating with Distinction.

Graham Currie specialises in research on urban public transport. He has published over 300 research papers in leading peer reviewed journals/conferences; more in this field than any other researcher in the world. He is an associate editor of the international research journal *Transportation* and is Chair of US Transportation Research Boards sub-committee on International Developments in Light Rail Transit. Professor Currie won the inaugural William B Millar prize for best research paper from the US Transportation Research Boards Annual Meeting in Washington, DC, the largest transport conference in the world. In 2013, Professor Currie authored two papers in the top 20 most cited in *The Journal of Transport Geography*. Professor Currie is Director of Research in the Department of Civil Engineering, Monash University which is the only Civil Engineering research group at a leading Australian University to have the top 5 star rating in the Research Excellence Australia.

Simon Dale has worked for Nottingham City Council since 1998. He has over 20 years of data collection and monitoring experience. He has been involved with the Nottingham Workplace Parking Levy (WPL) from 2001 onwards and was responsible for collecting the data required to formulate the WPL Business Case and assisted in producing the draft WPL Order. From 2010 to 2012, Simon worked within the WPL implementation team interpreting the underpinning legislation and formulating policy. Simon is currently responsible for the evaluation of the WPL package. As part of this, he is studying for an Engineering Doctorate via a joint evaluation project between Loughborough University and Nottingham City Council.

Matthew Frost is a Senior Lecturer in the School of Civil and Building Engineering at Loughborough University, UK. As a Civil Engineer, his main background is in Infrastructure (Highways and Railways) and Geotechnical Engineering. He has worked on a number of high profile research projects in the area of transport including investigating climate change resilience in UK transport infrastructure and sustainability in infrastructure design. He also has an interest in Light Rail system design and operation. He is currently working on a project in partnership with Nottingham City Council to investigate the impact of the work place parking charges as part of a wider package of transport demand interventions.

Norman Garrick is Associate Professor of Civil Engineering at the University of Connecticut. Dr. Garrick is also a member of the national board of The Congress for the New Urbanism (CNU). He specializes in the planning and design of urban transportation systems especially as they relate to sustainability, placemaking and urban revitalization. His writing has appeared in The Atlantic Cities, Planetizen, New Urban News, The Denver Post and The Hartford Courant. Dr. Garrick has worked as transportation consultant on a number of design charrettes including urban revitalization projects with the Prince of Wales Foundation in Jamaica and Sierra Leone. He is a recipient of the Transportation Research Board's

Wootan Award for Best Paper in policy and organization and a Fulbright Fellowship to Kingston, Jamaica. Dr. Garrick has also been visiting professor at the Swiss Federal Institute of Technology (ETH) Zurich and a lecturer in Oxford University's Masters of Sustainable Urban Planning Program.

Jason Gooding has a background of working in manufacturing and project management and joined Nottingham City Council in 2002 to work on the design, approval and implementation of the Workplace Parking Levy (WPL). Jason was also involved in the management of the councils Local Transport Plan and major programmes delivery during this time. From 2006 to 2012, Jason was the Team Leader of the WPL Implementation Team and thus oversaw the development of the scheme's detailed design and operation. At present, Jason is the City Council's Parking Manager and as such is in charge of the councils parking services including on and off street parking, WPL and also the Council's own staff parking management scheme.

Paul Hamer is a Senior Policy Manager with the Department of Transport, Planning and Infrastructure in Victoria and has worked extensively in the area of traffic and transport in the private and public sectors, including at both the local and state government level. Paul has co-authored a number of papers on parking policy and has presented at conferences through Australasia and in the United States. His research has also been profiled and referenced in the Australian print and radio media. Paul holds a Masters of Engineering Science from Monash University and is a Member of Engineers Australia.

Chinh Ho is a Senior Research Fellow in the Institute of Transport and Logistics Studies (ITLS) at The University of Sydney. He completed his PhD in 2013 on intra-household interactions and group decisions in travel mode choice, with a particular focus on planning strategies and segments of car users to encourage the use of more sustainable travel modes. Chinh was awarded the John H Taplin Prize for the best paper presented at the Australasian Transport Research Forum 2012 and the Innovation Grant from World Conference on Transport Research 2013. Chinh also holds a Bachelor of Civil Engineering with first class Honours in Bridge and Highway Engineering from Ho Chi Minh City University of Technology, Vietnam, where he was a full-time lecturer. Before joining ITLS Chinh obtained a Masters degree in Transport Planning from Nagoya University, Japan.

Stephen Ison is Professor of Transport Policy in the Transport Studies Group, School of Civil and Building Engineering, Loughborough University, UK. He has published widely in the area of transport demand management and parking in particular. He has guest edited a number of Journal special issues including 'Parking' for the Journal of Transport Policy Vol. 13, No. 6, 2006. He is a member of the Scientific Committee of the World Conference of Transport Research, Editor of the Journal of Research in Transportation Business and Management [Elsevier], Book Series Editor of Transport and Sustainability [Emerald Group Publishing] and has edited, authored or co-authored seven books.

Lisa Jacobson Senior Associate at Nelson\Nygaard Consulting Associates, is a skilled multimodal transportation planner who excels at combining both quantitative and qualitative data to craft comprehensive analyses. In her parking practice, Lisa has become fluent in state-of-the-practice parking technology and management structures that are closely linked with economic development and downtown growth. Before joining Nelson\Nygaard, Lisa was a fellow with the National Complete Streets Coalition, where she developed policies to encourage street design to incorporate all users, regardless of age and ability. Lisa's work at the Coalition was published in an AARP report, "Planning Complete Streets for an Aging America." She holds a Bachelor of Arts in International Affairs from The George Washington University and a Master of City Planning from the University of Pennsylvania.

Till Koglin holds a PhD in Transport Planning and is a researcher at Lund University. His main research competence is mobility studies and transport and urban planning with a focus on cycling and sustainability.

David Leibling is currently a freelance transport and motoring consultant, specialising in analysing published data in the fields of transport policy, motorists' behaviour, and parking. He was formerly the Director of Corporate Communications of the motoring group Lex Service PLC which acquired RAC, the motoring support organization in 1999. David has been a member of the RAC Foundation for Motoring's Public Policy Committee for many years and has written extensively for the RAC Foundation on topics such as motorists' shopping behaviour, commuting, parking, the cost of motoring and international transport statistics. He was Deputy Chair of London TravelWatch and a board member of Passenger Focus the watchdogs for users of London's transport system and for rail and bus passengers nationwide and he created, and continues to advise on, the RAC Report on Motoring, a detailed annual study of motorists behaviour, now in its 26th year.

Michael Manville is Assistant Professor of City and Regional Planning at Cornell University. He studies transportation, land use and public finance. He holds a PhD in Urban Planning from the University of California, Los Angeles.

Greg Marsden is Professor of Transport Governance at the Institute for Transport Studies at the University of Leeds. His research interests relate to understanding decision-making processes within local and national government, performance management, governance reform processes and citizen participation. He is currently working on issues relating to carbon governance, disruptions, resilience and energy demand reduction. He has acted as specialist adviser to the UK Parliamentary Transport scrutiny committee. He teaches on integrated land-use and transport planning and has an interest in the application of effective parking policy to manage travel demand.

Wesley E. Marshall is an Assistant Professor at the University of Colorado Denver, program director of the UCD University Transportation Center through the Mountain Plains Consortium, and co-director of the Active Communities/Transportation (ACT) research group. He received his Professional Engineering license in 2003 and conducts transportation teaching and research dedicated to creating more sustainable infrastructures, particularly in terms of road safety, active transportation, and transit-oriented communities. Other recent teaching and research topics involve: resiliency, parking, and street networks. Having spent time with Sasaki Associates and Clough, Harbour and Associates, Wes has been working on issues related to transportation for the last fifteen years. A native of Watertown, Massachusetts, Wes graduated with honors from the University of Virginia and received his master's and doctoral degrees from the University of Connecticut. He is a recipient of the Dwight Eisenhower Transportation Fellowship and winner of the Charley V. Wootan Award for Outstanding TRB Paper.

Christopher McCahill is a Senior Associate with the State Smart Transportation Initiative at the University of Wisconsin-Madison. He worked previously on the Project for Transportation Reform with the Congress for the New Urbanism in Chicago and as a researcher and course instructor in the Department of Civil Engineering at the University of Connecticut. In 2012, he was a fellow with the Eno Center for Transportation in Washington, DC. His research focuses on the policy and design implications of urban transportation and land use issues. He has written extensively for professional journals and popular media and spoken for audiences throughout the United States and in Europe.

Stuart Meek completed his PhD from Loughborough University in 2009 on the factors determining the effectiveness and implementation of car-bus interchange policies. His work focuses on the views of policymakers and other implementation agents, as well as park and ride users. He has since worked in the rail industry, both with London Underground and more recently the Southern train operating company, where he is a senior operations manager.

Steven Melia is a Senior Lecturer in Transport and Planning at the University of the West of England and author of *Urban Transport Without the Hot Air* (UIT Cambridge, 2015). His area of research concerns the relationship between transport and the built environment, with a particular focus on carfree and low car development. He coined the phrase 'filtered permeability' in the design of streets and cycling networks. He advised the UK Departments of Transport and of Communities and Local Government on transport aspects of the Eco-towns programme in 2008/ 2009. The guidance produced by the DfT and the Town and Country Planning Association for CLG on transport for Eco-towns both reflect his input in respect of carfree development. He has advised the Olympic Park Legacy Company on the transport plans for the Olympic site, and the RAC Foundation on parking policy. He was previously a parliamentary candidate and freelance journalist.

Anthony Mifsud is a transport planner in Sydney with an interest in urban design, parking policy and car sharing policy. He holds a Bachelor of Economics (Social Science) from the University of Sydney.

Corinne Mulley is the founding Chair in Public Transport at the Institute of Transport and Logistics Studies at the University of Sydney. Since her appointment to Newcastle University as a transport economist she has been active in transport research at the interface of transport policy and economics. More recently Corinne has concentrated on specific issues relating to public transport. She led a high profile European and UK consortia undertaking benchmarking in urban public transport and has provided both practical and strategic advice to local and national governments on benchmarking, rural transport issues, and public transport management.

Professor Mulley's research is motivated by a need to provide evidence for policy initiatives and she has been involved in such research at local, regional, national and European levels before moving to Australia. Since her appointment to Sydney University, Corinne has been active in public transport policy addressing issues of importance to NSW and the Federal governments as well as contributing to more local issues including travel planning, the health impacts of public transport, community transport and flexible transport services and, of course, parking.

Graham Parkhurst is Professor of Sustainable Mobility and Director of the Centre for Transport & Society, University of the West of England, Bristol, UK. Graham's qualifications are in psychology (BA), physical anthropology (MSc) and transport geography (DPhil) and he has more than two decades of experience researching and teaching transport policy and practice, previously at the University of Oxford and at University College London. The relationships between urban and regional transport policy have been a key theme in Graham's research interests, including work on urban parking, park and ride, and public transport supply policy and their interactions with commercial vitality and traffic restraint policy. Most recently, Graham's work has been focussed on the relevance of the new models of shared ownership and use of transport assets to sustainable mobility objectives.

Mohammed Quddus is Professor of Intelligent Transport Systems at the School of Civil and Building Engineering at Loughborough University. He holds a BSc degree in Civil Engineering from BUET, Bangladesh, an MEng degree in Transport Engineering from the National University of Singapore and a PhD in Intelligent Transport Systems from Imperial College London. Professor Quddus has widely published in the areas of road safety modelling, transport modelling, ITS and GIS. He serves as an Associate Editor of two leading transport journals: Transportation Research Part C: Emerging Technologies and Journal of Intelligent Transport Systems. His current research focuses on the enhancement of underpinning algorithms behind autonomous vehicles and connected vehicles with respect to improving safety.

Tom Rye is a Professor of Transport Planning at Lund University and research director of K2 National Research Centre in Sweden. His research areas are transport training, mobility management, transport policy evaluation and implementation, parking policy and planning for slow modes of transport.

Donald Shoup is Distinguished Professor of Urban Planning at UCLA, where he has served as Chair of the Department of Urban Planning and Director of the Institute of Transportation Studies. His book, *The High Cost of Free Parking*, has drawn widespread praise for revealing how better parking policies can improve cities, the economy, and the environment. In the book, Shoup recommends that cities should charge fair market prices for on-street parking, use the meter revenue to finance added public services in the metered neighborhoods, and remove off-street parking requirements. Shoup is a Fellow of the American Institute of Certified Planners, an Honorary Professor at the Beijing Transportation Research Center, and the Editor of *ACCESS*.

Peter Warren joined Nottingham City Council in 1998 having worked for Nottinghamshire County Council since 1979. He has over 35 years of data collection and monitoring experience. In his current post of Team Leader, Highway Metrics he is responsible for all transportation data collection and monitoring in the City of Nottingham and strategic monitoring in the wider Greater Nottingham conurbation. The Highway Metrics team carries out a wide range of survey work and data analysis, including road traffic, public transport, cycle, pedestrian and parking surveys and produces reports on transport trends and for transport scheme assessments. The team carried out the initial data collection work for the Workplace Parking Levy (WPL) Scheme in Nottingham and has continued to support the scheme since that time in terms of its operation and evaluation.

Rachel R. Weinberger, Principal and Director of Research and Policy at Nelson\Nygaard Consulting Associates, is an expert on sustainable urban transportation. Rachel has more than 20 years of planning experience in the private and public sectors and in academia. Her areas of expertise include land use transportation interactions, travel behavior, planning methodologies, urban economics, econometric analysis, travel demand management, and urban parking. She served as the senior policy advisor on transportation in the development of PlaNYC, New York City's much-lauded 2030 sustainability plan and she is an advisor to the Clinton Climate Foundation's Climate Positive Development program. A former University of Pennsylvania Professor, Rachel is the author or co-author of more than 50 research articles, reports, book chapters, and papers including the award-winning "Integrating Walkability into Planning Practice." She holds a Master of Urban Planning from Hunter College of the City University of New York and the degrees Master of Science in Civil

Engineering and PhD in Urban and Regional Planning from the University of California, Berkeley.

William Young is Chair of Civil Engineering, Monash University. He has a distinguished professional and academic career, having worked at Monash University for 39 years and prior to joining Monash in the transport industry in England, Germany and several States of Australia for 4 years. Professor Young has wide-ranging interests and has researched, consulted and published widely in the land-use/transport/environment interaction, traffic, parking, engineering management and education areas. He has published over three hundred papers and co-authored four books on transportation.

INDEX

Acceptance
  and employer-provided parking,
    171
  public, of parking policy, 177–8
  WPL, as congestion levy, 351–3
Access-time, and parking choice,
    119–20
Age, and parking choice, 126–7
Air pollution, 226, 247
Airports, 190
Amsterdam, 220–1, 229
Apartment buildings (*see also* Flats)
  carfree development, 220
  parking requirements, 99–102,
    104–5, 107
  underground parking, 100–1
Arlington, Virginia, 38–40, 43–4,
    45
Austria, carfree development, 215,
    217
Automobile/s (*see* Car/s)

Bath, UK, 197, 198
Berkeley, California, 38–40, 43–4,
    45, 241–3
Bicycles
  carfree development, 225–6, 228
  commuting, 24–5
  corrals, 376, 377
  P&R, 197, 199, 200
  retail spending, 21–2
  space requirements, Guangzhou,
    389
  workplace travel, 354

Bozeman, Montana, 138–9
Break points, in costs of parking
    structures, 100–1
Bristol, 353
Building setbacks, 371, 385–6
Buildings, reuse and minimum
    requirements, 241–4
Bureau of Public Roads (BPR),
    238
Bus lanes, and transport capacity,
    404
Bus services (*see also* Park and
    Ride (P&R))
  and local authorities, 195, 209n
Businesses (*see also* Commuter
    parking; Workplace
    parking)
  inward investment, 177, 357
  location decisions, 25
  parking management schemes,
    354–6
  parking requirements, 241–4
  parking space management,
    170–1
  PSL (Sydney), 319, 329, 331–2
  WPL (Nottingham), 346,
    350–1, 352–3

California, 105–6, 108
Cambridge, Massachusetts, 38–40,
    43–4, 45–51
Cambridge, UK, 196, 204
Camden, London, 174–5, 222–3
Canterbury, UK, 167

427

Car-bike trips, and P&R, 199
Car clubs, 175, 214, 218–19
Car-free housing (*see also* Carfree
    development; Low-car
    development), 215, 222–3,
    229, 230
Car ownership or use, 3, 4, 17–18,
    416
    car-free housing, Camden,
        222–3
    carfree development, 216–17,
        218–19, 225–6, 227–8, 230
    economic factors, 283–5
    Europe, 159–60, 173–4
    Guangzhou, 384, 385, 394–5,
        396, 401–2
    increase in parking, 49, 52
    increase in Philadelphia, 239–40
    land use, 40
    London, 269–70, 277–8,
        282–5, 286, 288–9
    low-car development, 223, 224
    P&R, 192–3, 207
    parking and driving times, 83
    parking demand, 84, 105
    parking supply, 41–4
    reasons for non-ownership,
        284–5
    residential parking, UK, 61–9,
        262–3
    retail spending, 21–2
    shopping, US, 254–5
    Utrecht, 179
Car park owners/operators
    Melbourne levy, 295, 297
    PSL (Sydney), 323–4, 331
Car parks, and parking choice, 121,
    123, 125–6, 129–30
Car sharing, parking standards, 17,
    29

Carbon (CO_2) emissions, 193, 201,
    227, 247
Carfree development (*see also*
    Car-free housing; Low-car
    development), 7, 16, 18,
    214–15
    benefits of, 216–17, 225–8,
        230–1
    potential UK demand, 224–5
    problems of, 228–9
Cars
    and cities, 41
    value of, and cost of parking
        spaces, 90–1
Casual parking
    price and supply, Melbourne,
        295–6, 309–10, 313
    PSL (Sydney), 323–5
CBD Parking Levy, Melbourne, 8,
    291–315, 413
    impacts, 306–15
    parking supply, 298–306
    pricing, 294–7
Central business districts (CBDs)
    (*see also* CBD Parking Levy,
    Melbourne; Parking Space
    Levy (PSL), Sydney), 40, 42
    and cruising, 145–7
Chicago, 149–50
Children, carfree and low-car
    development, 219,
    224, 226
China (*see* Guangzhou)
Churches, parking requirements,
    241, 242
CIVITAS MIMOSA project
    2008–2012, 179
Cologne, 220, 229
Commercial off-street parking,
    Melbourne, 302–3

Communication
  acceptance of parking policy,
    177–8
  information for commuters, 328
Commuter parking (*see also*
    Destination parking;
    Workplace parking),
    412–13
  bicycles, 24–5
  funding, Sydney, 327, 328
  P&R, 188, 190
  parking behaviour, 24
  parking duration, 72
  parking pricing, 121, 295–7
Commuter trips
  car-free housing, 222–3
  Melbourne, 311
  New Haven and Cambridge, 49
Compliance, WPL (Nottingham),
    350–1
Concessions (*see* Exemptions)
Condominiums, and parking
    requirements, 104–5
Congestion
  charges, 148, 265–6
  levy (*see* CBD Parking Levy,
    Melbourne)
  management, Guangzhou,
    382–4
  Nottingham, 338, 341–2, 343
  on-street parking, 368–9
  and parking choice, 117
  Sydney, and PSL, 318, 330, 331,
    332
Connectivity, 341, 343
Construction costs
  apartment buildings, 100–2
  off-street parking, 89–90, 162,
    174, 252
  office buildings, 91–3, 94–5

shopping centres, 96, 97–9
Consultation, WPL (Nottingham),
    342, 344–6, 358
Controlled parking zones (CPZ),
    4, 165–6, 174–5, 222,
    264–5
Coordination, management and
    policy, Guangzhou, 383,
    386–8, 390–3, 402
Crash severity, 369–70, 372, 378
Cruising, 6, 145–7, 369
  impacts of, 116
  search costs, 139, 140
  search-time, 119–20, 121, 124,
    125, 128
Curb parking (*see* On-street
    parking)
Cycling (*see* Bicycles)

Demand for access, 398–9, 412
Demand restraint, and parking
    policy, 25–8
Destination parking (*see also*
    Commuter parking;
    Workplace parking), 57–8,
    61, 69–84
  duration and purpose, 70–5
  and labour market, 84
  location and purpose, 76–8,
    79–81
  London, 266–7, 270–6
Developers, development
  Guangzhou, 392, 398, 401
  parking requirements, 27, 36,
    47, 89, 102, 111, 171–3
Digital parking, 179–80
Disability parking, 107, 119, 127,
    265, 399
Discounts (*see* Early-bird parking;
    Exemptions)

Displaced parking (*see also* Overspill parking/Spillover)
WPL (Nottingham), 345, 357
Double-taxation, and priced parking, 150–1

Early-bird parking
Melbourne, 295–6, 302, 306, 308–10, 313
Sydney, 323
Earmarking (*see* Hypothecation)
Economic development
Guangzhou, 403
Nottingham, 341, 343
P&R, 193–4
and parking policy, 175–7
Edinburgh, 129, 166, 227
Education level, and parking choice, 128
Egress-time, and parking choice, 119–20, 121, 127
Eindhoven, 123
Electric vehicles, adoption of, 18, 29, 265
Employees or employers (*see* Businesses; Workplace parking)
Employment
and destination parking, 84
parking demand and supply, 301, 310–11, 313
Employment status, and parking choice, 128
Enforcement, 167–8, 265
carfree development, 228–9
new technology, Utrecht, 179–80
parking choice, 118
residential on-street parking, 175
WPL (Nottingham), 350–1

Environmental impacts
carfree development, 216, 231
P&R, 193, 194, 201, 202
Ethnicity, and parking choice, 127
Exemptions
PSL (Sydney), 320, 323–5, 331, 332
WPL (Nottingham), 347, 348–9
Exeter, UK, 223
Expenditure, on parking, 82

Fairness, of priced parking, 150–3
Fines/penalties, 118, 167–8, 265, 351
First-come-first-served, 298
Flats (*see also* Apartment buildings)
car-free housing, 223
on-street parking, UK, 65–6
parking availability, London, 277, 278–9
Free parking (*see also* Workplace parking)
effects, 298, 299
on-street in London, 270, 271–3
on-street in US, 138–9, 141–4, 144–7
retail, 19, 176
and sales tax revenues, 108
UK, 78, 81–2
Freiburg (*see* Vauban)

Garages (UK)
reduction in use, 61
residential parking, London, 267–8, 277, 280
Garages (US) (*see* Car parks; Underground parking)
Gardens, converted for off-street parking, 269

Germany
  bicycle use and P&R, 197
  carfree development, 215, 217
Grocery stores, and parking layout,
  254–5
Groningen, 221–2
Guangzhou, 8–9, 381–405, 412
  car ownership and use, 401–2
  mixed-use developments, 392–7,
    401, 402–3
  oversupply, 393–4, 402
  parking demand management
    strategies, 403–4
  parking policy goals, 395,
    397–402

Hague, The, 199–200
Hamburg, 217, 219–20
Hartford, Connecticut, 38–40,
  41–2, 43–4, 364
Health, and carfree development,
  216–17, 226
Historic buildings, parking
  requirements, 102–5
Home ownership, and parking
  space, 16, 18
Housing
  new build and parking policy,
    15–18
  overnight parking, UK, 61–7
  parking availability, London,
    277–80
Hypothecation, 325–6, 331, 413
  public transport improvements,
    337, 338, 342
  Sydney, 327–8, 329–30

Illegal parking, 118, 127, 266, 267
Incentive schemes, and workplace
  parking, 23–5

Incomes, and parking choice, 127,
  151–3
Induced traffic, and travel
  behaviour, 41
Information, for commuters
  (*see also* Parking Guidance
  Information (PGI)), 328
Institute of Transportation
  Engineers (ITE), parking
  space requirements, 37, 243,
  244, 245
Integrated transport policy, 14,
  25–9, 207–8
Integrated urban mobility plans,
  163, 340–1
International Finance Center (IFC)
  (Guangzhou), 392–7, 401,
  402–3
Intersections, as barriers to access,
  253–4
Inventory, of parking supply, 50
Inward investment, 177, 357

Jefferson National Expansion
  Monument (Gateway
  Arch), St Louis, 249,
  251–2
Jobs, and parking
  demand, 301
Journey purposes, 14, 15, 72–5
  parking choice, 124–5
  parking locations, 76–8, 79
  parking pricing, 121–2

King County, Washington, 38

Land use (*see also* Minimum
  parking requirements), 3–4,
  34, 410–11
  carfree development, 227

Land use (*Continued*)
  costs of on- and off-street
    parking, 366−8, 378
  parking policy, 11−14, 26−8
  parking standards, Europe,
    171−3
  physical impacts of parking,
    40−1
  pricing, 298−9
Las Vegas, 91, 93
Leased spaces, 246, 297, 321−3
Licensed spaces, 51, 297, 347
Limited access model, carfree
    development, 219−21, 229
Link and ride (L&R), interchange
    strategy, 202, 203, 204−6
Local authorities (*see also* Cities by
    name; Hypothecation;
    Workplace Parking Levy
    (WPL), Nottingham)
  maximum standards, 172−3
  P&R, 194−5, 209n
  parking controls and pricing,
    158−9
  parking enforcement, 167−8
  parking management, 161−2,
    164−5
  revenues from charges and
    penalties, 265−6
Local Transport Plans (LTP), UK,
    340−1
London
  changes in car ownership, 68−9
  controlled parking zones (CPZ),
    174−5
  minimum and maximum
    requirements compared,
    107−8
  parking supply and demand,
    259−89

parking surveys, 59
Swiss Re and demand for
    access, 399
wheel-clamping, 118
London boroughs (*see also*
    Camden), 261, 288−9
Long-stay parking (*see* Early-bird
    parking)
Los Angeles, 100−1, 103−4, 106,
    362, 375
Los Angeles County, 96
Low-car development (*see also*
    Car-free housing; Carfree
    development), 7, 215, 223−5
Low-income people, regressive
    effect of parking charges,
    151−3
Lowell, Massachusetts, 38−40,
    43−4, 45

Marginal costs, of parking spaces,
    100−1
Market pricing, for on-street
    parking, 148−50, 154
Maximum parking standards (*see
    also* Minimum parking
    requirements; Parking
    standards)
  compared with minimum
    requirements, 107−8
  developer pays, 111
  public transport accessibility, 27
  residential parking, London,
    279−80
  spillover, 411
  street capacity, 403−4
  traffic reduction, 247
  UK, 16, 172−3
  Zurich, 50
Medford, Massachusetts, 252−4

Melbourne (*see* CBD Parking Levy)
Meters (*see also* Illegal parking;
    On-street parking –
    controlled)
  capabilities, 148–9
  on-street, London, 263–4, 265
  privatization, 149–50
  revenue tools, 141–2, 148
  and shoppers, 248
Minimal parking requirements,
    110–11
Minimum parking requirements
    (*see also* Maximum parking
    standards; Parking
    standards), 35–7, 87–111,
    236–7, 411
  elimination of, 103, 240–1, 247,
    403
  Guangzhou, 385, 397–8
  mispricing of street parking, 147
  New Haven and Cambridge,
    46–8
  oversupply of off-street parking,
    15–16, 245–6
  reuse of buildings, 241–4
  transit-rich areas, 105–8
Misallocation, 139, 140, 145
Mixed instruments, WPL
    (Nottingham), 338–9, 340
Mixed-use developments,
    Guangzhou, 392, 394–7,
    401, 402–3
Mobile phone parking, 180
Mode choice or share
  Guangzhou, 394–5, 402
  impacts of Melbourne levy,
    311, 314
  on- and off-street parking
    compared, 374–5
  P&R, 189–90

retail spending, 21–2
  workplace parking, 24–5
Multi-storey car parks, and
    security, 129–30

National Travel Survey (NTS)
    (UK), 59–60
Netherlands (*see also* Amsterdam;
    Groningen; Utrecht),
    26, 118
  car park size and parking
    choice, 123
  free parking at work, 24
  P&R, 188, 189, 197, 199–200
  regional parking policy, and
    retail centres, 176
New England, 365–6
New Haven, Connecticut, 38–40,
    43–4, 45–51
New York City, 17, 93
  building reuse, 243–4
  free on-street parking, 138–9
  garage fiasco, New York
    Yankees, 246
  oversupply of retail parking,
    245–6
  performance parking, 248
Newcastle, UK, and parking
    enforcement, 168
Non-car accessibility, 26–7
Non-residential parking (*see* Private
    non-residential parking)
Norway, 176, 326
Nottingham (*see also* Workplace
    Parking Levy (WPL)), 117
Nuclear family, and minimum
    parking requirements, 245

Occupancy (*see also* Parking
    accumulation), 123–4

Occupancy (*Continued*)
  car parks and parking
    information, 117−18
  CBD off-street parking, 146, 147
  Guangzhou, 392, 395, 397
  London, 266−7, 280−2
  New England, 366
  on-street parking and vehicle
    speeds, 371
  parking requirements, 99−100,
    105
  performance standards, 248−9,
    250
  PSL (Sydney), 330−1
  tracking by sensors, 149
Off-street parking (*see also*
    Apartment buildings;
    Construction costs;
    Minimum parking
    requirements; Parking levies;
    Retail parking; Surface
    parking; Workplace
    parking), 5, 6, 7
  Guangzhou, 381−405
  increase in Philadelphia, 239−40
  local authorities in Europe,
    160−2
  Melbourne, 293−4, 302−6, 313
  oversupply in new build
    housing, 15−16, 18
  parking duration, 125
  physical impacts, 40−1
  pricing, 139
  public, 270, 271−3, 385, 400
  residential parking, UK, 262−3,
    276−8
  retail activity, US, 364
  six U.S. Cities, 38−51
Office buildings

cost of parking requirements,
    91−6
cost of underground parking,
    91−3
parking spaces for, Los Angeles
    County, 96
reuse as residential units, 103−4
Office parking, 5
Oklahoma City, 248
On-street parking (*see also* Meters;
    Performance parking;
    Permits; Urban design), 5, 8,
    361−78, 400
  banned in US, 362, 363−4
  car ownership, 17
  controlled parking, London,
    267−75, 280−2
  enforcement, 118, 175, 179−80
  impacts of, 362, 365−75, 377−8
  non-controlled parking,
    London, 270, 271−3
  parking duration, 125
  policy and management,
    Europe, 161, 163, 164−5,
    173−4, 181
  population and housing density,
    UK, 61−7
  pricing, Europe, 165−8
  pricing, US, 137−54
  road safety, 365, 369−72, 378
  traffic flow, 363−4
Oslo, 176
Overnight parking at home, 61−8
Overspill parking/ Spillover (*see
    also* Displaced parking),
    228−9, 230, 236, 411
Owner-occupancy, and parking
    requirements, 104−5
Oxford, 172, 188, 200

Park and Ride (P&R), 6–7, 20,
185–209, 414
bus-based, UK, 167, 188, 195
effects, 169–70, 195–7, 200,
203–8
Europe, 168–70, 178–9, 194
overlapping and unintended
uses, 199
parking choice, 119
rail-based, Netherlands,
199–200
sociotechnical system, 187–92
sustainable development policy,
201–6
sustainable mobility strategy,
207–8
Park and Share (P&S), 208n
Parking accumulation, and journey
purposes, 74–5
Parking acts
by day of week, 70, 72
by duration, 15, 71–2
and journey purposes, 15, 72–5
by start times, 72
by time of day, 23, 70–1
Parking availability (*see also*
Cruising; Parking spaces;
Performance parking;
Waiting-time)
car ownership and use, 42–4,
68–9
economic vitality, 176–7
journey choice, 3, 4
P&R, 189–90
retail centres, 21
Parking capacity
P&R, 169, 201, 202
and parking choice, 123
Parking cash-out, 23, 24

Parking charges (*see also*
Enforcement; Meters;
Permits; Pricing), 415
fairness and low-income people,
151–3
fees paid, 78, 81–2, 153
inconvenience of payment
options, 84
Melbourne levy, 295–7
off-street, Guangzhou, 387, 390
on-street, London, 263–4
on-street residential parking,
UK, 67, 68
P&R, 189
parking choice, 121–2
parking duration, 125
PSL (Sydney), 320–1
sex and age, 126–7
travel-time and parking choice,
120
Parking choice (*see also* Cruising),
115–31
Parking controls (*see also*
Controlled parking zones
(CPZ); Enforcement), 164–5
and car ownership, 282–5
carfree development, 229–30
controlled parking, London,
267–75
parking choice, 118
Parking, cost of (*see also* Cruising;
Minimum parking
requirements; Parking
charges; Parking spaces;
Pricing), 6, 265, 366–8, 378
Parking demand (*see also* Parking
management; Parking
supply), 4, 57–84, 159–60
car ownership, 84, 105

Parking demand (*Continued*)
  estimates of, 36–8
  jobs, Melbourne, 301
  London, 259–89
  minimum parking requirements,
    398–9
  on-street parking, New England,
    365–6
  oversupply, US, 238, 256
  parking types, 123
  pricing, 37, 121–2
Parking duration, 15
  destination parking, 69, 70–5
  parking choice, 125
  parking demand, 59
Parking familiarity, and parking
  choice, 128–9
Parking Guidance Information
  (PGI), 117–18, 125, 129
Parking habits, and parking choice,
  128
Parking layout, 249, 254–5
Parking levies (*see also* CBD
    Parking Levy, Melbourne;
    Parking Space Levy (PSL),
    Sydney; Workplace Parking
    Levy (WPL), Nottingham),
    413
Parking locations
  information on, 117
  journey purposes, UK,
    76–8, 79
  parking placement, 249,
    254–5
  residential, UK, 61–2, 65–6,
    267–70
  traveller choice, P&R, 190
Parking management (*see also*
    Parking demand;
    Performance parking), 414

lack of coordination,
    Guangzhou, 383, 386–8,
    390–3, 402
  parking policy, 157–82
  problems and solutions, 162–3,
    180–2
  strategies, 45, 52, 130–1, 403–4
  workplace parking, 23–4,
    170–1, 354–6
Parking placement, 249, 254–5
Parking policy (*see also* Park and
    Ride (P&R); Pricing), 7,
    11–29, 414–15
  economic development, 175–7
  Guangzhou, 384–90
  Melbourne, 299–300
  New Haven and Cambridge,
    45–51
  objectives, 163–4
  parking choice, 118–19
  parking demand management,
    157–82
  parochial, 59, 108
  public acceptance, 177–8
  residential parking, 15–18
  retail parking, 19–22
  shopping centres, Europe,
    175–7
  travel demand restraint, 25–8
  trends, US, 240–56
  workplace parking, 22–5
Parking requirements (*see also*
    Maximum parking
    standards; Minimum parking
    requirements; Parking
    standards)
  Guangzhou, 386, 387, 388, 389
  and land development, 401
Parking restrictions (*see* Parking
    controls)

Parking search (*see* Cruising)
Parking shortages (*see also*
    Occupancy), 139, 140, 145
    Medford, Massachusetts, 252–4
    minimum parking requirements,
        236–7
Parking Space Levy (PSL), Sydney,
    317–32, 413
    evaluation, 330–2
    implementation, 320–5
    objectives, 319
    revenue allocation, 327–8,
        329–30
Parking spaces (*see also*
    Enforcement; Meters;
    Minimum parking
    requirements; Occupancy;
    Parking availability), 34
    construction costs, US, 89–90
    cost of, 90–1, 368
    decoupling from home
        ownership, 16, 18
    London, 266–7, 270–80
    requirements, US, 37, 243, 244,
        245
    turnover, 20, 124, 266
Parking standards (*see also*
    Maximum parking
    standards; Minimum parking
    requirements)
    London boroughs, 288–9
    Melbourne and Victoria,
        299–300
Parking supply (*see also* Parking
    capacity; Parking demand;
    Parking levies; Parking
    placement), 33–52
    car ownership and use, 41–4,
        282–5
    economic performance, 20

Guangzhou, 381–405
inventory, Zurich, 50
London, 259–89
oversupply, US, 238–40
parking requirements, 35–6, 96,
    99
parking types, 123, 160–2
residential parking policy,
    17–18
Parking turnover, 20, 124, 266
Parking types, 5, 160–2
    London, 267–71, 278–9, 288–9
    and parking choice, 122–3
Parklets, 376, 377
Pedestrian access (*see also* Walking)
    barriers to, 253–4
    Guangzhou, 394–5, 396
Pedestrian environment
    carfree development, 221–2
    on-street parking, 372–5, 378,
        411
    setback parking, 404
Penalties/fines, 118, 167–8, 265,
    351
Performance parking, 237, 240,
    247–9, 250, 252–3
Permits (*see also* Illegal parking;
    On-street parking -
    controlled)
    designated parking, 118–19
    incentives not to drive, 25
    residential parking, 16–17, 18,
        68, 166, 264–5, 269
    Utrecht, 179
    workplace parking, 23–4,
        170–1
Perth, Australia, 51
Philadelphia, 239–40, 254–5
Planners, and minimum parking
    requirements, 88–9, 108–9

Police, and parking enforcement, 167–8
Poole Quarter, low-car development, 224, 225
Population density, on-street parking and car ownership, UK, 62–4
Poverty (*see* Low-income people)
Price controls, results of, 139–40
Pricing (*see also* Leased spaces; Licensed spaces; Meters; Parking charges; Parking controls; Parking levies), 6, 20, 21, 29, 413, 415
  fairness, 150–3
  Guangzhou, 385, 390–1, 399
  Melbourne levy, 291–7, 311–12
  occupancy, San Francisco, 377
  on-street parking, Europe, 165–8
  on-street parking, US, 137–54, 365
  P&R, 169
  parking demand, 37
  parking supply, 298–9, 306–11, 313
  performance parking, 237, 240, 247–9, 250
  workplace parking, 41–2
  WPL (Nottingham), 346–7
Private non-residential parking (*see also* Retail parking; Workplace parking), 5, 160–1, 412–13
  London, 267, 270–3, 399
  Melbourne, 303–4, 305
Public acceptance, 177–8, 351–3
Public consultation, 342, 344–6, 358
Public opposition, 46

Public policy instruments, 338–40
Public referendum, 50
Public transport (*see also* Mode choice or share; Park and Ride (P&R); transit)
  accessibility, 17, 26–7
  business, politics, Nottingham, 352–3
  commuter trips, Melbourne, 311
  demand for access, 398–9, 412
  improvements, Nottingham, 337, 338, 342, 343, 344
  PSL (Sydney), 331
  retail spending, 21–2
  separate culture of, 191
  spending, Sydney, 327–8
  use, and on- and off-street parking, 374–5
  use, and P&R, 197, 201

Rail stations, P&R, 188, 191, 207
Rail systems, P&R, 187, 190–1, 199–200
Railheading, 191
Rationing, 170–1, 298
Regional parking policy, Netherlands, 176
Rent controls, US, 139
Residential parking (*see also* Car-free housing; Carfree development; Low-car development), 161, 410–12
  demand and supply, Europe, 173–4
  demand and supply, London, 259–89
  demand, US, 38
  enforcement, 175
  minimum requirements, 245

Residential parking (*Continued*)
  overnight, UK, 7, 61–8
  permits, 119, 166
  policy, 15–18
  Utrecht, 179
Residual land value, 102
Restaurants, parking requirements, 99, 244
Retail business, and on-street parking, 375
Retail parking (*see also* Private non-residential parking; Shopping), 412
  mixed-use developments, Guangzhou, 392, 394–5
  oversupply, US, 245–6
  policy, 19–22, 47, 175–7
Retail spending, and transport mode, 21–2
Revenue allocation (*see* Hypothecation)
Revenue generation
  alternatives, Nottingham, 345
  local authorities, London, 265–6
  Melbourne levy, 293
  metered parking, 141–2, 148
  parochial parking policies in US, 108
  PSL (Sydney), 319
Road capacity, 368–9, 378, 400–1, 403–4
Road pricing, and hypothecation, 326
Road safety (*see also* Setback parking)
  on-street parking, 365, 369–72, 378
  parking restrictions, 164–5

Road user charging (RUC), 312, 345
Rotterdam, 199–200

Sacramento, 247
Safety (*see also* Road safety)
  personal, and parking choice, 129–30
St Louis, 249, 251–2
San Francisco, 142–3, 150, 248, 250, 362, 377
Santa Monica, 247
Search costs, 139, 140
Search-time, 119–20, 121, 124, 125, 128, 263–4
Seattle, 93, 99–100, 249, 250
Security
  P&R, 169
  parking choice, 129–30
Setback parking, 385–6, 404
Sex, and parking choice, 126
Shadow markets, 139, 140
Shared parking, 400
Shopping
  car use, US, 254–5
  journey purpose, 14, 15
  on-street meters, 248
Shopping centres (*see also* Retail parking)
  off-street parking, UK, 177
  out of town, 19, 22
  parking requirements, 37, 96–9
Social cohesion, and carfree development, 226
Socio-demographics, of parking choice, 126–7
Socio-economics, of parking choice, 127–8
Spillover/Overspill parking (*see also* Displaced parking), 228–9, 230, 236, 411

Sports stadia, 199, 246
Street capacity, 368–9, 378, 400–1,
    403–4
Street design, 253–4, 365,
    370–1
Suburban parking, 37, 99–100,
    239, 254–5, 314
Surface parking (*see also* Off-street
    parking), 34, 91, 365–8, 374,
    378
  construction costs, 162
  and sprawl, 93
Surrey County Council, 26–7
Sustainable development policies,
    P&R, 201–6
Sustainable mobility strategies,
    P&R, 207–8
Swiss Re (London), 399
Sydney (*see* Parking Space Levy
    (PSL))

Tactical urbanism, 375–7
Taikoo Hui (Guangzhou), 392–7,
    401, 402–3
Technology, new
  funding, Sydney, 328
  paid public parking, Europe,
    165
  parking meters, 148–9
  performance parking, 248
  tracking occupancy, 377
  Utrecht, 175, 178–80
  variable-message signs, 117
Tenant parking (*see* Leased
    spaces)
Time, and parking choice, 119–21
Toronto, 17
Tourist attractions, 251–2
Town centres (UK), parking
    policies, 21, 22

Traffic congestion (*see* Congestion)
Traffic flow, 164, 363–4, 368–9
Traffic network policy, Parking
    Guidance Information
    (PGI), 117–18
Traffic reduction
  car-free housing, 222
  China, 382
  Guangzhou, 388
  P&R, 193, 195–7, 200, 203–6
  parking maximums, 247
  WPL (Nottingham), 357
Traffic safety, 369–70
Traffic speed, 401
Transit (*see also* Public transport)
Transit demand, Guangzhou, 399,
    404
Transit fares, compared with
    parking charges, 152–3
Transit-rich areas, and minimum
    parking requirements,
    105–8
Transit speed, and car use, 401
Transport demand management
    (*see also* Parking Space Levy
    (PSL), Sydney; Workplace
    Parking Levy (WPL),
    Nottingham), 1–9, 130–1
Transport funding (*see*
    Hypothecation)
Transport modes (*see* Mode choice
    or share)
Transport operators, P&R, 193,
    201
Transport planners, P&R, 193
Transport policy
  integrated, 14, 25–9, 207–8
  Nottingham, 341–2
Transportation allowances, for
    low-income people, 152–3

Travel behaviour (*see also* Bicycles; Destination parking; Journey purposes; Mode choice or share; Parking acts; Walking), 2–3, 41–4, 60
  alternative, to P&R, 199–200, 206, 207–8
  carfree development, 227–8
  New Haven and Cambridge, 49
  on- and off-street parking compared, 373–5
  residential parking, 411–12
Travel demand
  Melbourne levy, 297, 311–12
  P&R, 201–2
  price and supply, 299
  restraint, and parking policy, 25–8
  and urban planners, 109
Travel demand management, Perth, 51
Travel plans
  low-car development, 224
  workplace parking, 171, 338
Travel time, parking choice, 117, 119–21, 125–6
Trip frequency, and parking choice, 129
Trip purposes (*see* Journey purposes)

Uncertainty, and parking choice, 120, 124
Underground parking (*see also* Construction costs)
  Guangzhou, 385, 400–1
  London, 264, 286
Urban design, 237–8, 240, 249, 251–4
  street design, 365, 370–1

Urban intensification, and carfree development, 228, 230
Urban mobility plans, integrated, 163, 340–1
Utilities, compared with parking, 141, 151
Utrecht, 175, 178–80

Value-of-time, and parking choice, 130
Variable-message signs, and parking choice, 117
Vauban
  carfree development, 218–19, 225–6, 227, 228
  overspill parking, 228–9
Vehicle speeds, on-street parking, 365, 370–2, 378
Vehicular access, and carfree development, 219–21, 229
Vienna, 225–6

Waiting-time, and parking choice, 121
Walking (*see also* Pedestrian access/environment)
  carfree development, 225–6
  on- and off-street parking compared, 374, 375
  P&R sites, 199
  retail spending, 21–2, 254–5
Walking-time, and parking choice, 119–20, 121, 127
Washington, DC (US), 246
Washington State (US), 38
Wheel-clamping, 118
Willingness-to-pay, 122, 127, 130, 298

Workplace parking (*see also*
      Commuter parking; Private
      non-residential parking), 14,
      15, 22–5
   demand management, 23–4
   labour market, 84
   lease agreements, 246
   levies, 24
   parking by purpose, 72–5
   permits for employees,
      118–19
   pricing and travel behaviour, 37,
      41–2
Workplace Parking Levy (WPL),
      Nottingham, 8, 335–59,
      412–13

barriers to implementation,
      351–3
   consultation, 342–6
   enforcement, 350–1
   evaluation, 354–9
   policy issues and legislation,
      340–2, 347–50, 358
   pricing, discounts, 346–7
Workplace travel plans, 171, 338,
      345, 354
Worship, places of, parking
      requirements, 241, 242

Zoning codes (*see* Minimum
      parking requirements)
Zurich, 50